Merchant Princes and Charlatans or Makers of Money?

Henry Sless

Merchant Princes and Charlatans or Makers of Money?

Decoding Icons of Nineteenth Century British and International Finance

palgrave
macmillan

Henry Sless
University of Reading
Reading, UK

ISBN 978-3-030-86603-7 ISBN 978-3-030-86604-4 (eBook)
https://doi.org/10.1007/978-3-030-86604-4

Cover credit: whitemay/GettyImages
Cover Image Caption: Where to keep your money for the best? With so many confidence tricksters anxious to part you from it, you need to consider the matter carefully - sleight of hand and misdirection can fool even the most sensible of men. From "Punch, or the London Charivari", Volume LXVIII (68), published in London in 1875.

This Palgrave Macmillan imprint is published by the registered company Springer Nature Switzerland AG
The registered company address is: Gewerbestrasse 11, 6330 Cham, Switzerland

Acknowledgements

I am indebted to my Ph.D. supervisors, Professor Peter Miskell, and Associate Professor Lucy Newton, for their encouragement in turning my interest in cartoons and financial history into reality. To my Ph.D. reviewers, Professors Mark Casson of the University of Reading, and Martin Daunton Emeritus Professor at the University of Cambridge, for their helpful comments and their encouragement to turn my ideas into a book. And to two members of the Oxford Department of Continuing Education, Dr. Kate Watson, and the late Dr. Cathy Oakes. To Kate whose course on political cartoons all those years ago inspired me to begin my path towards becoming a cultural historian, and to Cathy for encouraging my interest in studying cartoons as a source of historical evidence.

To my editors at Palgrave, Lucy Kidwell, and Tula Weis, whose encouragement and support has been so welcome over the past year. And to my copy editor, Anthony Sarankin, who has turned my less than grammatically perfect prose into something polished.

And of course, to my wife Debs who has put up with my often-obsessive interest in financial cartoons over the past ten years, and without whose support I would not have reached the end of this journey.

Any errors and omissions are my own….

Key Books/Articles Per Chapter

Chapter 2 Financial Context

Akerloff, George A., & Robert J. Schiller, *Animal Spirits How human psychology drives the economy, and why it matters for global capitalism* (Oxford, Princeton University Press, 2010).

Crosthwaite, Paul, "Animality and ideology in contemporary economic discourse Taxonomising Homo Economicus", *Journal of Cultural Economy*, 2013, 6: 1.

Itkowitz, David C., "Fair Enterprise or Extravagant Speculation: Investment, Speculation and Gambling in Victorian England", pp. 98–119, in Henry & Schmitt, (eds.), *Victorian Investments New Perspectives on Finance and Culture* (Bloomington, Indiana University Press, 2009).

Johnson Paul, "Civilizing Mammon: Law, Morals and the City in Nineteenth Century England", in *Civil Histories: Essays Presented to Sir Keith Thomas*, (eds.) Peter Burke, Brian Harrison, and Paul Slack (Oxford, Oxford University Press, 2000).

Klaus, Ian, *Forging Capitalism Rogues, Swindlers, Frauds, and the rise of Modern Finance* (Yale, Yale University Press, 2014).

Kynaston, David, *City of London: A world of its own 1815–1890*, Volume 1 (London, Chatto & Windus, 1994).

Taylor, James, *Boardroom Scandal, The Criminalization of Company Fraud in Nineteenth-Century Britain* (Oxford, Oxford University Press, 2013).

Toms, Steven, “Financial Scandals: a historical overview”, *Accounting and Business Research*, 45: 5.

Tucker, Sir Paul M.W., “Solvency as a fundamental constraint on LOLR policy for Independent Central Banks: Principles, History, Law”, *Journal of Financial Crises*, 2: 1.

Turner, John. D., *Banking in crisis the rise and fall of British Banking Stability, 1800 to the present* (Cambridge, Cambridge University Press, 2014).

Van Driel, Hugo, “Financial fraud, scandals and regulation: A conceptual framework and literature review”, *Business History*, 61: 8.

Chapter 3 Visual Culture

Allen, Ann Taylor, *Satire & Society in Wilhelmine Germany Kladderadatsch and Simplicissimus 1890–1914*, (Lexington, University of Kentucky Press, 1984).

Altick, Richard. D., *Punch: the lively youth of a British institution, 1841–1851* (London, Ohio State University Press, 1997).

Banta, Martha, *Barbaric Intercourse, Caricature and the Culture of Conflict, 1841–1936* (Chicago, The University of Chicago Press, 2003).

Burke Peter, *Eyewitnessing: the use of images as historical evidence* (London, Cornell University Press, 2001).

Finel-Honigman, Irene, *A Cultural History of Finance* (Abingdon, Routledge, 2010).

Goldstein, Robert Justin, *Censorship of political caricature in nineteenth-century France* (Kent, Kent State University Press, 1989).

Gombrich, E. H., *Meditations on a Hobby Horse and Other Essays in the Theory of Art* (London, Phaidon Press, 2007).

Miller, Henry, *Politics Personified Portraiture, Caricature and Visual Culture in Victorian Britain, c 1830–1880* (Manchester, Manchester University Press, 2015).

Scully, Richard, “Accounting for transformative moments in the history of the political cartoon”, *IJOCA*, Fall/Winter 2014.

Taylor, James, “Business in Pictures: Representations of Railway Enterprise in the Satirical Press in Britain 1845–1870”, *Past and Present,* No. 189 (November 2005).

"The debate over censorship of caricature in nineteenth-century France", *Art Journal*, 48: 1, Nineteenth-Century French Art Institutions (Spring, 1989).

Chapter 4 Merchant Princes

Ferguson, Niall, *The House of Rothschild: Vol. 1 Money's Prophets 1798–1848* (New York, Viking Penguin, 1999).
———, *Vol. 2 The World's Banker 1849–1999,* (New York, Viking Penguin, 1999).
Osborne, "The Journal Vanity Fair and later Victorian politics", *The Journal of the Rutgers University Libraries*, 2012.
Ziegler, P., *The sixth great power: Barings 1762–1929* (London, Collins, 1988).

Chapter 5 Charlatans

Davenport-Hines, R.P.T., (ed.) *Speculators and Patriots Essays in Business Biography* (London, Frank Cass and Company Limited, 1986).
Robb, George, *White-Collar Crime in Modern England: Financial Fraud and Business Morality, 1845–1929* (Cambridge, Cambridge University Press, 1992).
Stratmann, Linda, *The Crooks who conned millions True stories of fraudsters and charlatans* (Stroud, Sutton Publishing, 2006).

Chapter 6 Financial Iconography

Burns Sarah, "Party Animals: Thomas Nast, William Holbrook Beard, and the Bears of Wall Street" *American Art Journal*, 30: 1/2, 1999.
Fraser, Steve, *Every man a speculator A History of Wall Street in American Life* (New York, Harper Perennial, 2006).
John, Richard R., "Robbers Baron redux: Antimonolopy reconsidered", *Enterprise & Society*, 13: 1, 2012.
Taylor, James, "Business in Pictures: Representations of Railway Enterprise in the Satirical Press in Britain 1845–1870", *Past and Present,* No. 189 (November 2005).

Chapter 7 Women

Green, D. R., A. Owens, J. Maltby and J. Rutterford (eds.), *Men, Women and Money: Perspectives on Gender, Wealth and Investment, 1850–1930* (Oxford, Oxford University Press, 2011).

Healey, Edna, *Coutts & Co 1692–1992: The Portrait of a Private Bank* (London, Hodder & Stoughton, 1992).

Poovey, *Genres of the Credit Economy: Mediating value in eighteenth century and nineteenth century Britain* (London, University of Chicago Press, 2008).

Chapter 8 The Other

Arendt, Hannah, *The origins of totalitarianism* (London, Penguin Classics, 2017).

Rubens, Alfred, "The Rothschilds in caricature", *Transactions & Miscellanies (Jewish Historical Society of England)*, 22.

Stern, Fritz, *Gold and Iron Bismarck, Bleichroder, and the Building of the German Empire* (London, George Allen & Unwin, 1977).

Wohl, Anthony S., 'Ben JuJu' -representations of Disraeli's Jewishness in the Victorian political cartoon, *Jewish History*, Vol. 10, No. 2. (Fall, 1996).

Chapter 9 The Law

Meisel, Martin, *Realizations Narrative, Pictorial, and Theatrical Arts in Nineteenth-Century England* (Princeton, New Jersey, Princeton University Press, 1983).

Wilson, Gary, and Sarah Wilson, "The pursuit of "socially useful banking" in Twenty-First Century Britain and exploring Victorian interactions between law, religion, and financial marketplace values", 22 *Nottingham Law Journal*, 53, 2013.

Key Words

Animal spirits

Animal spirits come from the Latin spiritus animalis: 'the breath that awakens the human mind'. It was coined by British economist, John

Maynard Keynes in 1936. It refers to the ways that human emotion can drive financial decision making in uncertain environments and volatile times.

Anti-Semitism
The belief or behaviour hostile toward Jews just because they are Jewish. It may take the form of religious teachings that proclaim the inferiority of Jews, for instance, or political efforts to isolate, oppress, or otherwise injure them. It may also include prejudiced or stereotyped views about Jews.

Bank discount rate
The bank discount rate is the interest rate for short-term money market instruments like commercial paper and Treasury bills offered by a Central Bank.

Behavioural economics
Behavioural economics studies the effects of psychological, cognitive, emotional, cultural, and social factors on the decisions of individuals and institutions and how those decisions vary from those implied by classical economic theory.

Bestiary
The symbolic use of animals to convey meaning.

Bill broking
A person or organisation that buys bills of exchange for a lower amount of money than they are worth and makes a profit by selling them for more or keeping them until they are paid.

Caricature
A caricature is a portrait that is full of additional elements, whether these are simple physical exaggerations or deliberate misrepresentations and analogies designed to make a political point.

Nowadays the caricature is seen as a type of cartoon but in fact, although caricature had been around since the mid-1600s, the first modern use of the word 'cartoon' was two centuries later, in an 1843 edition of Punch.

Charlatans
Someone who resorts to bogus means of impressing people to swindle his victims by selling them worthless goods or services that will not deliver on the promises made for them.

Company Promoters
A company or a person who does the preliminary work incidental to the formation of a company, including its promotion, incorporation, and flotation, and solicits people to invest money in the company, usually when it is being formed.

Devil-fish
Also known as the octopus.

Director of Public Prosecution
Appointed by the Government (in the Victorian period) to advise the police and personally act in cases of importance.

Emotional discourse
Defines and illustrates discursive psychology in terms of how people describe and invoke emotions in everyday talk and text.

Gambling
Gambling is the betting of money or something of value (referred to as 'the stakes') on an event with an uncertain outcome, with the primary intent of winning money or material goods.

Gentlemanly Capitalists
Cain & Hopkins put forward the theory that British imperialism was driven by the business interests of the City of London (the gentlemanly capitalists).

Gilded Age
The term *Gilded Age* for the period of economic boom after the American Civil War up to the turn of the century was applied to the era by historians in the 1920s, who took the term from one of Mark Twain's lesser-known novels.

Golden Age
The flowering of British caricature during the late eighteenth century embodied in the works of James Gillray (1756–1815), Thomas Rowlandson (1756–1827), and George Cruikshank (1792–1878), It is taken to end with the death of Gillray in 1815.

Homo economicus
The term *homo economicus*, or economic man, is the portrayal of humans as agents who are consistently rational and narrowly self-interested, and who pursue their subjectively defined ends optimally.

Iconography
The study of icons or common symbols.

Joint-Stock company
A business that is owned by the group of people who have shares in the company.

Laissez-faire
Laissez-faire economics is a theory that restricts government intervention in the economy. It holds that the economy is strongest when all the government does is protect individuals' rights. Laissez-faire is French for 'let do' or 'leave us alone'.

In other words, let the market do its own thing. If left alone, the laws of supply and demand will efficiently direct the production of goods and services.

Lender of Last Resort
A lender of last resort is an institution, usually a country's central bank, that offers loans to banks or other eligible institutions that are experiencing financial difficulty or are considered highly risky or near collapse.

Letterpress
Text as distinct from pictorial illustrations.

Limited liability company
Shareholders' liabilities in the event of a company failure are limited to the amount of their share capital.

Mammon
Money and possessions.

Merchant banking
The merchant-banking families dealt in everything from underwriting bonds to originating foreign loans, bullion trading and bond issuance (the modern term is investment banking).

Merchant Princes
A mercantile plutocrat: a man who wields great de facto political power by virtue of economic assets derived from trade and commerce.

Napoleon of Finance
Symbols of Napoleon referencing his financial acumen.

Narrative painting
The painting of everyday life subjects.

Official Receiver
To act as a receiver, trustee, or liquidator in personal or corporate situations.

Puffing
Exaggeration of the value of goods offered for sale.

Reflux principle
The law of reflux asserts that banks do not cause inflation through over-issue of money, since any excess money would quickly return to the issuing bank, usually as deposits, loan repayments, or for redemption in base money.

Satire
Satire is a genre of literature and performing arts, usually fiction and less frequently in non-fiction, in which vices, follies, abuses, and shortcomings are held up to ridicule, ideally with the intent of shaming individuals, corporations, government, or society itself into improvement. Although satire is usually meant to be humorous, its greater purpose is often constructive social criticism, using wit to draw attention to both particular and wider issues in society.

Speculation
In finance, speculation is the practice of engaging in risky financial transactions in an attempt to profit from short-term fluctuations in the market value of a financial instrument—rather than attempting to profit from the underlying financial attributes embodied in the instrument such as value addition, return on investment, or dividends.

Storyboard
A sequence of individual frames telling a story.

The New Journalism
Coined by Matthew Arnold in 1887, it symbolised popularising journalistic techniques, such as the use of illustrations, bold headlines, competitions, short snippets adopted by the mass market penny weeklies of the late nineteenth century.

The Old Lady of Threadneedle Street
The icon of a withered old-lady first used by Gillray to describe the Bank of England.

The Other
A nineteenth-century racist view that aliens, or those of other races, were inferior to white Anglo-Saxons.
Tropes
A commonly used term.

Unlimited liability company
Shareholders' liabilities in the event of a company fault are unlimited.

White-collar crime
It was first defined by the sociologist Edwin Sutherland in 1939 as 'a crime committed by a person of respectability and high social status in the course of their occupation'. Applied to business fraud undertaken by businesspeople, white-collar workers.

Contents

About the Author

Dr. Henry Sless is a research associate at the Henley Business School at the University of Reading. After qualifying in Modern Languages at the University of Bristol, Henry embarked on a thirty-year career in Accountancy and Tax, working in the commercial, public, and latterly private sectors. A third interest beckoned in retirement. Henry retrained as a cultural historian, completing a master's at the University of Kent before completing a Ph.D. at the University of Reading. He is keenly interested in the use of visual culture depicting financiers and their world as key elements in providing historical evidence.

Abbreviations

BL	British Library
BM	British Museum
BM	British Museum digital collection
CGB	City of Glasgow Bank
ILN	MaryEvans picture library
LOC	Library of Congress Prints and Photographs Department
NPG	National Portrait Gallery
RBB	Royal British Bank
RM	Railway Mania
UoF	University of Florida digital collections
UoG	University of Glasgow Special Collections
UoH	University of Heidelberg digital collections

List of Figures

List of Tables

CHAPTER 1

Introduction

> In two seconds, illustrators can say more to the public than writers can in 500 lines[1]

Altick in his review of the first ten years of *Punch*, refers to this image as: An anamorphic (vertically) elongated drawing of an investor, horror on his face, yelling so vividly as to be almost audible to a reader a full century and a half later.[2] The term 'anamorphism' was itself coined contemporaneously with this drawing[3] (Fig. 1.1).

These two references, one an image and one a quotation, embody the purpose of my book—the exploration of the use of visual images of finance in the nineteenth century. The cartoon encapsulates the shock and horror felt by investors at the height of the Railway Mania. This vertical image conveys emotions that would take many words to explain, hence the appositeness of the *Le Trombinoscope* quote.

My definition of visual images has been mainly limited on space grounds. I have decided to concentrate on cartoons in comic periodicals, as well as pictorial drawings and cartoons in the realistic periodicals and newspapers. There will be occasional comparative references to paintings and photographs. There will be no coverage of other aspects of visual images such as architecture, advertisements, posters.

To date little academic research has been carried into links between visual culture and financial history in the nineteenth century. Finel-Honigman provides a global summary of the impact of cultural history on

H. Sless, *Merchant Princes and Charlatans or Makers of Money?*,
https://doi.org/10.1007/978-3-030-86604-4_1

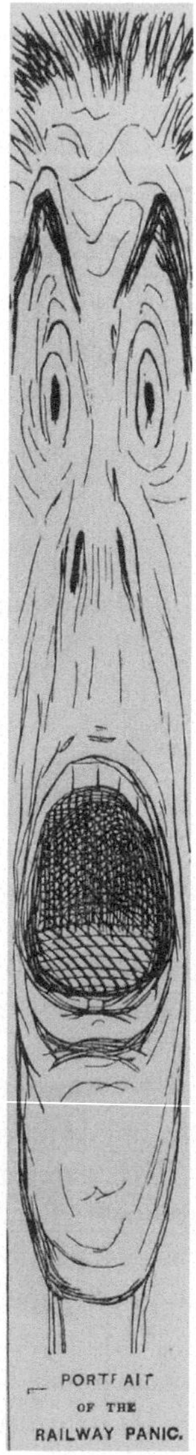

Fig. 1.1 *Punch*, *Portrait of the railway panic*, 8 November 1845. Courtesy of UoH

finance, and it is also echoed more recently in a book '*Show me the money*' which accompanied an exhibition of the same title.[4] Walcot, an art historian, provides a useful benchmark for an earlier period.[5] The only direct example is James Taylor's review of attitudes towards big business 1845–1870 and his more comprehensive analysis of visual and literary sources in relation to joint-stock companies during the same period.[6] My book expands on Taylor's coverage, specifically in relation to the iconography of finance and to provide a comprehensive coverage of visual images of finance in the whole of the nineteenth century.

That there is still a gap to be filled is supported by comments by two eminent economic historians, Michie and Daunton. Michie wanted to explore how the City of London was perceived by the Victorians.[7] He sought a homogeneous selection of works/sources to review over the Victorian period, and he concluded that novels, *rather than cartoons or paintings* (my emphasis), provided the best foundation for his review. His reasoning for rejecting cartoons or paintings was his assessment that there was a lack of homogeneous content/sources to support his review, which he summarised as 'finance only rarely lends itself to visual display'. This is reflected in the difficulties that a banking archivist, Fitzmaurice, encountered in writing a history of British Banking: 'Banking is a trade which keeps its records in print rather than pictures and with a traditional secrecy destroys them when no longer of use'.[8]

Secondly, Daunton, in his afterword to *Victorian Investments* which appeared in 2009, comments on the trouble Victorians experienced in distinguishing between legitimate investment and illegal speculation (AND SINCE!):

> It would be interesting to consider the definitions of speculation and investment in the Victorian period in a more systematic way (compared with the collection of articles in *Victorian Investments*), not through a few major novels by Conrad or Trollope but through a much wider analysis of a variety of sources (my emphasis): stories in popular magazines, comments by judges, discussion in the financial press.[9]

The traditional approach of financial historians to cartoons has been to use them to illustrate the written word rather than to use them as the primary source itself.[10] I have sought to address these comments by using, as my primary source, cartoons appearing in periodicals and newspapers over the whole of the nineteenth century.

This is the visual story of people involved in financial activities in the nineteenth century, the heroes, the villains (the white-collar criminals), those who were just 'makers of money' as *Vanity Fair* called them, as well as the victims of financial fraud/collapses. It depicts both themselves as well as the financial events through which they lived.

It contrasts visual depictions with other cultural representations, whether in other media such as paintings or photographs, or in literary and journalistic forms. Both contemporary literature as well as journalistic writings provided consistent warnings about dubious financial activities and unscrupulous financial figures. The negative portrayal of fictitious bankers in Dickens and Thackeray, the sensationalist journalistic writings of the erstwhile crime reporter, David Morier Evans, full of fact-filled warnings, or the more sober cautionary comments by Walter Bagehot all demonstrated the 'herd mentality' which still drove Victorian investors to ignore these warnings. It also highlights how the Victorians found it difficult to balance the entrepreneurial instincts of capitalist activities with traditional Christian moral principles.

The images themselves represent the primary source of historical evidence. Academic sources relying on written documents are referred to by way of context. The source for my book was an analysis of over 500 images, based on two unique datasets which I have compiled from digital and hard copy sources. The first dataset, comprising over 300 images of financial figures and financial events during the nineteenth century was compiled using digital resources of British Library and the British Museum, and includes images from the serio-comic periodicals such as *Punch*, *Fun*, and *Judy*, as well as the realistic periodicals such as the *Illustrated London News* and the *Graphic*.

My second dataset comprised my unique survey of 1695 caricatures from *Vanity Fair*, which identified the importance of finance as a profession. *Vanity Fair*, the bellwether of attitudes of the Victorian ruling elite, began in 1869 and continued beyond the end of the century. The dataset of over 200 caricatures of financiers constituted the largest profession depicted (absent MPs themselves who total 450).[11] It reflects both images of the Merchant Princes, those wealthy financial families (merchant bankers) who exercised political influence (the Rothschilds and the Barings) alongside caricatures of lesser-known individuals involved in Stock Exchange activities (stockbrokers, commodity brokers, private bankers, merchant bankers). Together these two datasets represent a homogeneous compilation of financial images spanning the pre-Victorian as well as the Victorian periods. The book includes a detailed review of 150 images of the period.

Interpretation of the images in this book requires an in-depth understanding of the political, financial, and cultural background to the period under review. It reflects a deep multi-disciplinary approach to attempt to capture what one of the great historians of the nineteenth century, Ranke, expressed as 'wie es eigentlich gewesen' (literally 'how things actually were'). His exhortation to 'Einfuhlen', the ability to get under the skin of historical events, to imagine what it was like in the times which were being studied, is reflected in the study of visual images of a given period.[12]

Appendix 1 provides an example of how this in-depth approach can be applied to one single image. On the grounds of space, the book itself is designed to introduce the reader to a representative sample of the images of finance in the era, whilst providing a flavour of the in-depth review possible in its analysis of selective images.

This is a unique book as other non-visual studies typically centre around either the villains (e.g., Robb, Taylor, Stratmann) or the Merchant Princes (e.g., Ferguson re the Rothschilds, or Ziegler re the Barings).

The book begins with a detailed discussion around the financial and visual culture contexts for the review of images. The financial context provides a historiography of financial history of the period. Through the overarching theme of private trust, I explore differing nineteenth century perceptions of Stock Exchange transactions as investment activities, or pure gambling or speculation. As I point out later, visual images tend to concentrate on emotional responses to events, so my discussion on financial crises concentrates on the impact rather than the causes. The main areas for discussion relate to business morality and the behaviour of investors faced with the uncertain financial climate of the period. Business morality covers the climate in which financiers operated in during the period, including the influence of the press and the role of regulators. The nineteenth century reflects a period when the distinctions between trading, speculation, and gambling were blurred. Whilst business trading represented acceptable legal investment activity, trading in stocks and shares only became respectable following the abolition of Barnard's Law in 1860. Yet even here, the boundaries between speculation and gambling (with the latter being unacceptable if carried on by the lower classes) were blurred (*Vanity Fair* features 'reputable' gamblers who won and lost monies on the racecourse, or at the card table). The role of the press is presented in terms of their influence on the 'court of public opinion' (as well as providing the cartoonists with the information on which to base their cartoons) especially as Governmental legal reforms lagged the consistent occurrence of financial fraud. Governments of the period followed 'laissez-faire' policies and were reluctant to introduce safeguards for investors. As the scale and rate of financial fraud increased during the century, the Government of the time was forced to introduce more and more company law reforms. The role of the other regulator, the Bank of England, in assuring financial stability) is also covered. The second area of focus centres on the behaviour of investors (what I have termed the 'emotional discourse') in the face of turbulent financial events. It analyses recent developments in the field of 'behavioural economics' (the work of Kahneman, Thaler, Shiller etc.), echoing Keynes's use of 'animal spirits', as well as changing definitions of 'homo economicus'.[13]

The visual context also provides a historiography, whilst covering recent research in the fields of Women Studies, and the Other. I suggest an approach to print methodology which synthesises the views of art historians like Gombrich and his reference to the 'cartoonists' armoury' as well as cultural historians like Maidment, Burke et al. who stress the need for a deep contextual analysis of prints including understanding contemporary references. This approach which I call a PEARL approach concentrates on the symbiotic relationship between the publisher, the editor, the artist, and the reader, whilst mindful of any legal constraints on publication. I comment also on the emerging fields of financial iconography as well as the study of the 'collective unconscious', the impact of the repetition of symbols over a long period of time in arriving at collective unconscious memories. What were the typical icons depicting financial events of the period, and what is the significance, if any, of the repetition of those icons over the centuries?

It is then followed by two chapters covering the visual depiction of the merchant princes and the charlatans. VanArsdel comments on the fascination that ordinary Victorians felt about the exploits of the 'merchant princes', a way of life which they never properly understood yet which they secretly admired.[14] Taylor discusses the importance of visual culture, including cartoons, as a medium used to comment critically on the unscrupulous practices of the charlatans. The latter, who succeeded briefly in making vast some of monies before their nefarious exploits were discovered, ended up being punished, either in the court of public opinion or increasingly as the century wore on, by receiving prison sentences.[15]

Having dealt with financial individuals, I then analyse the financial setting in which they operated through four chapters covering specific tropes which illustrate the zeitgeist of the period (Financial Iconography, Women, The Other, The Law). The imagery is often *complex* with themes overlapping each other.

Chapter 6 on Financial Iconography outlines the major themes present in images of the period covering financial crises. They depict the visual effect of emotions such as:

> Frenzy (especially crowd scenes, depictions of runaway engines, or the use of animals as visual personifications of the bestial impact of stock market activities), or
> Visual puns to depict Stock Exchange terminology, or
> Contrasting images of buildings of financial institutions representing the opposites of solidity (especially in the case of the Bank of England) and instability (buildings crashing down, corrupt business practices being carried on inside buildings).

Chapter 7 depicts women involved in finance (either as innocent investors or upright successful bankers like Harriot Coutts, or her niece, Angela Burdett Coutts, the great Victorian philanthropist), the embodiment of the Goddess Justice administering punishment to charlatans, or the embodiment of fiscal rectitude in the role of the Bank of England in bailing out failed banks (the Old Lady of Threadneedle Street).

Chapter 8 charts the treatment of the Other in the field of finance—the trope representing people of a different race (Jews, Scots, Irish). The initial anti-Jewish depiction of Nathan Rothschild in the early part of the century gives way at least in England to acceptance of Jews in the elite by the 1870s onwards. This is contrasted with the vicious satire afforded to the Jew turned Christian Benjamin Disraeli in the mid part of the century onwards. The impact of anti-Semitism from the 1870s onwards (and arguably before) is reflected in the crude satire of European and US Jewish financiers by artists in those countries. The chapter concludes by analysing the treatment of the Scots and the Irish. The Scots are treated in a non-satirical manner, their woes viewed as the same as their English brethren who had all lost monies in financial crises. Indeed, one image at the time of the 1825 banking crisis positively eulogises the thriftiness of Scottish bankers in comparison with their English counterparts. The

Irish, by contrast, are viewed as ignorant in keeping with non-financial depictions of them, though eschewing any true caricature.

Chapter 9 analyses the increasing number of images devoted to scenes of white-collar criminals being tried before the courts. This trend which accelerates after the trial of the City of Glasgow Bank (CGB) directors in 1879 reflects the impact of new journalism (e.g., *Illustrated Police News* where CGB directors are depicted on the same front page as domestic murder scenes and exotic animals from far-away places). The images appear in both the comic periodicals as well as in the realistic periodicals. In the case of the former the images reflect moral disapproval of the actions of bank directors, whereas in the latter there is a sense of schadenfreude at seeing white-collar criminals in the dock.

The coverage is international and comparative in scope, reflecting contrasting US and European visual responses. Figures covered include cartoonists such as Nast and Keppler in the US, painters such as Beard in the US, and Degas in France, and periodicals such as *Puck* and *Judge* in the US, *Kladderadatsch* in Germany, and *La Libre Parole* and *Musee des Horreurs* in France. What is significant is the cross-over of similar financial icons between the various countries at similar periods. Despite the similarities, the generally more genteel representation of financial figures and financial events in Britain is contrasted with the more extreme anti-monopolistic images in the US and the extreme anti-Semitic treatment of Jewish financiers in France and Germany.

The Merchant Princes were depicted in illustrated periodicals, despite them not being the charlatans beloved of cartoonists for being unscrupulous. Selection for inclusion in *Vanity Fair*, the society periodical, was a sign of acceptance so the number and type of financiers, not just the Merchant Princes, was significant. Whilst the Rothschilds were attacked for being the epitome of capitalist success as well as being Jewish in many countries, in Britain their positive contribution to society was reflected in the number of individual caricatures of the family which appeared in *Vanity Fair*.

The book indicates that in the visual arena white-collar criminals were invariably secretly admired. In Britain they were rarely satirised and were typically depicted at the height of their fame, rather than at the time of their demise (though this changed towards the end of the century). When their fall was depicted, it was either in a humorous tone or reflecting empathy with their plight. For *Vanity Fair* the characterisation as a charlatan was not recognised. Those who later in life and posthumously would clearly be viewed as financial charlatans were depicted in *Vanity Fair* at the pinnacle of their success.

Notes

1. Robert Justin Goldstein, *Censorship of Political Caricature in Nineteenth-Century France* (Kent, Kent State University Press, 1989), quoting *Le Trombinoscope* of April 1882, p. 35.
2. Richard D. Altick, *The Lively Youth of a British Institution 1841–1851* (London, Ohio State University Press, 1997), p. 458.
3. http://www.oed.com.idpproxy.reading.ac.uk/view/Entry/7058, accessed 10 April 2019. The word means a distorted projection or perspective, first used as noun in 1836.
4. Irene Finel-Honigman, *A Cultural History of Finance* (Abingdon, 2010). Paul Crosthwaite, Peter Knight, and Nicky Marsh (eds.), *Show Me the Money the Image of Finance, 1700 to the Present* (2014).
5. Clare Walcot, 'Figuring Finance: London's New Financial World and the Iconography of Speculation, Circa 1689–1763 in Two Volumes', unpublished PhD Thesis, University of Warwick, September 2003.
6. James Taylor, 'Business in Pictures: Representations of Railway Enterprise in the Satirical Press in Britain 1845–1870', *Past and Present*, No. 189 (November 2005), pp. 111–145 and *Creating Capitalism: Joint-Stock Enterprise in British Politics and Culture 1800–1870* (London, 2006).
7. Ranald C. Michie, *Guilty Money: The City of London in Victorian and Edwardian culture, 1815–1914* (London, Pickering & Chatto, 2009).
8. R. M. Fitzmaurice, *British Banks and Banking: A Pictorial History* (Truro, D. Bradford Barton, 1975), p. xx.
9. Martin Daunton, 'Afterword', pp. 202–219, in Nancy Henry and Cannon Schmitt (eds.), *Victorian Investments New Perspectives on Finance and Culture* (Bloomington, Indiana University Press, 2009), p. 205.
10. See, for example, Martin Daunton, *Trusting Leviathan the Politics of Taxation in Britain 1799–1914* (Cambridge, Cambridge University Press, 2007) and Niall Ferguson, *Vol. 2: The World's Banker 1849–1999* (New York, Viking Penguin, 1999).
11. See Appendix 2 for further details of my analysis of *Vanity Fair* caricatures.

12. Cited in www.umass.edu/wsp/history/ranke/index.htm#past, accessed from web 2 October 2018.
13. See Chapter 2 for references.
14. J. Don Vann and Rosemary T. VanArsdel, *Victorian Periodicals and Victorian Society* (Toronto, University of Toronto Press, 1995), p. 199.
15. James Taylor, *Boardroom Scandal: The Criminalization of Company Fraud in Nineteenth-Century Britain* (Oxford, Oxford University Press, 2013), pp. 250–252.

CHAPTER 2

Financial Context

2.1 Introduction

This is the story of nineteenth-century British financiers, whether those involved in the haute finance of merchant banks, the more prosaic retail bankers, the ordinary stockbrokers, or the sharp-practising company promoters. It is also the story of the financial world in which they lived: a period of frequent economic uncertainties with failures of British banks and the involvement of the Bank of England (BoE) in providing monetary liquidity to prevent financial crises getting worse.[1] The failures were sometimes the result of economic causes, but more often corporate fraud perpetrated by greedy managers, and unscrupulous company promoters exploiting a lax regulatory regime, was to blame. In between it was a period of extraordinary growth, powered by the rise of gentlemanly capitalists, who financed domestic and international expansion.

Despite the occurrence of bank frauds and failures throughout most of the century, investors did receive more and more protection as the century wore on. The safety of the financial system evolved through the successful regulation of the banking system, which began with the Bank Charter Act of 1844, and successive changes to how banks operated (specifically the introduction of limited liability in 1855).[2] The introduction of the Bank Charter Act was promoted by the followers of the Currency School (led by Samuel Jones-Loyd, later Lord Overstone) who advocated that restricting Bank of England note issuance to the amount

H. Sless, *Merchant Princes and Charlatans or Makers of Money?*,
https://doi.org/10.1007/978-3-030-86604-4_2

of gold reserves would prevent inflationary pressures building, thereby limiting the possibility of asset bubbles. Details of the debates between the Currency School and the Banking School are covered in the discussion about Lord Overstone in Chapter 4, "Merchant Princes", and in the discussion of the diagram entitled 'Lord Overstone's Trade Cycle' at the beginning of Chapter 6, "Financial Iconography". Successive changes to corporate law were supplemented by the Bank of England's adopting a de facto Lender of Last Resort (LOLR) responsibility from the 1870s. Even as investor protection increased, there remained the need for investors to seek redress from the courts for past management misdemeanours. In an era of government laissez-faire approaches to corporate behaviour, changes to legal protection were slow to evolve.

Klaus defined finance during the Victorian era as one characterised by the existence or absence of trust in the financial system.[3] Private trust, he argued, encompassed the often complex but ultimately symbiotic relationship between shareholders, directors, managers, company promoters, and financial journalists, which governed the corporate world in the Victorian era. As Walter Bagehot, the leading Victorian journalist on financial matters commented in relation to the relationships between investors and the banks: confidence had to be earned over time. Credit had to 'grow'; it could not be 'constructed'.[4]

Where confidence was absent, it led to what Robb characterised as 'white-collar crimes' (though the term itself was coined many years later) which affected the economy and led to breakdown of trust.[5]

2.2 Financial Crises and Their Causes

As has been previously mentioned, images of financial events are almost exclusively connected with their (emotional) impact, rather than with their causes. Nevertheless, in the interests of completeness, a brief survey of the literature associated with financial crises is included.

There has been much debate about the definition of a financial crisis, and the causes of such failures. Reinhart & Rogoff's classic definition of a banking crisis refers to bank runs that lead to the public sector's having to take over financial institutions or, if not taking them over, providing financial liquidity to stabilise the financial system. They comment on the occurrence of financial crises in clusters, which are often repetitive. This is echoed by Kindleberger, who refers to a rhythm of peaks and falls in the markets. He points to overtrading (speculation or gearing) as the prime reasons for such crises. He goes on to comment on the influence of exogeneous shocks to the financial system such as the onset or end of a war, a series of good harvests and a series of bad harvests, the opening of new markets, new sources of supply, financial deregulation, and new technologies (railways, etc.).[6] Elements of these shocks are outlined in the summary of financial crises which follows at the end of this chapter.

This leads to a discussion of contemporary views of these events. The concept of a 'business cycle' dates to the works of the Mercantilists, the Physiocrats, and even Adam Smith. The concept that crises are periodic—something that comes and goes and returns, i.e., a cycle rather than a singular incident—took some time to take off.

Inevitably, there are problems of linguistic semantics. What did the word 'cycle' mean in the nineteenth century? Besomi comments that the Overstone diagram and subsequent illustrations by Mountiford and Longfield were predicated on a single cycle (a singular incident) rather than the modern-day meaning of a regular cycle. Similarly, did depictions of Overstone's phases as a circle indicate recurrence or one-off singularity?[7]

Periodicity dates to Langton (1857) and Mills (1867) who put forward the idea of personal feelings and credit, whilst Jevons (1862, 1867) identified sunspots and harvests. But it is the work of Juglar (1862) which firmly established the business cycle as an area of research. He postulated cycles of 9–10 years.

In the banking context Turner uses share prices and failure rates to challenge the traditional narrative view (Collins, Rogoff, and Schwartz) that nineteenth-century British banking lurched from one crisis to another (involving bank failures and economic crises seemingly every ten years from 1825 through to 1878).[8] Turner reviews the crises in British financial history in the nineteenth century using a detailed statistical analysis expanding on the views of Reinhart and Rogoff that look at the proportion of commercial bank failures and the capital of such banks to overall totals of such banks and their capital. He supplements this with his own analysis of relative changes in bank share prices to argue that only the years1825–1826 really impacted the financial sector severely.

Turner's statistical view, though, does not reflect the contemporary anger at the seemingly all too frequent episodes of financial mismanagement which were conveyed in newspapers and cartoons of the period. The titles of the works of the major economists covering this period (Kindleberger, Reinhardt & Rogoff, Akerlof & Shiller, as well as the work of the contemporary journalist Mackay) testify to the use of emotional language to characterise these events. 'Manias, panics and crashes', 'Eight centuries of financial folly', 'Animal spirits', 'Extraordinary popular delusions and the madness of crowds' evoke the language in vogue during this period.[9]

Any history of financial crises is littered with references to symbolic icons—bubbles/balloons/puffs of air for the Tulip Mania of the 1630s and the South Sea Bubble of 1720, buildings crashing down for the 1825 crash, the engine out of control at the time of the Railway Mania in the 1840s. The association of such emotional responses to financial crises has been well documented contemporaneously by Mackay and Evans. Today economists regard asset bubbles occurring when the asset's price temporarily exceeds its fundamental value—the contagion of expectations. Mackay said: 'Men, it has been well said, think in herds; it will be seen that they go mad in herds, while they only recover their senses slowly, and one by one'.[10] Keynes appreciated that most economic activity resulted from rational economic motivations, but also that much economic activity is governed by 'animal spirits'.[11]

Throughout the nineteenth century and beyond the concept of 'homo economicus'—the self-interest construct that is deemed to be the primary human driver beloved by neoclassical economists—has undergone radical changes in definition. For most of the early nineteenth century Mill's concept of rational wealth creation was dominant. 'Mill took man out of nature'.[12] Homo economicus was viewed as a rational calculating machine—Adam Smith's 'invisible hand' that ensures the common good.

This is relevant for my review of imagery of financial crises. The emotional human responses depicted—which convey greed, frenzy, the herd mentality—anticipate twentieth-century behavioural economics rather than classical economics. Akerlof and Shiller expanded on Keynes's reference to 'animal spirits' by identifying five psychological factors which drive the modern economy—*confidence*, fairness, *corruption,* money illusion, and *stories* (my emphasis).[13] These factors help economists to understand the role of ambiguity and uncertainty in markets. The factors identified in italics above are emotions which are highlighted in my review of images. Trust, which I commented earlier is the key factor (as is the absence of trust), driving the market is the ultimate form of confidence as it transcends rational beliefs (market information)—people trust the information because they want it to be true.[14] This leads on to corruption, antisocial behaviour. Similarly, the impact of 'stories', of people and their lives, adds to the confusion. The two remaining factors, fairness (the setting of wages and prices), and money illusion (the public's confusion by inflation or deflation) are not represented in the images under review.

Crosthwaite references Keynes's discussion of 'animal spirits', giving credence to the study of human economic behaviour being informed by animal behaviour (e.g., self-propelled organisms such as migrating birds, lemmings, and ants—reflective of mimetic behaviour during market bubbles and crashes).[15] This also overlaps with the new field of neuroeconomics—which studies how economic behaviour can shape our understanding of humans and animals and roots 'animal spirits' in relationships between genes, hormones, and neurological circuits.

The 'Animal turn' in economics overlaps with the multi-disciplinary subject of 'animal studies'. Animal behaviour economics posit using the study of primates as 'evidence that humans are naturally predisposed not to be 'profit maximisers' driven by pure selfishness, as 'classical economics' maintains, but instead to seek 'reciprocity, the division of rewards, and cooperation'.[16]

2.3 Gambling and Speculation

Underlying the debates about private trust in the nineteenth century is the all-pervading predilection for forms of gambling and speculation. An inadequate regulatory and judicial framework resulted in constant tensions between ever-eager investors seeking 'quick' profits, and unscrupulous managers exploiting the inadequacies of Corporate Law to dupe the often-naïve investors. Gambling and speculation were at the heart of the financial failures during this period: in 1825, Sir Francis Baring, a scion of the Barings Bank family, stated in Parliament that it was impossible to distinguish between what he called 'fair enterprise and extravagant speculation'.[17]

During the Victorian era stock exchange traders fought for respectability against the backdrop of banking and stock scandals. By the 1870s when economic prosperity was at its zenith, commentators might have thought the battle was won. But the twenty-year economic depression which followed (admittedly, a mainly agricultural depression) fuelled people's fears about the monetary system of which they were part. To add to this nervousness there were still more banking scandals in the 1890s, and the rise of betting shops and bucket shops brought gambling into sharp focus again.[18]

2.4 The Impact of Government Laissez-Faire Business Policies

The business climate of 'laissez-faire' meant there was a constant struggle for Governments to maintain a balance between permissive company law and unduly restrictive practices.

Klaus points to the development of 'taxes on distrust'—the costs of doing business involving litigation claims, wherever scheming promoters and directors seemed always to be one step ahead of the regulators—the result, he claims, of a laissez-faire legal climate.[19] Robb supports Klaus's theory, but also talks about 'the class bias which pervaded law and politics'. Robb characterizes this in terms of there being one law for the rich (rarely successful prosecutions until 1870s), whilst others were not so lucky.[20] Atiyah and Butler argue in more nuanced terms that the legal climate was unsympathetic to corporate structures, and this impeded economic progress.[21] Taylor positions his 2013 work as a revisionist account contradicting Robb; he demonstrates that the UK did clamp down on white-collar crime through criminal prosecution and regulatory changes during the latter quarter of the nineteenth century.[22]

2.5 Banking and Corporate Law Regulation

The pre-Victorian period is dominated in monetary economics by the figure of Samuel Jones-Loyd (later Lord Overstone), a private banker, who lived from1796 to 1883. His formative years saw him exposed to the Bullionist/Anti Bullionist debates of the 1810s and 1820s, whilst he himself was the chief proponent of the Currency School, which was the prime influence on Peel's Bank Charter Act of 1844 despite the arguments of the Banking School.

The Bank Restriction Act of 1797 stopped the redemption of bank paper into gold (because of war shortages). Debates then emerged in early 1800s about whether paper notes should be made convertible to gold on demand. The Bullionists (Ricardo, Wheately, Parnell, and Horner) argued for convertibility. Without any restriction on amount of gold reserves, they believed banks would be tempted to issue notes more than their reserves and cause an excess supply of money which would lead to inflation.

Anti-Bullionists (dating back to John Law, and Adam Smith, including contemporaries in the nineteenth century such as Vansittart, Torrens) argued for the status quo of suspension: notes would not be issued beyond the trade needs of banks, the so-called 'reflux principle' whereby liquidation of 'bills of exchange' issued by banks would limit their activities going forward.

This merged into the debate in the 1840s about whether Bank of England notes should have gold parity. Overstone protested the evils of allowing more than one bank to issue notes and pushed for higher gold reserve-liabilities ratio, essentially 100%.

The Currency School (Overstone, McCulloch, Mountiford, Longfield, and Torrens) supported restrictions introduced in the Bank Charter Act, whilst the Banking School (Tooke, Fullarton, and John Stuart Mill) preferred the status quo. They argued that concerns about inflation were better dealt with by restrictions on bank credit, not note issuance.

The suspension of the Bank Charter Act in 1847, 1857, and 1866 gave credence to Banking School ideas (see below for details of financial events associated with these three dates). Nevertheless, the Currency School views prevailed over time and the restrictions on note issuance introduced in 1844 lasted on and off until World War One.

Victorian regulatory responses to consistent episodes of banking fraud and mismanagement centred on the merits of unlimited versus limited liability. The growth of joint-stock companies brought with it demands for limited liability to increase liquidity and wider share ownership, but this was resisted in the case of banks. For the latter, unlimited liability was considered for a long part of the century necessary to retain investor confidence. Owners of banks were viewed as 'completely on the hook' and excessive risk-taking was theoretically curbed by the personal consequences of such actions.

With a broadening shareholder base, investors were seen increasingly as passive actors. In the absence of sufficient shareholder protection by corporate governance and company law reform, these investors could be protected from themselves only if there was a credible threat that fraudsters would be prosecuted.

The prevailing view of those in government was that investors needed to realise that no one was going to bail them out, but their behaviour defied rationality. Gladstone refused to permit prosecution of the Overend & Gurney directors 'it would effect the future prudence and self-restraint of a generation too greedy of money and too ready to adopt one of the most doubtful means of making money'.[23]

Where the frauds involved wealthy investors, this remained the view for a long time. In the case of less affluent investors the situation was different. Investors in savings banks generally involved the working class. Several savings bank officials were successfully prosecuted in the criminal courts between the 1840s and the 1860s.[24]

In response to a series of bank failures in the mid-1850s the Liberals promoted legislation between 1857 and 1861 which created new criminal penalties of up to seven years for embezzlement of company monies, falsification of company books, and the publication of false statements with intent to defraud. Whilst limited liability had been introduced in 1858, and taken up by English banks, the Scottish banks still maintained that investors' confidence was best assured with unlimited liability.[25]

Nevertheless, the failure of the CGB in 1878 resulted in a loss of confidence so significant that the call for limited liability for banks became overwhelming. Belatedly the government of the day realised that low-wealth investors had become sizeable (in overall monetary terms) shareholders in banking concerns, and that unlimited liability had consequently become a worthless security.

The CGB collapse led not only to the successful prosecution of management by the Scottish public prosecutor, but also to the appointment of a Director of Public Prosecutions (DPP) for England and Wales. In 1890 the post of Official Receiver was created to investigate insolvent companies and make recommendations for fraud prosecutions to the DPP. Whilst regulatory reform sought to address fraudulent activities, during the century it went hand in hand with the increasingly interventionist role of the Bank of England.

2.6 Emerging Role of the Bank of England

The Bank of England emerged by the latter half of the nineteenth century as the lender of last resort (LOLR), but it became accepted as the bastion of security only after a series of financial scandals during the century tested its abilities as a private company to provide public confidence in the operation of state finances. Clapham provides the classic 'in-house' view of the history of the Bank during this period, more factual than critical in its commentary.[26] Howe provides an extra dimension by analysing the extent of the professional qualifications of the Bank's directors[27] and their growing competence to undertake the increasingly complex and onerous responsibilities. Many commentators have analysed the regulatory impact of the emerging role of LOLR (Turner, Collins, Button, Knot, et al.).[28] Their emphasis is on understanding how the Bank assumed this role (without any official legal requirement) during the 1870s. The contemporaneous agreement with the emerging role of the Bank of England by the 1870s is expressed by Bagehot.[29]

In the case of Overend & Gurney (O &G), Schneider has recently argued that it was sacrificed on the altar of moral hazard (not because it was too big to fail). Or as Kynaston suggests, public interest was set aside by self-centred central bankers wishing to make an example.[30] Tucker posits a different interpretation based on the reports that BoE commissioned a confidential report by Glyn, Bevan, and Hodgson (a former BoE governor), deputised by BoE to examine O&G's books and decide whether assistance from the BoE or other commercial banks was merited.[31] The report concluded that no rescue should be attempted since the firm was so rotten.[32]

Capie echoes others in commenting that not all financial crises caused such pressures on the banking system that BoE intervention was required.[33] The CGB failure was viewed as a financial fraud, but the financial system itself coped with liquidity concerns.

The rescue of Barings in 1890 involved amongst other things, a review of Baring's financial books. Currie's review concluded that the bank did have a margin of solvency, and this dictated the course of rescue action.

But was it a necessary rescue? Barings was not a commercial bank but a merchant bank. An alternative explanation is provided by Ziegler who commented emphatically that the establishment saved 'one of its own'.[34]

In the end Barings was supported by a guarantee provided by a syndicate of London banks, including the BoE (itself partly indemnified by the Treasury). This was followed by a splitting of the bank in to a 'good' bank and a 'bad' bank (reflecting respectively the assets liquid enough to be managed separately (what we now call 'good' assets from other more illiquid assets- what is now called 'bad' assets).[35]

2.7 The Role of the Press

For a long period, the press blamed investors for their greed and naivete.[36]

Taylor likens the interest in criminal trials to the Georgian interest in salacious sex scandals with lawyers, politicians, and journalists adopting novelistic 'conventions and melodramatic tropes' to excite the public.

Both Taylor and Wilson stress the impact of public opinion; however, though very few directors or promoters were successfully imprisoned, their appearance in court and subsequent reports in the press generated bad publicity which ensured that several of them were forced to resign as MPs or were ruined professionally (see for example the discussion on George Hudson in the chapter on Charlatans).[37]

Lee's review of the press coverage of the CGB failure found that newspapers were engaged in a propaganda campaign to change the law on unlimited liability by a twin-pronged attack on its unfairness: first by highlighting (incorrectly as it turns out) the impact of the CGB failure on small, financially vulnerable shareholders[38] and, second, by seeking to assure investment confidence by protecting the position of the dominant investing class, the wealthy shareholders.

Newspaper editors repeatedly accepted payments from company promoters, and bucket shop operators.[39] Nevertheless, the press was seen to have had a positive impact in exposing corporate fraud; 'watchdog journalism filled the regulatory vacuum that the inadequacy of legislative safeguards against fraud had caused'.[40]

The press, and in particular the financial press, were important in the dissemination of information about companies to investors. Whilst the information could be informative (see the works of David Morier Evans, Bagehot, and Oliphant) journalists faced a dilemma: whilst they wanted to have reliable sources on which to base their comments they could not reveal everything they knew for fear of upsetting these very same sources.[41] This dichotomy is illustrated by the case of Harry Marks discussed in the chapter on Charlatans. Marks exploited his 'public' exposé of fraudulent companies in his newspaper *Financial News* to personally benefit from financial fraud. He was bribed by promoters (amongst them Hooley) to 'puff' the companies they were floating as well as to benefit from companies in which he held financial stakes.

2.8 Business Morality

Bankers were viewed as morally repugnant yet commercially necessary and successful. It reflected overall the dilemma: Christian principles of morality on the one side, and belief in the virtue of entrepreneurial capitalist activities on the other.[42]

For most of the century Stock Exchange brokers were viewed suspiciously by society. Whilst they oiled the wheels of the economy, providing finance to the joint-stock companies, their business practices were often considered immoral. Itkowitz points to the 1860s as the time when speculation became viewed as reputable. The repeal of the 1737 Barnard's Act in 1860 signified the acceptance that Stock Exchange transactions (even futures transactions) were legitimate activities. Ironically, when 'bucket shop keepers' and 'turf accountants' developed share trading activities in the 1880s, far from casting doubt on the validity of Stock Exchange activities with which they were inextricably linked, it reinforced, in the public's minds, the illegitimate nature of off-Exchange transactions.[43]

Contemporary attitudes towards bankers (specifically the theme of socially useful banking pursued by Archbishops of Canterbury Carey and Welby) have been examined in the light of Victorian attitudes by Wilson.[44]

Businessmen often used the defence that their contested acts were 'business as usual' or common practice.[45] Klaus echoes these comments in relation to the activities of Harry Marks 'it takes place every day'.[46] Van Driel comments that directors used the defence of 'honest intent'—to enable the company to survive difficult times and return to profitability.[47]

Johnson comments that historical explanations of nineteenth-century morals have not considered sufficiently the sources affecting the real commercial world. He analyses differing explanations from leading commentators (Hilton, Garnett, and Collini). In Hilton's view, the waning influence of evangelicalism and the introduction of limited liability in 1855 permitted increases in speculative activity. There was no longer the risk of personal insolvency as in the case of old partnership structures, but instead there was potentially unlimited upside with the downside limited to capital invested. Johnson comments that Hilton used as his primary sources parliamentary debates and tracts and magazines. But what was the impact on real-life Lombard Street?

He contrasts this view with that of Garnett—she finds that evangelicals began to stress individual responsibility, honesty, and a renunciation of selfish accumulation. Garnett's sources were writings on social ethics drawn from the evangelical community. Johnson comments that she did not demonstrate the extent to which this literature was read by anything other than a small minority of people.[48]

Finally, Johnson refers to Collini who stresses the 'culture of altruism' which did flourish in the period 1850–1880 amongst Victorian intellectuals. Here Johnson comments that Collini concentrated on the leading minds of the day and ignored any evaluation on more broadly based social norms and values.

Johnson concludes his review by using the examples of two real-life figures, financial 'charlatans', Lord Cochrane and Harry Marks, to comment on nineteenth-century morals (see chapter on Charlatans for detailed commentary on these two figures). For Johnson, Mammon gained the upper hand over morality during the century with the acceptance of fraud in society as a price of a risk-taking economy.[49]

Toms and Van Driel have recently summarised the historiography of fraud. They both refer to the major contribution of Taylor (2013 etc.) who attributes the rise in fraud opportunity in the Victorian era to the emergence of the joint-stock company and the lack of funding for effective regulation.[50]

Up to c. 1840 fraudulent activity was characterised mainly by petty financial crime and corruption, not headline financial scandals (though the case of Lord Cochrane is an exception not mentioned by Robb).[51] Subsequent incidences of corporate frauds were minor and associated with individual confidence tricksters (counterfeiting, bills of exchange, petty bank fraud). As Robb notes, elite misconduct was a relatively minor social ill.[52] Financial crime was viewed as a private offence requiring a private rather than a public prosecution—an expensive proposition for many investors.

Odyluzko quotes Sir Henry Cole, a contemporary of the time, on the Railway Mania (RM):

> In this year, 1845, England was visited with one of its periodical epidemics of commercial folly, the Railway Mania as it was called, which rivalled in intensity the South Sea Bubble of 1720. *Peers, peeresses, commoners, merchants, tradesmen, domestic servants, operatives, were all involved in the madness, and the ruin entailed by it. There was no sign of a serious understanding of the Mania* [my emphasis].[53]

The key themes of trust and confidence which pervade the century are also subjective emotional characteristics, which can vary over time. They lend themselves readily to visual depiction, reflecting negative connotations about monies (greed, avarice, corruption).

Alongside legislative changes driven by banking abuses, Wilson argued (echoing Taylor) that those involved in such activities needed to be 'named and shamed' to keep at bay the disastrous potential loss of confidence in the financial system that contemporary commentators feared could result from banking scandals.

Whilst the courts came down heavily on lower social classes (clerks), for those of a higher social class, remorse and social disgrace were usually deemed adequate punishment. But surely the clerks and managers learned from their superiors, so was such social disgrace too little, too late?

2.9 Gentlemanly Capitalists

As Disraeli expressed in *Vivian Grey*, to enter high society it was necessary to have '*blood, a million, or a genius*'.[54]

The term 'Gentlemanly Capitalists' was first coined by Cain & Hopkins in relation to the emergence of British Imperialism. At the same time, the characteristics of these 'gentlemanly capitalists' also embody the universal virtues that Victorians came to see in all their financiers. The financiers discussed in this book who belong to this category feature in the society periodical *Vanity Fair*, notably the Merchant Princes—the highest of the financial elite—personified by the Rothschilds and the Barings families. The analysis of images of financiers also includes the charlatans, those who did not demonstrate the high standards of the gentlemanly capitalists, as well as mere 'makers of money', but whose role in finance and society led them to be depicted in *Vanity Fair*.

According to Cain and Hopkins, how wealth was acquired was also a fundamental feature of the gentlemanly capitalists.[55] As opposed to gaining capital through work in the factories, it was highly desirable that gentleman attained their wealth through the trade of 'invisibles', such as insurance and banking services, or by serving on the boards of companies. Corporate standing meant that such individuals were able to intertwine themselves in Whitehall, in so doing, to gain information and influence as the financiers of those who dictated policy whilst bankrolling the expeditions derived from such policies.[56]

These links were as much due to the power of money in providing a common bond of education (at the top public schools and universities) as they were to owning land as the aristocracy. Furthermore, it was important that a gentleman engaged in gentlemanly endeavours, which enabled him to solidify social and familial bonds. The financiers exhibited both honourable and dishonourable traits, and frequently failed to live up to the trust placed in them by their investing public.[57]

The growing conservative nature of traditional banking and the impact of close familial and business ties is examined in Kynaston.[58] His description of a myriad personal histories of Stock Exchange brokers led, he believed, to the development of personal connections which saved the ultimate establishment banking firm, Barings, in 1890. Cassis reinforces this view, demonstrating the close personal (i.e., family) relationships between major bankers, especially towards the end of the nineteenth century.[59]

Rubinstein's study of probate values reinforced the view that the richest in society came from commerce and finance rather than industry or manufacturing. Nicholas, however, disputed this view using statistical data from the *Dictionary of Business Biography* to argue that wealth was more evenly distributed amongst these professions. But as Daunton comments, wealth holding was surely just one determinant of status and power.[60]

2.10 The Financial Events to Be Covered

This section summarises chronologically the major financial events in the nineteenth century generating visual images reviewed in this book.

1814	**Lord Cochrane and the Stock Exchange scandal**. There was an alleged conspiracy by Lord Cochrane to fraudulently drive up the price of Omnium stocks by spreading false rumours of Napoleon's death. Cochrane and others were each sentenced to twelve months imprisonment. There were subsequent successful efforts by Cochrane to rehabilitate his name. This is not an event mentioned by Reinhart & Rogoff as it resulted in a short-term fluctuation in Stock Exchange prices with no lasting impact on the financial system
1825	Banking crisis caused by improvident finance provided by the **country banks** Resumption of specie payments by BoE had recommenced in 1819, followed by favourable harvests, and a thriving export industry. Investors chased high returns (higher than traditional Government stocks) and sought to invest in large numbers of domestic and overseas infrastructure projects, many of which were extremely far-fetched and risky. Country banks fuelled this expansion by taking advantage of BoE's reduction of its discount rate to overissue their own notes and invest in often illiquid domestic and foreign currency investments. When calls upon the unpaid capital of the new share projects became due, the financial system could not cope. The BoE was forced to raise the discount rate: sixty-six provincial banks failed as did some London-based banks

(continued)

(continued)

1847	**The Railway Mania**—The 1840s saw an explosion of railway prospectuses at the same time as aggressive discounting by BoE. There was also a fall in wheat prices and disruption to money markets by calls on railway shareholders Campbell, Turner and Walker comment that during this period, hundreds of new railways were 'promoted,' and railway stocks experienced a substantial asset price reversal. Contemporaneous and modern commentators have both suggested that this period was one of the greatest bubbles in economic history[61] The period was associated with the rise and fall of George Hudson, the 'Railway King'. Though pilloried in the press he was not prosecuted for any crimes. McCartney and Arnold conclude that unlike the situation in other frauds, governance structures in place prevented Hudson committing substantive fraud (the frauds were limited as a result to fewer companies in which Hudson was involved)[62] Taylor goes on to comment that as the concept of profit was not legally defined at the time, the appropriation of company money by Hudson was accepted, at least by some observers, as legitimate compensation for his services, given the minimal amount of directors' salaries handed out at the time[63]
1856	This was the year of **three major banking failures**: the 'gigantic swindle' of Strahan, Paul & Bates; the 'thunderclap' of the Tipperary Bank which led to the suicide of John Sadleir and culminating in the failure of the **Royal British Bank** (RBB) later in the year; and the major commercial frauds committed by Redpath and Robson[64] The causes of the collapse of RBB represented common themes during the Victorian period and can be summarised as: (1) Risky investments in Welsh coal mines (see similar comments in respect of O&G and CGB failures) (2) Paying dividends out of capital (a familiar refrain from the RM) (3) Directors' taking monies out of the bank by way of personal loans[65]
1866	**Overend & Gurney failure**—Known as the 'Corner House' because of the location of its offices at the corner of Lombard Street and Birchin Lane, O&G was part of the wider trading group of the Gurney family, East Anglian Quaker merchant gentry. It rose to become the largest bill broker in London, however its activities had become increasingly aggressive in the ten years prior to its collapse, challenging the role and authority of BoE in the money markets O & G failed primarily because it entered the lending business with weak lending controls and inadequate risk management. It was unable to meet the demand for repayment of its deposits and, when BoE refused to step in, it was forced to suspend payments. Taylor attributes the failure to lax regulation on short-selling and credit expansion[66] The clamour for justice grew following the failure and two directors were eventually committed for trial in 1869 but acquitted by the end of that year Tucker makes two points: first that the real-economy effects of the failure of O&G were limited and, second, that its failure reflected its own idiosyncratic risks rather than systemic sources of failure common to many institutions across the UK financial sector. The real-economy fallout was low in part because while O&G has often been regarded as a bank, its primary business was bill broking. It did little screening of its borrowers—meaning that it lent to very few productive firms—and consequently the direct loss to the real economy of its failure was small[67]
1873	**The Vienna Stock Market crash**—War reparations paid to Germany after the Franco-German war of 1870–1871 fuelled overtrading and speculation. This is covered in Chapter 8, 'The Other'

(continued)

(continued)

1878	**CGB failure** - Its failure in 1878 was due as much to lax regulation of company accounts, and corporate strategy as to the financial consequences of unlimited liability on shareholders. Acheson & Turner have explored the impact of this failure on shareholders' investments in financial institutions and the disappearance of unlimited liability (after the regulatory changes in 1879 when investors' demands for more protection could no longer be ignored).[68] This research has revealed that despite the banking scandals of the mid to late 1870s, depositors were always paid in full. CGB had over 1200 shareholders and the response to its failure has been partly attributed to an influx of low wealth individuals unable to meet calls in unlimited liability companies.[69] Shareholders were by and large 'rich' enough to withstand calls on unpaid share capital Capie did not view the CGB failure as a financial crisis—the bank was fraudulently run, but the financial system was not at risk. It involved significant misstatement of company accounts to cover up interpersonal lending and other bad loans granted by negligent directors. Two of its directors, Stronach and Potter were sentenced to eighteen months imprisonment (no penal servitude)- other defendants received sentences of five months each
1882	The rise and fall of the **Union Générale Bank** in France (discussed in Chapter 8, 'The Other')
1890	**Barings Bank failure**—A major merchant bank not involved in the payments system. Reinhart and Rogoff viewed it as a banking crisis as its rescue averted a financial panic. Barings was overexposed to the Argentinian bond market because of the quantity of unsold Argentinian bonds it owned. Combined with an increasing illiquid bond market due to market rumours of instability, this was enough to render Barings unable to meet its short-term financial needs despite having a surplus of assets over liabilities[70] There was no systemic financial fallout from the collapse of Barings. Its partners bore the extent of the losses and by 1895 Barings had been reconstituted on a sound footing
1892	**The failure of the Liberator Building Society**—The Liberator closely followed the model of another mutual society, the Alliance National Land Building and Investment Society formed in 1862 and which had been named to suggest a link with the leading temperance organisation, the United Kingdom Alliance. In a similar vein, the name 'Liberator' was designed to align its ideals (or at least to appear to do so) with those of the non-conformist Liberation Society Its founder, Jabez Balfour used the Liberator as a conduit to pass money drawn from unsuspecting public depositors to invest in property speculation (the Lands Allotment Company which Balfour had controlled since 1867) Balfour was able to get away with what he did because of a compliant set of directors and an auditor/director, Morell Theobald, who, in common with several of his contemporaries, failed to stand up to a dominant senior executive.[71] The scheme began to unravel in 1892 because the economy was in recession and the flow of savings began to dry up. At the time of its failure, Liberator was the largest building society in the country. The crash cost investors and savers £8m[72] The eventual successful prosecution of the directors revealed that from the inception of the group it had existed on the deposits of its stakeholders, which had been used to pay directors' dividends, even when the group was operating at a loss. Furthermore, the group had misrepresented, fraudulently, its fiscal health, 'cooking the books' to retain investors and encourage new investment. Balfour's use of what would now be called related party-transactions exemplified 'the criminal potential of company groups'.[73] Moreover, the stakeholders' deposits had funded the directors' lavish lifestyles through unagreed 'loans'[74]

2.11 Conclusion

This review of the financial literature has inevitably omitted discussion of every nineteenth-century financial failure. It has been based on those events which generated the visual images identified from my database research. What is significant is the nature of the two events which did generate the most images identified. The first was the Railway Mania of 1845–1847 and the second the CGB failure of 1878. Just in terms of numbers of images identified, the events, separated by just over thirty years, clearly captured the imagination of the public.[75] The first event encapsulates the frenzy, the 'herd' mentality of investors, and is the dominant theme in financial images throughout the century. The frenzy had both optimistic as well as negative phases, the optimism of the boom period as investors made money, to be followed by the pessimism when the bubble burst and fortunes were lost. The second highlighted the nature and impact of corporate banking fraud on victims and villains. This was a theme which developed over the period, as white-collar crime began to be successfully prosecuted.

The review of images highlights the ambivalence of the gentlemanly capitalists' morals. The charlatans, the financial fraudsters, were depicted as pillars of the society when their exploits brought wealth to their investors. When the charlatans were exposed, the opprobrium towards them was expressed in the court of public opinion, and in images in the comic-serious periodicals.

The inclusion, however, in *Vanity Fair*, alongside Merchant Princes, of 'makers of money' who derived their wealth from gambling, as well as the charlatans, indicates that the elite society viewed all these financial figures as accepted members of society. It also demonstrates that the blurring of distinctions between legitimate trading, gambling, and speculation was ever present.

Notes

1. See Geoffrey Williams, *Fraud in the Development of Victorian British Banking*, 2013 for details of banking losses suffered by banks in these earlier years, p. 10. See John D. Turner, *Banking in Crisis: The Rise and Fall of British Banking Stability, 1800 to the Present* (Cambridge, Cambridge University Press, 2014), pp. 74–75 for details of the failures in the 1830s and 1840s.

2. See James B. Jeffreys, *Business Organisation in Great Britain 1856–1914, a study of trends, with Special Reference to the Financial Structure of Companies, the Mechanism of Investment and the Relations Between the Shareholders and the Company* (New York, Arno Press, 1977) and Joseph Sykes, *The Amalgamation Movement in English Banking, 1825–1924* (London, King, 1926).
3. Ian Klaus, *Forging Capitalism Rogues, Swindlers, Frauds, and the Rise of Modern Finance* (2014), p. 4.
4. Ibid., p. 23.
5. George Robb, *White-Collar Crime in Modern England Financial Fraud and Business Morality 1845–1929* (Cambridge, Cambridge University Press, 1992), p. 10.
6. Charles P. Kindleberger and Robert Z. Aliber, *Manias, Panics and Crashes: A History of Financial Crises* (Basingstoke, Palgrave Macmillan, 2005).
7. Daniele Besomi, 'Graphical Representations of Overstone's Cycle of Trade', in C. Gehrke, N. Salvadori, I. Steedman and R. Sturn (eds.), *Classical Political Economy and Modern Theory: Essays in Honour of Heinz D. Kurz* (London, Routledge, 2011).
8. Turner (2014). M. Collins (1990), and 'The Banking Crisis of 1878', *Economic History Review*, 2nd ser., XLII, 4 (1989), C. M. Reinhart and K. S. Rogoff, *This Time Is Different: Eight Centuries of Financial Folly* (Princeton, Princeton University Press, 2009), A. J. Schwartz, 'Real and Pseudo-Financial Crises', in F. Capie and G. E. Wood (eds.), *Financial Crises and the World Banking System* (London, St Martin's Press, 1986).
9. Charles McKay, *Extraordinary Popular Delusions and the Madness of Crowds* (Ware, 2006, reprint of 1852 edition). The title indicates his view of the impact of financial crises on individuals. David Morier Evans, *Facts, Failures and Frauds: Revelations Financial, Mercantile, Criminal* (New York, 1968 reprint of 1859), pp. 1–5. Charles P. Kindleberger and Robert Z. Aliber, *Manias Panics and Crashes: A History of Financial Crises* (Basingstoke, Palgrave Macmillan, 5th edition, 2005), pp. 36/37, George A. Akerlof and Robert J. Shiller, *Animal Spirits: How Human Psychology Drives the Economy, and Why It Matters for Global Capitalism* (Oxford, Princeton University Press, 2009), p. 3.
10. Mackay, p. xv.
11. Akerlof and Shiller, p. xxiii.

12. Margaret Schabas, *The Natural Origins of Economics* (Chicago, University of Chicago Press, 2007), p. 150.
13. Akerlof and Shiller, pp. ix and 4.
14. Ibid., p. 12.
15. Paul Crosthwaite, 'Animality and Ideology in Contemporary Economic Discourse, Taxonomising Homo Economicus', *Journal of Cultural Economy*, 6:1, 2013, p. 97. Crosthwaite, 'Blood on the Trading Floor, Waste, Sacrifice, and Death in Financial Crises', *Angelaki: Journal of Theoretical Humanities*, 15:2, 2010, p. 5.
16. Crosthwaite, 2013, p. 103.
17. Edward Chancellor, *Devil Take the Hindmost: A History of Financial Speculation* (New York, Plume, 2000), pp. 9–10.
18. Itkowitz, 'Fair Enterprise or Extravagant Speculation; Investment, Speculation, and Gambling in Victorian England', in Henry and Schmitt (eds.), *Victorian Investments, New Perspectives on Finance and Culture* (Bloomington, Indiana University Press, 2009).
19. Ian Klaus, *Forging Capitalism Rogues, Swindlers, Frauds, and the Rise of Modern Finance* (Yale, Yale University Press, 2014).
20. George Robb, *White-Collar Crime in Modern England: Financial Fraud and Business Morality, 1845–1929* (Cambridge, Cambridge University Press, 1992).
21. P. S. Atiyah, *The Rise and Fall of Freedom of Contract* (Oxford, Oxford University Press, 1979). H. N. Butler, 'General Incorporation in Nineteenth-Century England: Interaction of Common Law and Legislative Processes', *International Review of Law and Economics*, 6:2, 1986.
22. Taylor, p. 701.
23. Taylor, 'White-Collar Crime and the Law in Nineteenth-Century Britain', *Business History*, 60:3, 2018, p. 346.
24. Ibid., p. 346.
25. Michael Collins, 'The Banking Crisis of 1878', *Economic History Review*, 2nd ser., XLII, 4 (1989), p. 504.
26. J. H. Clapham, *The Bank of England: A History, Vol. 11 1797–1914* (Cambridge, Cambridge University Press, 1944).
27. Anthony C. Howe, 'From Old Corruption to New Probity: The Bank of England and Its Directors in the Age of Reform, *Financial History Review*, 1, 1994, pp. 23–41. https://doi.org/10.1017/S0968565000001542.

28. M. Collins, *Money and Banking in the UK: A History* (London, 1990). John. D. Turner, *Banking in Crisis: The Rise and Fall of British Banking Stability, 1800 to the Present* (Cambridge, 2014). Richard Button, Samuel Knot, Conor McManus, and Matthew Willison, 'Desperate Adventurers and Men of Straw: The Failure of City of Glasgow Bank and Its Enduring Impact on the UK Banking System', *BOE Quarterly Bulletin, Q1*, 2015.
29. Vincent Bignon, Marc Flandreau, and Stefano Ugolini, 'Bagehot for Beginners: The Making of Lender-of-Last-Resort Operations in the Mid-Nineteenth Century', *Economic History Review*, 65:2, 2012, p. 580.
30. Sir Paul M. W. Tucker, 'Solvency as a Fundamental Constraint on LOLR Policy for Independent Central Banks: Principles, History, Law,' *Journal of Financial Crises*, 2:2, 2020, p.18.
31. Ibid., p. 19.
32. Ibid., p. 20.
33. Forest Capie, '200 Years of Financial Crises: Lessons Learned and Forgotten', *Conference Paper, Madrid, Spain*, December 2011.
34. Ziegler, *The Sixth Great Power: Barings 1762–1929* (London, Collins, 1988), p. 266, also quoted in Turner, p. 157.
35. Tucker, p. 20.
36. James Taylor, *Boardroom Scandal: The Criminalization of Company Fraud in Nineteenth-Century Britain* (Oxford, Oxford University Press, 2013), p. 88.
37. Gary Wilson and Sarah Wilson, 'The Pursuit of "Socially Useful Banking" in Twenty-First Century Britain and Exploring Victorian Interactions Between Law, Religion, and Financial Marketplace Values', *Nottingham Law Journal*, 22, 2013, p. 53.
38. T. A. Lee, 'A Helpless Class of Shareholder: Newspapers and the Failure of the City of "Glasgow Bank"', *Accounting History Review*, 26, 2012, p. 144.
39. Van Driel, p. 1273.
40. Taylor, 'Privacy, Publicity, and Reputation: How the Press Regulated the Market in Nineteenth-Century England', *Business History Review*, 87, 2013, p. 693.
41. Mary Poovey, *Genres of the Credit Economy: Mediating Value in Eighteenth-Century and Nineteenth-Century Britain* (London, University of Chicago Press, 2008).

42. Geoffrey Searle, *Morality and the Market in Victorian Britain* (London, Clarendon Press, 1998). Irene Finel-Honigman, *A Cultural History of Finance* (Abingdon, Routledge, 2010).
43. Itkowitz, pp. 98–99.
44. Gary Wilson and Sarah Wilson, 'The Pursuit of "Socially Useful Banking" in Twenty-First Century Britain and Exploring Victorian Interactions Between Law, Religion, and Financial Marketplace Values', *Nottingham Law Journal*, 22, 2013, p. 53.
45. Robb, p. 171.
46. Klaus, p. 196.
47. Hugo Van Driel, 'Financial Fraud, Scandals, and Regulation: A Conceptual Framework and Literature Review', *Business History*, 61:8, p. 1275.
48. Paul Johnson, 'Civilizing Mammon: Laws, Morals, and the City in Nineteenth-Century England', in Peter Burke, Brian Harrison, and Paul Slack (eds.), *Civil Histories: Essays Presented to Sir Keith Thomas*, published in Oxford Scholarship Online, p. 7. https://doi.org/10.1093/9780198207108.003.0017.
49. Ibid., pp. 22/23.
50. Hugo Van Driel, 'Financial Fraud, Scandals and Regulation: A Conceptual Framework and Literature Review', *Business History*, 61:8, pp. 1259. Steven Toms, 'Financial Scandals: A Historical Overview', *Accounting and Business Research*, 45:5, p. 479.
51. Toms, p. 481.
52. Robb, p. 147.
53. Andrew Odyluzko, 'Collective Hallucinations and Inefficient Markets: The British Railway Mania of the 1840s', p. 26. (Preliminary version, 15 January 2010), http://www.dtc.umn.edu/_odlyzko.
54. Quoted in Sarah Bradford, *Disraeli* (London, Grafton Books, 1985), p. 32.
55. P. J. Cain and A. G. Hopkins, *British Imperialism: Innovation and Expansion 1688–1914* (New York, Longman, 1993).
56. Jake Jacobs, 'Defalcations, Swindles, and Fraud: Ungentlemanly Capitalism in Victorian Babylon, 1800–1899, *King's Law Review*, 9:1, 2018, p. 51, downloaded from HeinOnline.
57. Ibid., p. 52.
58. David Kynaston, *City of London: A World of Its Own 1815–1890*, vol. 1 (London, Chatto & Windus, 1994).

59. Youssef Cassis, *City Bankers 1890–1914* (New York, Cambridge University Press, 2009).
60. Tom Nicholas, 'Wealth Making in Nineteenth- and Early Twentieth-Century Britain: Industry v Commerce and Finance', *Business History*, 41:1, 1999, p. 17.
61. Gareth Campbell, John D. Turner, and Clive B. Walker, 'The Role of the Media in a Bubble', *Explorations in Economic History*, 49 (2012), p. 461.
62. Van Driel, p. 1270.
63. Taylor, 2013a, pp. 84–89.
64. Quoted in James Taylor, *Boardroom Scandal: The Criminalization of Company Fraud in Nineteenth Century Britain* (Oxford, Oxford University Press, 2013), p. 109.
65. See James Taylor, 'Commercial Fraud and Public Men in Victorian Britain', *Historical Research*, 78:200, May 2005, pp. 230–252. This is the only major study of this banking crisis.
66. Taylor (2013). See also Rhiannon Sowerbutts, 'The Demise of Overend Gurney', *BoE Quarterly Bulletin*, Q2 2016, Turner (2014), Bignon et al. (2012), Geoffrey Elliott, *The Mystery of Overend & Gurney: A Financial Scandal in Victorian London* (London, Methuen, 2006), Kynaston (1994). See also M. Collins, 'The Banking Crisis of 1878', *Economic History Review*, 2nd ser., XLII, 4 (1989) and 'The Bank of England as Lender of Last Resort, 1857–1878', *Economic History Review*, New Series, 45, February 1992, pp. 145–153.
67. Tucker (2020).
68. G. G. Acheson and J. D. Turner, 'The Death Blow to Unlimited Liability in Victorian Britain: The City of Glasgow Bank Failure', *Economic History Review*, 59, 2006, pp. 320–346.
69. G. G. Acheson and J. D. Turner, 'Shareholder Liability, Risk Aversion, and Investment Returns in Nineteenth-Century British Banking', in D. R. Green, A. Owens, J. Maltby, and J. Rutterford (eds.), *Men, Women and Money: Perspectives on Gender, Wealth and Investment, 1850–1930* (Oxford, Oxford University Press, 2011).
70. See H. S. Ferns, 'The Baring Crisis Revisited', *Journal of Latin American Studies*, 24:2, May 1992, pp. 241–273 and Youssef Cassis, 'Crises and Opportunities: The Shaping of Modern Finance', accessed online from www.oxfordscholarship.com on 5 January 2016.

71. Jacobs, p. 342.
72. Ibid., p. 343.
73. Robb, p. 142.
74. Taylor, 2013, p. 230.
75. My review identified that 50%, or 70 of the total images of financial crises identified during the period, were attributable equally to these two events.

CHAPTER 3

Visual Context

> A historiography that was alert to memory's shadows - those sleeping images which spring to life unbidden and serve as ghostly sentinels of our thought - might give at least as much attention to pictures as to manuscripts or print. The visual provides us with our stock figures, our subliminal points of reference, our unspoken point of address.[1]
>
> —Raphael Samuel, Theatres of Memory

3.1 Introduction

This quote from Samuel sums up some of the qualities of visual images to be explored in this section of the book. It prefigures later comments in this chapter on the impact of memory, of the unconscious. Patten comments in relation to the Golden Age of Georgian satire that it tends to depict negative aspects of topical events and figures, because giving praise rarely sold prints.[2] As the century develops the advent of realistic periodicals such as *ILN* or the *Graphic* provides an antidote in the form of positive realistic portrayals of leading financial figures. When *Vanity Fair* caricatures appeared in 1869, a cross-over between realistic portrayals and light caricature emerged.

The traditional view expressed by Kunzle, Maidment, and others is that the Victorian period—characterised by a more polite society in which even the popular press exercised self-censorship[3]—was a reaction to the mores of the Georgian period. In contrast to the extreme scatological and violent

H. Sless, *Merchant Princes and Charlatans or Makers of Money?*,
https://doi.org/10.1007/978-3-030-86604-4_3

satire of the Golden Age, a lighter Victorian satire reflected the overall zeitgeist and a return to formality and politeness characterized using puns to convey humour rather than outright caricature. Nevertheless, during the Victorian period caricatures of famous figures (especially parliamentarians such as Disraeli and Gladstone) became acceptable. Rather than offensive distortion of a person's physiognomy (which is more characteristic of caricature), the mild caricature displayed in *Vanity Fair* permits an analysis of contemporary attitudes towards the elite. The success of the periodical reflected the difficult path followed by its editors and artists in trying to provide amusement to its readers—including some of most famous, who were the subject of caricature—without offending them.[4]

The late 1870s onwards saw the reappearance of financial icons associated with the 1820s and even earlier. The financial settings (e.g., balloons, puffs of air) conjure up the ephemeral, chimerical world of financial bubbles used in the depictions of the boom years of 1824/5 and the era of the South Sea Bubble in 1720.

By the early 1890s parliamentarians were being satirised more directly; Harry Furniss and Francis Carruthers Gould depicted Sir William Harcourt (Chancellor of the Exchequer in the early 1890s) variously as an elephant, a hedgehog, an old maid, and Mammon—in the form of a Pharaoh.

3.2 Image Analysis

3.2.1 PEARL Template

The use of images provides a different perspective to text-based news—it shows the selective use of news to drive the editorial content of cartoons. There was a symbiotic relationship between the publisher (whose publication reflected a political bias), the editor (who had to choose which events to comment on to keep the publication's readers interested), the artist (whose role was to interpret the requirements of the editor), and the readers (who would buy only what they wanted to see and read at the right price)—all in the context of the legal restraints if any on the degree of caricature permitted. I have used the acronym PEARL (Publisher, Editor, Artist, Reader, Legal) that results from this interrelationship to offer a critical perspective on the images reviewed in later chapters.

Images in weekly periodicals provided a more immediate response to current events than literary sources and monthly periodicals published sometime after the events. But equally, and especially a problem for a modern-day reader of cartoons from the past, Furniss's comment on the ephemeral topicality of caricatures highlights the need for in-depth hermeneutic interpretation. This is what the PEARL approach seeks to uncover. It is illustrated in Appendix 1 in relation to one specific image.

3.2.2 Publisher/Political Bias

The increasing importance of political bias as particular publishers (and artists) pushed a pro- or anti-Government agenda during this period should not be underestimated. In the Victorian period it is most prominent in the attitude of rival periodicals to the foreign policies of Disraeli and Gladstone (see section on Merchant Princes).

In the financial area there was general agreement amongst the political parties on the ruling government's laissez-faire approach towards regulation of companies. *Vanity Fair* ushers in a trend of polite satire on leading politicians and financiers. But it is only as the century wears on that the more irreverent periodicals (*Funny Folks*, *The Cycle*, etc.,) reflected the era of new journalism by introducing overt criticism of the unscrupulous company promoters of the day.

Any discussion about the role of the publisher in producing visual images needs to take account of what Maidment described as the major technical and economic developments of graphic media within a particular historical period.'[5]

Leary has noted how the full-page cartoon may have drawn on the stand-alone satirical print for inspiration, but it also 'hastened that genre's demise': the market for the Hogarth, Gillray, or even Doyle style of print had entirely evaporated by the 1840s, partly because readers could purchase entire issues of magazines filled with cartoons for a fraction of the price of an old-fashioned, stand-alone print.[6]

The abolition of the stamp tax on knowledge between 1853 and 1861, the fall in paper prices, as well as the growth of advertising reduced costs of publication all encouraged publication of cheaper periodicals including newspapers.

The introduction of photo-chemical and photo-mechanical techniques in the 1870s and 1880s allowed photographic images to be reproduced in newspapers and books. Since steel engraving's *raison d'etre* was primarily economic, both these and traditional woodcuts became obsolete quickly.

3.2.3 *Editorial Input*

As comic periodicals came of age from the 1830s, editorial influence resulted in the strategic positioning of cartoons at the beginning or the centre of publications, as well the use of single- or double-page cartoons to accentuate the importance of a particular cartoon.

Periodicals such as the *ILN* and the *Graphic* (founded 1869) relied as much, if not more, on images as on words in their representations of the world. The editor of the *Strand* (founded 1891) went as far as to demand an image on every page.[7] Campbell comments on the effect of the trend of 'new journalism'—a growing emphasis on metropolitan papers, dating to mid-century, signifying the use of headlines, sketches, interviews, and illustrations.[8]

The relationship between text and cartoon is key to understanding the latter's meaning. Madsen argues that images should not simply be analysed in terms of print culture but as separate conversations with the printed text.[9] Thus, the impact of a cartoon can be influenced by the absence of text, the use of text within the cartoon itself, as a caption to the cartoon, or with text positioned on the previous or subsequent pages.[10] Maidment points to the gradual dominance of the text over the visual image in the Victorian period, though this is disputed by Flint, who argues more broadly for the gradual domination of the visual in the minds of the Victorians.[11]

Sometimes *Punch* published a textual commentary (on an adjacent page) to remind readers of the context and visual imagery being depicted. In the case of the realistic periodicals, *ILN* published (on a page towards the back of the issue) an explanation of the detailed drawings they had included as images at the front. The explanation sometimes offered an editorial comment.

Overall, the nineteenth century saw an increase in economic and secular topics in visual images reflecting the long-lasting influence of Hogarth from the previous century. Briggs and Briggs, in their social history of *Punch* commented that one of the reasons that *Punch* was often more successful than the *Times* in pursuing social causes was the power of the visual image, specifically the use of the Big Cut.[12]

3.2.4 *Artistic Style*

Overlap Between Cartoonists and Painters

Thomas, Meisel, and others have commented on the overlap between cartoons and paintings—many of the artists in the periodicals also were painters—especially narrative painting.[13] This blurring of distinctions in the Victorian period between what is traditionally associated with 'high art' (i.e., painting) and what is commonly known as 'low art' (i.e., cartoons) is another reason why discussion about images of finance should not be limited to low art alone.

There is an overlap in the discussion above about high vs. low art in relation to *Vanity Fair*. This periodical forms the basis for my chapters on Merchant Princes and Charlatans: it was a collection in colour of individual caricatures and accompanying letterpress. It was aimed at the society elite and is revealing as much about those individuals who were excluded as about those who were included. The accompanying letterpress commentary by the editor, Bowles, who masqueraded under the pseudonym, Jehu Junior, provided much of the contemporary 'gossip' and political commentary on the characters being caricatured.

Cartoonists like Tenniel would mix with artists like Millais, whilst artists such as Luke Fildes and Hubert Herkomer would take illustrations they had done for periodicals such as the *Graphic* and *ILN* and turn these realistic drawings into social realistic paintings.[14] Inspiration for Frith's *The Road to Ruin* was to be found in Hogarth's *The Rake's Progress* and *Mariage a la Mode*, as well as *Reynolds Miscellany, The Gamesters Progress* published in 1849. Frith's *The Race for Wealth* series was itself even satirised in the comic periodical *Fun* soon after the paintings were exhibited.

The popularity of Victorian painters has been equated to that of Charles Dickens, with security measures in place to prevent crowds of visitors to the Royal Academy damaging the works presented there.[15] Indeed, the excitement felt by spectators seeing these paintings must have had much in common with the feelings evoked at the height of the Georgian Golden Age of Satire sixty years earlier.[16]

For most of the nineteenth century, narrative painting dominated the Victorian artistic landscape. Telling a story was as, if not more, important than any stylistic concerns. The form of such representation centred around two distinct topics—the urban crowd and the sin against domesticity (prostitution). Meisel comments that gambling as depicted in paintings was a form of 'illicit commerce, an alternative to the iron laws of economic life and financial accountability'.[17] Except for the limited number of paintings dealing with gambling in the 1860s and 1870s, Victorian artists largely eschewed coverage of the financial world. As we saw in the chapter Financial Context, gambling represented an economic activity which was associated in contemporary minds with speculation, and was viewed ambivalently, with both moral disapproval of the depravity of gambling, as well as tacit acceptance that it was widely pursued and admired (where it was successful).

Stylistic Devices

Treuherz commented that many artists began to extend their narratives beyond 'the confines of a single time and place' using a serial format derived from Hogarth.[18] This serial format is prevalent across several media, from paintings to cartoons in periodicals and newspapers. The subsequent use of the storyboard (e.g., at the time of City of Glasgow Bank collapse) led to the comic strips of Ally Sloper in the late nineteenth century onwards.

At the risk of generalisation, popular imagery between 1830 and 1880 had been largely dominated by black-and-white linear images; after 1880 tone and colour became much more important and prominent.[19]

The period saw the rise of comic-serious periodicals (*Punch, Fun, Judy, Moonshine, Picture Politics,* etc.) as well as realistic periodicals like the *Illustrated London News* (*ILN*) and the *Graphic*, as well as the popular sensationalism of the *Illustrated Police News* (*IPN*).

Generally, this was reflected in the difference between static, iconic portraits that sought to 'fix' the sitter, and the spread of more dynamic imagery after 1850, such as illustrated newspapers and *cartes de visite*, which provided snapshots that placed the subject within the contemporary context rather than detaching them from it.[20]

Photographs/Portraits

Portraits in the pictorial press were increasingly based on photographs from the late 1840s. But photography was still limited in its ability to capture the sitter: standardised props and compositions were used whilst long exposure times also contributed to the stilted appearance of many sitters.[21] Furniss comments on the techniques used by photographers to alter almost everything about the sitters other than their clothes.[22]

Miller commented that there were four main purposes for political portraits. First, the shaping of national narratives through depiction of great statesmen and politicians involved in important events. Second, they formed and reflected political identities. Third, they satisfied the eagerness to see who the people—who engaged in great political acts—were. Fourth, in shaping the public image and reputation of politicians, both individually and collectively, politicians could exert control and influence over their image.[23]

I illustrate this phenomenon when discussing visual representations of the Liberal Chancellor of the Exchequer, Sir Vernon Harcourt, in the Chapter Merchant Princes. In this context the periodical *Picture Politics* juxtaposes 'official' photographs of the parliamentarian Harcourt with cartoon representations to highlight different often comic aspects of his personality.

3.2.5 *Readership*

Don Vann and VanArsdel comment that in the nineteenth century the circulation of periodicals and newspapers was larger and more influential than that of printed books.[24]

Altick points to the significance of the introduction of illustrations in the development of a mass working-class readership of periodicals with the publication of the *ILN* in 1842.[25] However, it should be borne in mind that *Punch* and other London periodicals were minority publications which were far outstripped in circulation numbers by more mass-market publications.[26]

Huggett in his social history of *Punch* saw its readership as being composed of two extremes, the modern money makers, and the new landed interest, those earning thousands of pounds every year, as well as those just above £200 per annum, the minimum level at which income tax was payable.[27] By the 1870s they were joined by the ever-increasing numbers of the professional classes, the bookkeepers and bank clerks, etc., who could now afford to buy newspapers and magazines thanks to the technological and distribution advances which had driven prices down following the repeal of paper duties, initially in 1855 and the final one in 1861.

Punch's readership, roughly equal to that of Harper's in the US, was many times that of *Le Charivari* in France (though the circulation of *Le Petit Journal* did reach one million in the 1890s). This was extended by the fact that no sooner did the week's *Punch* spread over the country when 'a mass of newspapers, both in England and in the colonies', described and discussed ""this week's cartoon" for the edification of their readers'.[28]

In England, *Punch* was not only read; it was studied. Because of the emphasis on a classical education in the public schools—to the exclusion of modern history, geography, modern literature, and the practical sciences—the regular newspapers would have been the main source of information for the young during a substantial part of the century.[29]

There was a geographical dimension to the explosion of reading habits amongst working and middle classes. In the early part of the nineteenth century readers of cartoons would peer through shop windows in the metropolis or peruse bound copies of latest series of cartoons in society drawing rooms. Later in the century improved transportation and distribution techniques would see cartoons displayed as advertisements in railway stations, as well as reading cartoons in libraries, coffee houses, or at home.[30] The regularity, even repeat viewing of periodicals is an aspect discussed below.

3.2.6 Legal

Goldstein highlights the historic view that caricatures were more dangerous than the written word because they communicated more directly to the audience's senses and emotions than the traditional written word did. Allied to this was the fear of the ruling elite (specifically in France) that because sizeable numbers of the population were illiterate, they would be more easily swayed by pictures. As a result, drawings though not print were subject in France to censorship almost continually from 1820 to 1881.[31]

As we shall see below, there were similar censorship restrictions in Germany. In the case of the US there were no such restrictions. In the UK self-censorship after the excesses of Georgian vulgarity was exercised by publishers throughout the Victorian period. This reflected the mores of the time, though the advent of new journalism in the 1870s onwards meant that many of the newer periodicals were less reverent in their depictions of major financial figures of the day.

3.3 Image Theory

Traditionally, research into Victorian periodicals has concentrated on specific periodicals, artists, editors, or thematic analyses, especially *Punch*. More recently articles on editors of periodicals other than *Punch* have emerged, e.g., books and articles on *ILN*, the *Graphic*, and *Judy*[32] or coverage of events or individuals (e.g., thematic analyses of wars of Empire (Bryant), or Victorian cartoon responses to the German Kaiser Wilhelm II (Scully) are two examples).[33] In relation to *Punch*, there have been numerous articles and books covering a detailed review of its early years (Altick) to broader reviews by Briggs and Briggs, and Huggett.[34]

M. D. George's systematic cataloguing of the prints in the British Museum Collection of Political Prints and Personal Satires (1600–1832) in the 1940s and 1950s formed the basis for future cultural historians' analysis of prints.[35] Her approach was deemed by later historians to have been too literal, and it is the pioneering cultural historians in the late 1960s and 1970s—such as Streicher, Coupe, and Kemnitz—who began to challenge historians to use cartoons as another form of historical evidence.[36] Freels comments that they ignore the study of the symbols in the cartoons which is as important as understanding the background of the artists themselves.

Porter's seminal 1988 article stressed that 'prints display short-hand artistic conventions' that we need to deconstruct.[37] He stressed the need to understand the multiple signs and codes that artists used to convey politics, women, and cultural contexts. His comments were taken up by Maidment and others to advance the now commonly accepted interpretative approach towards visual images which relies on understanding the complex symbiotic relationship between publisher, editor, artist, and reader.[38] This leads to the PEARL acronym (which includes Legal as an additional element) which I have adopted as my interpretive lens.

3.3.1 Use as Historical Evidence

One of the challenges in analysing visual images is assessing academically how visual images can be used as historical evidence. The potential use of images as historical evidence is best illustrated by the cultural historian, Burke, in *Eyewitnessing*.[39] He sets out provisional rules of source criticism; his rules (or, more precisely, questions which need to be addressed) can be grouped into two categories, the first dealing with the truth of the image (verification and authenticity), and the second with cultural contexts, conventions of representations, visual traditions, and attitudes to the past. He has been taken to task by art historians such as Ades for dismissing aesthetic considerations as unnecessary to his source criticism.

Nevertheless, Burke's systematic analysis of image interpretation has proved extremely influential. Jordanova has expanded on Burke's research in *The Look of the Past*. She has consistently argued that images should not be regarded as mere decorative embellishment of written historical sources (as is evidenced in traditional historical studies) but as objects worthy of discussion as primary source material.[40]

My book serves as evidence that such primary source material does provide valuable insights into how financial events and figures were viewed contemporaneously. This is especially true when considering the repetition of financial iconography which recurs both in Britain and abroad in relation to financial events and figures.

3.3.2 Cartoonists' Armoury

Image theory has been greatly influenced by early works in the twentieth century by Gombrich, a celebrated art historian. Gombrich brought the study of cartoonists into mainstream art when he discussed 'the cartoonists' armoury', the array of artistic techniques available to the cartoonist to convey caricature.[41] These were:

Figures of speech,
Condensation and comparison (images more than words),
The (political) bestiary (animal/human) visualisations (e.g., Harcourt as a cat or a hedgehog; stock characters like John Bull, Mr Punch, and Mr Jeames),
Natural metaphors and powerful contrasts (juxtaposition).

For Freels, the pages of *Punch* reveal a gradual reduction in physiognomic caricature and replaced eventually by the more subtle use of captioning and image placement.[42]

Furniss commented that his methodology for the series of 'Puzzle Heads' involved looking at individual attributes which 'could not but be unpleasant pictures… one man's meat is another's poison'.[43]

Whereas puns and metaphors are often mentioned in connection with Victorian humour, it is Gombrich's identification of Bestiary or animal imagery which is the most fruitful area of research in the financial imagery field.

Animal imagery was represented in high art in Britain from Stubbs through to Landseer. Potts referenced the use of animal representations to convey a sense of elemental conflict and raw instinct—the blurring between the natural and the social in nineteenth-century discourse.[44] There was a cross-over from Landseer's paintings in the 1840s with the use by *Punch* and other comic artists of stag antlers to signify stock exchange behaviour. Tenniel in mid-century developed animal personifications of nations.[45] In the UK, Furniss, and others in the late 1870s onwards used animal personifications to portray parliamentarians (see the portrayal of Harcourt and Goschen in Chapter 4 dealing with Merchant Princes).

Burns stresses the trends in entertainment in the US (fairs/circuses) which fuelled the emotional depiction of speculation in both painting (Beard) and cartoons (Nast). John comments that sometimes, for example, the arch speculator Jay Gould was transformed into an animal: a predatory whale; a venomous python; a mischievous raccoon; or even a poisonous tarantula spider whose web, fashioned with telegraph wires, had ensnared the courts.[46]

In the case of France, the late 1880s onwards saw an expansion of imagery being used as anti-capitalist, anti-Semitic portrayals. Distorted animal images were used to influence public opinion by preying on fears of national infestation (deep *fin-de-siecle* concerns about the nation and the body).[47]

3.3.3 *Memory—Repetition*

A review of images that are repeated in terms of both text and visual representation over the whole Victorian period leads into an emerging discussion around 'emotional discourse' and the impact on Victorian readers' unconscious of recurring financial tropes. Mitchell analyses *Punch*'s Special Issues of 1887 and 1897 and comments on the existence of a collective unconscious created by the constant repetition of images and text over the Victorian period.[48] The repetition was reinforced by the marketing techniques that *Punch* and other comic periodicals introduced of publishing issues in addition to normal weekly issues (e.g., weekly issues, monthly parts, or half-yearly bound volumes[49]). In addition, annual Almanacks were introduced to be followed by Special and Summer numbers).

My book reveals that this collective unconscious is present in financial imagery in Britain and abroad during the nineteenth century.

3.4 The International Dimension

To assess the impact of British caricature during this period I have sought to refer to examples from other countries. I chose both European (France, Germany) as well as transatlantic (the US) as they embodied characteristics of British caricature though at different stages of historical development. In analysing images of financial events and financial figures from France, Germany, and the US, I was struck by both the similarities and differences in their various approaches to visual satire. Similarities were revealed in the choice of iconography, pointing to the dissemination of images from different periodicals across the world. This also reflected the relaxation of censorship rules in force in different countries). At the same time, differences occurred in the case of France and Germany in their treatment of Jewish financial figures reflecting the different phase of those countries' anti-Semitic reaction to the perceived abuses of capitalism. The imposition of censorship in France and Germany during the early part of the nineteenth century led to an explosive reaction once those censorship rules were relaxed in the latter quarter of the nineteenth century.

3.4.1 British Caricature

British caricature was originally quite radical in its approach although it reflected a 'cultural nostalgia' for the Regency period which belies its status as the epitome of Victorianism.[50] *Punch* became milder over time and adopted a deliberate policy of appealing and speaking to the middle ground and the middle class.[51] Freels comments that *Punch* reflected a world view that extolled industry, British fair play, and British world hegemony.[52]

From the 1870s, onwards with the advent of *Vanity Fair's* caricatures and the bestiary representations of Furniss and others, British caricature culminated in the renewed flourishing of 'satire without malice'.

3.4.2 *French Caricature*

In France, Philipon and Daumier inherited the mantle of Gillray and Rowlandson. The publication of *La Caricature* in 1830 by Charles Philippon was soon followed by *Le Charivari* in 1832, the model for *Punch* which appeared in 1841. They ridiculed Louis Philippe, (King of the French, 1830–1848) as a pear, taking advantage of the freedom to criticize under the Second Republic (1848–1852), and continuing the struggle even after Louis Napoleon (or Napoleon III, Emperor of the French, 1852–1870) imposed the heaviest and most calculated censorship regime ever faced by cartoonists for almost the duration of his long reign.[53]

The next flourishing of French caricature occurred in the period after the end of press censorship in 1881. Thereafter, periodicals such as *Le Petit Journal*, and then in the late 1880s the right-wing *La Libre Parole Illustree*, and *La Musee des Horreurs*, appeared. Caricatures satirising financial scandals (reflecting sympathy for the victims, and anti-Government big business) and anti-Semitism (the consequence of resentment over influence of Jews in business and in business scandals), appeared.

3.4.3 *German Caricature*

In the view of the cultural historian, Coupe, German caricature really began in 1848 due 'to the rapidity and relative cheapness of the lithographic process'.[54] Ironically, it was the conformist, ultra-Victorian Wilhelmine epoch which accelerated the rather innocuous humour of *Fliegende Blatter* (1845), *Kladderadatsch* (1848)[55] as well as the aggressive satire of *Simplicissimus* (1896).

Allen comments that *Simplicissimus* and *Kladderadatsch* were both liberal periodicals, attracting readers of all levels of intelligence and education.[56] The latter concentrated on middle classes and government policy, whilst the former was broader in scope and encompassed the working class as well. Yet the two periodicals exhibited stark differences:

1. *Kladderadatsch* mainly communicated through the written word, *Simplicissimus* through pictures.
2. *Kladderadatsch* reflected Berlin and Jewish humour of the time (two of the editors were Jewish). Jews were excluded from other liberal

professions—irony coming from detachment typical of the outsider, the Other. Liberalism and nationalism were its key tenets. *Simplicissimus* belonged to relaxed tolerant Munich just as *Kladderadatsch* belonged to discipline authority and obedience of Berlin.
3. *Kladderadatsch,* like most mid-century German periodicals, reflected a middle-class readership with 'the time and the leisure to appreciate its intellectual style. *Simplicissimus*, by contrast, illustrated the development of journalism (cf. UK 'new journalism') to attract a mass readership in a faster-moving urban environment which left little time for subtlety or complexity.
4. Everyday urban life was depicted in brash colour in *Simplicissimus*, compared with the classical mythology and black and white drawings of *Kladderadatsch.*

The main artist for *Kladderadatsch*, Scholtz, visualised the German people displaying their worst behaviour at times of speculation, especially after the Franco-Prussian war of 1870–1871.[57]

3.4.4 US Caricature

US progress on graphic satire was slow by comparison to France and Britain. The obstacles of costly print technology, bad roads, and vast distances all conspired to keep caricature on the fringes of the burgeoning US media. But the introduction of commercial lithography in the 1830s ushered in a new and dynamic period of caricature in the US. The democratisation of US culture and the quest for profit led many artists to take advantage of the opportunities afforded by the low cost of mass-produced lithographs.[58]

The introduction of *Harper's Weekly* from 1857 to the end of the century ushered in a second globally preeminent period in the US embodied in the lives of Thomas Nast, and Joseph Keppler. Even beyond his retirement in 1885, Nast's cartoons have proven to be some of the most enduring images in American history. The Republican elephant, the Democratic donkey, and the Tammany tiger are all inventions from the pencil of Nast and are testimony to his place in the history of US caricature.[59]

Keppler's style was milder and more subtle than that of Nast. Emulating *Punch's* diversity of artistic method, Nast and Keppler would employ similar techniques to relay their political and social messages to their audience. John comments on the origins of the robber baron epithet which, though literary, were most compellingly expressed in visual terms.[60] They are represented in the series of satirical cartoons published during the 1880s—the decade in which the robber baron became firmly enshrined in US visual culture—in the influential New York City-based weekly satirical magazines, *Puck*, and *Judge*. The magazines ran dozens of cartoons savaging Jay Gould, William H. Vanderbilt (son of Cornelius), and other like-minded business leaders as reckless monopolists unmindful of the public good.

Having set the scene for the review of financial images, it is now appropriate to consider the history of financial iconography in the nineteenth century.

3.5 Financial Iconography

The gap I have identified is that there is no one chronological piece of research analysing how financial themes were depicted across several periodicals during the whole Victorian period. Taylor (2005) and (2006) comments on the iconography of finance in relation to joint-stock companies rather than finance. His 2005 article comments on attitudes towards joint-stock companies during the period 1845–1870, whilst his 2006 book deals more broadly with the view of joint-stock companies during a longer period (1800–1870) as seen through popular culture (novels and cartoons).[61]

Whilst there is a dearth of research on financial themes in the Victorian era, research into the rich tradition of financial iconography in earlier periods can provide some useful insights. This tradition has historically dealt with financial scandals. The Dutch examples of the Tulip Mania in the 1620s and 1630s, and the South Sea Bubble of 1720, gave rise to images and symbols (both visual and textual) that associated financial scandals particularly with wind, hot air (balloons), and bubbles, for hundreds of years going forward.

3.5.1 Research into Pre Nineteenth-Century Examples

Two main sources from earlier periods provide a potential comparative approach. Walcot deals with the period 1689–1763, whilst Goetzmann and others deal with the Dutch crash of 1720 (which spilled over into England).[62] Walcot, an art historian, places the iconography used in the context of a *weltanschauung* emerging in England of respectable trade being tarnished by the evils of speculation (an analogous situation to the Victorian period where the virtues of rampant capitalism were also accompanied by the evils of widespread gambling and speculation). Goetzman adopts a multi-disciplinary approach in analysing events from a social, financial, and cultural perspective—essentially the approach that I follow in later chapters. In both works the overriding theme is that the types of imagery reflected the social mores of the time.

3.5.2 Research into Nineteenth-Century Examples

Miles Taylor highlights the differing political and fiscal uses of the imagery of John Bull imagery during the nineteenth century, picking up on the themes identified in the late eighteenth century.[63] Matthews and Mellini provide a thematic analysis of the various professions (including bankers) depicted in *Vanity Fair* during the latter half of the nineteenth century.[64] Their coverage, however, is brief and far from comprehensive in relation to bankers (the chapter on bankers for instance also covers businessmen, as well as builders!).

James Taylor and Popp are the only recent business historians who have written articles putting the image (in the case of Taylor, periodicals; for Popp, the postcard) at the forefront of analyses of contemporary events. Taylor, for example, views the use of visual images not as evidence of the realities of nineteenth-century business 'but for prevailing social attitudes and preferred social values'.[65] Barnes and Newton explore the visual context for studying bank portraiture in the early part of the nineteenth century.[66] Another recent area of study is explored by Shannon who comments on the liberalisation of men's business wear by the end of the nineteenth century.[67] Overall, it is Taylor's concentration on 'emotional discourse' which is at the forefront of my approach, supported by the rigor of Burke's rules, and the multi-disciplinarity espoused by Jordanova.

Finally, a book surveying financial images from 1700 to the present, *Show me the Money*, sets out the history and politics of representation—using cartoons, photographs, and other visual media. Intriguingly, it reveals no examples of financial images from the Victorian period; this period being reflected instead using US examples.[68] Did the authors feel that there were no suitable Victorian examples?

3.6 Literature and Finance

Another fruitful area with which to contrast the treatment of financial events and figures is the treatment of financial events and figures in contemporary literature. Whether it was in novels or journalism, there was plenty of written commentary on these events. It should also be remembered that the source of inspiration for the visual images being reviewed were the daily or weekly newspapers.

Much academic work has been produced on the uses and types of financial plots in Victorian novels (the infamous characters of Merdle in Dickens's *Little Dorritt*, or Melmotte in Trollope's *The Way We Live Now* are two examples of the satire aimed at unscrupulous individuals involved in finance). Russell's *The Novelist and Mammon* explored Victorian novelists' imaginative creations and the extent to which they were conditioned by actual events rather than the novelist's individual moral point of view.[69] More recently, O'Gorman, (ed.), and Henry and Schmitt (eds.) provide detailed analyses of contemporary attitudes towards investment and speculation in Victorian literature (and the dichotomy in contemporary views on where the dividing line was drawn during the period).[70] These more recent surveys illustrate the multi-disciplinary approach favoured by current cultural historians. There are contributions from academics working in the fields of English literature, History, Economic/Business History, as well as Law.

Finel-Honigman, in her *Cultural History of Finance,* covers a broad array of cultural sources—both textual and visual—in assessing views of finance over the centuries (however, the references to cartoons are extremely limited). She comments on the dichotomy at the heart of Victorian literature and of Victorian society, the fine line between being a gentleman banker and the greedy unscrupulous financier or speculator.[71]

Ferguson in his review of Michie's *Guilty Money*, a survey of Victorian novels dealing with the image of the City of London, refers to the power of isolated financial scandals involved with speculation in fuelling resentment towards bankers.[72] Michie takes issue with the traditional approach of literary critics in reviewing what he called 'the Greats'—the major works of the period. He seeks to understand to what extent (minor) novels (rather than other sources) can be used as historical evidence in relation to attitudes towards the City of London.[73] Michie decided that (minor) novels presented the best source of material to build up this view (he comments that visual sources, such as cartoons or paintings do not provide a homogeneous representative sample).

He concludes that attitudes towards bankers reflected changes in society's views during the period and were not uniformly negative. In this regard he sides with Reed who points to the shifting attitudes towards finance as evidenced in literary works of the Victorian period.[74]

As in the debate mentioned above about Burke's assessment of the role of aesthetic considerations, here Michie believes that literary scholars, concentrating as they do on the creative process (i.e., the existence or absence of artistic merit in novels), run the risk of assuming novels represent facts, rather than fiction. Facts, he argues as a historian, must be ascertained by a review of multiple sources to corroborate, or dispute, the views expressed in novels.

3.7 Conclusion

This book tests Michie's view by analysing visual images covering several representative episodes in financial history during the period rather than concentrating solely on what may be considered the major events. The use of sources other than novels is also reinforced by Daunton.[75] He exhorts scholars to consider a wider array of sources—from newspapers to judges' comments, to popular periodicals—to try to arrive at a more comprehensive analysis than is obtained from a rather narrow focus on novels.

Whilst literary scholars take issue with Michie's demarcation, what is clear in my mind is that a survey of multiple images over a long period can shed more light on contemporary mores than the review of a single image (what Burke refers to as '*images serielles*') can. This is highlighted in my review of A (rtistic techniques) which follows the primary research in each chapter, as well as the specific review of financial iconography in Chapter 6. In addition, it is necessary to assess the popularity (i.e., circulation figures) and the political persuasion of the author or artist to be able to judge whether the views expressed in novels or other media are not merely the views of the individual writer or artist. This is commented on in my review of P (ublishers bias) which summarises the findings at the end of each of the primary research chapters. Finally, it seems logical to carry out some sort of comparative analysis in relation to views expressed in one medium (cartoons primarily) to be able to draw more general conclusions about the contemporaneous nature of those views. I deal with this in Chapter 9 specifically where I compare the output of the renowned Victorian narrative painter, Frith, with Fun's comic riposte to Frith's series *Race for Wealth.*

Notes

1. Carlo Ginzburg, 'Your Country Needs You; A Case Study in Political Iconography', *History Workshop Journal*, 52:1, Autumn 2001, p. 1, quoting Raphael Samuel, *Theatres of Memory* (1964).
2. Patten, *George Cruikshank's Life, Times and Art Vol 2: 1835–1878* (Cambridge, The Lutterworth Press, 1996), p. 70. The Golden Age is usually referred to as the period from the beginning of the reign of George III, 1760, to the death of the most famous graphic artist of the period, James Gillray, in 1815.
3. David Kunzle, *A History of the Comic Strip*, 2 vols. (Berkeley, University of California Press, 1990), Brian E. Maidment, *Reading Popular Prints, 1790–1870* (Manchester, Manchester University Press, 1996).
4. Gareth Cordery and Joseph. S. Meisel, *The Humours of Parliament, Harry Furniss's View of Late Victorian Political Culture* (Ohio, Ohio University Press, 2014).
5. Brian E. Maidment, *Reading Popular Prints, 1790–1870* (Manchester, Manchester University Press, 1996), p. 14.
6. Patrick Leary, *The Punch Brotherhood, Table Talk and Print Culture in Mid-Victorian London* (London, The British Library Publishing Division, 2010), p. 35.
7. Raymond Williams, *The Long Revolution* (2001; Parthian Books, repr., 2011), p. 4.
8. Kate Campbell in 'Discourses of Journalism' (eds.), Brake, Bell and Finkelstein, *Nineteenth Century Media and the Construction of Identities*, p. 48.
9. Emily Madsen, 'Phiz's Black Doll: Integrating Text and Etching in *Bleak House*', *Victorian Literature and Culture* 41, 2013, pp. 411–433.
10. Louis James, 'Cruikshank and Early Victorian Caricature', *History Workshop*, 1978, pp. 107–120.
11. Brian Maidment, *Comedy, Caricature and the Social Order 1820–1850* (Manchester, Manchester University Press, 2013). Kate Flint,

The Victorians and the Visual Imagination (New York, Cambridge University Press, 2008).
12. Susan and Asa Briggs, *Cap and Bell, Punch's Chronicle of English History in the Making 1841–1861* (London, Macdonald and Company, 1972), p. xii, 'The Big Cut' being the main cartoon of each week's issue of *Punch*.
13. Julia Thomas, *Pictorial Victorians: The Inscription of Values in Word and Image* (Ohio, Ohio University Press, 2004). Martin Meisel, *Realizations Narrative, Pictorial, and Theatrical Arts in Nineteenth-Century England* (Princeton, Princeton University Press, 1983).
14. Stefanie Markovits, *The Crimean War in the British Imagination* (Cambridge, Cambridge University Press, 2009).
15. Julie F. Codell, 'Visual Culture Beyond Consumption and Finding Post-Colonial Victorians', *Journal of Victorian Culture*, 7:1, 2002, p. 129.
16. See Gillray's *Very Slippery Weather* BM11100 for example of crowds outside a print shop window observing the latest print satires.
17. Meisel, 1983, p. 340.
18. Julian Treuherz, *Victorian Painting* (London, Thames and Hudson Ltd, 1993), p. 112.
19. Henry Miller, *Politics Personified, Portraiture Caricature and Visual Culture in Britain, c 1830–1880* (Manchester, Manchester University Press, 2015), p. 220.
20. Ibid., p. 229.
21. Miller, p. 6.
22. Harry Furniss, *Confessions of a Caricaturist with Pen and Pencil*, vol. 1 (London, T. Fisher Unwin, 1901), p. 167.
23. Miller, p. 74.
24. J. Don Vann and Rosemary T. VanArsdel, *Victorian Periodicals and Victorian Society* (Toronto, Toronto University Press 1995), p. 3.
25. Altick, pp. 343/344.
26. Ibid., p. 358.
27. Frank E. Huggett, *Victorian England as Seen by Punch* (London, Sidgwick & Jackson, 1978), p. 117.
28. Freels, p. 26.
29. Morris, p. 322.

30. Richard D. Altick, *The English Common Reade: A Social History of the Mass Reading Public 1800–1900* (Chicago, University of Chicago Press 1957), p. 342.
31. Freels, p. 10.
32. See, for example, Leonard De Vries, comp., collab. Ilonka van Amstel, *History as Hot News 1865–1897: The Late Nineteenth Century World as Seen Through the Eyes of the Illustrated London News and the Graphic* (London, John Murray, 1973), Peter Sinnema, *Dynamics of the Pictured Page, Representing the Nation in the Illustrated London News* (Aldershot, Ashgate Publishing, 1998), Richard Scully, 'William Henry Boucher (1837–1906): Illustrator and Judy Cartoonist', *Victorian Periodicals Review*, 46:4, Winter 2013.
33. Mark Bryant, *Wars of Empire in Cartoons* (London, Grub Street Publishing, 2008). Richard Scully, 'The Other Kaiser: Wilhelm I and British Cartoonists, 1861–1914', *Victorian Periodicals Review*, 44:1, 2011.
34. Richard Altick, *Punch: The Lively Youth of a British institution, 1841–1851* (London, Ohio State University Press, 1997). Susan and Asa Briggs (coll. and eds.), *Cap and Bell, Punch's Chronicle of English History in the Making 1841–1861* (London, Macdonald and Company, 1972). Frank. E. Huggett, *Victorian England as Seen by Punch* (London, Sidgwick & Jackson, 1978).
35. M. D. George (ed.), *Catalogue of Political and Personal Satires Preserved in the Department of Prints and Drawings in the British Museum*, vols. vii–xi (London, British Museum Press, 1942–1954).
36. W. A. Coupe, 'Observations on a Theory of Political Caricature', *Comparative Studies in Society and History*, 11:1, January 1969, Thomas Milton Kemnitz, 'The Cartoon as a Historical Source', *Journal of Interdisciplinary History*, 4:1, The Historian, and the Arts (Summer, 1973), pp. 81–93, L. H. Streicher, 'On a Theory of Political Caricature', *Comparative Studies in Society and History*, 9:4, 1967.
37. Roy Porter (review), 'Seeing the Past: The English Satirical Print 1600–1832 by Michael Duffy; John Miller; J.A. Sharpe; Paul Langford; Peter. D.G. Thomas; John Brewer; H.T. Dickinson', *Past & Present*, no. 118, February 1988.
38. Brian E. Maidment, *Reading Popular Prints, 1790–1870* (Manchester, Manchester University Press, 1996). See also Patricia

Anderson, *The Printed Image and the Transformation of Popular Culture 1790–1860* (Oxford, Clarendon Press, 1991).

39. Peter Burke, *Eyewitnessing: The Use of Images as Historical Evidence* (London, Cornell University Press, 2001).
40. Ludmila Jordanova, *The Look of the Past Visual and Material Evidence in Historical Practice* (Cambridge, Cambridge University Press, 2013).
41. E. H. Gombrich, *Meditations on a Hobby Horse and Other Essays in the Theory of Art* (London, Phaidon Press, 1963, repr., 2007).
42. Ibid., p. 43.
43. Furniss, p. 253.
44. Alex Potts, 'Natural Order and the Call of the Wild: The Politics of Animal Picturing', *Oxford Art Journal*, 13:1, 1990, pp. 20/21.
45. Frankie Morris, 'John Tenniel, Cartoonist: A Critical and Sociological Study in the Art of the Victorian Political Cartoon', unpublished PhD, University of Missouri-Columbia, 1985, p. 126.
46. Richard R. John, 'Robbers Baron Redux: Antimonolopy Reconsidered', *Enterprise & Society*, 13:1, 2012, pp. 1–38. https://muse.jhu.edu/article/467915, p. 140.
47. David C. Jones, '"A Beastly Affair": Visual Representations of Animality and the Politics of the Dreyfus Affair', *Canadian Journal of History*, 46, 2011, p. 39.
48. Rebecca N. Mitchell, 'Before and After: *Punch*, Steampunk and Victorian Graphic Narrativity', in Anna Maria Jones and Rebecca N. Mitchell (eds.), *Drawing on the Victorians: The Palimpsest of Victorian and Neo-Victorian Graphic Texts* (Ohio, Ohio University Press, 2017).
49. Miller, p. 8.
50. Maidment, 2013.
51. See Altick, p. 11, Leary, pp 39–56.
52. Freels, p. 29.
53. Scully, 2011, pp. 147–180.
54. W. A. Coupe, *German Political Satires from the Reformation to the Second World War*, vol. 3. (New York, Kraus International Publications, 1993), p. xii.
55. *Kladderadatsch* was an onomatopoeic word meaning crash or collapse based on the North German word for rubbish, Kladde, as the usual word Quatsch.

56. Ann Taylor Allen, *Satire & Society in Wilhelmine Germany Kladderadatsch and Simplicissimus 1890–1914* (Lexington, University Press of Kentucky, 1984), p. 11.
57. Marsha Morton, 'Picturing the Perils of Greed; Kladderadatsch and the 1873 Financial Crash', *Journal of Illustration*, 4:2, p. 208.
58. Ibid., p. 45.
59. Ibid., p. 57.
60. Richard R. John, 'Robbers Baron Redux: Antimonopoly Reconsidered', *Enterprise & Society*, 13:1, 2012, pp. 15–16.
61. James Taylor, 'Business in Pictures: Representations of Railway Enterprise in the Satirical Press in Britain 1845–1870', *Past and Present*, no. 189, November 2005.
62. Clare Walcot, 'Figuring Finance: London's New Financial World and the Iconography of Speculation, Circa 1689–1763 in Two Volumes', PhD Thesis, Department of History of Art, University of Warwick, September 2003. William N. Goetzmann, Catherine Labio, K. Geert Rouwenhorst, and Timothy G. Younf (eds.), *The Great Mirror of Folly: Finance Culture and the Crash of 1720* (Yale, Yale University Press, 2013).
63. Miles Taylor, 'John Bull and the Iconography of Public Opinion in England c. 1712–1929', *Past & Present*, no. 134, February 1992.
64. Roy T. Matthews and Peter Mellini, *In Vanity Fair* (London, Scolar Press, 1982).
65. James Taylor (2005), p. 60, and Andrew Popp, 'The Broken Cotton Speculator', *History Workshop Journal*, no. 78, Autumn 2014, pp. 133–156.
66. Victoria Barnes and Lucy Newton, 'Constructing Corporate Identity before the Corporation: Fashioning the Face of the First English Joint Stock Banking Companies Through Portraiture', *Enterprise & Society*, 18:3, September 2017, pp. 678–720.
67. Brent Shannon, *The Cut of His Coat: Men, Dress, and Consumer Culture in Britain, 1860–1914* (Ohio University Press, 2006). ProQuest Ebook Central, http://ebookcentral.proquest.com/lib/reading/detail.action?docID=1773388.
68. Paul Crosthwaite, Peter Knight, and Nicky Marsh (eds.), *Show Me The Money: The Image of Finance, 1700 to the Present* (Manchester, Manchester University Press, 2014).

69. Norman Russell, *The Novelist and Mammon: Literary Responses to the World of Commerce in the Nineteenth Century* (Oxford, Clarendon Press, 1986).
70. Francis O'Gorman (ed.), *Victorian Literature and Finance* (2007), Nancy Henry and Cannon Schmitt (eds.), *Victorian Investments New Perspectives on Finance and Culture* (Bloomington, Indiana University Press, 2009).
71. Irene Finel-Honigman, *A Cultural History of Finance* (Abingdon, Routledge, 2010).
72. Christopher Ferguson (rev.), Michie, *Guilty Money: The City of London in Victorian and Edwardian Culture, 1815–1914* (London, 2009), *Victorian Studies*, 53:1, p. 136.
73. Ranald Michie, *Guilty Money: The City of London in Victorian and Edwardian Culture, 1815–1914* (London, 2009).
74. John R. Reed, 'A Friend to Mammon: Speculation in Victorian Literature', *Victorian Studies*, 27:2, Winter 1984.
75. Martin Daunton, 'Afterword', pp. 202–219, in Nancy Henry and Cannon Schmitt (eds.), *Victorian Investments, New Perspectives on Finance and Culture* (Bloomington, Indiana University Press, 2009).

CHAPTER 4

The Merchant Princes and the Makers of Money

Who keeps the world both old and new, in pain
Or pleasure? Who makes politics run glibber all?
The shade of Buonaparte's noble daring?
Jew Rothschild and his fellow- Christian Baring
—Lord Byron, *Don Juan*[1]

4.1 Introduction

This chapter will analyse depictions of the Merchant Princes, the internationally prestigious merchant bankers of the period: the 'great', as well as the 'good', the mere mortals who just made money. *Vanity Fair* described them as 'makers of money',[2] although the term, as we shall see in the following chapter, also included numerous financiers who are better described as charlatans because their financial frauds robbed their investors of millions of pounds.

The analysis will cover initially the depiction of the two dominant British merchant banking families of the century, the Rothschilds and the Barings. The reference to Napoleon Bonaparte came to be associated later in the century with several charlatans whose nomenclature was the 'Napoleon of Finance'.

H. Sless, *Merchant Princes and Charlatans or Makers of Money?*,
https://doi.org/10.1007/978-3-030-86604-4_4

The section on other bankers will include a range of financial activities, from stockbroking, to private banking, to merchant banking. The inclusion of self-professed gamblers (identified as gamblers on horses, cards, or the Stock Exchange) as caricatured figures in *Vanity Fair* indicated that they were celebrated by the elite.

The analysis is split into two sections, the first covering the pre-Victorian era, whilst the second covers the Victorian era itself.

4.2 Pre-Victorian Era

The main protagonists to be discussed in this section are Nathan Rothschild, as well as the scion of the Coutts banking dynasty, Harriot Coutts.

The depiction of the Rothschilds is also covered in Chapter 8, The Other, analysing the treatment of the Jewish merchant banking dynasty over the century in both UK and international periodicals.

Similarly, the depiction of Harriot Coutts is also covered in Chapter 7, Women, analysing the changing nature of the visual depiction of women in finance over the century.

4.2.1 Background on Representations of Financial Figures During the Pre-Victorian Period

Donald comments that 'the classic image of the banker, the entrepreneur, the international trader and the manufacturer is rarely present in Georgian iconography'.[3]

In the pre-Victorian era, portraits or prints of individual figures in the financial world are few and far between. The figures represented are also almost exclusively part of the London financial world. Important figures involved in the events of the period—for instance, the other founders of the Alliance Assurance Company (Samuel Gurney, Francis Baring, and John Irving), most of the Governors of the Bank of England, or leading government ministers—are not depicted at all.

Portraits of financial figures of the period were drawn almost exclusively by Richard Dighton. Bryant and Heneage summarise his output as 'mild caricatures of leading figures of the day' prefiguring the caricatures of *Vanity Fair* but without the same degree of satire.[4] They were portraits in profile of leading figures in the Stock Exchange, whether bankers, stockjobbers, or merchant traders. Coffee, tallow, and indigo brokers are depicted, reflecting the merchant traders.[5] They tend to be tall thin men (other than Nathan Rothschild himself)—stock figures instantly recognisable. Bills comments, in relation to Rowlandson's early nineteenth-century caricatures, that London tradesmen of the period tended to be depicted as fat, in contrast to the sinewy financiers are nuanced when one reviews the work of Dighton and others in the 1820s.[6] Dighton's bankers ranged from Nathan Rothschild[7] or his relatives and business associates (Moses Montefiore[8]; Benjamin Gompertz, a relative and the only actuary depicted[9]; Samuel Gurney[10]; and Thomas Wilson, a prominent City MP), to Curtis, a relative of Sir William Curtis; Stirling, a partner in a London-based bank; Goldsmid, a financier; and even a Bank of England director, Richard Mee Raikes.[11] Two Lloyds brokers, Lindsay and Dewar, also feature. It is interesting that other banking figures, such as the Barings, tend not to be represented (at least not until the late 1820s in the case of Alexander Baring). The formal treatment of Nathan Rothschild changed from that shown above to when he was more in the public eye in the late 1820s. Mini portraits in prints show him even more obese or subject to satire.[12] Overall, the absence of key banking and financial figures from the British Museum's collection of prints is unexplained.

Where other unnamed financial figures are shown, they tend to be stock figures, with elongated features and large heads, in top hats.[13] Not all of them are Jews, so in this early period there is less stereotypical association of stockjobbers or bankers with the Jews. Whilst the presence of the portraits suggests these individuals were important and had 'arrived' socially, the backgrounds to the portraits remain firmly financial. They are, however, static and do not show the figures at work (there is one stock representation of brokers at work).[14] More formal portraits showed landscape scenes and country residences associated with their subjects: these depicted the fruits rather than the source of their wealth. Hence the depiction of bankers and merchant traders at their place of work may be signalling the source of their wealth.

4.2.2 Nathan Rothschild

Nathan is depicted in England in several different guises during this period:

1. The straightforward depiction as a realistic figure (e.g., Figs. 4.1 and 4.2)
2. As a 'matchstick figure', part of an overall allegory of stock exchange activities (e.g., Figs. 4.3 and 8.1)
3. As a representative of the Other with caricatured Jewish features (e.g., Fig. 8.4)
4. As a personified allegory of stock exchange practices (Fig. 6.19).

The coverage in this chapter is of the first two categories. Category 3 is covered in the Chapter 8, The Other, whilst category 4 is dealt with in Chapter 6 on Financial Iconography.

Jones's depiction of Nathan Rothschild in Fig. 4.1 shows him alone, the epitome (a pun on pillar—Rothschild being the stalwart or pillar of the Stock Exchange, with the pillar also representing one of the real-life pillars of the exchange) of Stock Exchange activities.

Ferguson comments that these depictions were based on a common description of Nathan as 'a very common looking person, with heavy features, flabby pendent lips, and a projected fisheye. His figure, which was stout, awkward, and ungainly, was enveloped in the loose folds of an ample surtout.'[15] Rubens comments further that caricaturists also poked fun at the colour of his clothes, invariably black, which showed the influence of the Frankfurt ghetto. They also poked fun at his peculiar English.

When we come to Dighton the portrait of Nathan (Fig. 4.2) is rather flattering, a feature which enabled Dighton to obtain many private commissions.[16] They were typically full-length, in profile, precursors to images in the periodical *Vanity Fair*.[17]

Figure 4.3 is a complex allegory on the flotation of the Alliance Assurance Company in 1824. It concentrates on the role of Nathan Rothschild and his business associates, notably Moses Montefiore, and Montefiore's brother-in-law Benjamin Gompertz.

When we look at the depiction of Nathan Rothschild (see the figure in the blue jacket in Fig. 4.4), it is worth contrasting the early Dighton portrait shown above (Fig. 4.2), which depicts Nathan as obese, but smartly dressed. Here Nathan is depicted, only very slightly overweight, engaged in business conversation (indicated using French) with Montefiore (the taller thin figure with a tan jacket). Similarly, Moses Montefiore is depicted here more dynamically, stooping rather than stiffly upright as in an earlier Dighton print (see Fig. 4.5).

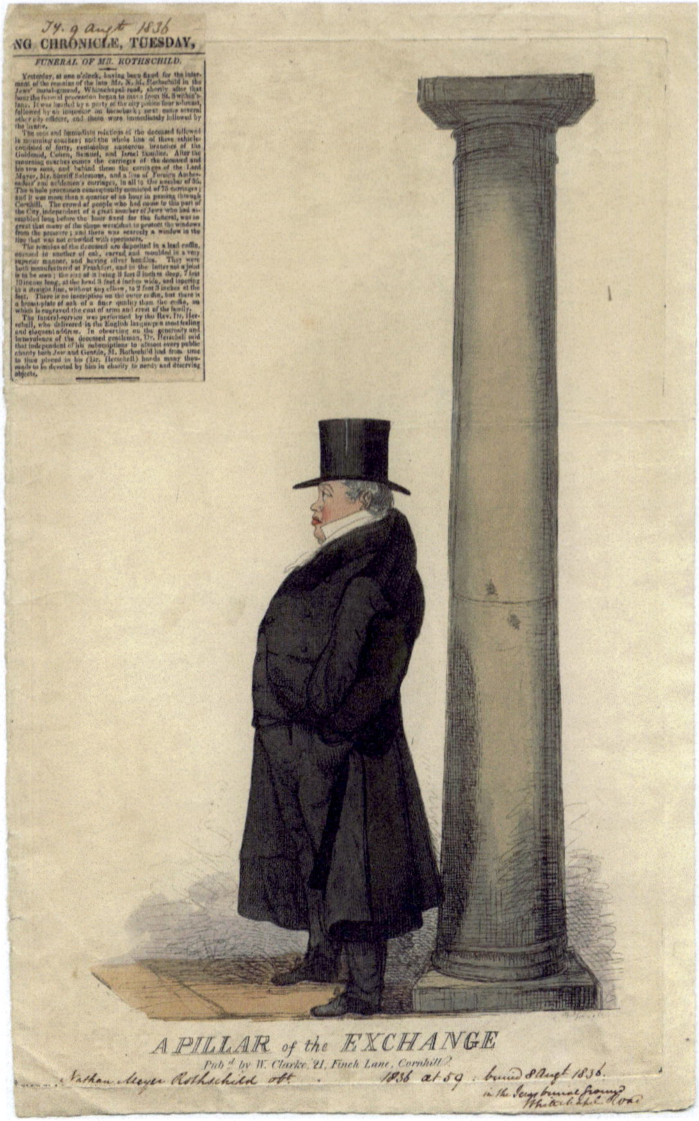

Fig. 4.1 BM 14822, *A Pillar of the Exchange*, 1825, Thomas Howell Jones (Courtesy of BM)

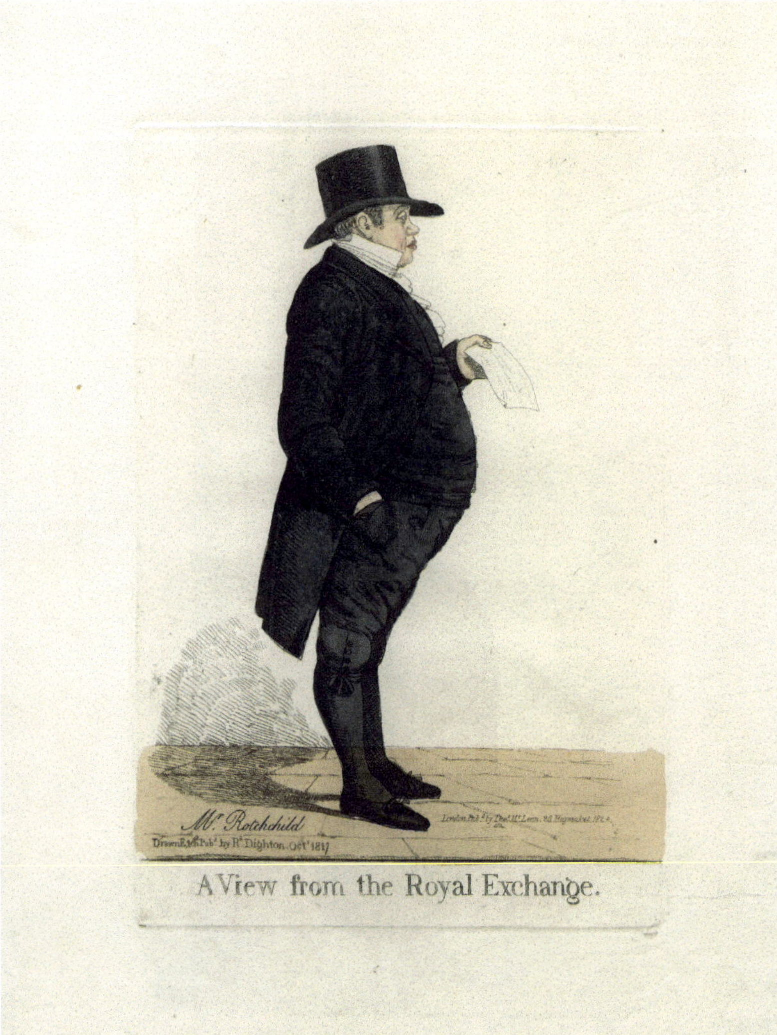

Fig. 4.2 BM 14678, *A View from the Royal Exchange*, Richard Dighton,1817 (Courtesy of BM)

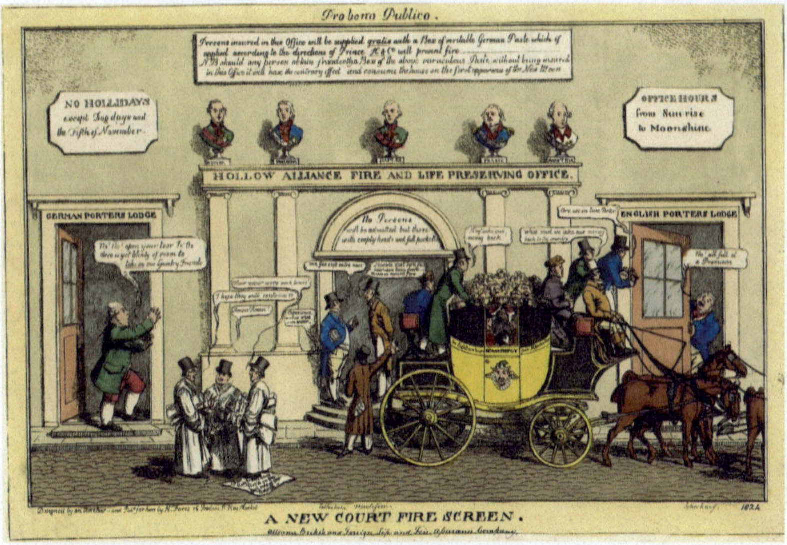

Fig. 4.3 BM 14666, *A New Court Fire Screen*, Charles Williams, 1824 (Courtesy of BM)

Overall, the depiction of the central figures in this print is more of a 'matchstick' style whereby the complex allegory is more important to depict than the actual key protagonists. The figures of Rothschild and Montefiore are not depicted satirically.

4.2.3 Harriot Coutts

The second financial figure for review is Harriot Coutts, an actress by profession, who had married into the Coutts banking family and on the death of her husband became a very influential woman. When they married legally on 12 April 1815, Thomas Coutts was seventy-nine; Harriot was thirty-seven. On his death seven years later, Thomas left Harriot his vast fortune and his partnership in Coutts Bank.[18]

As Mrs Arbuthnot expressed it in 1824, Harriot was 'a memorable example of the power of money. She lived with Mr Coutts many years before his first wife died, was an actress & now, because he has left her

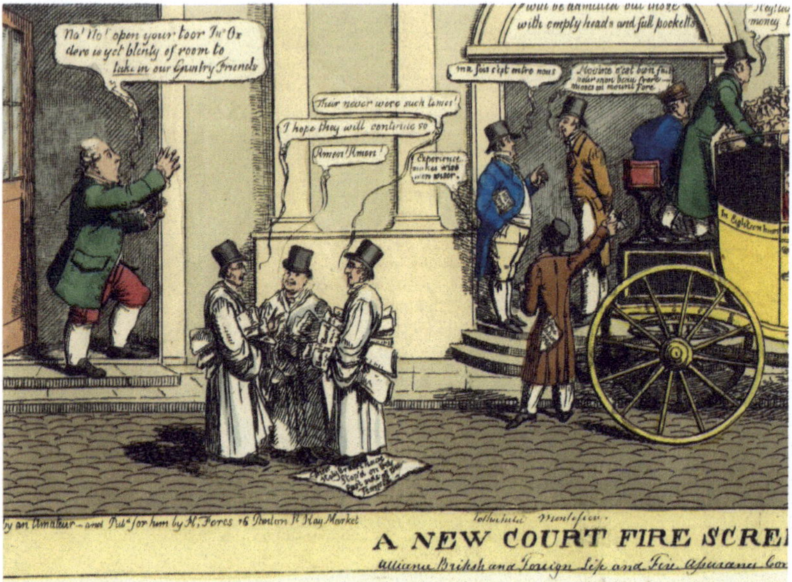

Fig. 4.4 *A New Court Fire Screen* (extract)

his whole fortune, she gives balls and breakfasts & is invited by every body'.[19]

Healey comments that in Harriot's early years, the Duke of Wellington advised her on how to understand and take care of money whilst Charles Dickens advised her on how to spend it.[20]

Harriot Coutts (nee Mellon) is depicted as in the early Rothschild images in various guises:

1. The straightforward depiction as a realistic figure (an actress)—Fig. 4.6.
2. As a caricature representing monied interests (*Croesus and Thaler*—Fig. 4.7 and *Stout as Ever!!!*—Fig. 4.8).

Discussion of Harriot Coutts as a woman is explored further in Chapter 7.

In Fig. 4.7, Thomas Coutts is depicted as Croesus; Harriot as Thaler. In Greek mythology, Croesus was extremely rich, and Thalia was one of the three Greek muses, famous for their beauty and art (reference to

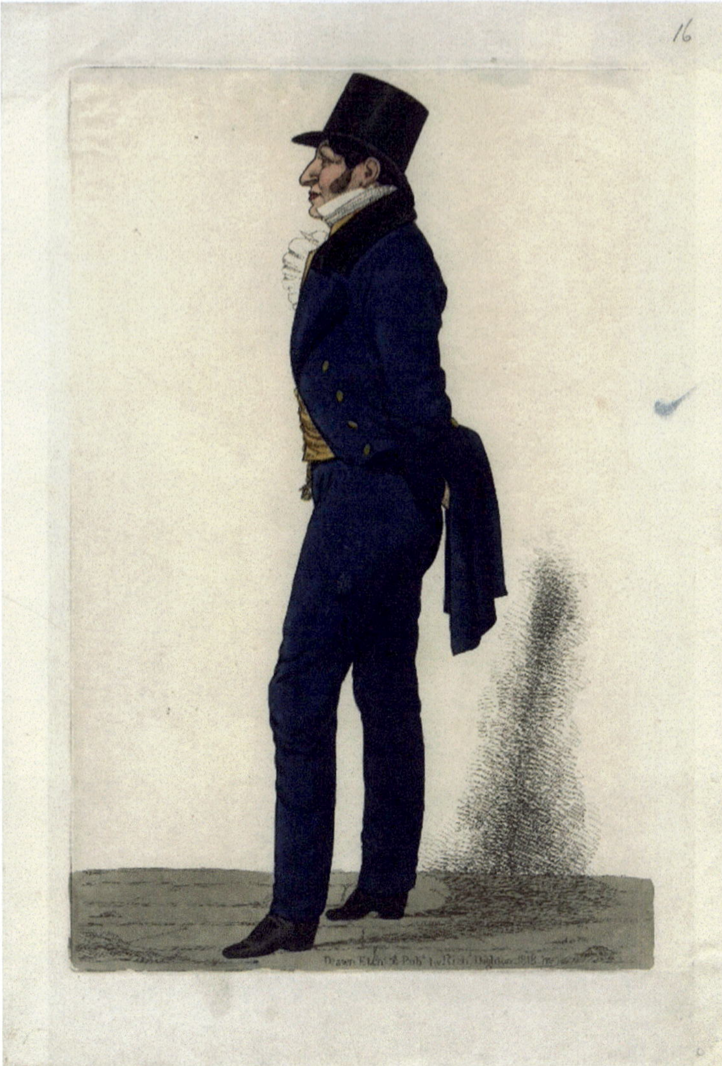

Fig. 4.5 BM 13021, *Moses Montefiore*, artist and publisher Richard Dighton, London, 1818 (Courtesy of BM)

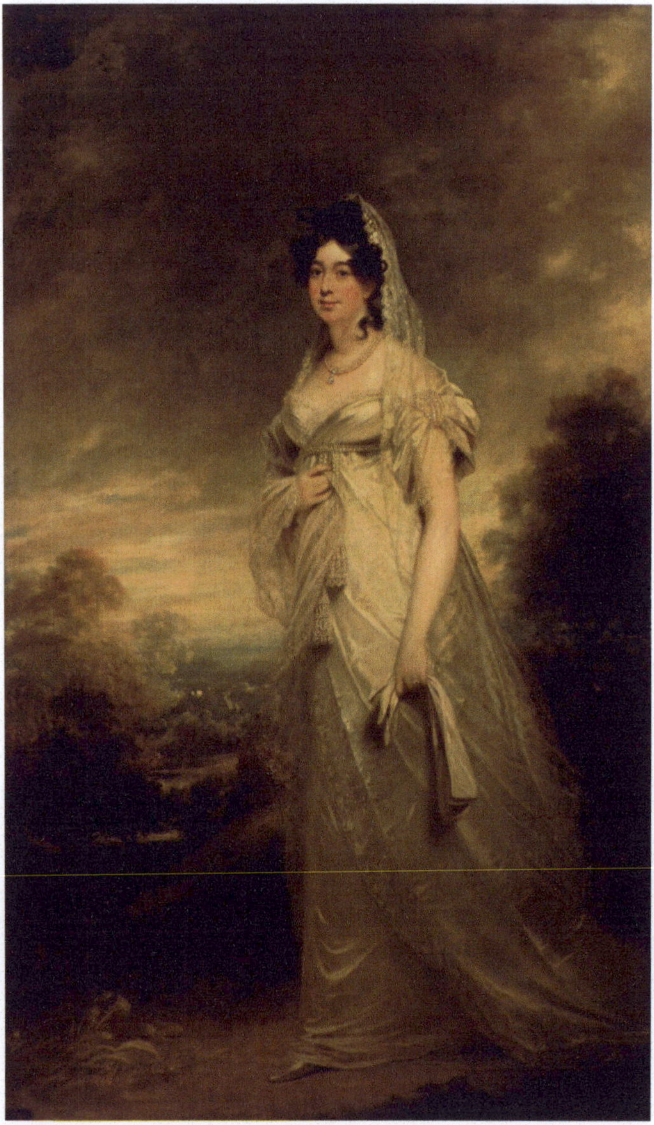

Fig. 4.6 Harriot Coutts (Courtesy of NPG)

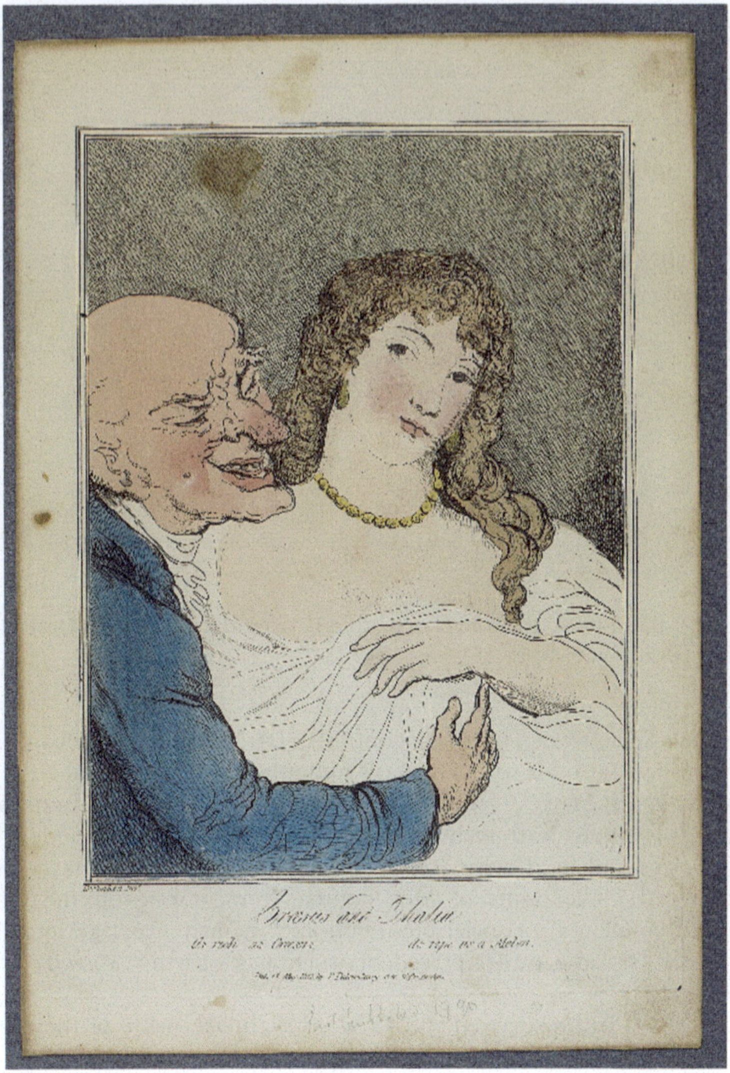

Fig. 4.7 Croesus and Thalia (Courtesy of Yale University Library)

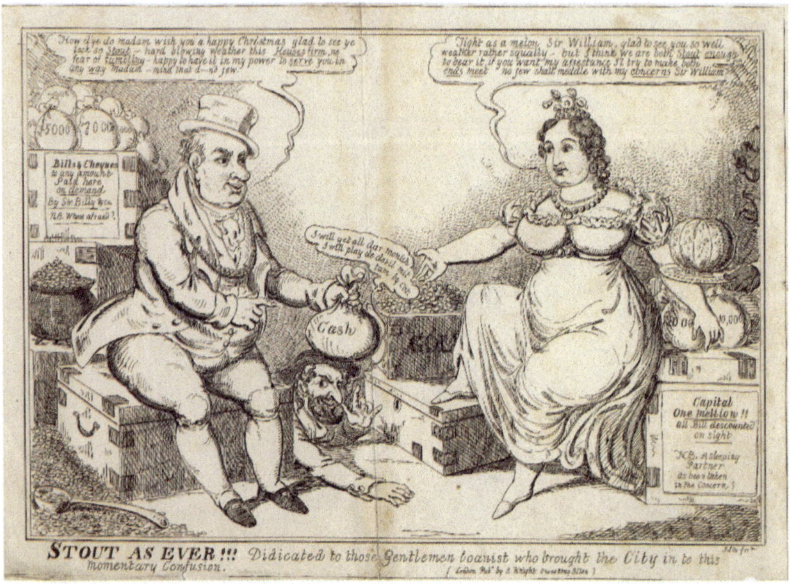

Fig. 4.8 BM 14809, *Stout as Ever!!!* artist J. L. Marks, London, c. December 1825[22] (Courtesy of BM)

Harriot as an actress). The image contrasts Harriot's purity with Coutts's lecherousness (at odds with Thomas's undoubted love for Harriot).

In *Stout as Ever!!!* (Fig. 4.8), Sir William Curtis and Coutts are depicted as obese, extremely expensively dressed, and surrounded by money bags and gold coins (representing the prosperous banks which they owned). The prints of Mrs Coutts represent one of 'the most powerful emblem(s) of social presumption'[21] namely marriage into the aristocracy (see also earlier precedents such as Hogarth's *Mariage à la Mode*).

These two banks survived the 1825 crisis (unlike many of the other banks of the period). They are discussing the state of financial affairs at Christmas time in 1825, just past the height of the crisis in London. They are depicted inside a bank vault, secure against the ravages of the financial crisis raging outside, surrounded by bags of gold. Money here is a virtue as it has protected these individuals against the fate, suffered by many others, of bankruptcy and ruin. In other prints of the period (e.g., *The*

Bubble Burst, *The Reign of Humbug!!*),[23] money is associated with failed projects, cant, and hypocrisy, whereas in *Stout as Ever!!!* Sir William Curtis and Mrs Coutts are associated with prudence and soundness in having sufficient cash to meet the demands of any creditors who might want to cash in their bonds.

The print is significant for two reasons. First, it is one of the very few images of the period which depict the survivors of the banking system, and second, it depicts a female banker, another rarity of the period. It illustrates the use of visual and verbal puns to comment on the stability of the two banks. It also uses stereotypical Jewish characterisation, here used to blame the Jews for the country's banking ills (see Chapter 8 for further discussion).

Often satirised because of his lowly origins (he started off life as a sailor), by the 1820s Sir William is depicted as an obese, illiterate man with a carbuncled nose, often dressed in sailor's trousers.[24]

Whilst Jews are associated with the Devil, the embodiment of Mammon, and the cause of the banking crisis, by contrast, Sir William and Mrs Coutts embody security, surrounded by money. The social innuendo references the state of Mrs Coutts's amorous affairs. The use of the word 'stout' to portray both the physical and financial strength is one example.

An analysis of the characterisation of Sir William Curtis and Mrs Coutts in *Stout as Ever!!!* reveals the absence of physical exaggeration (Figs. 4.9, 4.10, and 4.11).

Apart from a slight exaggeration of Sir William Curtis's nose. As well as of Harriot Coutts's face and bosom (rather fuller than in the original), Fig. 4.8 is not unkind in its portrayal of the two. Note that Harriot Coutts was not the only example of a woman heading up a private bank during this period—Sarah Childs, Lady Jersey, was the owner of Child & Co.

4.3 Victorian Era

4.3.1 *The Caricatures in* Vanity Fair

The letterpress provided by Jesu Junior (the editor of *Vanity Fair*, Thomas Gibson Bowles) accompanying each caricature gives an indication of the humour and light-heartedness intended to be conveyed in the caricatures. The letterpress also provides important commentary on the importance of the individuals chosen and their role in high society.

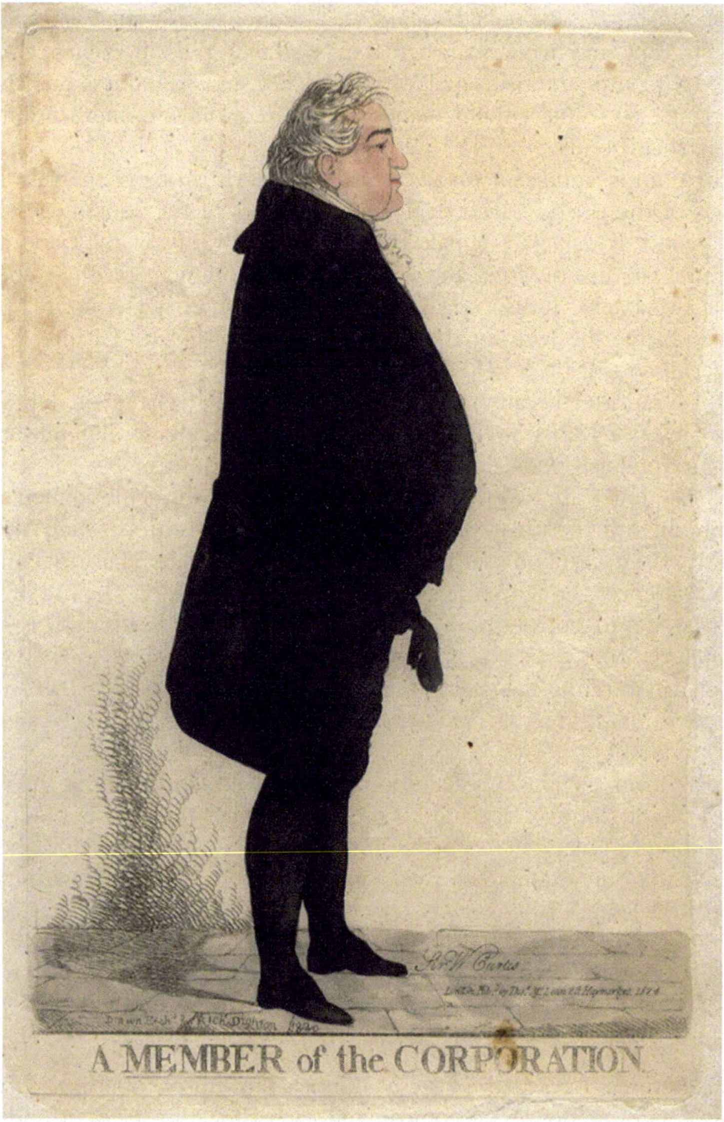

Fig. 4.9 BM 14063, *A Member of the Corporation* (Sir William Curtis), artist and publisher Richard Dighton, London, 1820 (reissued 1824) (Courtesy of BM)

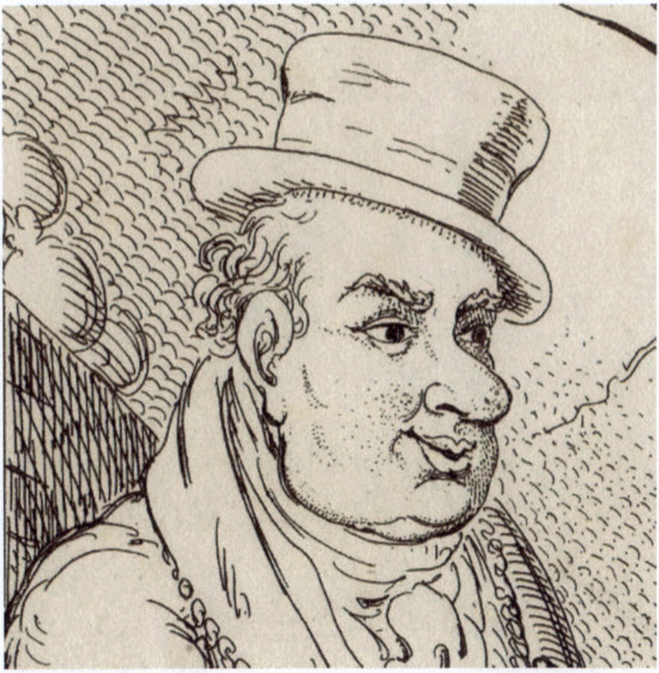

Fig. 4.10 The head of Sir William Curtis, an extract from *Stout as Ever!!!* (Fig. 4.8)

Whether representations of the Other (notably the Jews) or financiers, the caricatures in *Vanity Fair* are all (bar one—see reference to Harry Benson in Chapter 5, Charlatans) positive representations, representing models of behaviour and probity viewed approvingly by the readers of the periodical, the elite of society.

The device of letterpresses is accentuated using captions to introduce each caricature. The captions convey different characteristics (references below are to individual caricatures commented on later):

1. The use of informal first names (e.g., *Baron Lionel*, or *Alphonse* in relation to the Rothschilds, or *Tom* in the case of Tom Nickalls, the renowned stockbroker).

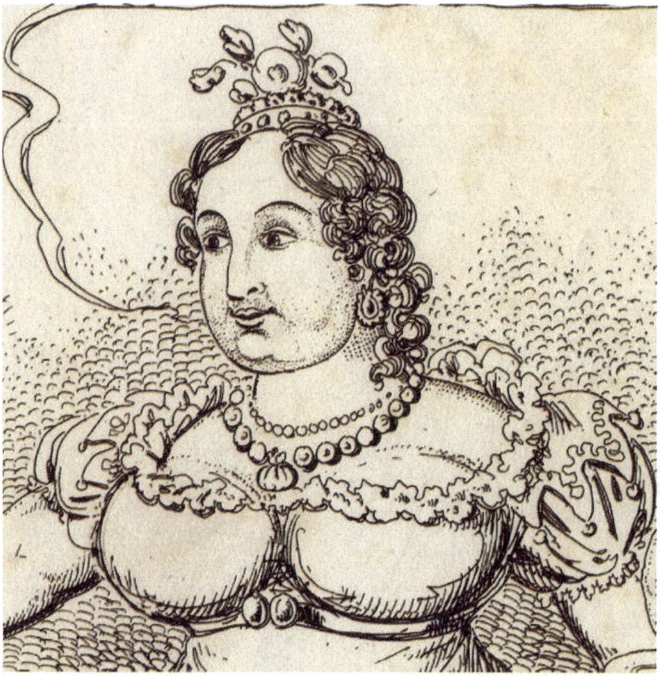

Fig. 4.11 The head of Mrs Coutts, an extract from *Stout as Ever!!!* (Fig. 4.8)

2. The use of impersonal surnames or formal titles (e.g., *Barings* (Lord Revelstoke), *Baroness Burdett-Coutts*).
3. Their association with their parliamentary seat or country residence, *Burnley* (Jabez Balfour), *Papworth* (Ernest Hooley).
4. The embodiment of financial activities (*Egyptian finance* (Sir Ernest Cassel), *Fair trade* (Sampson Lloyd), *The City* (Sir Robert Fowler), *Financial News* (Harry Marks), *The Stock Exchange* (Lionel Cohen).
5. The embodiment of their claim to fame/notoriety:

> *The Theory of Foreign Exchanges* (the financial work of George Goschen, a prominent Tory financial expert in Parliament), *Leicester Square* (referring to the philanthropic exploits of the soon to be exposed fraudster Albert Grant), *The Cape* (referring to the South African exploits of Cecil Rhodes), *The Leviathan* (Mr Steel), *the*

Jubilee Plunger (Henry Ernest Schlesinger Benzon), *The Turf Frauds*. (Harry Benson)

Overall, the use of these captions provides a witty summary of the individual being caricatured which is supplemented by the accompanying letterpress and the composition of the setting and dress for each individual caricature.

Finel-Honigman comments on the uniformity of depiction in paintings and photographs of major nineteenth-century bankers, whether respected bankers or the more disreputable brokers and speculators:

> large, portly, impeccably tailored, middle-aged men in black suits, silk cravats, and top hats, sporting elegant mustaches or beards, they impart solidity, calm, imperviousness, and trust. Around the world, for over a century, all bankers became British bankers in appearance, with few modifications in the cut of the suits and homburgs replacing top hats.[25]

Whilst this pattern is reflected in depictions of financiers in the realistic periodicals, the review of *Vanity Fair* caricatures reveals a more nuanced representation. *Vanity Fair*'s caricatures follow for the most part Finel-Hongiman's summary but crucially they occasionally depict financiers in garb and setting which are quite different. The examples of Tom Nickalls, the stockbroker, in hunting attire astride a horse, or Harry Benson, the turf fraudster, in convict attire, testify to the delight that *Vanity Fair* caricaturists took in going against the 'norm' (see Chapter 5 for discussion on Harry Benson).

The sample of caricatures to be commented on is based on my detailed analysis of caricatures of financial figures in *Vanity Fair*. The sample includes representatives from the two major merchant banking families of the period, the Rothschilds and the Barings. It then deals with other bankers (merchant bankers, retail bankers, and private bankers) as well as members of the government engaged in financial matters (Chancellors of the Exchequer). It finishes with examples of gamblers. Gambling was a widespread activity in Victorian society and as the Cassel quote indicates, it was often indistinguishable from banking activities.

My analysis of financial figures from *Vanity Fair* revealed an absence of figures from specific categories. The first is Bank of England governors, and the second major omission (or non-coverage) was Joint-Stock bankers. I can find no commentary to explain these absences so I can only speculate that they were not present at the various high society events or at the Houses of Parliament (as sitting MPs or members of the House of Lords), which otherwise provided the choice of subject matter for *Vanity Fair*'s editors and artists.

4.3.2 *The Rothschilds*

The Victorian period saw a toning down in Britain of caricatures satirising Jews and the Rothschilds in particular.

The depiction of the Rothschilds is found to be more nuanced when reviewing images other than those in *Vanity Fair*. In *Vanity Fair*, the Rothschilds were accepted members of the elite and their banking and philanthropic dealings praised. Caricatures of the Rothschilds (numbering ten) appeared in *Vanity Fair* at regular intervals from 1871 to 1900, demonstrating the esteem in which they were held consistently during this period.

Lionel Nathan Rothschild

> His capacity for work great, his assiduous very great, and his caution above all quite wonderful he was while a young man, by virtue of his own qualities, no less than of his name, the undisputed [Emperor of Legitimate Finance].[26]

A revealing comment was given that the Rothschilds were predominantly involved in Stock Exchange trading, an activity which differed little from gambling which was viewed slightly less favourably. The inclusion of gamblers in *Vanity Fair* is discussed below (Fig. 4.12).

Continental views of the Jews, especially the Rothschilds, are discussed in Chapter 8. There is a very pointed contrast in the images of Alphonse de Rothschild, the head of the French Rothschild family, where the *Vanity Fair* caricature is distinctly favourable, with a virulent anti-Semitic image in *Musee des Horreurs* from 1899–1900[27] (Fig. 4.13).

The impression here is that of a man of society in plush surroundings and at ease.

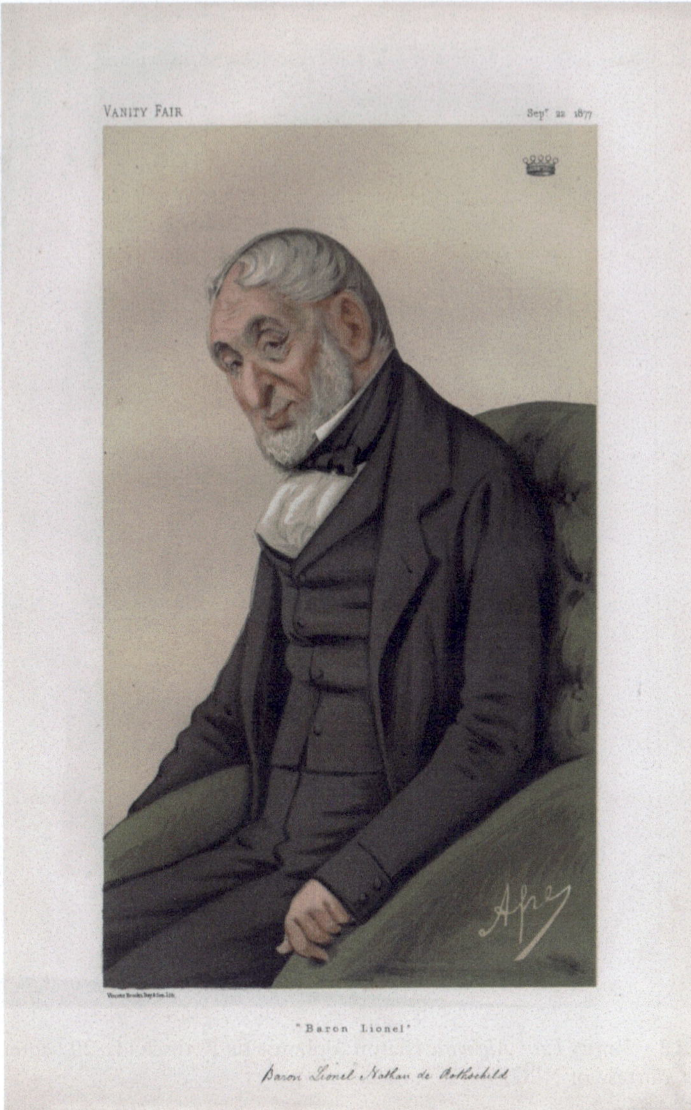

Fig. 4.12 *Vanity Fair*, *Baron Lionel* (Baron Lionel Nathan de Rothschild), 22 September 1877 (Courtesy of NPG)

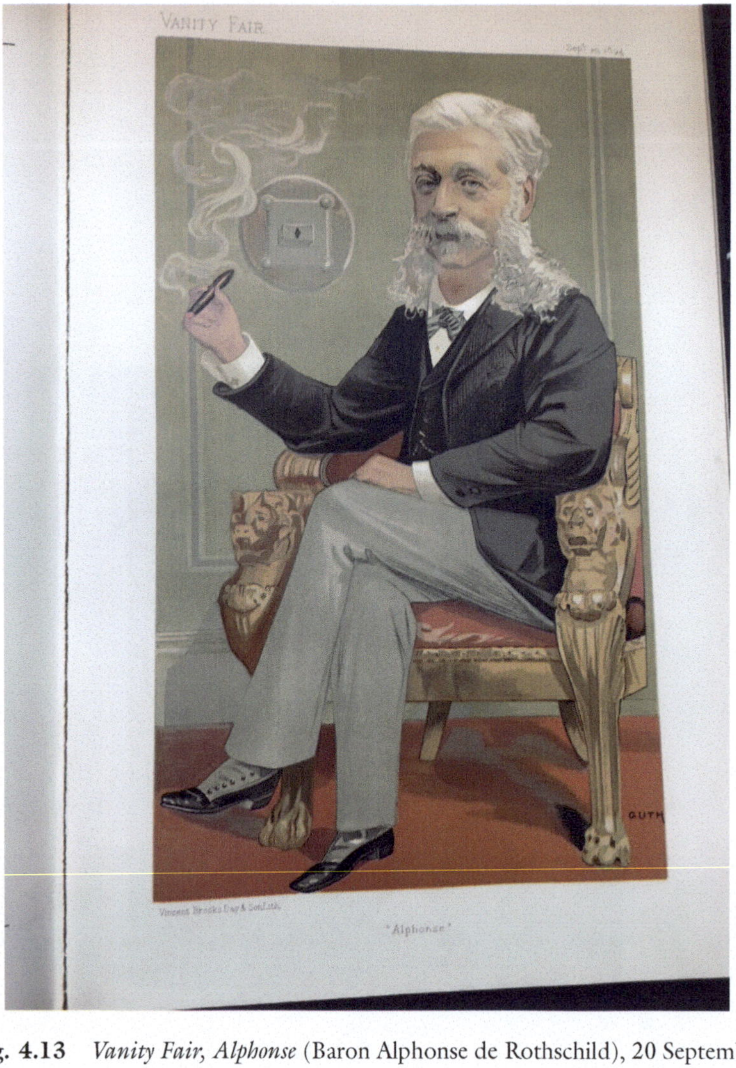

Fig. 4.13 *Vanity Fair*, *Alphonse* (Baron Alphonse de Rothschild), 20 September 1894 (Courtesy of NPG)

He has great financial power and he is supposed to have done much to spoil the newest Russian loan, by way of reprisal for that country's unkindness to poorer Jews than himself. He is very rich; and he is brother-in-law to Lord Rothschild.[28]

In Fig. 4.14, Lord Nathaniel Rothschild, recently raised to the peerage (another sign of the Other trope not applying to prominent Jewish bankers) is seen in a benevolent light: keeping the Egyptians on side. The Egyptians are shown as uncivilised, with crocodile features, easily

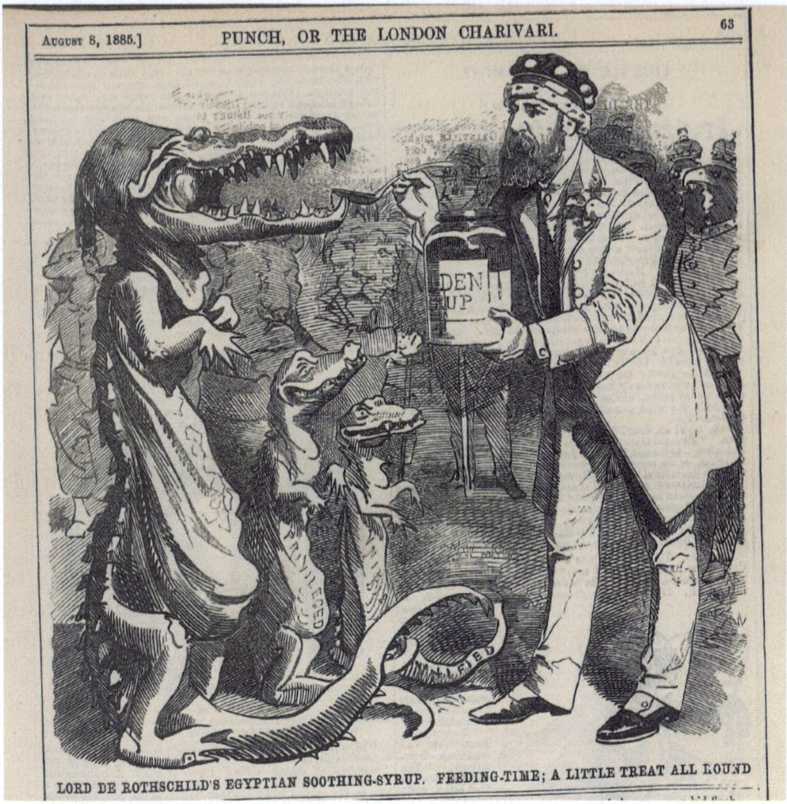

Fig. 4.14 *Punch*, *Lord de Rothschild's Egyptian Soothing-Syrup*, 8 August 1885 (Courtesy of UoH)

soothed by sweet liquids (golden syrup). In keeping with the general tone of Victorian attitudes, foreigners were depicted as animals, part of the 'Other' trope.[29] The Russian bear, the Austrian eagle, and the British lion observe proceedings. By contrast, Rothschild is depicted wearing a crown, a symbol of aristocracy and deference and acceptability within society, far removed from the crude anti-capitalistic, anti-Semitic representations to be found on the continent.

A joint Rothschild loan of over nine million pounds to the Egyptian government in 1885 (the 'golden syrup') helped calm an often-turbulent country and reinforced Britain's role in Egypt without openly antagonising rival powers. The absence of financial iconography is echoed in the cartoon illustrating the role of Disraeli and Rothschild ten years earlier in securing the funds to buy the Suez Canal Shares (see below). Golden syrup had been invented by Lyle in 1881 so this may have been another pun on British invention prowess with the added element of being used to soothe an irascible Egyptian ruler. Note, though, that despite the depiction of financial elements of the transaction, no financial iconography is present in this cartoon.

In Fig. 4.15 a more typical representation of the power and influence of the Rothschilds is shown by this approving realistic drawing in the *Graphic* in 1891.

The drawing evokes memories in its title and scene to Thomas Howell Jones's caricature of Nathan Rothschild in 1825, more than sixty years earlier (Fig. 4.1). The title reflects public pride (Pillars of the City) in the financial operations of the stock market (as well as the stability of its institution) and depicts the first Lord Rothschild ('Natty'), with his back to the pillar, his bulky son Walter and, between them, Carl Meyer, Rothschild's trusted adviser.

The *Graphic* image depicts the pillars as the key members, not all of them Jewish. They all stand erect (upstanding members of the community). An accompanying article describes in sober and approving terms the activities of the lead characters in the image.

4.3.3 *The Barings*

The Barings feature prominently throughout the nineteenth century as part of an international banking elite. The family reached such heights within the London banking elite that it was reported in 1818, that the

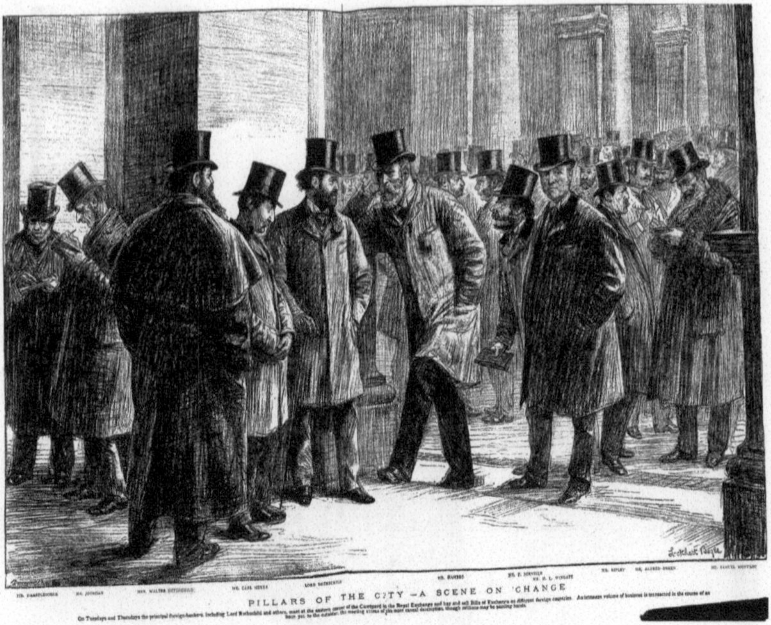

Fig. 4.15 *Graphic*, *Pillars of the City—A Scene on Change*, 9 May 1891 (Courtesy of BL)

Duc de Richelieu, prime minister to Louis XVIII, named six great European powers: Britain, France, Prussia, Austria, Russia, and the Baring Brothers.[30]

Their success can be measured by the number of the family members who were ennobled during this period (four). The sheer variety of the positions they occupied, in the diplomatic service, as well as political posts, testifies to the all-embracing acceptance by the elite of these descendants of Lutheran bankers from Bremen (Fig. 4.16).

Lord Revelstoke

In relation to Lord Revelstoke the tone of the letterpress accompanying his caricature is admiring and reverential:

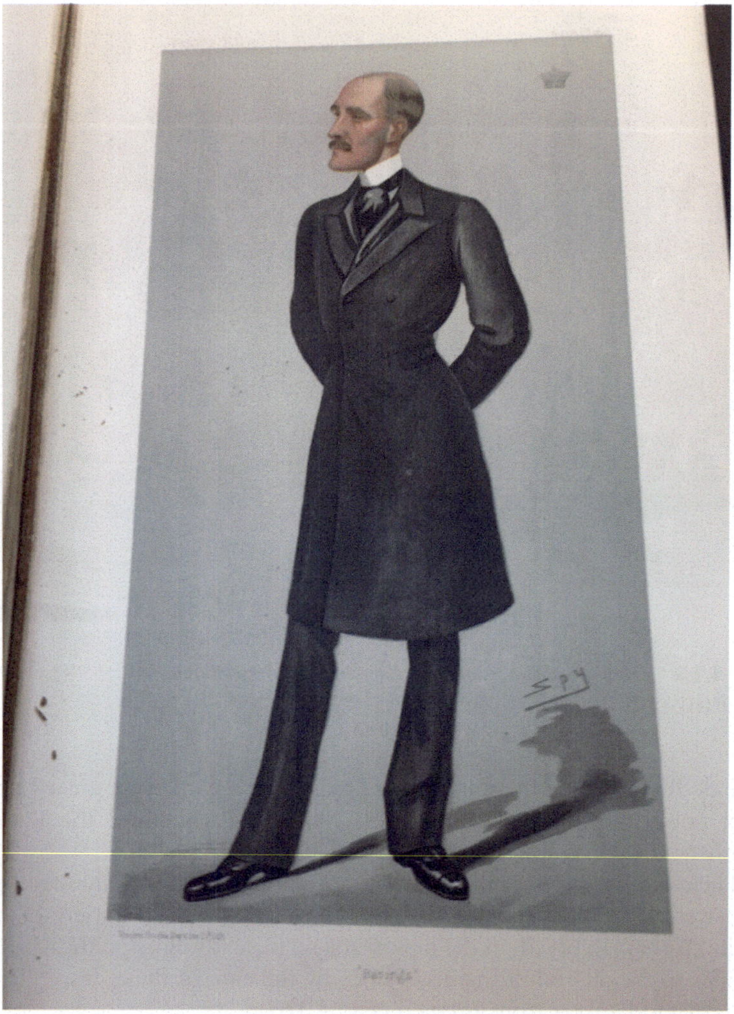

Fig. 4.16 *Vanity Fair*, *Barings* (Lord Revelstoke), 15 September 1888 (Courtesy of NPG)

> They lent money to needy Monarchs and struggling States; the mysteries of finance were to them an open book: and as bankers and Baronets, Viceroys of India, and Cabinet Ministers, various descendants of the Bremen Baring have left their mark on the land of their adoption. Edward Charles Baring opened his credit account sixty years ago. He has lived, and intends to die, a great and wealthy banker [how the mighty fall-the rescue of Barings would occur just two years later—my words]. He is related to Lord Northbrook, who may apply himself, in a spirit of solemn devotion, to the trade of politics; but Edward Charles prefers the wild excitement that attends the floating of a loan or the discounting of a bill.......He promoted Guinness.[31]

His upright bearing, almost painfully thin, evokes the image of a confident banker (but certainly not of the corpulent variety beloved of caricaturists of other periodicals, notably *Fun*).

The Barings collapse in 1890 is illustrative in that although Lord Revelstoke was clearly the architect of the downfall of his bank, his role in the collapse is not mentioned in any *Vanity Fair* depiction of him.[32]

Almost certainly, the speed of the actual collapse of the bank, and the secretive successful attempt to retain public confidence in the financial system, militated against sustained press commentary. The written commentary of the time centred more around the 'noble' actions of the Barings family in accepting total financial responsibility for the imprudent actions of their family company.

Mr Liddderdale

The only representation that does appear is a drawing of the public face of the rescue of Barings, William Lidderdale, the then Governor of the Bank of England (see below). He does not appear in *Vanity Fair,* which supports the argument that Governors were not viewed as members of the elite as only three Governors (Hubbard, Lawford, and Sandeman) feature in *Vanity Fair* throughout the thirty-two years of caricatures reviewed (there were thirty-one Governors during Victoria's reign) (Fig. 4.17).

The collapse of Barings is covered from an institutional perspective in the discussion around the role of the Bank of England as lender of last resort (see the section on the 'Old Lady of Threadneedle Street' in Chapter 7).

The attitude of the Barings family to the collapse is instructive. Lord Revelstoke's unbridled vanity and self-confidence had exploded after a hugely profitable floatation of Guinness in 1887. Speculation in

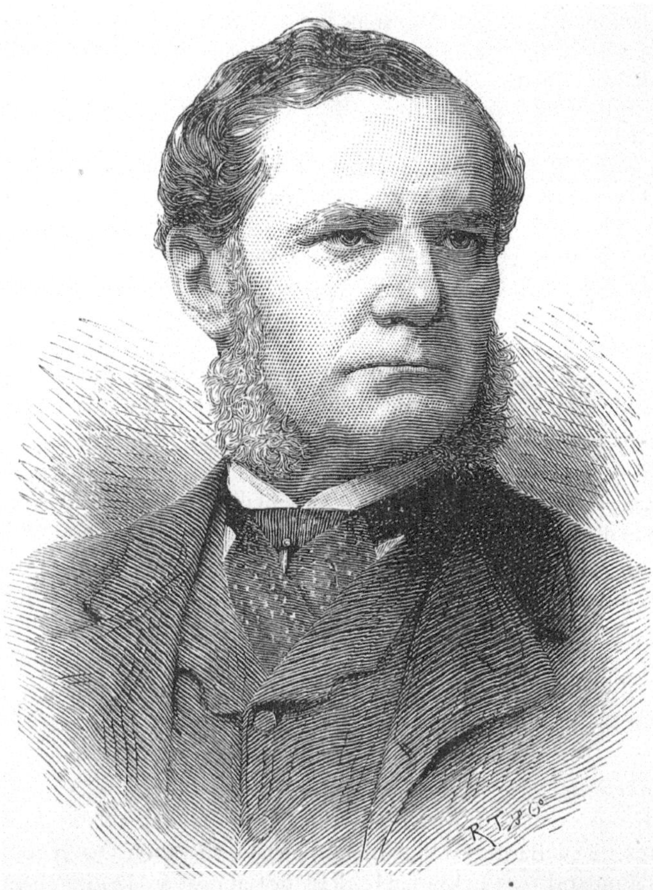

Fig. 4.17 *ILN*, *Mr W Lidderdale*, 9 May 1891 (© Illustrated London News/Mary Evans)

foreign markets, combined with rivalry with Rothschild, led to Barings deep involvement in Argentina. Then came the collapse of Barings in November 1890.

Barings was a partnership with partners, largely family members, who were personally liable for losses. The general view in the City was that Barings had behaved honourably (the individual partners used personal funds to meet obligations, in addition to the orderly disposal of the partnership's assets) and had managed successfully after 1895 to re-emerge as a major banking force.

4.3.4 Other Bankers and Financiers

Next to the banking dynasties of the Rothschilds and the Barings, there were other individuals who were part of what has been called 'the aristocratic bourgeoisie'. The main figure to be discussed here is Sir Ernest Cassel.

Sir Ernest Cassel

Sir Ernest Cassel was an important figure in banking circles because he was close to Edward VII and his financial acumen, alongside that of the Rothschilds and the Barings, was prized by the Treasury. Cassel falls into the category caricatured by one unkind contemporary as 'Britishers' who sing 'God save the King' in broken English. He was born a Jew but baptised as a Christian (cf. Disraeli). Indeed, he was referred to wittily and perhaps somewhat sarcastically as 'Windsor-Cassel—the last Court Jew'.[33] Coming from humble beginnings, he was essentially divorced from his own class, whilst sharing the interests of the class above him.

A commentary in relation to his 1899 caricature in *Vanity Fair* encapsulates his success:

> Born to a Cologne Banker eight-and-forty years ago, he early imbibed some of the secrets of real Finance: which have helped him to the position that he now occupies. Commerce and Finance, indeed, interested from the first; and to them, since he came to England at the age of sixteen, he has devoted his chief attention.[34]

Cassel made his money alone, not as part of any merchant bank, but using his connections. One of his methods, not illegal at the time, was called 'Cassel's greasing system; whereby he sold shares or provided loans on easier than market terms where he felt that this would assist in overcoming opposition to his ventures in overseas markets'[35] (Fig. 4.18).

Figure 4.19 is a representation of the entourage of the future Edward VII. Cassel, on Edward's immediate left, is whispering to Edward holding a bag of gold. Cassel was known to have supported the financial affairs

Fig. 4.18 *Vanity Fair*, *Egyptian Finance* (Sir Ernest Cassel), 7 December 1899 (Courtesy of NPG)

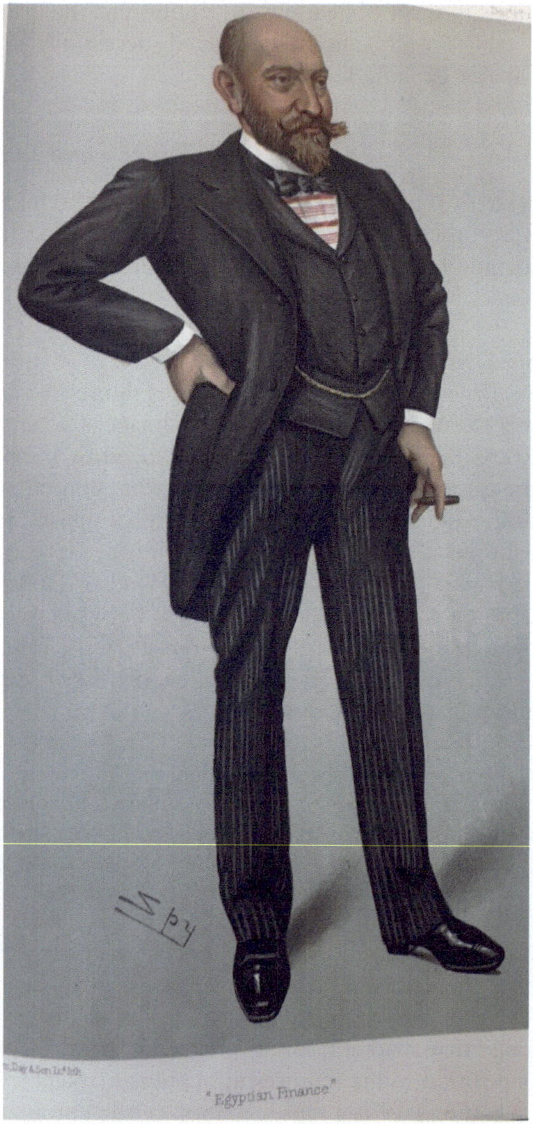

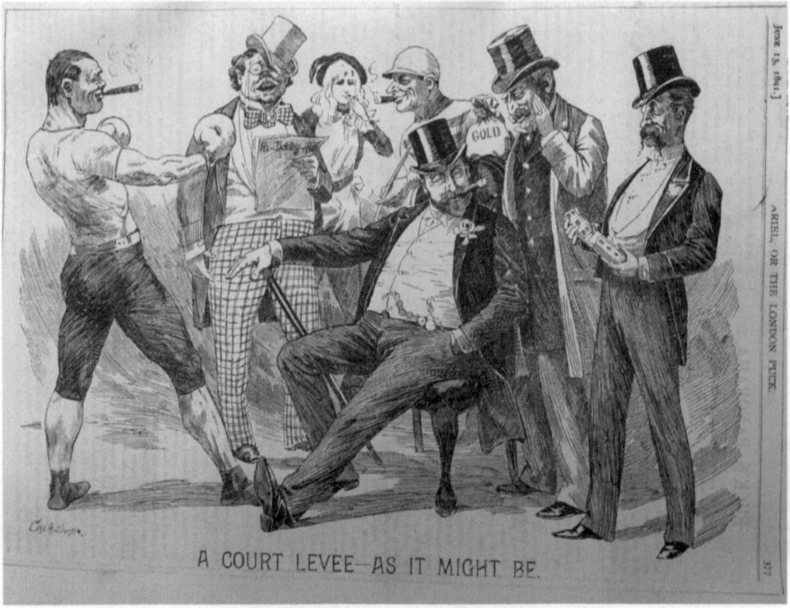

Fig. 4.19 *Ariel, or the London Puck, A Court Levee—As It Might Be*, 13 June 1891 (own photo) (@ BL Shelf Mark, LOU.LON 236 [1891])

of Edward. The cartoon reflects Edward's predilection for cards, horse racing, boxing, and women.

The Retail Bankers

Sampson Lloyd

Figure 4.20 shows Sampson Lloyd, a member of the Lloyds banking family; he became Chairman of Lloyds Bank in 1884 shortly after this caricature. An extract from the letterpress commentary below indicates the favourable impression that retail bankers such as Lloyd made on readers of *Vanity Fair*:

> is an excellent example of the results of commercial training upon a robust mind..... He is a shrewd man of much industry and tenacity.

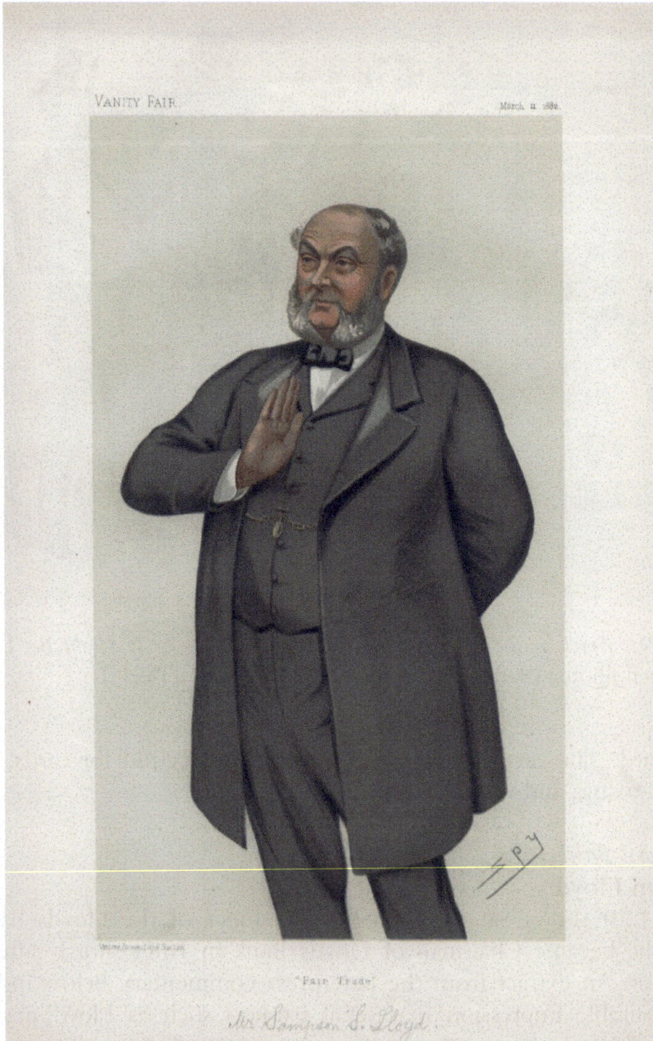

Fig. 4.20 *Vanity Fair*, '*Fair trade*' (Sampson Lloyd), 11 March 1882 (Courtesy of NPG)

Lord Overstone (Samuel Jones-Loyd)

Samuel Jones-Loyd, known as Lord Overstone after 1850, joined his father's bank, Jones Loyd & Co, and took control of the bank after his father retired in 1844. In 1864 the bank became incorporated with the London and Westminster Bank (now part of Royal Bank of Scotland due to its acquisition of National Westminster Bank). He died in 1883, aged 87.

His major achievements as head of the so-called 'Currency School'—which argued for a stricter, more cautious banking reserve ratio for the Bank of England (he heavily influenced Sir Robert Peel's drafting of the Bank Charter Act of 1844) predated the appearance of *Vanity Fair.* His exclusion, therefore, is unremarkable.

Figure 4.21 reveals the retail banker and essayist, in an almost 'saintly' characterisation, the epitome of stability and steadfastness. His head-wear probably represents a head warmer, perhaps quite common in aged people, so it is quite possible that a modern-day lens attaches a quasi-spiritual significance that would not have been visible to Victorian viewers. Nevertheless, it suggests a sense of seriousness and of piety that is absent from other depictions of financial figures, which tend towards self-aggrandisement or mild caricature.

The Private Bankers

There were numerous private bankers illustrated in *Vanity Fair*. The letterpress commentary below—in this case relating to J. J. Hubbard but in fact a typical example—reveals the links between bankers and aristocracy, and their knowledge of finance.

> In due course of time he became a merchant in the Russian trade, married a daughter of the eighth Lord Napier, and acquired money and a reputation for knowledge of finance.... He has been the Governor of the Bank of England; he is a great authority on Income Tax.[36]

Sir Michael Biddulph

The letterpress on Michael Biddulph illustrates the humour contained in some of the editorial commentary and offers a favourable view of the science (note, not art) of banking:

> He has since been completing his education and rounding off his corners in the highly respectable bank of Messrs Cocks, Biddulph, and Company;

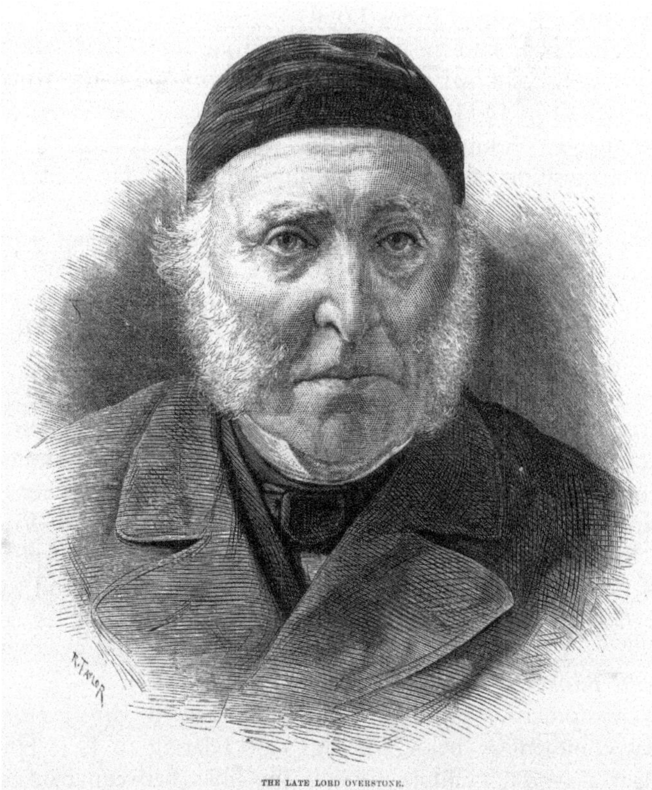

Fig. 4.21 *ILN*, *The Late Lord Overstone*, 1 December 1883 (© Illustrated London News/Mary Evans)

> of which firm he is now a partner. He is a shrewd man, who knows a good deal about the science of banking and some other things. He is rich; and his hat is a work of art.[37]

Sir Robert Fowler

The epitome of the successful private banker (he became a Lord Mayor of London) is used as an example of how financiers were accepted into the 'elite' of *Vanity Fair* readership.

Sir Robert Fowler was 'an expansive man, good-natured and kindly and an excellent bugle-man for his party'.[38] He was a City banker, a country squire (frequenting the Badminton Hunt, and part of the Wiltshire gentry), yet also a Quaker by background, and a member of the Anglican establishment.

The two prints (Figs. 4.22 and 4.23), one a caricature from *Vanity Fair*, and one a portrait, depict some of these characteristics. The *Vanity Fair* caricature was presumably drawn soon after he became an MP in 1880 and reflects his love of the good life (his ruddy complexion and wide girth indicating his love of drink and fine food), and his membership of the House of Commons. As the letterpress 25 June 1881 in *Vanity Fair* states: 'He drives in a gilt coach to the [Carlton] Club and gives dinners'. The crucial distinction between the two images is their sizing; in the case of *Vanity Fair* the image is of a full-length Fowler, whereas the portrait reflects a typical seated position. The first emphasises his self-importance and joie de vivre, the latter is a more sober representation reflecting the propriety of his position in society.

For Malchow, the election of Fowler as Lord Mayor of London 1885 represented a return to traditional attitudes: 'For both men [Fowler and his Liberal friend, William McArthur, the previous Lord Mayor] the Lord Mayor of London was important as symbol and model for upper-class behaviour'. He goes on to comment that Fowler was a symbol for the renewal of philanthropic traditions and Evangelical views.[39]

The Prime Ministers

Reference needs to be made also to Gladstone and Disraeli, both of whose political posts encompassed roles as Chancellor of the Exchequer and Prime Minister.

Disraeli

Disraeli served as Tory Chancellor of the Exchequer three times (1852, 1858/1859, 1866/1868). A typical representation of Disraeli in his financial role is depicted below. An interesting use of the icon of a bubble, normally associated with financial speculation. The effect here is ironic, the view being that Disraeli's budget is nothing but soap and water, a mirage in effect (Fig. 4.24).

The purchase of shares in the Suez Canal in 1875 was one of the few events in which cartoonists specifically linked Disraeli with financial matters (Fig. 4.25).

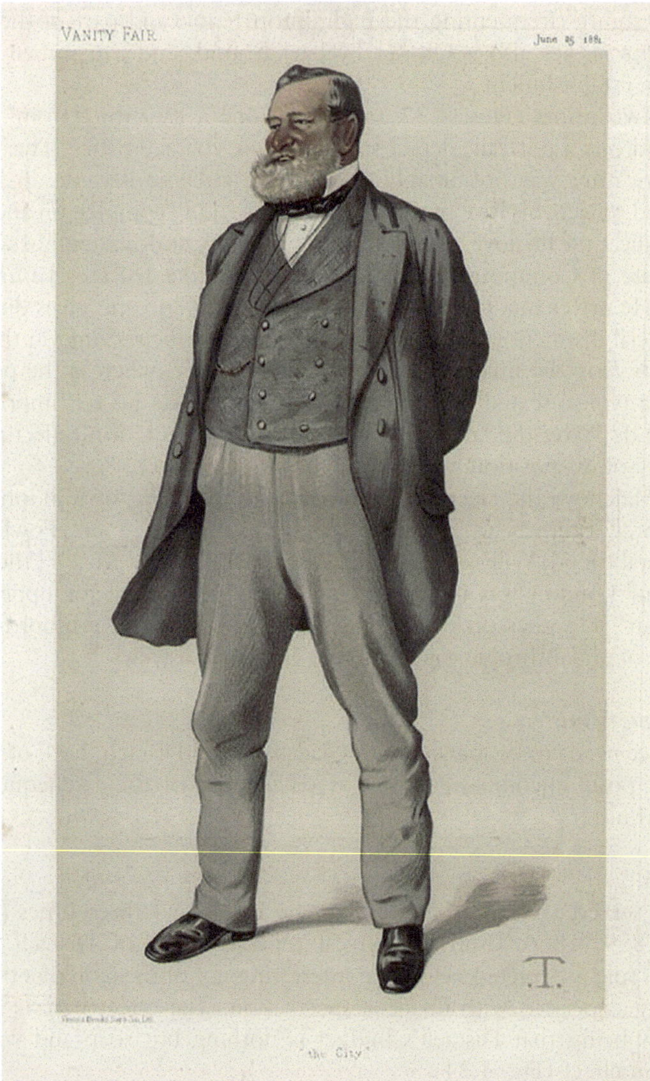

Fig. 4.22 *Vanity Fair: The City* (Sir Robert Fowler), 25 June 1881 (Courtesy of NPG)

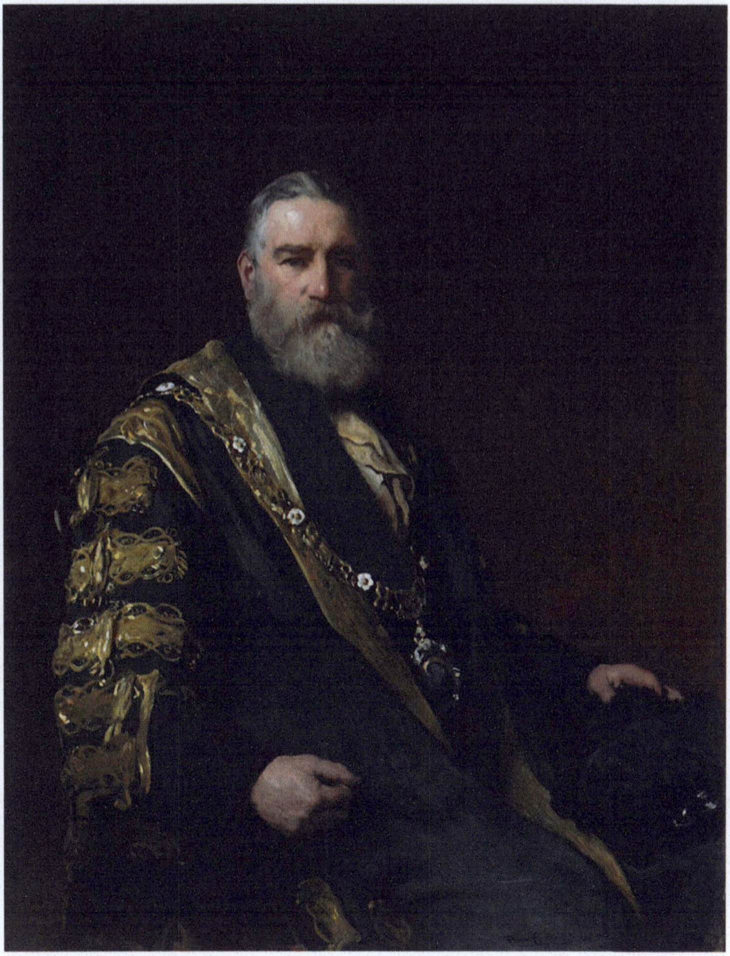

Fig. 4.23 *Sir Robert Fowler* 1885 as Lord Mayor (Courtesy of NPG)

Gladstone

Gladstone was a Liberal Chancellor of the Exchequer on four occasions (1852/1855, 1859/1866, 1873/1874, 1880/1882).

Figure 4.26 shows Gladstone, the prime minister, as Pierrot controlling his puppet (the then chancellor, Childers) and is typical of the imagery

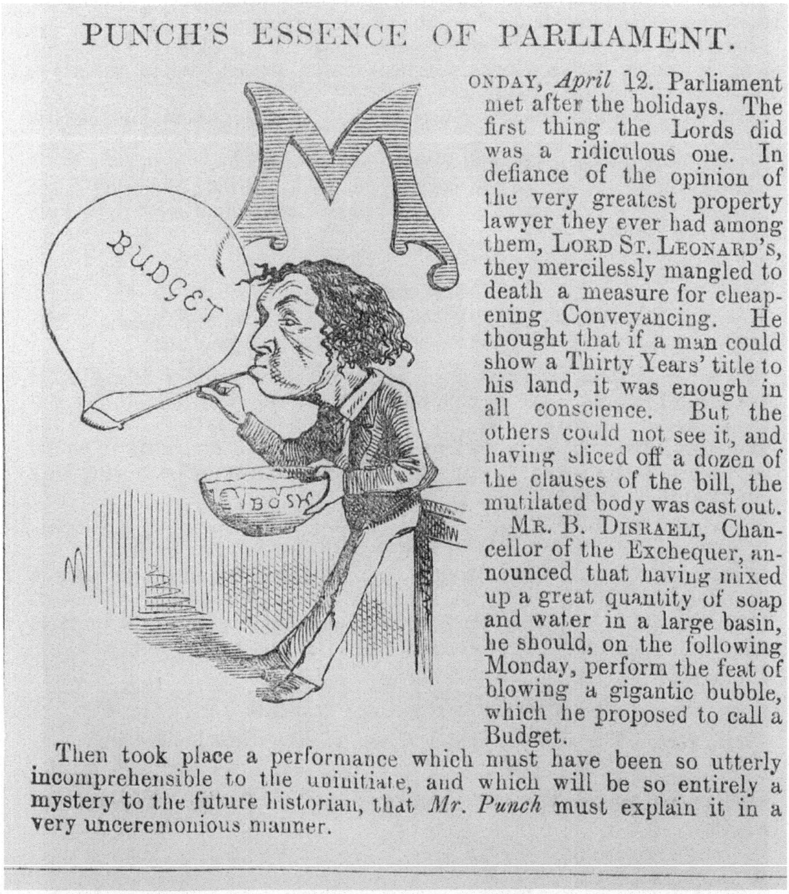

PUNCH'S ESSENCE OF PARLIAMENT.

MONDAY, *April* 12. Parliament met after the holidays. The first thing the Lords did was a ridiculous one. In defiance of the opinion of the very greatest property lawyer they ever had among them, LORD ST. LEONARD'S, they mercilessly mangled to death a measure for cheapening Conveyancing. He thought that if a man could show a Thirty Years' title to his land, it was enough in all conscience. But the others could not see it, and having sliced off a dozen of the clauses of the bill, the mutilated body was cast out.

MR. B. DISRAELI, Chancellor of the Exchequer, announced that having mixed up a great quantity of soap and water in a large basin, he should, on the following Monday, perform the feat of blowing a gigantic bubble, which he proposed to call a Budget.

Then took place a performance which must have been so utterly incomprehensible to the uninitiate, and which will be so entirely a mystery to the future historian, that *Mr. Punch* must explain it in a very unceremonious manner.

Fig. 4.24 *Punch*, *Essence of Parliament*, 24 April 1858 (Courtesy of UoH)

displayed in comic periodicals of the time to depict events surrounding the fiscal budget.

Other Chancellors of the Exchequer

Caricatures of financial figures dominated in *Vanity Fair* (see Appendix 3 for the analysis I have performed). I have highlighted here the

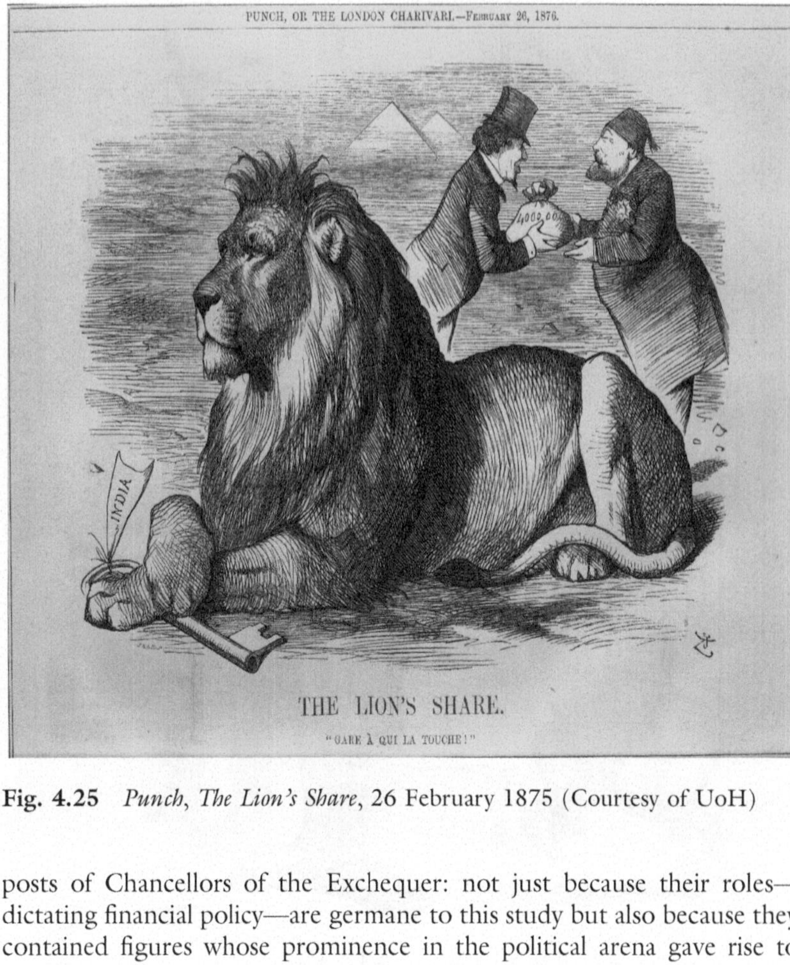

Fig. 4.25 *Punch*, *The Lion's Share*, 26 February 1875 (Courtesy of UoH)

posts of Chancellors of the Exchequer: not just because their roles—dictating financial policy—are germane to this study but also because they contained figures whose prominence in the political arena gave rise to constant caricature. In the latter half of the century there were two Chancellors of the Exchequer, Sir William Harcourt and George Goschen, who were prominent in their financial policies (Disraeli and Gladstone as Chancellors of the Exchequer in earlier periods have already been discussed above).

From opposing parties (Harcourt was a Liberal, and Goschen a Tory), their involvement in finance and tax matters during the 1880s and 1890s gave rise to frequent caricatures in *Vanity Fair* and other periodicals. This

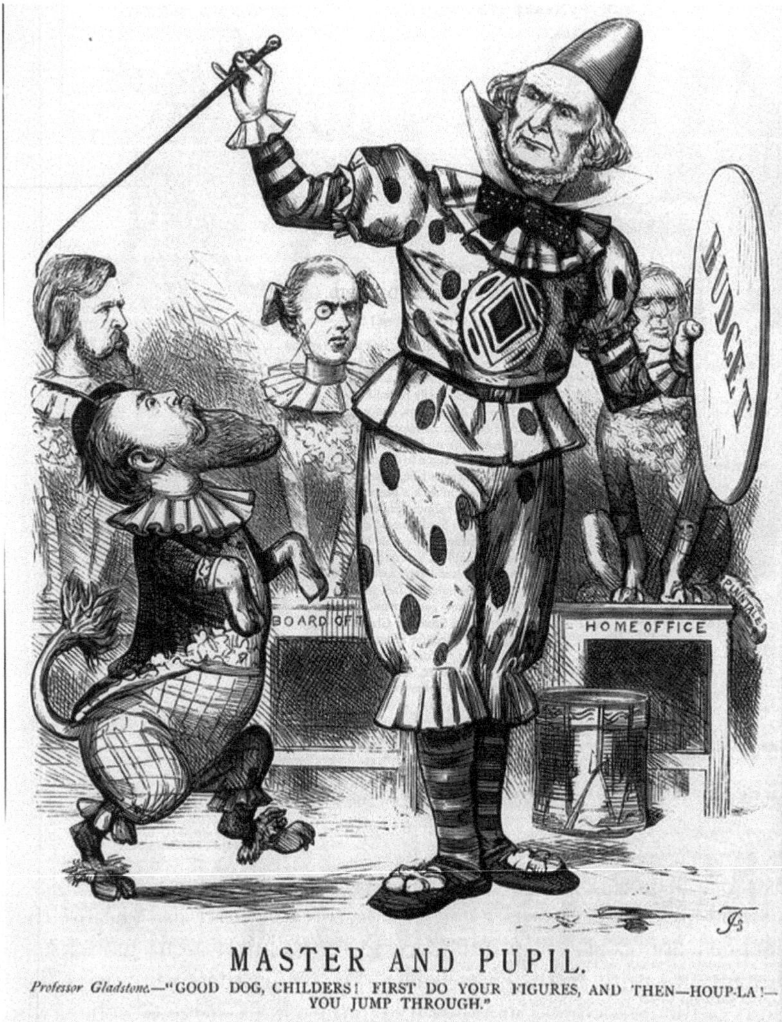

Fig. 4.26 *Fun*, *Master and Pupil*, 4 April 1883 (Courtesy of UoF)

was, as I have outlined above, a period when, owing to the public's fascination with the workings of parliament, cartoons of MPs became popular. It was also characterised by a more satirical depiction of MPs exemplified in the work of Harry Furniss. He introduced the personification of such individuals using slight exaggeration of their physical characteristics as well as animal features to embody their emotional or physical attributes. In the case of *Vanity Fair*, both Harcourt and Goschen are depicted in the same way as other MPs with no trace of outright satire.

George Goschen

A Tory Chancellor (1887–1892), Goschen was the first to have had active banking experience. He entered the family firm of Fruhling & Goschen and was a director of the Bank of England from 1858 to 1866.

He appears only once in *Vanity Fair* in 1869 (see Fig. 4.27) at the beginning of his distinguished political career. The letterpress commentary comments favourably on his exploits up to 1869:

'As Commerce first gave power to England so it still continues to shed lustre upon its name from the Mansion House to the Pole'. He wrote *The Theory of Foreign Exchanges* referred to in the caption.

The representation of Goschen accentuates his lean physique and the intensity of his facial expression. His frequent clashes in parliament with his Liberal opponent, Sir William Harcourt, provided fodder for parliamentary cartoonists such as Harry Furniss. Frequent images of the two of them appear sparring in animal form (e.g., cats fighting each other), especially during the tortuous process of the debates over the 1894 Finance Bill.[40]

An antidote to *Vanity Fair*'s depiction is Harry Furniss's portrayal of him in his series '*Mr Punch's Puzzle-Headed People*'. This series provoked praise and fury equally amongst supporters and opponents. Furniss himself commented that these caricatures inevitably were rarely flattering. He felt that allowances needed to be made for an 'ugly caricature provided that it was a good drawing, prophetically correct, and therefore historically interesting'.[41]

Figure 4.28 reveals complex imagery typical of the period. The focus for the image is Goschen's arguably most memorable achievement, the successful consolidation of government debt (reducing the cost of the debt to the country).[42] See also his right eye, which takes the form of a Victorian coin signifying his interest in monetary matters. The reference to Union over his left eyebrow represents Goschen's support of

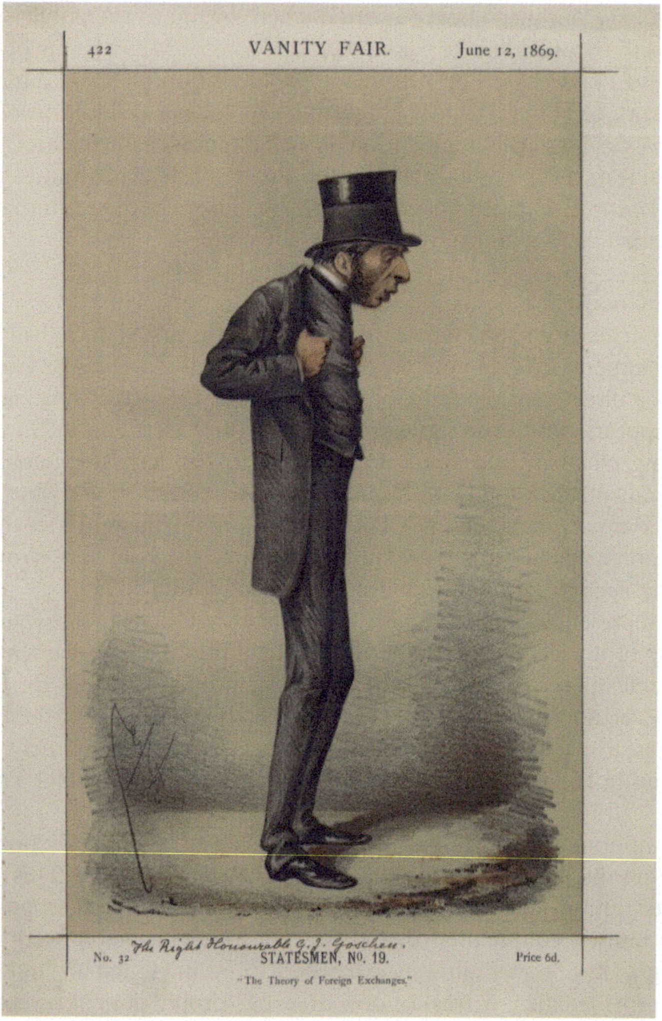

Fig. 4.27 *Vanity Fair*: *The Theory of Foreign Exchanges* (George Goschen), 12 June 1889 (Courtesy of NPG)

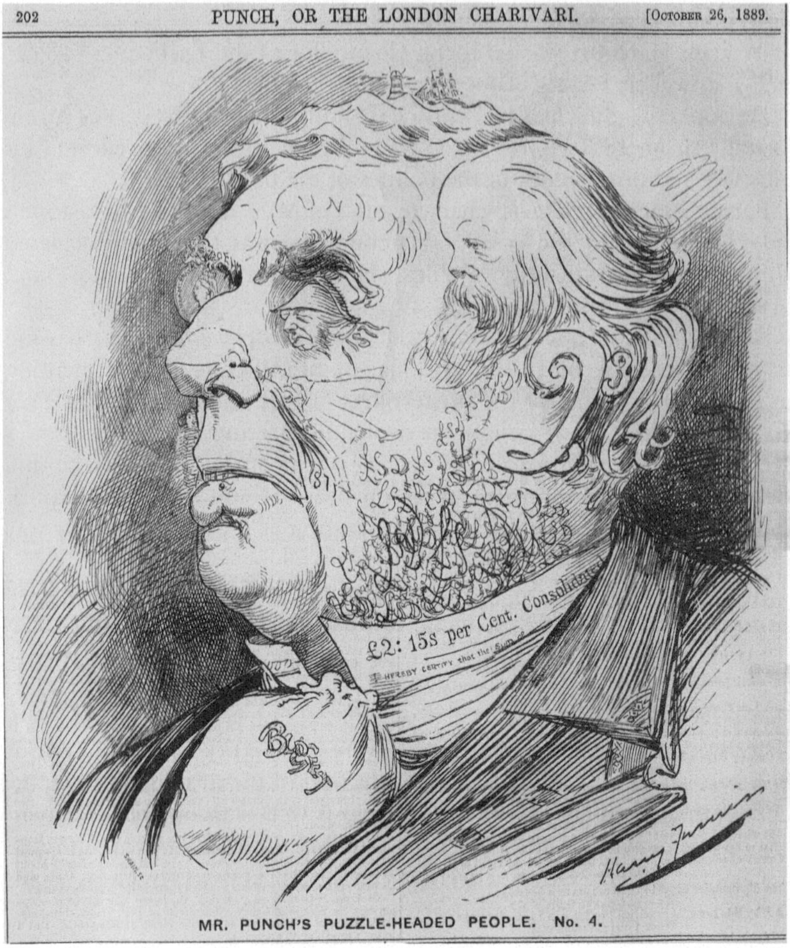

Fig. 4.28 *Punch*, *Mr. Punch's Puzzle-Headed People*, *No. 4* (George Goschen), 26 October 1889 (Courtesy of UoH)

Unionism. Two other proponents of Unionism are depicted here. In Goschen's left eye is the figure of Lord Hartington, (later Lord Devonshire, the leader of the Liberal Unionism), and in Goschen's left ear, literally, is the figure of John Bright (a leading Liberal MP who opposed Home Rule for Ireland).

Sir William Harcourt

Sir William Harcourt was a Liberal Chancellor of the Exchequer (1892–1895), as well as Leader of the Opposition (1896–1898).

He appears eight times in *Vanity Fair* both singly and as part of group portraits (from 1870 to 1899). The number of appearances reflected his longevity and prominence in the politics of the time.

Furniss exaggerated facial characteristics of MPs, especially Gladstone's and Harcourt's. In the case of Harcourt, he was frequently depicted with an 'unknown quantity of chins'. Hence the reference in the *Punch* cartoon to '*all Harcourts*' (Fig. 4.29).

At the time of Harcourt's greatest political achievement, the passing of the Finance Bill of 1894, cartoons appeared frequently commenting on the arduous nature of the proceedings in Parliament. In *Picture Politics* Furniss takes great delight in depicting Harcourt in various guises (see Fig. 4.30), appropriate to specific elements of the Finance Bill (death duties, naval estimates, taxes on beer) as well as various expressions of humour, exasperation, and exhaustion as the Bill wound its way tortuously through Committee Stages.

In Fig. 4.31, *Judy*, by contrast plays the difficult (knotty) task of getting the bill through Parliament, using a visual pun: planing out knots of wood.

The Stockbrokers

There were numerous stockbrokers covered in *Vanity Fair*. The term is used here to include bookmakers. A selection of them is discussed below representing the quirkiness of the entries, as well as favourable commentary on the activity of Stock Exchange trading. Other entries are covered in Chapter 8, The Other, covering Jewish stockbrokers such as Louis Cohen.

Mr Steel

Figure 4.32 is one of two prints (the other being Mr Oil and Gas) in which the subjects are not named, but merely referred to by their nicknames. In the case of Mr Steel, he was a 'Native of Sheffield' and owned steel works there—he made his fortune as a bookmaker. The size of his transactions earned him the title 'The Leviathan'.

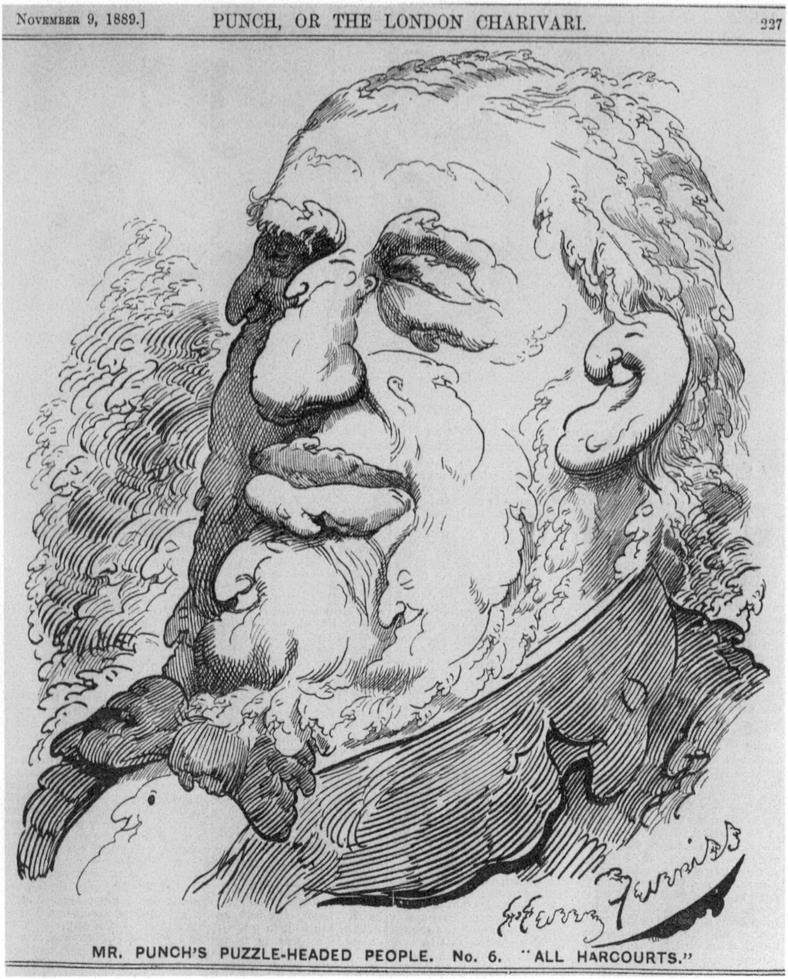

Fig. 4.29 *Punch, Mr. Punch's Puzzle-Headed People, No.6 'All Harcourts'*, 9 November 1889 (Courtesy of UoH)

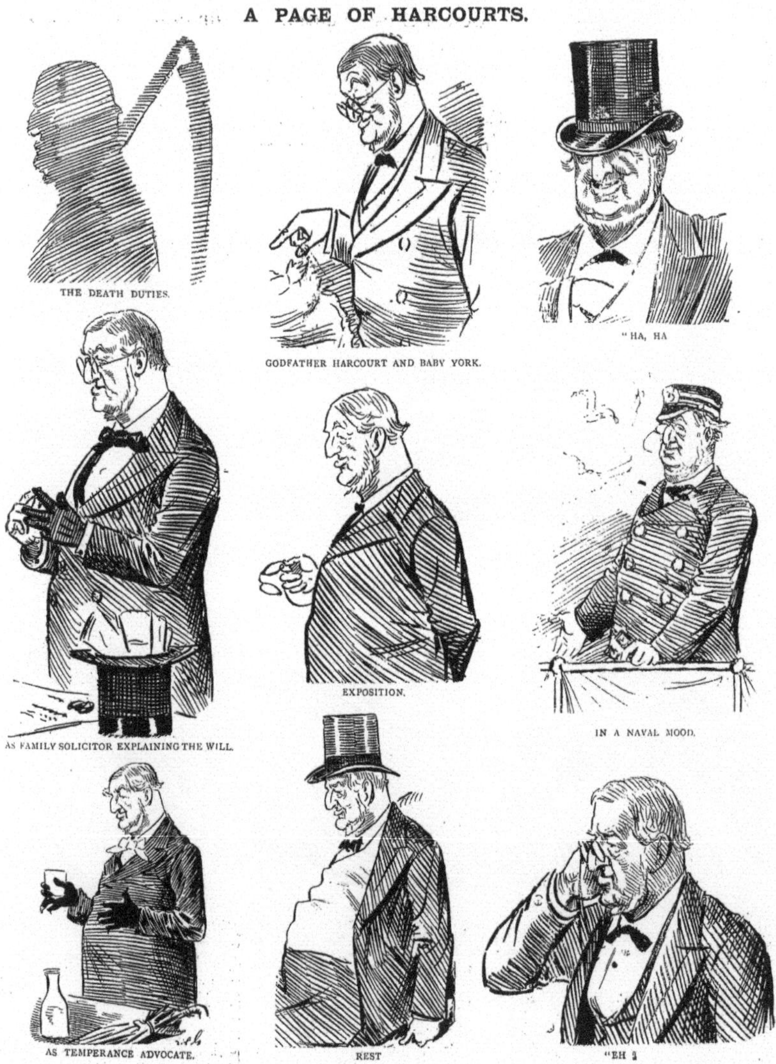

Fig. 4.30 *Picture Politics: A Page of Harcourts*, Furniss, 16 July 1894 (@ BL Shelf mark PENP.NT180, Issue 5, p. 13)

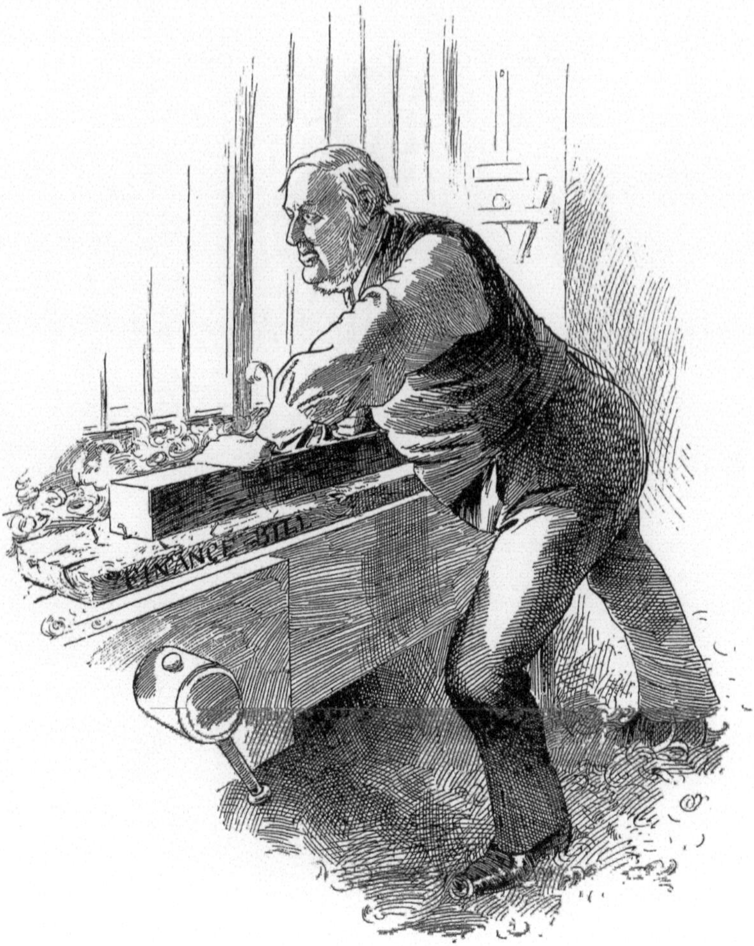

KNOTTY.

Fig. 4.31 *Judy*, *Knotty*, 20 June 1894 (@ BL Shelf mark P.P. 6014.be, p. 289)

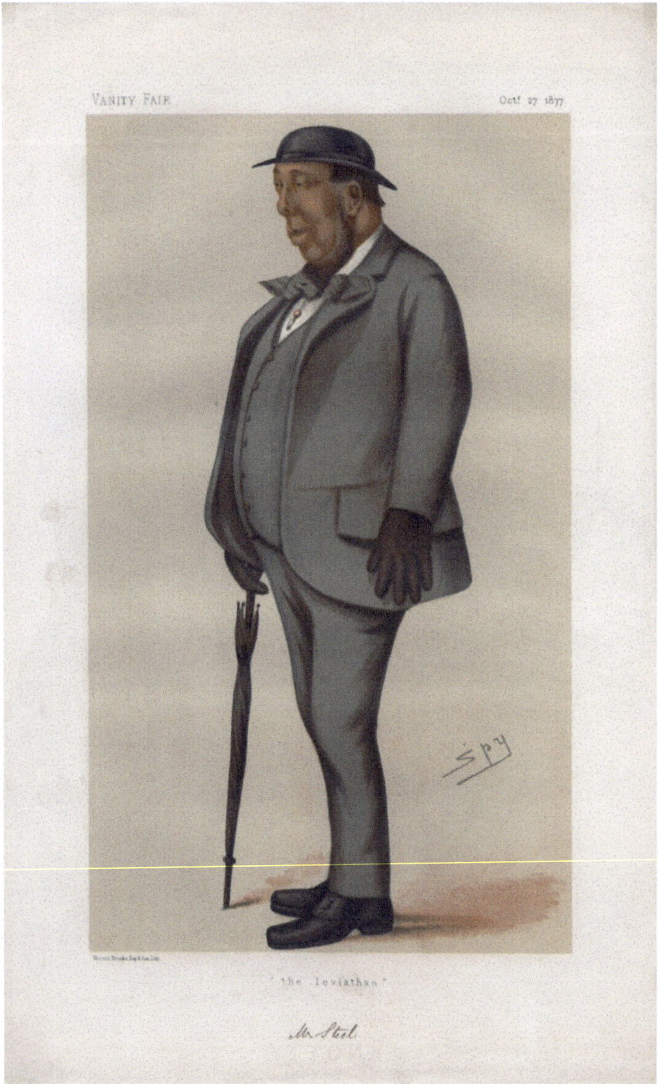

Fig. 4.32 *Vanity Fair*, *The Leviathan*, (Mr Steel), 27 October 1877 (Courtesy of NPG)

John Thomas North (Col North)

North was a company promoter. 'He is now quite a big man in the City, and holders of "Primitivas" and such-like stocks hang upon his lips in simple faith ... unlike most promoters, he boasts that he had never paid a penny of promotion money; nor, so far as his own Companies are concerned, has he ever allowed a Director to take fees before the shareholders have received a dividend......He has dabbled in collieries and in water gas and in race-horses and in other bubbles; but his luck is great'.[43]

The letterpress references his refusal to pay monies for his companies to be 'puffed' (promotion monies), nor to engage in dubious accounting practices such as paying directors' fees before paying shareholders dividends (common tactics of the dubious company promoters mentioned in the next chapter). He is depicted in racing garb (with binoculars); his activities whether in commerce or in gambling are 'dabbling' (i.e., not actually carrying out any serious professional activities), and all are associated with speculative intentions (hence the use of bubbles). There is a clear link between Stock Exchange trading (the role of a company promoter) and gambling (on horses). This is continued in the next section where individuals are named in *Vanity Fair* specifically as gamblers.

Whilst *Vanity Fair* and the public at large lauded his civic and philanthropic exploits, he was not without his critics. In Chile where he made his name and earned his sobriquet, the Nitrate King, 'his name was a byword for ambition and greed'[44] (Fig. 4.33).

Tom Nickalls

> The leading dealer in the American railway market, and one of the best known men on the Stock Exchange, is Mr. Tom Nickalls. He was born three-and-fifty years ago, and made his first mark in the City on that Black Friday when Messrs. Overend Gurney and Co. closed their doors. As a man of business, he displays the intelligence, the rapidity of decision, and the courage which go to make the successful jobber, and his success has been very great.[45]

An unusual representation in *Vanity Fair* (see Fig. 4.34). One of the leading Stock Exchange jobbers, Nickalls is not depicted in business attire but as a sportsman, a rider (probably in connection with a hunt). The letterpress waxes eloquent on the business skills he displayed successfully in his stockjobber role.

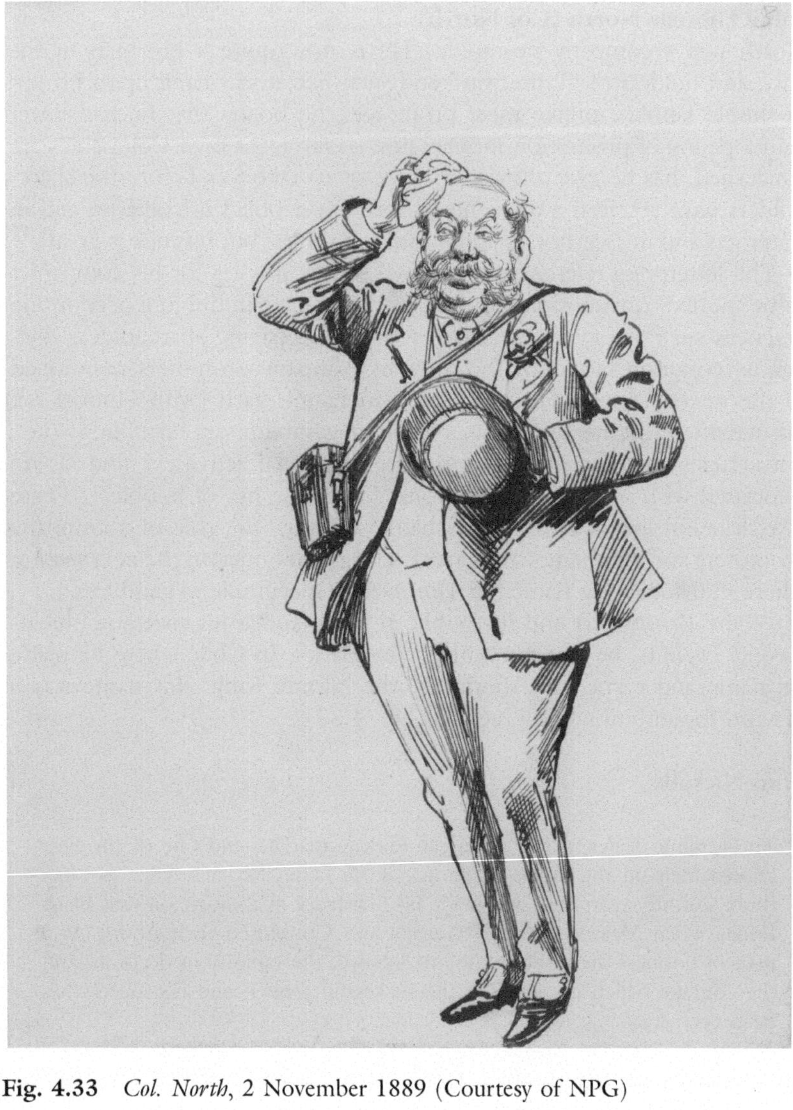

Fig. 4.33 *Col. North*, 2 November 1889 (Courtesy of NPG)

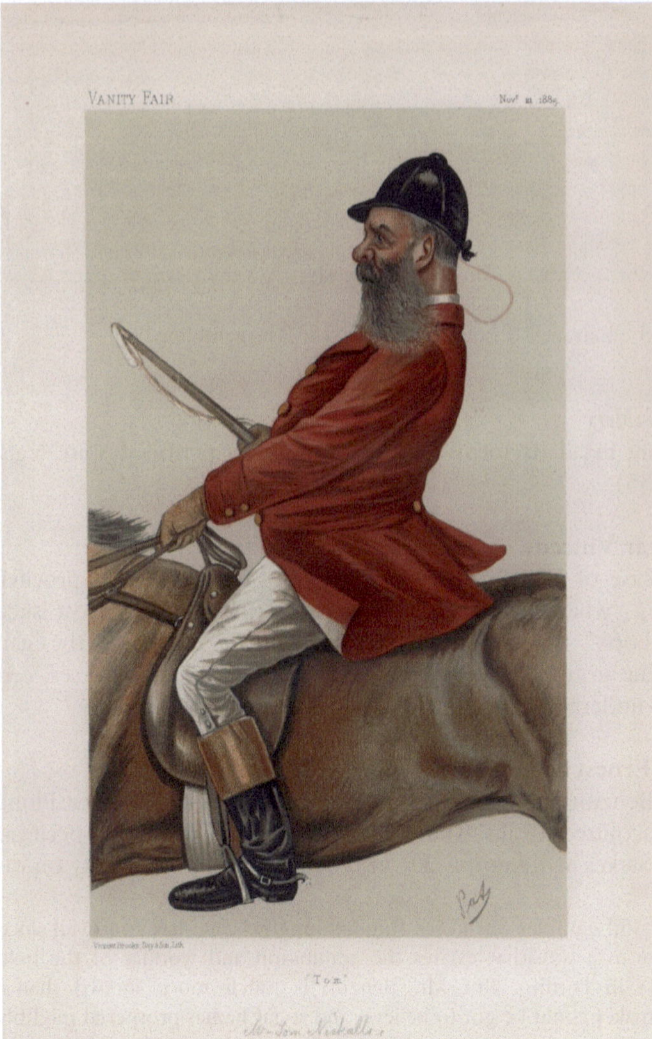

Fig. 4.34 *Vanity Fair*, *Tom* (Mr Tom Nickalls), 21 November 1885 (Courtesy of NPG)

But the spirit of gambling, we regret to confess, enters still far too largely in the people's pleasures, and while it does so, there will always be holes and corners found to gratify it in. Although it is partially hunted from the magnificent abodes of the west, yet London abounds with places where fortunes may be staked on the throw of the dice or the dealing of the card. The legislative eye destroyed the bold front that gaming assumed in past days; but it has not blotted it from the metropolis. But this, perhaps, is beyond all power of law to do, and until the love of it is conquered in society, so long, as we before said, enactments will be defied, and places will be found in which the gambler may carry on his nefarious avocation—and nefarious it is, whether carried on for pleasure or profit. Hardly now is there a tavern to be

Fig. 4.35 Extract Robson & Redpath 1857 re gambling[46]

The Gamblers
Gambling in all its forms thrived during this period despite legislation (Fig. 4.35).

Sir Edgar Vincent
In the case of Vincent, his early days at Eton revealed a proclivity for gambling 'when, at the age of fourteen, he made a most successful Derby book'. He also illustrates the extent to which the gamester spirit—the urge to stake money recklessly, whether on horses, cards, or shares—underlay speculation in the 1890s and subsequently.[47]

Henry Ernest Schlesinger Benzon
Henry Benzon was known in popular culture as the 'Jubilee Plunger', a title he acquired for his 'wild' betting activities at the races, specifically the Jubilee Stakes at Kempton. He also bet large sums of money on cards.

> Successful gambler on horses 'Jubilee Juggins'... he has contrived since to plunge in a way that excites the admiration and wonder of the boldest traders in betting. But Mr. Benzon is much more shrewd than any bookmaker could be got to believe, and so far he has prospered mightily.[48]

The letterpress praises Benzon's gambling activities, so endorsing these activities as honourable activities carried out by 'one of their own', members of the readership of *Vanity Fair* (Fig. 4.36).

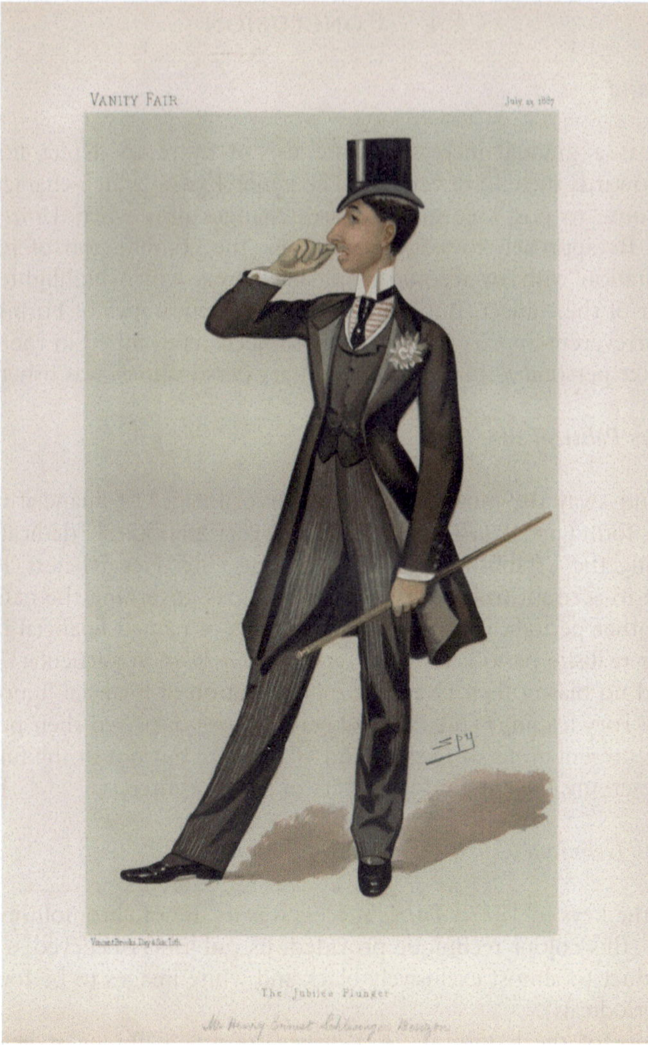

Fig. 4.36 *Vanity Fair: The Jubilee Plunger* (Mr Benzon), 23 July 1887 (Courtesy of NPG)

4.4 Conclusion

Background

There was a gradual increase in the use of satire to depict financial figures towards the end of century. The genteel satire which characterises the response to post-Georgian excesses changes only when *Vanity Fair* appears. Its approach to satire was to use the combination of realistic representation with an accompanying letterpress which highlighted the character of the subject. But it is not until the appearance of Furniss that a more irreverent approach to financial subjects, epitomised in the use of animal-like personifications in parliamentary personalities, was ushered in.

Publishers Political Bias

By far and away the most prolific number of images of financial figures is to be found in *Vanity Fair*. It was a Tory periodical, dedicated to supporting the Establishment, the governing elite. Nevertheless, it held this elite to account to be worthy of their duties governing the nation.

The other periodicals which carried images of named financial figures were the realistic periodicals (*ILN* and the *Graphic* in particular). They displayed no bias in their choice or representation of financial figures.

Judy (Tory leaning) and *Fun* (Liberal leaning) displayed their political bias in representations of Disraeli and Gladstone, but not in the financial arena, reserving their satire for matters of political interest.

Editorial Techniques

One of the keys to *Vanity Fair*'s success was its use of chromolithograph printing (this colour technique provided, its publishers believed, a superior product to almost exclusively black and white images to be found in other periodicals).

The use of the letterpress in *Vanity Fair* was a unique style in the Victorian era as it deliberately and consistently used text to comment on its focus, the caricature, which was positioned on the opposite page. Other periodicals such as *Punch* might comment on their cartoons with text which appeared, on occasions, somewhere near the cartoon, or *ILN* or the *Graphic* would provide factual commentaries on their drawings somewhere else in their periodical. It was *Vanity Fair*, however, which contained no text other than the commentary on the image itself, which distinguished it from its contemporaries. In addition, the caption for each *Vanity Fair* caricature attempted to capture the essence, or the character, of the personality being caricatured.

Artistic Techniques

Whereas depiction of named financial figures is rare in the comic press until the late 1880s (there were a few cartoons of Rothschild in *Punch*), the realistic periodicals of the day, *ILN*, *Graphic,* and *IPN*, did feature named financial figures in realistic mode.

The framing of financial individuals in family settings (e.g., Rothschild) accentuated their accepted position in society (the paintings were reminiscent of classical portraiture of the period).

As we have seen, named financial figures are rarely depicted in a financial setting, or indeed a setting which reflects financial iconography. The exceptions occur at the beginning and end of the period. In the 1890s the financial doyens of the stock exchange world are depicted realistically, standing ironically between the pillars of the exchange, echoing the image of Nathan Rothschild in the 1820s.

Notes

1. Extract from Byron's *Don Juan* (1824), Canto X11.5, lines 1–8 from Project Gutenberg.
2. Preface, vol. 1, *Vanity Fair*.
3. Diana Donald, 'Mr Deputy Dumpling and Family: Satirical Images of the City Merchant in Eighteenth Century England', *The Burlington Magazine*, 131:1040, November 1989, p. 755.
4. Bryant and Heneage, p. 60.
5. BM 14532 *A View on the Baltic Walk*, 14532A, *A View on the Royal Exchange*, 14533 *Coffee's the Thing*, 14536 *A Near Guess*, 14538 *A Scene on the Baltic Walk.*
6. Mark Bills, *The Art of Satire: London in Caricature* (London, 2006), p. 116.
7. BM 12906, *A View from the Royal Exchange*, is a typical example.
8. BM 13021, *Moses Montefiore.*
9. BM 14666, *A New Court Fire Screen.*
10. BM 14529, *Is Friend Rothschild on Change.*

11. BM 14678–14683 (Raikes, Wilson, Lindsey, Stirling, Goldsmid, Dewar).
12. BM 15522, *The Jew and the Doctor or Secret Influence Behind the Curtain*, BM 15523, *New Scene for the Old Farce of the Jew and the Doctor*, BM 15156, *Beauties of Brighton.*
13. BM 14340, *The Royal Exchange—Tom Pointing Out to Jerry a Few of the Primest Features of Life in London.*
14. See BM 14538, *A Scene at the Baltic Walk, Royal Exchange, November 1822.*
15. Ferguson, vol. 1, p. 260.
16. Alfred Rubens, 'The Rothschilds in Caricature, *Transactions & Miscellanies (Jewish Historical Society of England)*, 22.
17. Mark Bryant and Simon Heneage (comp.), *Dictionary of British Cartoonists and Caricaturists 1730–1980* (Aldershot, Scolar Press, 1994), p. 60.
18. "In February 1815, after the death of his first wife, they were married at St Pancras Church, but the marriage was declared invalid, and they went through a second ceremony on 12 April 1815."
19. Francis Bamford, and The Duke of Wellington (eds.), *The Journal of Mrs Arbuthnot, 1820–1832*, vol. 1 (London, repr., 1950), p. 408.
20. Edna Healey, *Coutts & Co 1692–1992: The Portrait of a Private Bank* (London, Hodder & Stoughton, 1992), p. 305.
21. Donald, p. 762.
22. *The Metropolitan Magazine*, vol. 3, p. 78. *Metropolitan*, established by Thomas Campbell in 1831, changed name to *The Metropolitan Magazine* in 1833. Accessed from the Web 24 June 2013. The word 'loanist' does not appear in the OED, but the reference here indicates that the word signifies those who loan money: 'The Jews always were, and now are, (from David, the inspired harpist, down to Rothschild, the inspired loanist) doatingly fond of music'.
23. See Chapter 8 for further commentary.
24. http://www.oxforddnb.com.chain.kent.ac.uk/view/article/6964, article by Norman Gash accessed 24 June 2013.
25. Finel-Honigman, pp. 135/136.
26. *Vanity Fair*, Letterpress, 22 September 1877.
27. See Chapter 8.
28. *Vanity Fair*, Letterpress, 20 September 1894.

29. OED definition: To become conscious of by viewing as a distinct entity; (in later use) *spec.* to conceptualize (a people, a group, etc.) as excluded and intrinsically different from oneself OED https://www.oed.com/view/Entry/263193?rskey=sVWA4g&result=2#eid, accessed 14 November 2020.
30. Quoted in Asha Banerjee, 'The First Modern Bailout: The Barings Crisis of 1890 and the Bank of England', Master's Thesis, Department of History, Columbia University, 2017, No. 46, p. 25.
31. *Vanity Fair*, Letterpress, 15 September 1888.
32. See detailed commentary on Barings collapse in Chapter 7 when discussing the depiction of the Old Lady of Threadneedle Street.
33. R. P. T. Davenport-Hines (ed.), *Speculators and Patriots Essays in Business Biography* (London, Frank Cass, and Company Limited, 1986), p. vii.
34. *Vanity Fair*, Letterpress, 7 December 1890.
35. Thane, 'The Case of Sir Ernest Cassel', in Davenport-Hines, p. 96 (footnote 7).
36. *Vanity Fair*, Letterpress, J. J. Hubbard, *Old Mother Hubbard*, 4 October 1884.
37. *Vanity Fair*, Letterpress, Michael Biddulph, *South Herefordshire*, 25 July 1891.
38. Quoted in H. L. Malchow, *Gentlemen Capitalists: The Social and Political World of the Victorian Businessman* (Stanford, CA, 1992), p. 242.
39. Malchow, p. 215.
40. See *Pall Mall Gazette: A Fair Share of Taxation*, 5 June 1894.
41. Furniss, vol. 1, p. 253.
42. Though Goschen was involved later in the high profile, successful financial rescue of Barings.
43. Letterpress, *Vanity Fair*, 2 November 1889.
44. https://doi.org/10.1093/ref:odnb/37816.
45. *Vanity Fair*, Letterpress, 21 November 1885.
46. Hathitrust, p. 27.
47. Davenport-Hines, p. vii.
48. *Vanity Fair*, Letterpress, 23 July 1887.

CHAPTER 5

The Charlatans

5.1 Introduction

When as a young and unknown man I started to be successful, I was referred to as a gambler. My operations increased in scope. Then I was a speculator. The sphere of my activities continued to expand and presently I was known as a banker. Actually, I had been doing the same thing all the time.

—Sir Ernest Cassel, banker to royalty and aristocracy, quoted in the late 1890s.[1]

Cassel's quote reflects his bemusement at the different classifications attached to the unchanging nature of his business activities. Though the quote refers to Cassel's working life from the 1870s onwards, the sentiments apply to the whole of the Victorian period (and to the rest of the century I would argue based on my review of images of the era).

Whether real-life speculator, gambler, or banker the images of the era portray individuals almost always at the height of their fame (their rise not their fall). Grudging respectability of named individuals is the theme in visual culture of this period until the era of 'new journalism' in the late 1880s onwards; disapproval is reflected in their loss of social status but not in satirical visual representation. It is left to visual representations of the impact of their actions on anonymous investors (see Chapter 6) to display such disapproval.

H. Sless, *Merchant Princes and Charlatans or Makers of Money?*,
https://doi.org/10.1007/978-3-030-86604-4_5

This was a period of lax regulation, with the 'poor investors' (an emotional connotation here as the investors were invariably well off) duped by a seemingly endless number of fraudsters. Imperfect market information, the need to find increased annual income (pensioners, widows, etc.), the lure of the crowd (the herd instinct or what is popularly now known as animal spirits),[2] all combined to allow unscrupulous directors, company promoters, and fraudulent bank managers/staff, free rein to perpetrate financial fraud on often greedy, naïve investors. The emotional response of investors to the lure and dangers of risky investments was, as I will show later, mirrored by cartoonists seeking ever more sensationalist visualisations to convey non-verbal responses.

A list of those mentioned in this chapter is included in Table 5.1.

Where visual depictions do occur, the depictions do not show the charlatans in satirical mode.[3] And not all financial scandals resulted in images of charlatans appearing in the popular periodical press.

The dilemma for Victorians, and editors and artists in the popular press, was that not all these financiers were considered 'bad'. The dividing lines between gambling, investment, and speculation were problematic; so also, was the propriety of identifying the perpetrators by name in cartoons. As Flavin expresses it 'Gambling ethos (was) at the centre of Victorian society'.[4] Taylor comments that the absence of the deterrent of strong

Table 5.1 List of Charlatans

Name	*Occupation*	*Year*
Thomas Cochrane	Naval officer	1814
George Hudson	Financier	1845–1849
Strahan, Paul & Bates	Private bankers	1855
John Sadleir	Bank director	1856
William Robson	Chief clerk, transfer department, Crystal Palace company	1856
Leopold Redpath	Registrar, Great Northern Railway	1856
Albert Grant	Company promoter	1874–1877
Harry Benson	Fraudster	1877
CGB directors (various)	Bank directors	1878
Harry Marks	Journalist	1889
Jabez Balfour	Chairman, Liberator Building Society	1892
Ernest Hooley	Company promoter	1898

corporate governance rules meant that the only way of 'shaming' white-collar criminals was in the court of public opinion by naming them in the written press. But no such naming and shaming occurred in the popular pictorial press, until the early 1890s.

5.2 Pre-Victorian Figures

5.2.1 Lord Cochrane

In February 1814, Lt-Col R du Bourg, aide-de-camp to Lord Cathcart, British military attaché to the Czar, spread false information that Napoleon had been killed by Cossacks. Hopes and expectations had been driving up the price of Govt Consols since early February. Specifically, the price of Omnium (a combination of government stock and public annuities) fluctuated wildly. A Stock Exchange investigation took place because of the deliberate way in which the rumour was spread. Lord Cochrane, Cochrane-Johnstone (his uncle), and Richard Butt (a Stock Exchange trader and financial adviser to Lord Cochrane), were charged with having conspired, by disseminating false information using the auspices of another conspirator De Berenger, to raise the price of government funds 'with a wicked and fraudulent intention' to 'cheat and defraud' the King's subjects. According to the prosecution the fraud was intended to prevent them from losing more monies. They had speculated heavily on purchasing large quantities of stock in the previous weeks expecting as 'bulls' that prices would continue to rise. They had contracted to buy over a million in stock but news from France kept prices flat and reports of Napoleon's victory over Blucher on 14 February depressed prices.

The chief conspirators each received a sentence of twelve months in prison, a fine of £1000 and an hour in the pillory outside the Royal Exchange. Cochrane's public profile as a naval hero and prominent anti-corruption campaigner made his fall from grace even more poignant.

Yet as Cobbett and others pointed out newspapers and individuals had for years engaged in similar activities without any legal recourse. The error, in this case, was to have caused financial loss by way of creating and supplying false information (Rothschild could trade on his own information but not mislead others).

Although Cochrane regained his rank and honours he did not become accepted by the mid-Victorian elite.[5]

The events are portrayed in a Cruickshank cartoon *Gambling in the Stocks*, Fig. 5.1. Cochrane is seated on a thistle playing dice with de Berenger, even as these two are entrapped in the stocks (Cochrane-Johnstone and Butt are playing cards).

The use of visual symbols (dice, stocks, ducks, etc.) is discussed in detail in the chapter on iconography. The focus here is on the figure of Cochrane himself and his fellow conspirators.

The depiction is sensationalist in tone: Dukes, and military officers (a Frenchman to boot) are being subjected to ridicule.

Chronologically the review of visual images of charlatans moves to George Hudson, the 'Railway King', who personified the excesses of the Railway Mania of the 1840s, and Leopold Redpath, who perpetrated one of the greatest financial swindles of the 1850s.[6]

5.3 Victorian Figures

5.3.1 George Hudson

A review of the *Punch* Historical Archive revealed only seven cartoons identifying George Hudson, whereas a review of the NPG revealed three images, two portraits, and a family portrait.[7] The Artemis search revealed no additional images. Given the numerous images covering the Railway Mania in many other often short-lived periodicals[8] cartoons of George Hudson did not dominate the visual press even if he was a dominant figure in the commercial world of the time. Arnold & McCartney (2004) quote one of Hudson's supporters at the height of his powers: 'he wields at command and presides over an amount of pecuniary capital exceeding that of any other man in the empire'.[9] Hudson used unscrupulous (though not illegal) accounting practices to supplement his meagre director's fees.

So how was George Hudson depicted? A larger-than-life character: a physically imposing man, his bulk mirrored the brute force of the railways he directed. His head, according to a contemporary was 'a formidable-looking engine.... as round and as stern-looking as a forty-two pounder' and set on his massive frame without the formality of a neck.[10] A typical representation of him is shown in Fig. 5.2 which reflects these characteristics.

The image in Fig. 5.2, the portrait is side-on and depicts him in business mode, serious, in gentleman's business attire. The portrait signifies

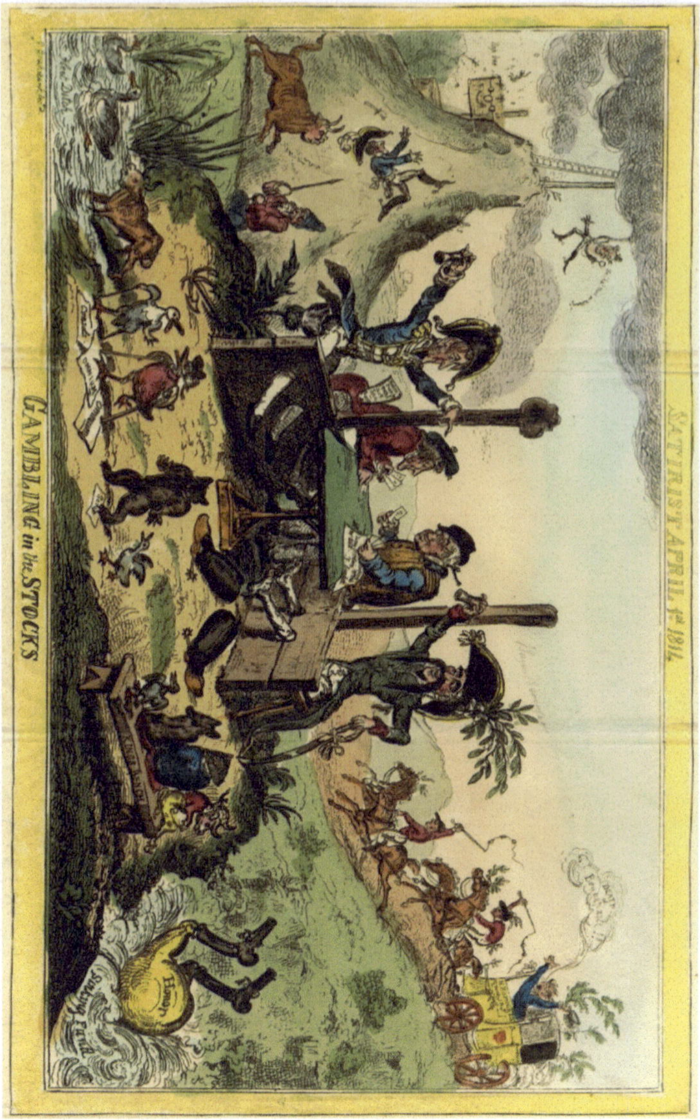

Fig. 5.1 BM 12209, *Satirist*, *Gambling in the Stocks*, 11 April 1814 (Courtesy of BM)

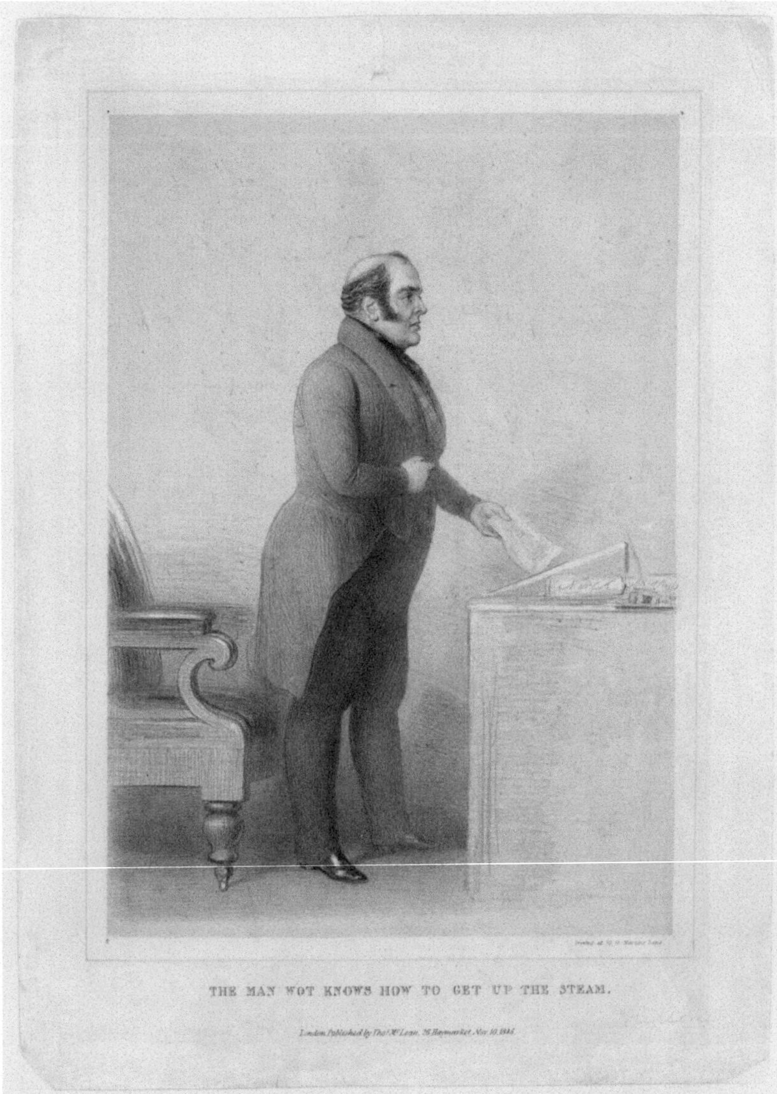

Fig. 5.2 *The Man wot Knows how to get up the Steam* (George Hudson), 1845 (Courtesy of NPG)

respectability. This is echoed in a striking family portrait of the same period (Fig. 5.3) which is presented almost in silhouette and reflects the close-to-aristocratic status of the Hudson family at the time.

Altick quotes *Punch* on Hudson's many virtues: 'he was; everything at once: a large shareholder, a comprehensive projector [in modern day language a promoter], a chairman, a trustee for shareholders, an agent for particular transactions, a broker, a contractor, a banker, a confidential friend of landowners, and a good deal more besides'.[11]

In Fig. 5.4, an image from *ILN* shows Hudson in a glowing light, very dapper, almost reverential in aspect a sharp contrast to the NPG portrait of the same period. Here, no portliness is portrayed, and a top hat hides his baldness.

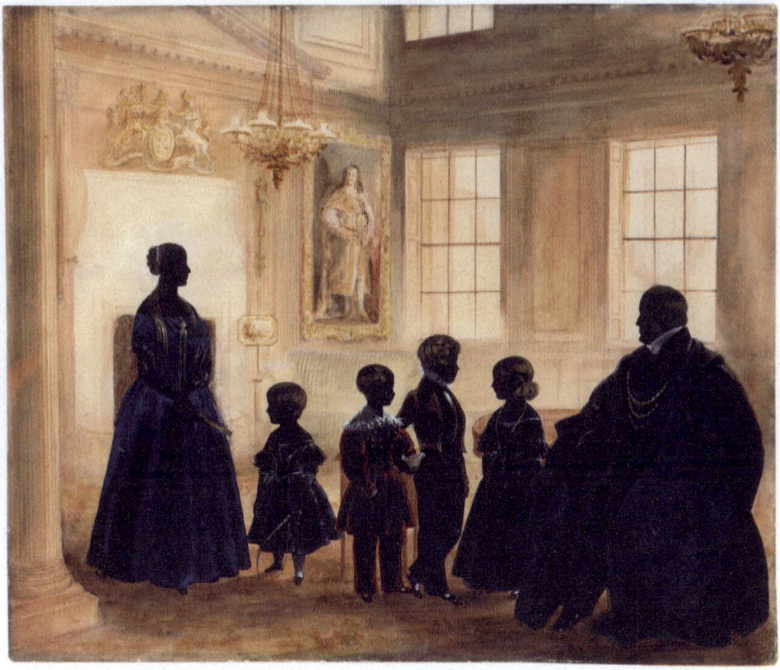

Fig. 5.3 *The Hudson family*, 1845 (Courtesy of NPG)

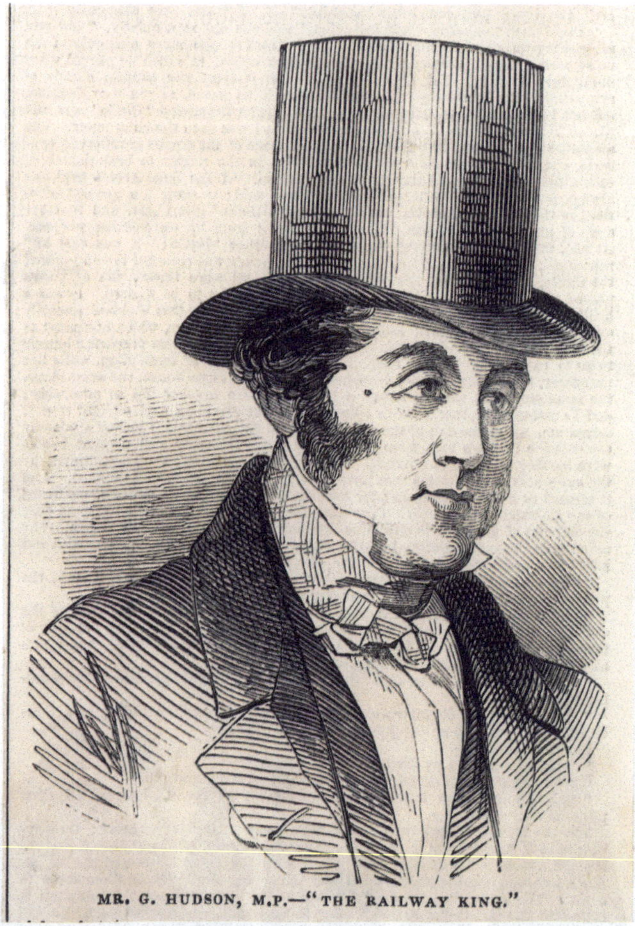

Fig. 5.4 *ILN, Mr G. Hudson, MP—"The Railway King"*, 6 September 1845 (© Illustrated London News/Mary Evans)

For Taylor, Hudson was 'a gift to cartoonists, in whose depictions he could be found blending and blurring into his railways'.[12] Taylor encapsulated his personification in cartoons of the time: 'Such representations made the point that this man shared the destructive powers of the trains he directed'.[13]

In *Punch*, as in other periodicals of the time, Hudson is named—there is no suggestion of libel being associated with naming individuals. *Punch* is constantly ironic about the 'exploits' of Hudson. It satirised the fawning admiration that the public showed for him. In Fig. 5.5, representatives from all walks of life—royalty, courtiers, women, etc—pay homage to the king of Mammon, King Hudson, sitting on a throne, with a railway worker bearing an iron staff as his attendant. The figure of Hudson is life-like, closer in appearance to the *ILN* caricature than the NPG one.[14]

Even in the *Hudson Testimonial* (see Fig. 5.6), Hudson is depicted life-like, but the irony of portraying him astride a horse disguised as a railway engine, the statue itself bestriding his two houses that he had bought in the very fashionable Albert Gate, is not lost.

Punch refers to an effigy of Hudson in Madame Tussauds, 'an honour that as Punch pointed out had not, as yet, been accorded to two other luminaries of the moment, Jenny Lind and Pope Pius IX'.[15] 'For those who preferred to ***worship in private***, the print-seller Colnaghi commissioned an engraving to be made of a portrait of Hudson painted by the fashionable artist Francis Grant' [my emphasis on ironic use of words].[16]

In other images, Hudson is Leporello to John Bull's Giovanni[17] and then in keeping with Taylor's earlier comments, on a run-away throne careening off the tracks[18] as a railway clown facing indignant shareholders.[19] In the ironically named '*The Great Railway Guy for 1849*',

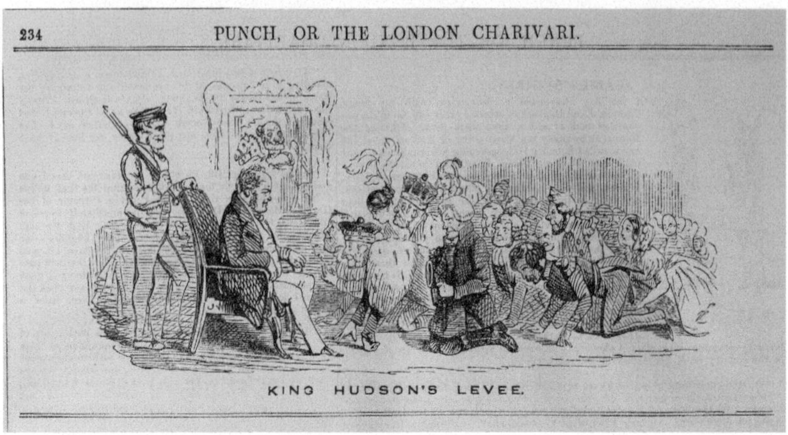

Fig. 5.5 *Punch, King Hudson's Levee*, 29 November 1845 (Courtesy of UoH)

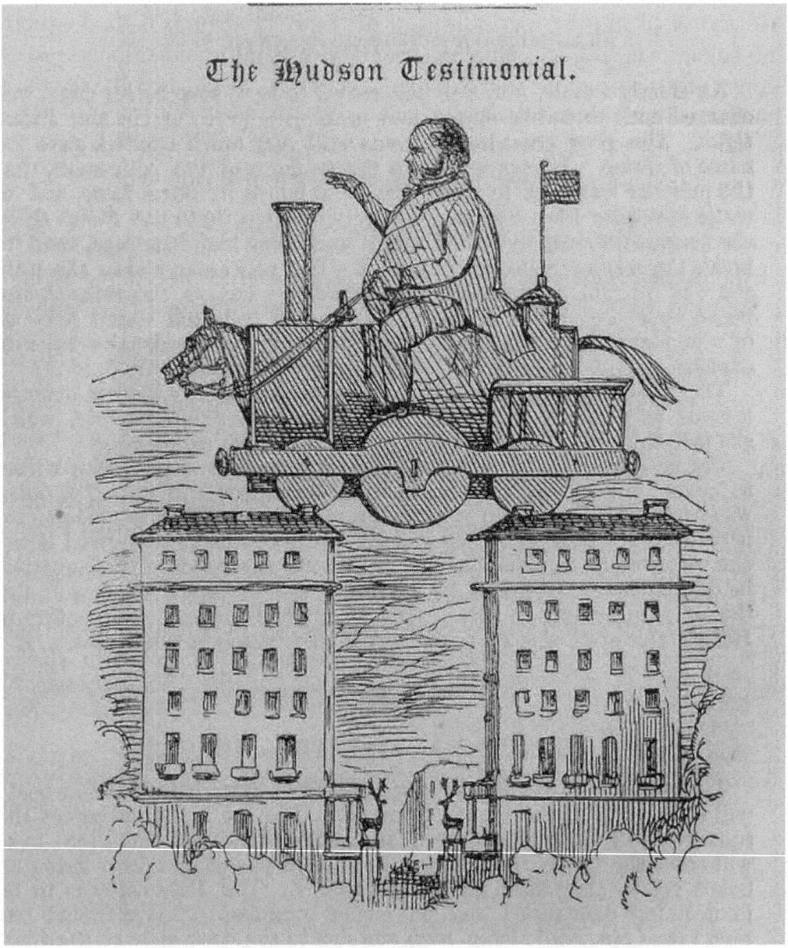

Fig. 5.6 *Punch*, *The Hudson Testimonial*, 24 October 1846 (Courtesy of UoH)

Hudson was depicted holding fistfuls of shares, and being borne on poles carried by two men, both of whom had stag's antlers growing out of their heads. In the background is a poster referring to the Hudson Testimonial (monies to be subscribed by the public to honour Hudson's achievements—the statue was never erected!).[20]

Hudson was made the scapegoat for all the follies of the Railway Mania, i.e., the personification of the evils of the period, although many contemporary commentators berated management and shareholders.[21]

5.3.2 *Leopold Redpath*

The year 1856 was one 'prolific in fraudulent discoveries'[22] In the case of John Sadleir's suicide in early February of that year, *Punch* merely observes '.... It was evident that he had contemplated suicide for some days, as he was no longer able to bear the self-reproach of the ruin he had brought upon hundreds by his frauds and forgeries'.[23]

Scenes from the Lives of Robson & Redpath published in 1857 detailed the exploits of Robson and Redpath. Robson's frauds (forged transfers of shares, and other frauds on the Company and the public) amounted to £28,000. By contrast, the fraudulent activities of Redpath amounted to some £250,000 (almost £19 million in today's terms).[24] Robb describes Redpath's fraud as 'perhaps the most notorious company fraud of the 1850s'.[25]

As outlined in the introduction to *Scenes from the Lives*:

> The wildest fiction is distanced by the dread realities of the newspaper disclosures. Felons of every day – commercial swindlers, despairing suicides, false seducers, blood-stained murderers_- abound on every hand, and the great world we live in has considerably increased in great criminals. Now we have time-honoured bankers doomed for fraud to finish their hoary age in prison cells...[26]

The images convey a melodramatic representation, reminiscent of illustrations in serialisations of Dickens's novels. The book was published just two weeks after Redpath's trial, and like Dickens's novels of the period was serialised.[27]

The images which follow (Figs. 5.7 and 5.8) illustrate various aspects of Redpath's life. The depiction of the investigation of the company's accounts (Fig. 5.8) displays the emotional reaction to one director having recently met Redpath socially, and becoming suspicious about the origins of the monies that would have justified his social status. The book contains no illustrations depicting the financial crimes of which Redpath was accused.

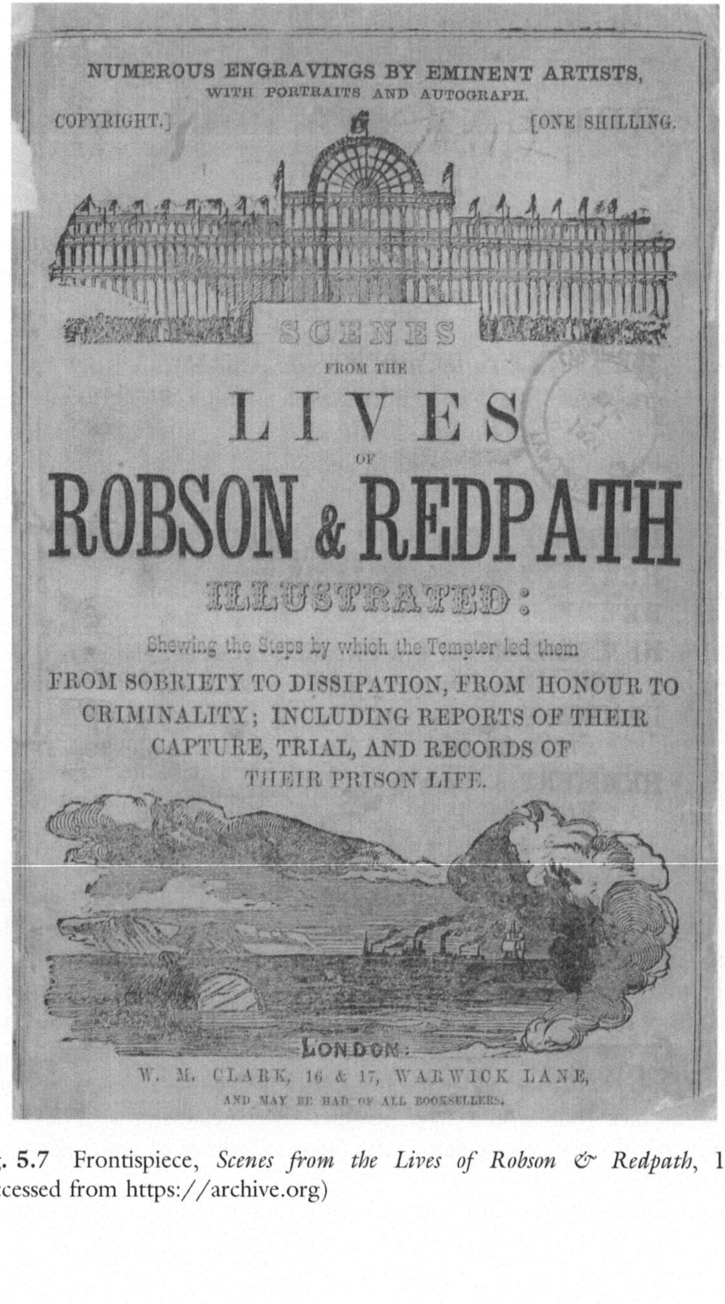

Fig. 5.7 Frontispiece, *Scenes from the Lives of Robson & Redpath*, 1857 (Accessed from https://archive.org)

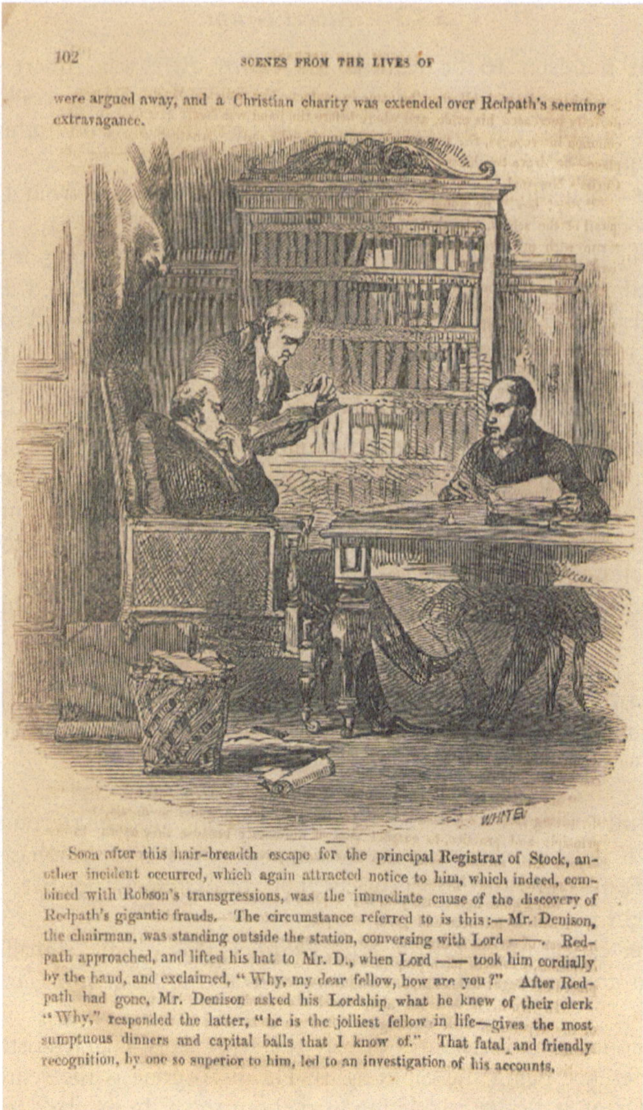

102 SCENES FROM THE LIVES OF

were argued away, and a Christian charity was extended over Redpath's seeming extravagance.

Soon after this hair-breadth escape for the principal Registrar of Stock, another incident occurred, which again attracted notice to him, which indeed, combined with Robson's transgressions, was the immediate cause of the discovery of Redpath's gigantic frauds. The circumstance referred to is this:—Mr. Denison, the chairman, was standing outside the station, conversing with Lord ——. Redpath approached, and lifted his hat to Mr. D., when Lord —— took him cordially by the hand, and exclaimed, "Why, my dear fellow, how are you?" After Redpath had gone, Mr. Denison asked his Lordship what he knew of their clerk "Why," responded the latter, "he is the jolliest fellow in life—gives the most sumptuous dinners and capital balls that I know of." That fatal and friendly recognition, by one so superior to him, led to an investigation of his accounts.

Fig. 5.8 Investigation of Redpath's accounts by bank directors

5.3.3 *Albert Grant*

The first fraudster to be featured in *Vanity Fair* was Albert Grant. Meredith comments that all speculators believed Grant could turn anything to gold 'but the gold eventually turned out to be nothing but waste paper'.[28]

Grant began life as Abraham Gottheimer, a poor Jew from Dublin. He specialised in floating companies involved in foreign railways, mining, and public utilities. He often 'puffed' companies by publishing or getting published articles about the companies in which he was involved. He also arranged for secret payments to be made to him (a sort of kickback) by constructors of infrastructure projects. Most of these activities led to legal disputes and allegations of fraud.

The monies he took from the public fed his social and philanthropic ambitions. The *Vanity Fair* caricature entitled '*Leicester Square*' (Fig. 5.9) referenced his philanthropic desire to clean up the area around Leicester Square. A similar effort in Milan which cleared the city centre slums and constructed an elaborate shopping arcade brought him a baronetcy from King Victor Emmanuel.

Bowles's letterpress commentary is again instructive on contemporary views:

> The making of Money is a trade of infinite variety, and Mr. Albert Grant is a striking example of the amount of success to be derived from the legitimate pursuit of the higher paths of commerce and finance.

Importantly, Bowles's commentary refers to the '*legitimate* pursuit of the *higher paths* of commerce and finance' (my italics for emphasis), and *Vanity Fair*'s view of finance places it in an extremely positive, almost noble light.[29]

A later caricature, '*Delicate Manipulation*' (Fig. 5.10), signalling his fall from grace appeared in a short-lived rival, the *Monetary Gazette*, in 1877.

The contrasting caricatures display the same facial characteristics, the only difference being the captions. In Fig. 5.10 gone is the representation of Grant as a calm calculating man about town. In its place are more props, legal papers, and a judge's wig, symbolising the litigious environment that Grant was experiencing. Grant himself is no longer insouciant; he is grave. Although there are no visual indicators of any form of financial

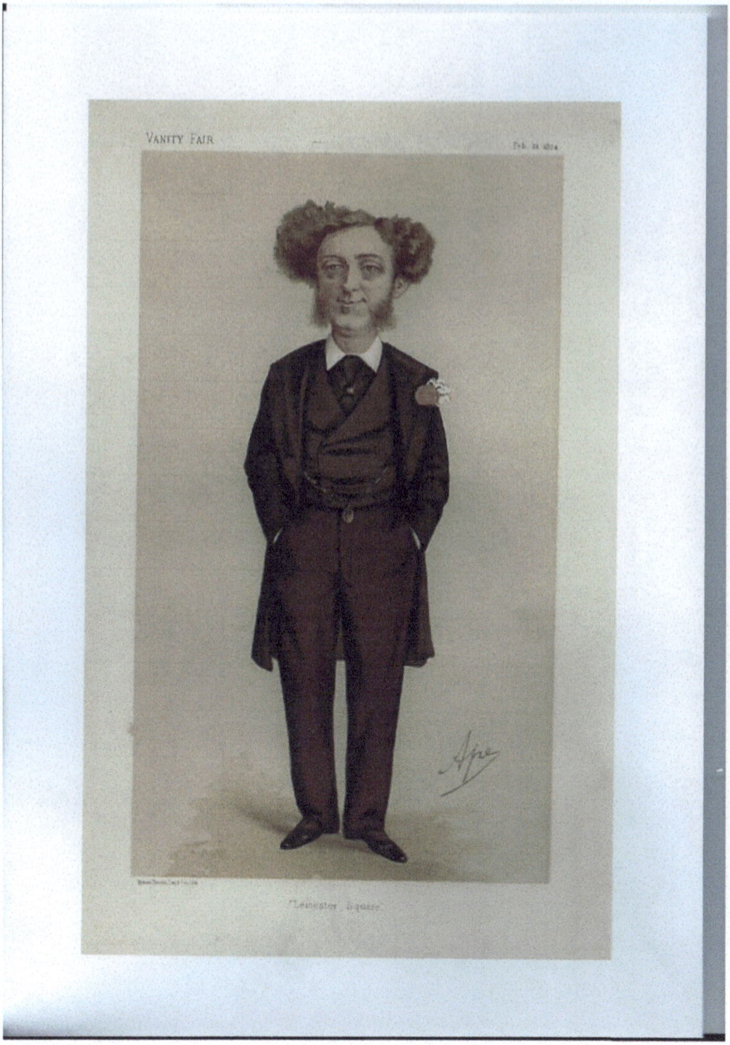

Fig. 5.9 *Vanity Fair, "Leicester Square"* (Albert Grant), 21 February 1874 (Courtesy of NPG)

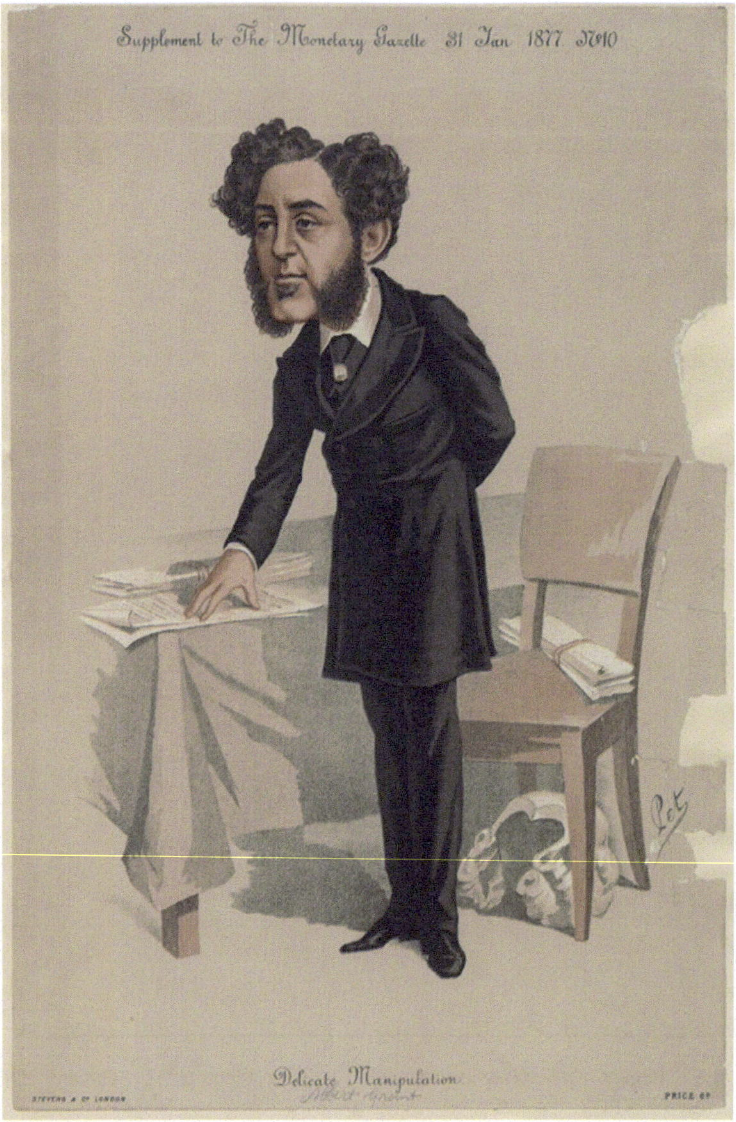

Fig. 5.10 *The Monetary Gazette*, *Delicate Manipulation*, 31 January 1877 (Courtesy of NPG)

chicanery, the depiction of Albert Grant suggests a degree of ambivalence. Feted by society whilst he was at the height of his fame, he was not depicted scurrilously in *Vanity Fair*. It was left to the comic periodicals, specifically *Fun* to mock, anonymously, his exploits (see Chapter 6). And, of course, he left his mark in the literary sphere, in the embodiment of his character in Trollope's Merdle. He was also the inspiration for Frith's series on business morality '*The Spider and the Flies*' also discussed in detail in Chapter 6.

5.3.4 *Harry Benson*

'The Turf Frauds', Fig. 5.11 depicts Benson in prison garb (the only caricature in *Vanity Fair* that makes so direct comment on the state of the perpetrator). The Turf Frauds involved Benson and associates persuading naïve investors to invest in fictitious betting scams at racecourses. Benson and his chief associate William Kurr were tried in April 1877. Benson, the architect of the frauds, received a prison term of eighteen years, whilst Kurr was sentenced to ten years. Kurr then used incriminating information to implicate two Scotland Yard detectives, Meiklejohn and Druscovich, in aiding and abetting Benson and Kurr in return for bribes.

The letterpress comments: 'Benson is assuredly one of the most splendid rogues any age or country has produced. And it is ominous that London produces both men and women with effrontery to manifest sympathy for him'.[30] This description can be thought to be almost eulogising his exploits (use of the word 'splendid') and indicates that for many he was a loveable rogue.

Benson had been tried and sentenced in April; *Vanity Fair*'s caricature, which appeared in September, is intriguing in its composition. As the detectives were arrested in September 1877, it is likely that *Vanity Fair* was reflecting retrospectively society's verdict on the actions of the fraudster against his own kind as well as commenting on his role in the imminent trial of the detectives.

A contrast can be made with the realistic depiction in the sensationalist *Illustrated Police News* (*IPN*), which depicts Kurr and Benson before their conviction (see Fig. 5.12). It is intriguing that the *IPN* depiction shows the two fraudsters, not the accused policemen (the caption entitled '*The Great Detective Case*' refers to the November 1877 trial of the detectives at which Kurr and Benson gave evidence). Arguably, depicting the detectives would have provided more of a shock to *IPN*'s readers,

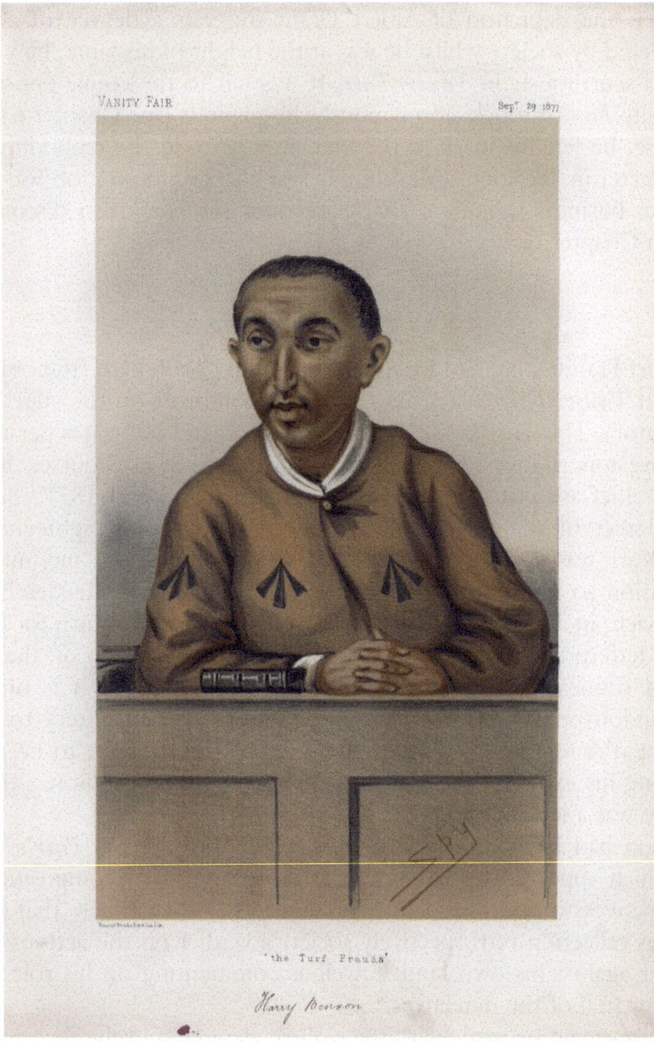

Fig. 5.11 *Vanity Fair*, *'The Turf Frauds'*, 29 September 1877 (Courtesy of NPG)

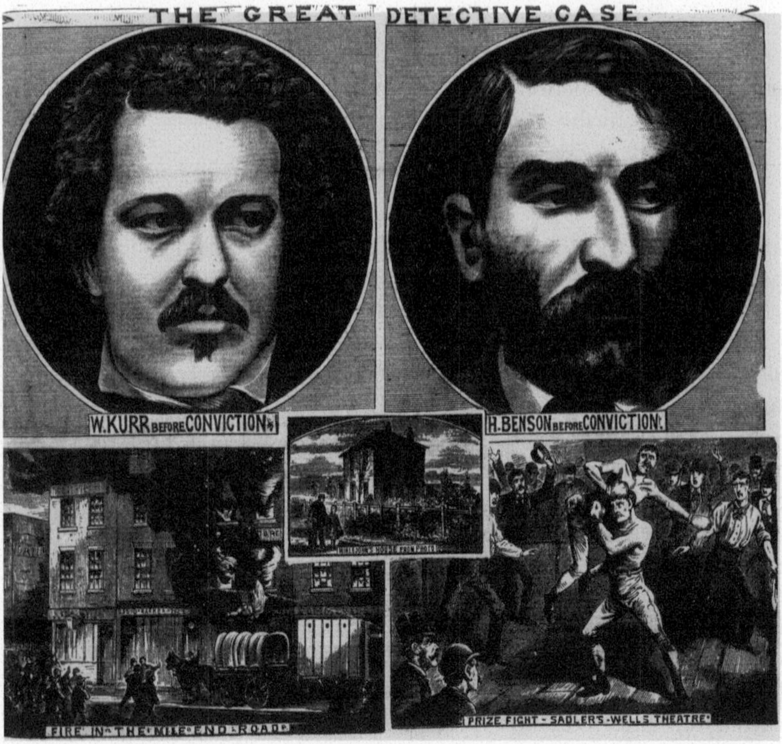

Fig. 5.12 *IPN*, *The great detective case*, 10 November 1877 (@ BL, Issue 717)

who would not have expected upholders of the law to be indicted. On the other hand, because *IPN* had not covered the earlier trial of Kurr and Benson, they possibly felt obliged to show the two criminals.

The *IPN* depiction of Kurr and Benson is illustrative of its approach to white-collar crime. Because readers of this periodical were more accustomed to stories of murder, or exotic animals, the juxtaposition between criminals involved in financial crime with stories of fire and prize fighting added to the sensationalism of its coverage of the Benson case. This juxtaposition is repeated in its depiction of the CGB directors.

The contrast between the drawing of Benson before his conviction and his caricature whilst in prison is striking. If, as might be expected, many highbrow readers read both periodicals then the disparity in fortunes would leave no reader in any doubt that certain crimes do not pay—the distinguished respectability, if shifty countenance, of the *IPN* drawing stood in sharp distinction against Benson's fall from grace, indicated by his shaven head in the *Vanity Fair* caricature.

5.3.5 CGB Directors

Within a year of the Turf Frauds the CGB failure occurred. The discussion which follows is centred around the depiction of named directors.

None of the directors prosecuted in the CGB collapse were depicted in *Vanity Fair*. Almost certainly this was because they were not household names in London (they were all upstanding members of the Scottish banking community). Nevertheless, representations of them do appear in the two realistic periodicals of the time, the *Graphic* and *ILN*. These are dealt with in detail in Chapter 9 (see Fig. 5.13).

IPN specialised in lurid accounts of sensational murders, crimes, and exotic creatures. Figure 5.13 portrays four of the directors in the failed bank alongside the main image of a boa constrictor and framed by murders above and below: this only emphasises the Victorian fascination with the exotic and sensational.[31] The snake's presence, in what appears to be an Indian location (turbans), evokes images of the Afghan Wars (the first of which had just started at the time of the *IPN* cartoon). Overall, this illustrates how periodicals juggled to include a myriad of contemporary events. Readers were meant to conclude that these 'pillars of the community', who had recently been arrested, were no better than (and just as newsworthy as) the murderers and the terrifying creature on the rest of the front page. Indeed, the image of the boa constrictor evokes more sinister overtones as the natives are clearly very fearful of this 'monster' given its size and its apparent ability to kill a dog. Does this larger-than-life representation influence readers' opinions on the four CGB directors? Do they need to be brought down to earth by being strangled by a snake as their most appropriate punishment? The boa constrictor normally associated with North or South America, or even India, was not native to Afghanistan, so the depiction is both fanciful and sensational.

Whilst the popular sensationalist periodicals delighted in exposing fraudulent financiers, it was ironic that the journalistic press which strived on the surface to be objective and provide useful information to investors

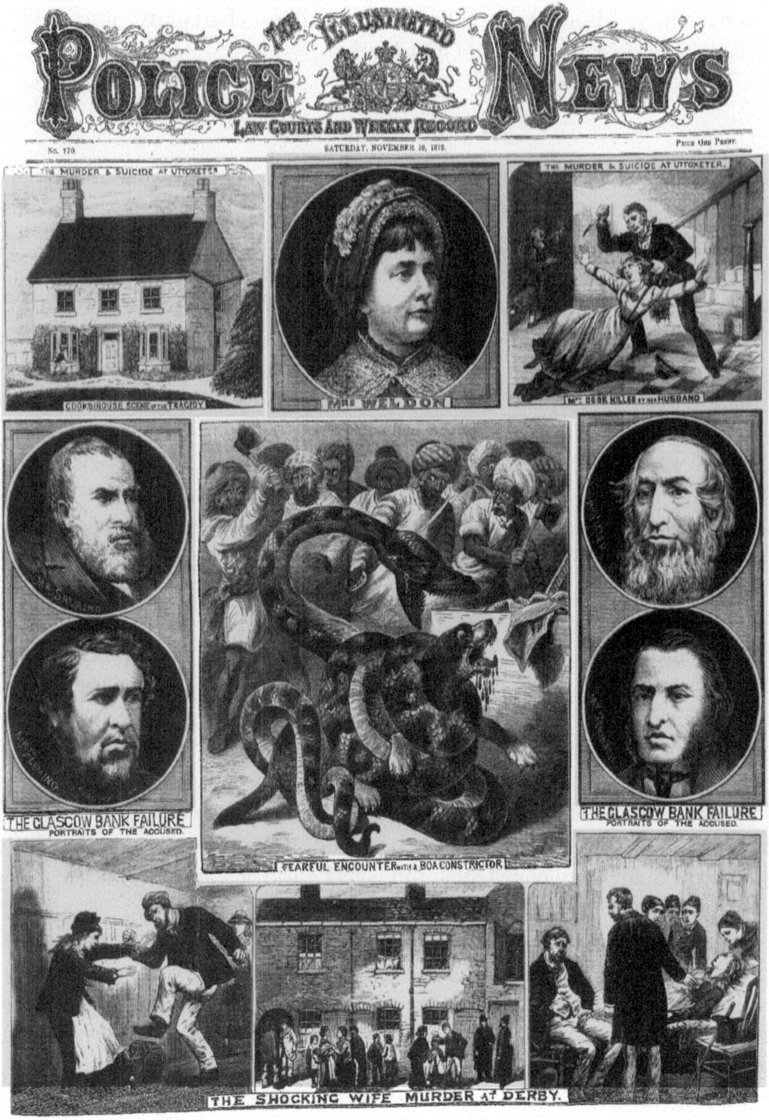

Fig. 5.13 *IPN*, Front Page, 16 November 1878 (@ BL, Issue 770)

to warn them about the techniques of these charlatans, also had a charlatan amongst its midst, Harry Marks.

5.3.6 Harry Marks

In *Vanity Fair*, the caricature of Harry Marks, the shady financial journalist is captioned '*Financial News*' (see Fig. 5.14).

The *Vanity Fair* letterpress alludes to the sensational nature of his activities: 'He fought and won eighteen libel suits in five years'.[32] Whilst 'puffing' (i.e., promoting companies without declaring any personal interests) was prevalent, Marks dominated the financial press arena in this regard. The letterpress makes no comment on the nature or reliability of his financial stock picking, which did cause substantial financial losses to many of its readers.

Marks is depicted as an affable rogue, with reams of ticker tape (providing detailed instant news on stock prices and stock events) streaming into a nearby wastepaper basket. The use of ticker tape is commented on further in Chapter 6.

The most prominent scandal involved Rae-Transvaal, a company puffed by Marks and his associates in 1886 in his paper, *Financial News*, which resulted in massive losses for the investing public. Marks praised the company in the press, thereby artificially pushing up prices for a short time. The directors then arranged for the issue of a large dividend to be followed by the speedy or slow decline of the stock and finally liquidation or reconstruction.

Despite his scandalous exploits, Marks remained managing editor of *Financial News*, was a member of the London County Council in 1889–1891 and again between 1895 and 1897, and a Conservative MP for Tower Hamlets between 1895 and 1900.

From 1890 Marks was subject to numerous unsuccessful libel suits. Significantly from a legal and public opinion point of view, no attempt was made to unseat him as an MP or prosecute him for market-rigging. Marks' escape from criminal sanctions was a consequence of the conventional laws and business morality that did not apply in his area. Market rigging was indeed indictable, but it was common practice in the City, a sign of the hypocrisy in those circles. As O'Hagan commented 'The mentality of members of the Stock Exchange is strange. Men who hold their heads high, who would be terrified if it were suggested that they were not the

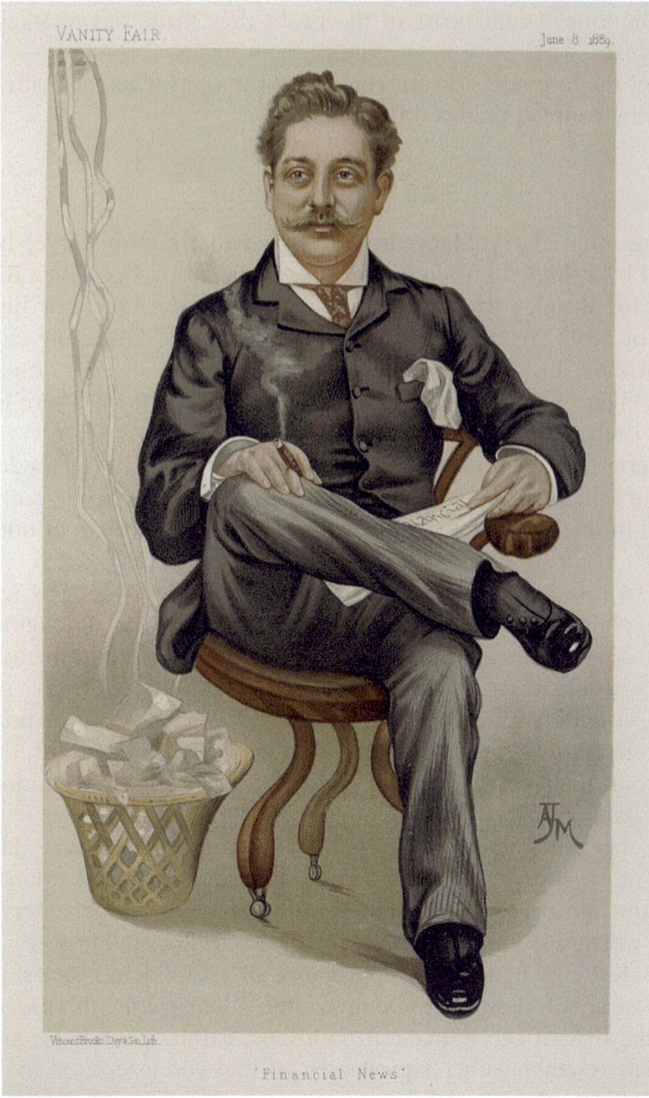

Fig. 5.14 *Vanity Fair*, '*Financial News*' (Harry Marks), 8 June 1889 (Courtesy of NPG)

soul of honour, would boast of the profit they made out of stagging a new venture'.[33]

One of the foremost corrupt company promoters whose activities were attacked by contemporaries was Jabez Balfour.

5.3.7 *Jabez Balfour*

Not long after Harry Marks first appeared in the public eye, he was followed by a shrewd but corrupt business operator called Jabez Balfour, the MP for Burnley who caused the collapse of the Liberator Building Society in 1892. A man of many talents, religious, financially clever, a philanthropist, his caricature was published in *Vanity Fair*, captioned 'Burnley' (Fig. 5.15) referencing the location of the town where he had recently been elected to Parliament.

The letterpress commentary is positive: 'Despite his Radical tendencies, the credit which is due to industry, energy, and public spirit cannot be denied him. He is a jovial person, upon whom hard work does not seem to tell'.[34]

The *Westminster Gazette* described Balfour as follows: 'His religion and his philanthropy lent unction to this politics. His religion, his philanthropy and his politics gave sanction to his financial schemes. His eminence as a financier gave him weight as a politician, solidity as a philanthropist, consideration as a man of religion'.[35] The date of the caricature precedes Balfour's demise by six months—on 6 September 1892, the first of the companies associated with the Liberator group, the London and General Bank, had its payments suspended.[36]

After the swindle was discovered, Balfour fled the country. He was arrested in Argentina by Inspector Frank Froest of Scotland Yard in 1895, tried at the Old Bailey and sentenced to fourteen years of penal servitude, most of which was served in harsh conditions in Portland prison.

As McKie puts it, the very appearance of a confident successful man meant that he was destined to be successful.[37] The picture in *Vanity Fair*, rather like that of other financial fraudsters, exudes confidence and the individuals resemble other typical men of the world depicted in *Vanity Fair*. O'Hagan, the successful company promoter, thought public outcry against Balfour had made a fair trial impossible—he had found him to be upright and honest in his dealings with him.[38]

Balfour started the Liberator Group aged just twenty-five. At one time he held thirteen directorships with separate companies, some outside of

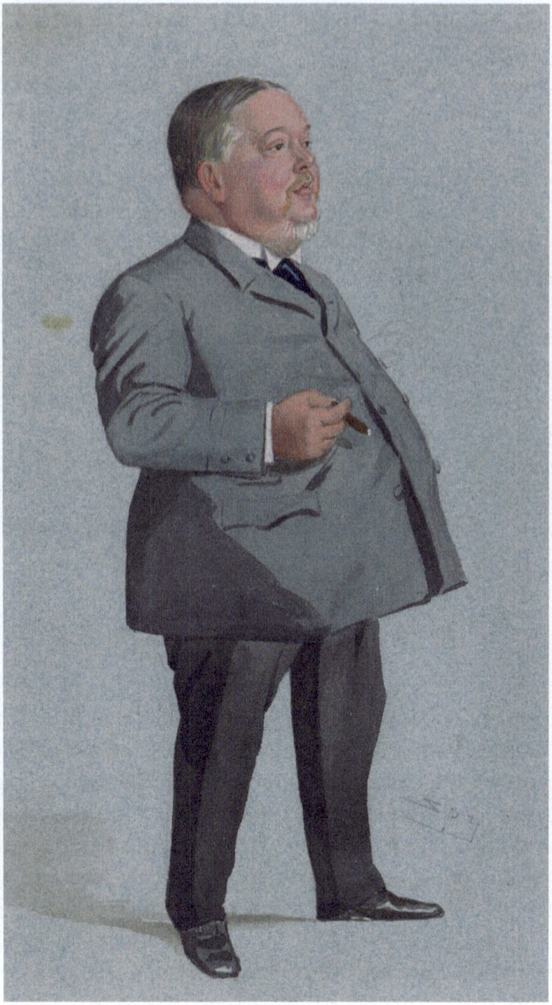

Fig. 5.15 *Vanity Fair, Burnley* (Jabez Balfour), 19 March 1892 (Courtesy of NPG)

the Liberator Group; it led to him being described as the 'Champion Director'.

To contemporaries, the name—Liberator Building Society—had a double meaning implying both a free home and free church whilst also hinting (falsely) at a connection with the *Religious Liberation Society.* In the main, the Group cultivated investment from the thrifty classes of non-conformist Christians, and often opportunistically employed unsuspecting ministers as promoters. The Liberator Building Society was established in 1868 and appeared to prosper; by 1879 it had supposedly surpassed the Leeds Permanent as Britain's largest building society.

Jacobs concludes that the combination of his religious inclinations, business prowess, and political standing, facilitated his disreputable activities. Moreover, his standing in each of these overlapping communities undoubtedly contributed to the notoriety his case generated. He suggests that a semblance of gentlemanly values appears to have allowed gentlemanly capitalists to commit disreputable crimes more easily.[39]

In the same vein as Balfour but whose activities resulted in a jail sentence was Ernest Hooley.

5.3.8 Ernest Hooley

Hooley was a financial fraudster. He achieved wealth and fame by buying promising companies (some of them to become very well-known, such as Bovril, Dunlop, and several bicycle companies such as Raleigh) and reselling them to the public at inflated prices. He used exaggeration in his prospectuses, as well as bribery of journalists and financial editors. He was eventually convicted and sentenced to prison for fourteen years.

Stratmann quotes an anonymous contemporary account of Hooley: 'He was determined to make a million or go smash'.[40] She goes on to comment '…he did both. In 1896 he was unknown; by 1897 his name was an international byword for conspicuous financial success; by 1898 he was bankrupt'.[41]

Figure 5.16 captures the smug satisfaction of an arch fraudster, his confidence in abundance, striding forth as a typical gentleman.

Vanity Fair's caricature of Hooley (Fig. 5.17) is entitled 'A chief secretary', or '*Papworth*' named after the estate he had purchased the previous year. The composition reflects Hooley's standing in society—the epitome of the country squire.

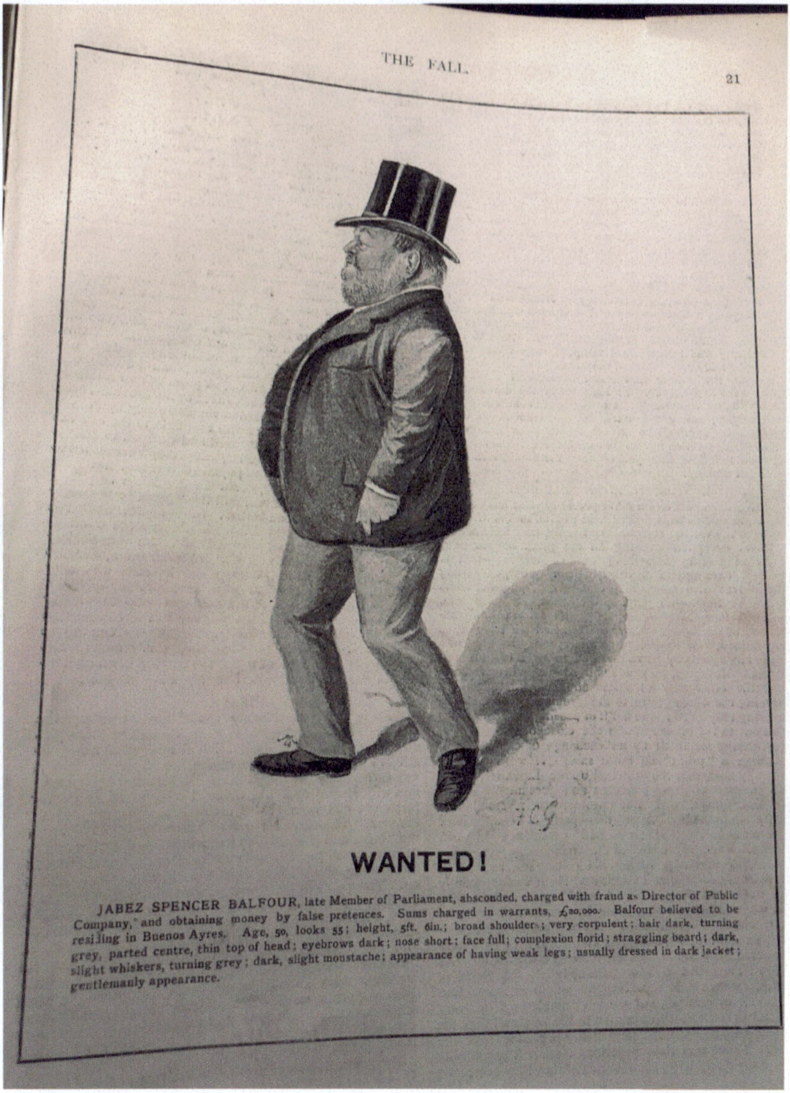

THE FALL. 21

FCG

WANTED!

JABEZ SPENCER BALFOUR, late Member of Parliament, absconded, charged with fraud as Director of Public Company," and obtaining money by false pretences. Sums charged in warrants, £20,000. Balfour believed to be residing in Buenos Ayres. Age, 50, looks 55; height, 5ft. 6in.; broad shoulders; very corpulent; hair dark, turning grey, parted centre, thin top of head; eyebrows dark; nose short; face full; complexion florid; straggling beard; dark, slight whiskers, turning grey; dark, slight moustache; appearance of having weak legs; usually dressed in dark jacket; gentlemanly appearance.

Fig. 5.16 *Wanted!*, *The Hooley Book*, Frederick Carruthers Gould, 1892 (own photo) (@ BL, GRC 10827.bb.36)

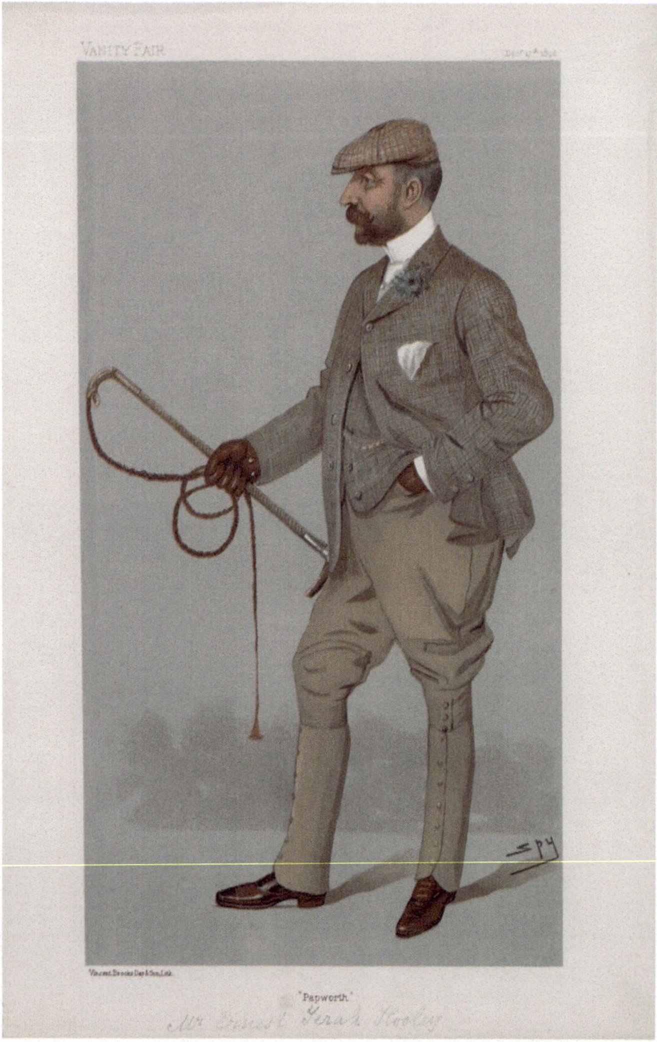

Fig. 5.17 *Vanity Fair, 'Papworth'* (Ernest Hooley), 17 December 1896 (Courtesy of NPG)

By this time, the mid-1890s the comic periodicals were beginning to show more bite to their caricatures. Whilst *Vanity Fair* portrays Hooley as a dignified member of the establishment, as his misdemeanours unfolded, periodical after periodical portrayed the chimerical speculative nature of his efforts.

The letterpress comment is revealing as to Hooley's business acumen: 'He does not look a very great financier, nor a very shrewd man of business; but he is: and he has shown by his faculty of never touching anything that he does not understand.... He is as generous as he is wealthy'.[42]

Figure 5.18 depicts Hooley at the tipping point of his career; it makes use of a pun (two-faced) to show the two sides of his character—one persuading investors to invest in his share schemes, the other his desperate attempt to remain insolvent in the face of numerous financial claims against him. The negotiations that Hooley had with the Chinese government illustrated the illusory nature of his success: led to believe that the

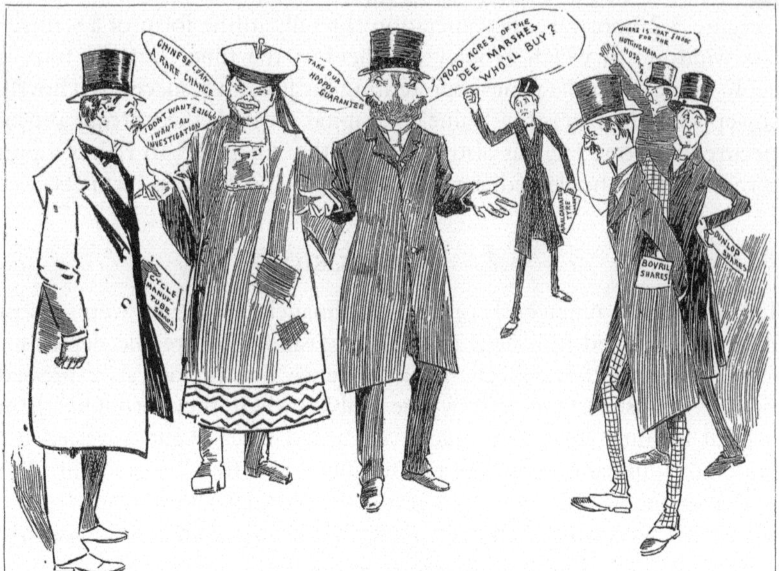

THE FIN-DE-SIÈCLE MILLIONAIRE.

Fig. 5.18 *Judy, The Fin de Siècle Millionaire*, 27 October 1897 (@ BL Shelf mark P.P. 6014.be, Issue 505)

Chinese government wanted him to lend them £16m (with a commission of £1m) Hooley entered negotiations which, after two months, came to nothing. The government probably intended all along to borrow from HSBC but had played Hooley off against it.[43]

Figure 5.19 provides a variation on the bubble iconography typical over the centuries. Here Hooley is depicted on the left in his ascendancy, the 'healthy' balloon transporting him into the skies. He is wearing the typical garb of a gentleman at leisure (see the galoshes), with a long cigar in his right hand. The balloon shows, in words, the names of the various companies that he has floated over the previous years. His fingers sport diamonds, and the caption reads, '*1897, Millionaire*'.

The counterpart to this is the depiction on the right of an anguished Hooley plunging into the sea, marked '*bankruptcy*'. The very balloon that had propelled him to his wealth has now been punctured, and with no gas, he plummets. In a desperate attempt to keep the balloon airborne, Hooley has jettisoned ballast emblazoned with names associated with the industries that he has been involved in, but this action cannot save him.

Figure 5.20 portrays the veneration (literally in the form of a stained-glass window) in which Hooley was held at the time. But the tone is deeply ironic, with the panes representing his flotation 'successes' (Bovril, Schweppes, Grappler), the 'value' of capital created, the corrupt use of sinecure directors. He was also known as the 'Grappler' to reflect a pun on the company he floated as well as to signify his fighting instincts.

5.4 Conclusion

Throughout the nineteenth century the financial fraudsters were almost uniformly depicted in a negative satirical fashion. Where the depictions are not negative they reflect the ambivalence that periodicals expressed towards fraudsters. Lauded by the public when they brought them financial fortune, they were quickly discarded when events revealed the fraudulent foundations of their rise to fame. This trend is exemplified in the depictions of Hudson which reveal in paintings and drawings in the realistic periodicals his stature in society. Even the comic periodicals do not initially revile Hudson—it is only as his financial crimes are exposed that he becomes exposed to ridicule.

As the century wears on the criminal activities of fraudsters in the realistic periodicals are conveyed by the depictions of their progress through the legal system. By contrast the comic periodicals increasingly attack the

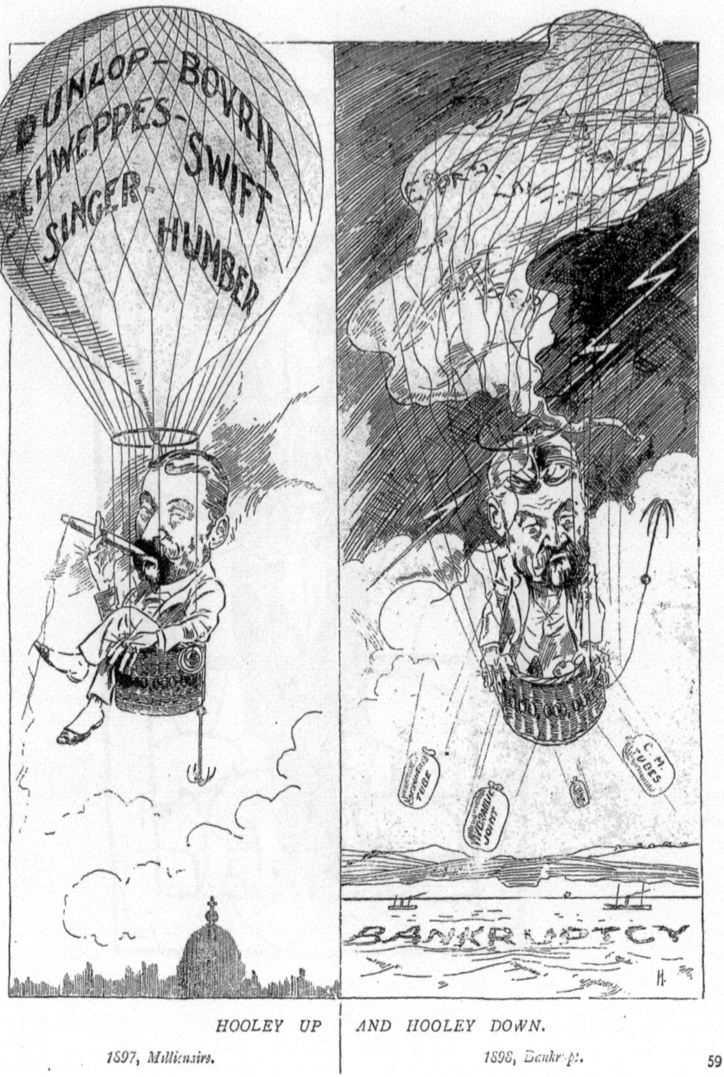

Fig. 5.19 *Cycling*, *Hooley Up and Hooley Down*, 18 June 1898 (@ BL, Vol. XV, Issue 387)

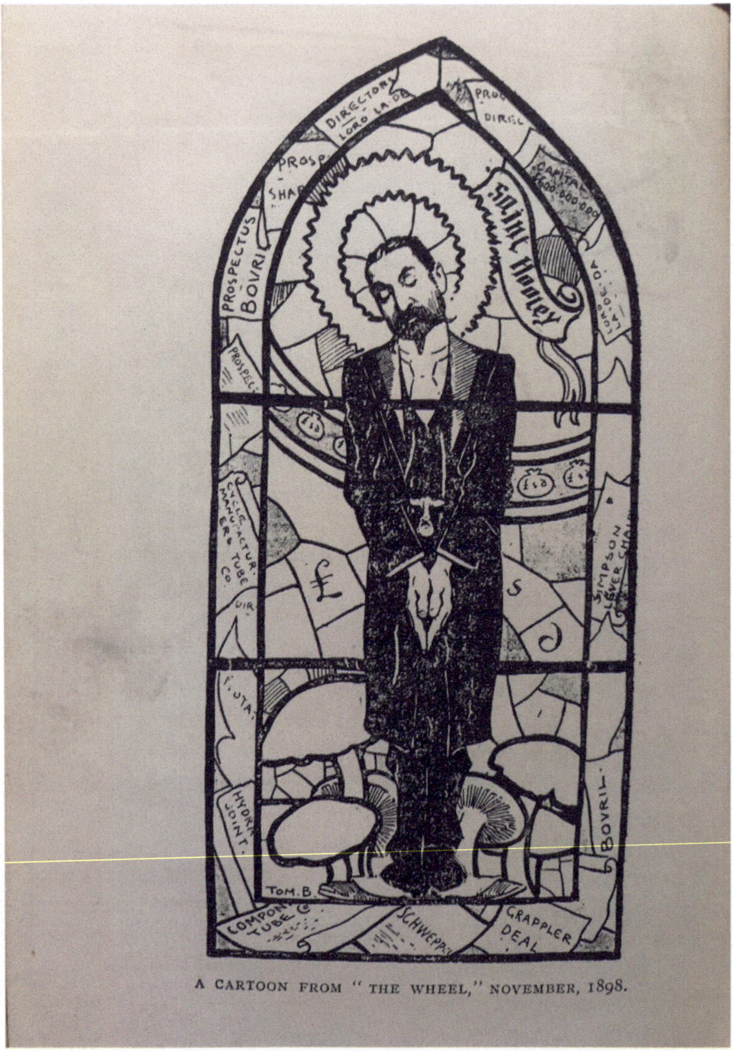

Fig. 5.20 *The Wheel, Saint Hooley*, November 1898, from the Hooley Book (own photo) (@ BL, GRC 10827.bb.36)

fraudsters (rather than just empathising with their victims as they had done earlier in the century) using ever more evocative icons.

Publishers Political Bias

As parliamentary parties were not in disagreement about the need to punish white-collar criminals there was no difference in their representation in periodicals.

What differed was the degree of irreverence displayed in the comic periodicals compared with the more dignified approach of the realistic periodicals.

Editorial Techniques

The rise in the public's interest in white-collar criminals led to editors employing a range of innovative techniques to bring the attention of the reader to these criminals, or financial crises. This was true of both the realistic and comic-serious periodicals. In the case of the realistic periodicals editors chose to place the financial figures and the events in which they were involved on the front page.

Artistic Techniques

The main development was the use of the 'staged 'storyboard' format to lead the reader to judge the unfolding events in a specific way. This was especially the case where legal proceedings were involved. In this way the cartoon images provided a more dynamic interpretation than that offered in photographs.

Notes

1. Carter Field, *Bernard Baruch, Park Bench Statesman* (New York, Kessinger Publishing, 1944), pp. 76–77.
2. See Chapter 2 for more detail.
3. A useful definition of Victorian satire is to be found in *Vanity Fair*. Jehu Junior writes of 'Artistic licence with no malice'. See footnote 22.
4. Michael Flavin, *Gambling in the Nineteenth Century English Novel: A Leprosy o'er the Land* (Brighton, Sussex Academic Press, 2003), p. 1.

5. He began a long campaign to have his sentence reversed. Eventually in 1832 he was granted a free pardon. Then followed more meritorious naval service and a restoration of all former honours and monies due to him.
6. See Robb, p. 31.
7. The *Punch* images were *The premier navigator*, 22 November 1845, *King Hudson's levee*, 29 November 1845, *The Hudson Testimonial*, 24 October 1846, *Lord George Bentinck Prince of Rails trying on Hudson's crown*, 20 February 1847, *Leporello reciting the railway loves of Don Juan*, 9 December 1848, *Celebrated comic scenes between the railway crown and indignant shareholders*, 4 August 1849 and *The great railway guy of 1849*, 10 November 1849. The NPG images are covered later.
8. Taylor, *Business in pictures*, pp. 114/115. A search of the *Punch* historical archive revealed 84 images from *Punch* alone of the railway mania.
9. A. J. Arnold and S. McCartney, *George Hudson the Rise and Fall of the Railway King* (London, 2004), p. x.
10. Taylor, 2005, pp. 120/121.
11. Altick, p. 461. Quoting *Punch*, 10 April 1849.
12. See Taylor, 2005, pp. 121/122, *Man in the Moon*, *The Railway King*, ii (1847), 255.
13. Ibid., p. 121.
14. See comparison with *Kladderadatsch* image satirising the German financier Bleichroder in Chapter 8.
15. Ibid., p. 462.
16. Ibid., p. 462. Just over a year later *Punch* comments gleefully on the announcement that Madame Tussaud had withdrawn its effigy of Hudson.
17. Ibid., p. 460, footnote.
18. Ibid.
19. Ibid., *Punch*, 4 August 1849.
20. Ibid., p. 462.
21. Robb, p. 51 for comments by Carlyle—'what a sordid hungry canaille are they all', and comments by David Morier Evans and the *Times*.
22. *Punch*, 1856, Frontispiece, p. 5.
23. Ibid., p. 4.
24. Accessed from www.moneysorter.com.

25. Robb, p. 53.
26. *Scenes from the Lives of Robson & Redpath* accessed from Archive.org. The reference to prison time is presumably to the sentencing of Strahan and Bates.
27. See David A. Hayes and Marian Kamlish, *The King's Cross Fraudster Leopold Redpath, His Life + Times* (Didcot, Marston Digital, 2013), p. 116. Also note the references to the display of white-collar criminals such as Robson, Redpath, Strahan, Paul, and Bates in Madame Tussaud's Chamber of Horrors (echoing Hudson's own effigy).
28. Hubert A. Meredith, *The Drama of Money-Making, Tragedy and Comedy of the London Stock Exchange* (London, 1931), p. 113. See also H. Osborne O'Hagan *Leaves from My Life*, vo. 1 (London, 1929), p. 32.
29. *Vanity Fair*, Letterpress, 21 February 1874.
30. *Vanity Fair*, Letterpress, 29 September 1877.
31. Stratmann, pp. 94/95. 'Animals often featured in the pages of the *IPN*, as the victims of human cruelty, the perpetrators of violent attacks, the innocent causes of accidents, or as daring and resourceful rescuers.'
32. *Vanity Fair*, Letterpress, 8 June 1889.
33. Dilwyn Porter '"A Trusted Guide of the Investing Public": Harry Marks and the Financial News 1884–1916', in R. P. T. Davenport-Hines (ed.), *Speculators and Patriots Essays in Business Biography* (London, Frank Cass, 1986), p. 12.
34. *Vanity Fair*, Letterpress, 19 March 1892.
35. Quoted in David McKie, *Jabez the Rise and Fall of a Victorian Rogue* (London, 2004), p. 255.
36. Taylor, *Boardroom Scandal*, p. 223.
37. McKie, p. 256.
38. H. Osborne O'Hagan, *Leaves from My Life* (London, Bodley Head, 1929), p. 141.
39. See Jacobs.
40. Stratmann, p. 130. "Smash" being colloquial for going bankrupt.
41. Ibid., p. 130.
42. *Vanity Fair*, Letterpress, 17 December 1896.
43. Stratmann, p. 142.

CHAPTER 6

Financial Iconography

6.1 Introduction

This chapter deals with the iconography associated with the financial events which were experienced by the financial figures under review. It covers the major banking and commercial crises of the nineteenth century, whether caused by fraud or other white-collar crimes. It reflects the position of both the victims of these crises as well as the villains, the charlatans covered in the earlier chapter. Figure 6.1 frames the visual icons associated with these events.

Overstone, the main proponent of the Currency school, and the architect of what became Peel's Bank Charter Act of 1844, outlined ten phases of business activity (Fig. 6.1, a later representation, illustrates six, probably for neatness of depiction).[2,3]

Its usefulness here is in framing the discussion around financial icons associated with phases of financial crisis, notably the excitement (or bubble) and convulsion (frenzy/mania) phases. The excitement phase references buildings raised in the air by balloons, as well as fictitious (bubble) companies (e.g., the image of the South Pole Warming Company), whilst the convulsion phase references the impact of the crisis in terms of text captions (scrip, stocks, shares) a Royal Bubble Bank which is depicted being blown up with all its contents (the Bank of England or the failure of the Royal British Bank in 1856). The villains (the company

H. Sless, *Merchant Princes and Charlatans or Makers of Money?*,
https://doi.org/10.1007/978-3-030-86604-4_6

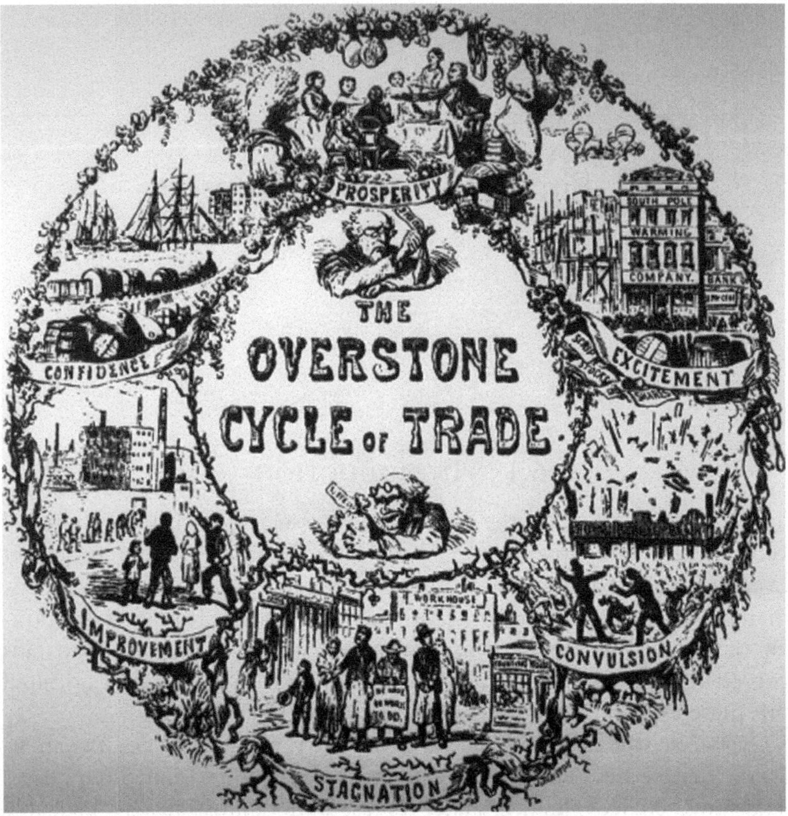

Fig. 6.1 *The Overstone Cycle of Trade cycle*[1] (Image accessed from the web)

promoters) are shown at the front and there are shades of an earlier 1825 print *Bubbles of 1825* (see Fig. 6.3).

The iconography reflects consistent themes throughout the nineteenth century derived from the rich tradition of financial iconography of speculation dating back to the Dutch Tulip Mania of the 1620s. Often these themes are present in the same image, but they can be characterised individually as follows:

Balloons/puffs—reflecting the ephemeral nature of speculative activities. Associated with wind, synonymous with the Dutch word 'windhandel' (speculative trade).

Frenzy—the emotional impact on the players in the speculative Stock Exchange. It is typically depicted as crowds of investors, 'herds', outside failed banking headquarters, or as investors on a train careening into the clouds, or into an abyss. Recurring images of creatures (Crowquill in *Illustrated London News* in the 1840s, Morgan in *Tomahawk* in 1867) were used as symbols of malevolence exercising evil influence on despairing investors). Also, images in the US and UK which depict the impact on the promoters, the Stock Exchange participants. As illustrated in the Overstone diagram above, the irrationality of crowds could be both positive or negative, leading to exuberance as well as to panic.

Financial institutions—several images use banks/bank counters as an ironic symbol of fraud (as compared with equivalent symbols used to depict the solidity of the Old Lady of Threadneedle St (see below). This also reflects the dichotomy between internal and external spaces. External depictions of financial institutions' buildings reflect the ambivalence of apparently solid edifices (see *A New Court Fire Screen* with the facade of an insurance company being the front for the evils of Mammon, or the O & G failure and US depictions of US financial crises) with shaky foundations of such institutions depicted in one image, the *Northern Looking Glass* image shown below).

Interiors tended to be depicted in the 1820s to reflect financial security: the interior of a thriving pawn shop; partners in a bank receiving deposits from customers; or a bank vault full of gold coins. The solidity of bank interiors is referred to again in the depictions of the Old Lady.

Successive bank frauds in the 1850s onwards lead to the internal areas of the bank being associated with corrupt activities (bank managers, out of sight, taking in deposits or absent from their offices having absconded) or the distress of investors clamouring for the return of their monies.

Stock Exchange terminology—the century is rife with depictions of visual puns summarising Stock Exchange terminology (bulls, bears, stocks, pillars, etc.) A comparison is drawn between high art (paintings) and low art (cartoons), distinguishing between representations in different countries. The association of animal bestiary with representations of Stock Exchange activities is covered.

Victims/Villains

The images overall depict both the victims and the villains of financial activities. Initially the focus is on the victims (the despair of the investor caught up in the maelstrom of investing) and the naivete of their 'lemming' like behaviour. As the century wears on there is increasing emphasis on the villains, their corruptness and hypocrisy, and the damage they have wreaked on the 'poor' investors.

Female figures are used to convey the purity of the ideals which basemen should aspire to but fail to reach (Goddesses of Justice). Whilst in the period of the Tulip Mania and through to the mid-1820s Fortuna, the Goddess of Fate, of Luck, was used to define fickleness and inconstancy.

The book reveals that similar iconography can be found in the US as well as in Continental Europe. The images analysed show that iconography 'travelled' globally—images from one country were seen by artists in another country and copied or altered to reflect topical events.

6.2 The Iconography

6.2.1 Balloons/puffs

The use of a wind-chariot indicating follies of speculation dates to 1602.[4] The image depicts a historical panorama with four cartoons at each corner of the print indicating elements of the mania—familiar usage to Dutchmen of the period. The female figure of Flora, Folly, dominates the centre of the print (Fig. 6.2). It illustrates the typical use of the feminine figure in seventeenth century onwards to denote inconstancy irrationality (cf. use of Fortuna in Lottery prints of early nineteenth century).[5]

Figure 6.3 is an unsophisticated depiction of the impact of the 1825 boom period. Balloons with text providing details of the names of the companies formed during this period are viewed as caused by steam/smoke (i.e., hot air, no substance). The creators of this smoke are the company promoters with long pipes, who are trading with enthusiastic would-be investors of all walks of life.

Williams' depiction of the balloon in *A King bestowing favors* gives rise to ambivalent and amusing interpretations. The symbol of the balloon is associated in other prints with kites or bubbles, the manifestation of failed projects (for further details see Fig. 8.1).

Here it is associated with economic prosperity as it is carrying aloft the king of capitalism, Nathan Rothschild, who is off to collect more dividends from his successful trading strategies.

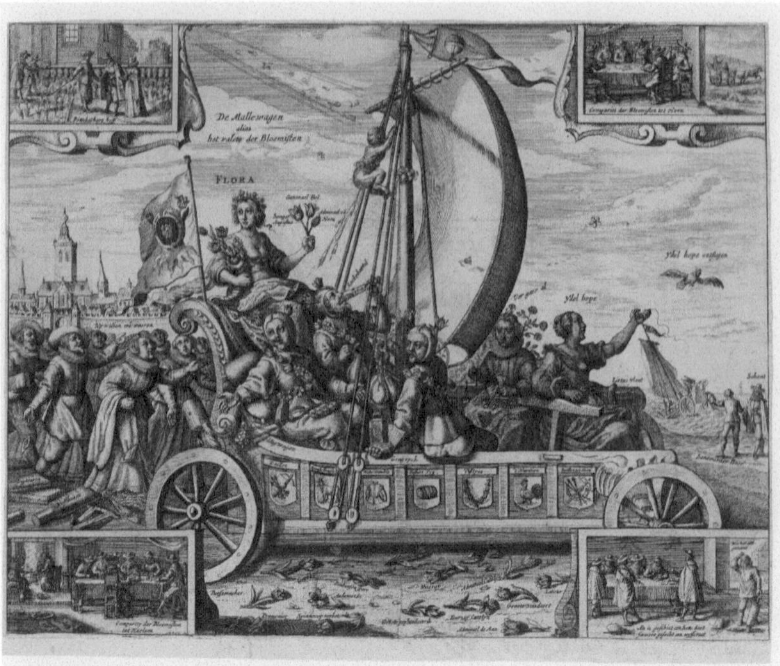

Fig. 6.2 *Floraes Mallewagen* (Car of Fools), 1637 (Courtesy of Rijksmuseum)

Later in the century the figure of Hooley is depicted riding both a balloon symbolising the chimerical ephemeral nature of his rise as well as a punctured balloon symbolising his fall into bankruptcy (see Fig. 5.18).

6.2.2 Frenzy

An example of both the use of text to convey 'bubbles' and the anguish or frenzy of John Bull faced with the monetary crisis of late 1825. In *Moon Rise* the collapse of the 'country' banks in 1825 is depicted by the word 'bubbles' being associated with a particular county in England (Fig. 6.4). By inference the counties without the word 'Bubbles' had been unaffected (see Appendix 1 for detailed commentary on this image).

Figure 6.5 contrasts the panic in England with the calm in Scotland during the 1825 banking crisis. In England banks are seen crashing down

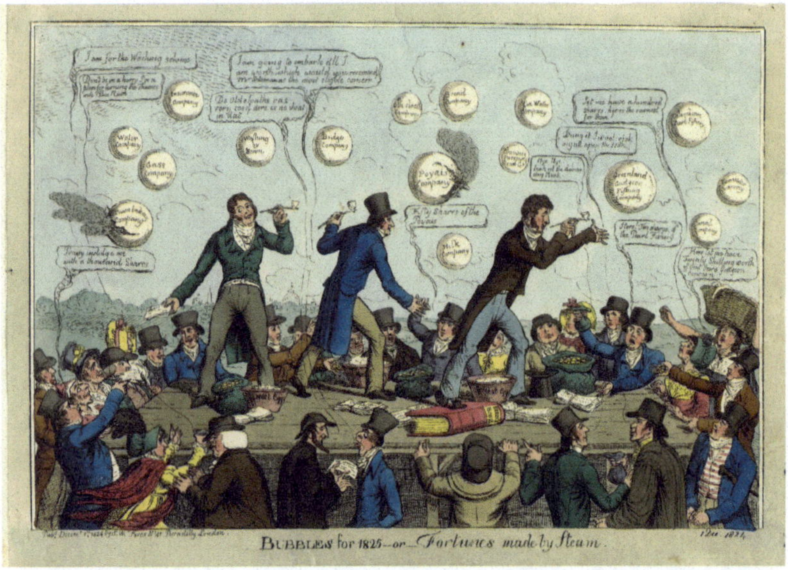

Fig. 6.3 BM 14669, *Bubbles for 1825—or—Fortunes made by steam*, 1 December 1824 (Courtesy of BM)

on the poor investor (symbolised by the figure of John Bull), whilst in Scotland Scottish depositors (depicted in national garb) are shown handing over their deposits to eager bank managers (with piles of gold behind them).

The Railway Mania affected all walks of life as everyone sought to take advantage of the frenetic share activity of the time.[6]

This image published at the end of 1825 illustrates in sharp contrast the relative stability of the English and Scottish banking systems at the time. The ability of the Scottish banks to withstand the shocks down south was reported on favourably at the time.[7] Indeed, the legislative reforms introduced after the crisis incorporated some of the perceived benefits of the Scottish system.[8]

In the Fig. 6.6 the impact of the RM is shown by crowds being crushed under the weight of the great engine, Mammon—an allegory of the misfortunes to affect many investors. The crushing of individuals in the foreground would surely have evoked memories of the notorious

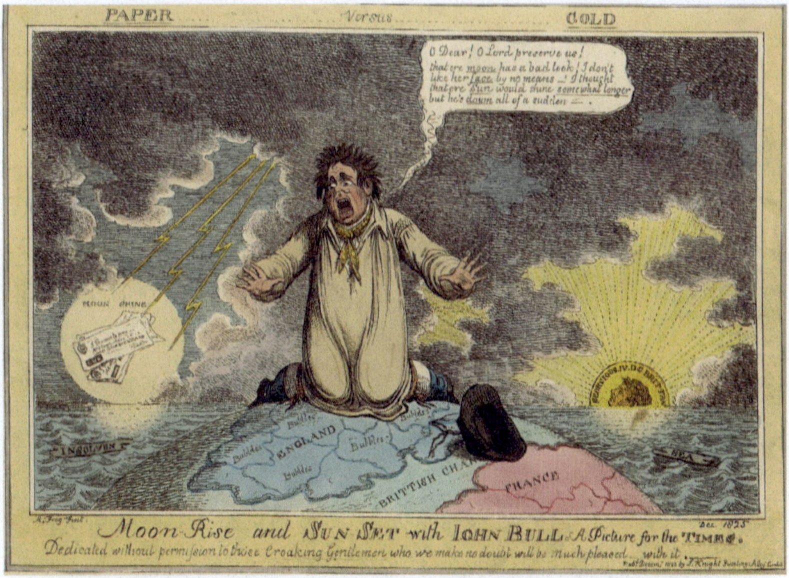

Fig. 6.4 BM 14814, *Moon Rise and Sun Set with John Bull A picture for the times*, 1825 (Courtesy of BM)

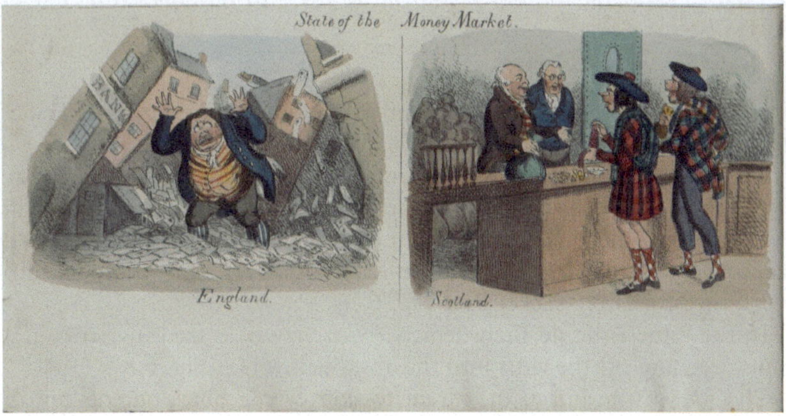

Fig. 6.5 BM 14812, *Northern Looking Glass, State of the Money Market*, 1825 (Courtesy of UoG)

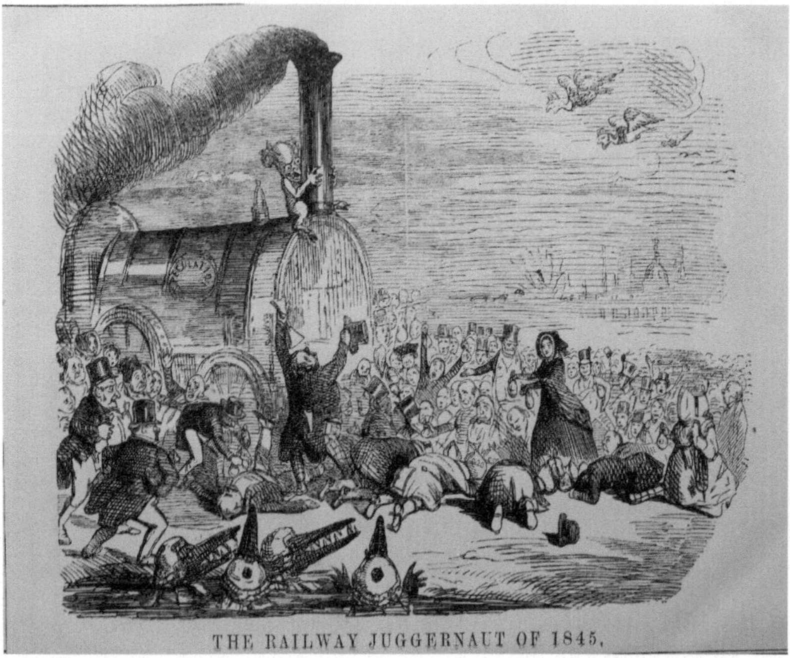

Fig. 6.6 *Punch*, *The Railway Juggernaut of 1845*, 26 July 1845 (Courtesy of UoH)

death of William Huskisson, MP, former President of the Board of Trade, at the launch of Stevenson's Rocket in 1830.

These types of images (Figs. 1.1 and 6.6) convey the panic and frenzy of the events. The sheer terror at the events unfolding is represented in *Punch* by this image (Fig. 1.1) of an elongated face with a strangulated expression. Crowquill expressed it in terms of a vortex or whirlpool into which investors were sucked (see Fig. 6.7).

In the same issue he then depicts the frenzy of crazed investors in a train careening off the cliffs into the abyss below (see Fig. 6.8).

The use of the image of a train to convey machines out of human control was popular throughout the RM and since (see Fig. 6.15 for an example at the time of the O&G collapse twenty years later).

US

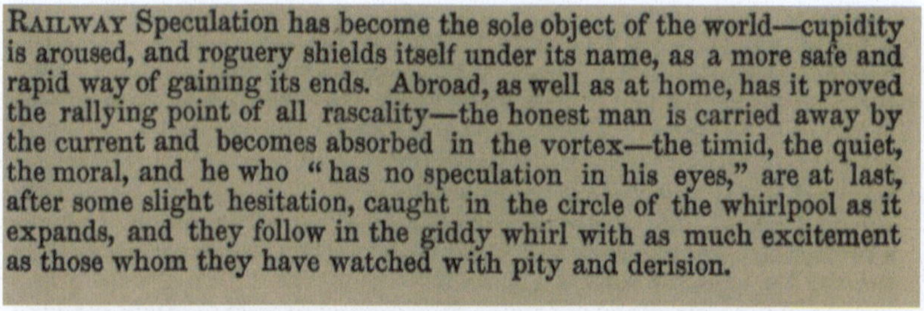
RAILWAY Speculation has become the sole object of the world—cupidity is aroused, and roguery shields itself under its name, as a more safe and rapid way of gaining its ends. Abroad, as well as at home, has it proved the rallying point of all rascality—the honest man is carried away by the current and becomes absorbed in the vortex—the timid, the quiet, the moral, and he who "has no speculation in his eyes," are at last, after some slight hesitation, caught in the circle of the whirlpool as it expands, and they follow in the giddy whirl with as much excitement as those whom they have watched with pity and derision.

Fig. 6.7 *ILN*, *Railway Mania* (text), 18 October 1845 (© Illustrated London News/Mary Evans)

US painters such as Cafferty and Beard depicted Stock Exchange crises in contrasting modes. On 13 October 1857, panic struck the New York Stock Exchange (NYSE) when the Ohio Life & Trust Company declared bankruptcy, setting off a chain reaction that plunged hundreds of other banks and individual investors into ruin. In the oil painting *Wall Street, Half Past Two O'clock, October 13, 1857*, by James H. Cafferty and Charles G. Rosenberg (Fig. 6.9), crowds of soberly dressed top-hatted brokers and speculators react to the disaster with grave decorum and self-restraint. Only the newsboys and a couple of men at the centre display any excitement.

By contrast, images of the 1893 and 1873 crises (see Figs. 6.10 and 6.11) show much more disorderly crowds, shoving and gesticulating. The difference between the images reflects a hierarchy that allowed for crude, raucous excess in the popular graphic arts whilst reserving a greater dignity for painting commensurate with its elite status in the art world (but see Beard below).[9]

The comic periodicals were in no doubt about the panic caused to investors by financial crises. The *Daily Graphic* depicts a grotesque giant is depicted clearing Wall Street of various ills (depicted as strips of paper, rotten railways, shaky banks, bogus brokers, speculative puts). Behind the giant people are panicking outside the offices of the broker Drexel & Co (Fig. 6.12).

The cross-over between high and low art is finally realised in Beard's *Bulls and Bears in the Market* of about 1879. In this painting, exhibited at the National Academy of Design in 1880, animals surge between the staid classical facades of Wall Street, furiously trampling, goring, hurling,

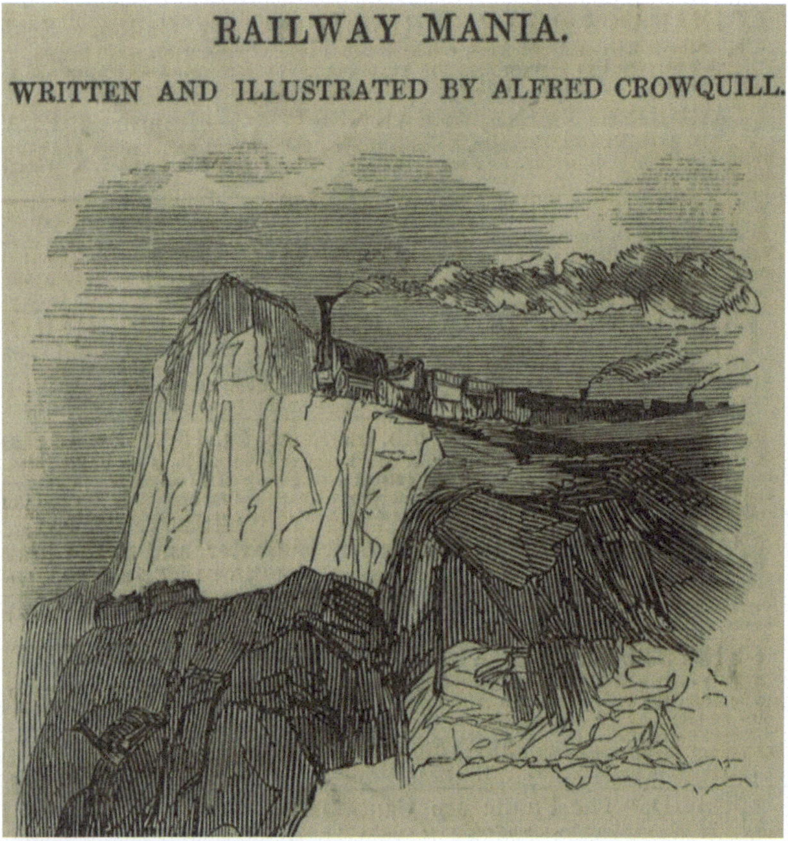

Fig. 6.8 *ILN*, *Railway Mania*, 18 October 1845 (© Illustrated London News/Mary Evans)

kicking, clawing, one another in an atmosphere of utter mayhem. Beard's painting reflects the pandemonium in Stock Exchange markets echoing the savage attacks on Stock Sxchange operators to be seen in *Puck* (see *Cut-throat business* below).

In the UK, by contrast, images of the victims of financial crises were depicted more sedately. In Fig. 6.13, below depicting the failure of Overend & Gurney (O&G) in 1866, the victims are in a crowd swirling around the headquarters of the discount house.

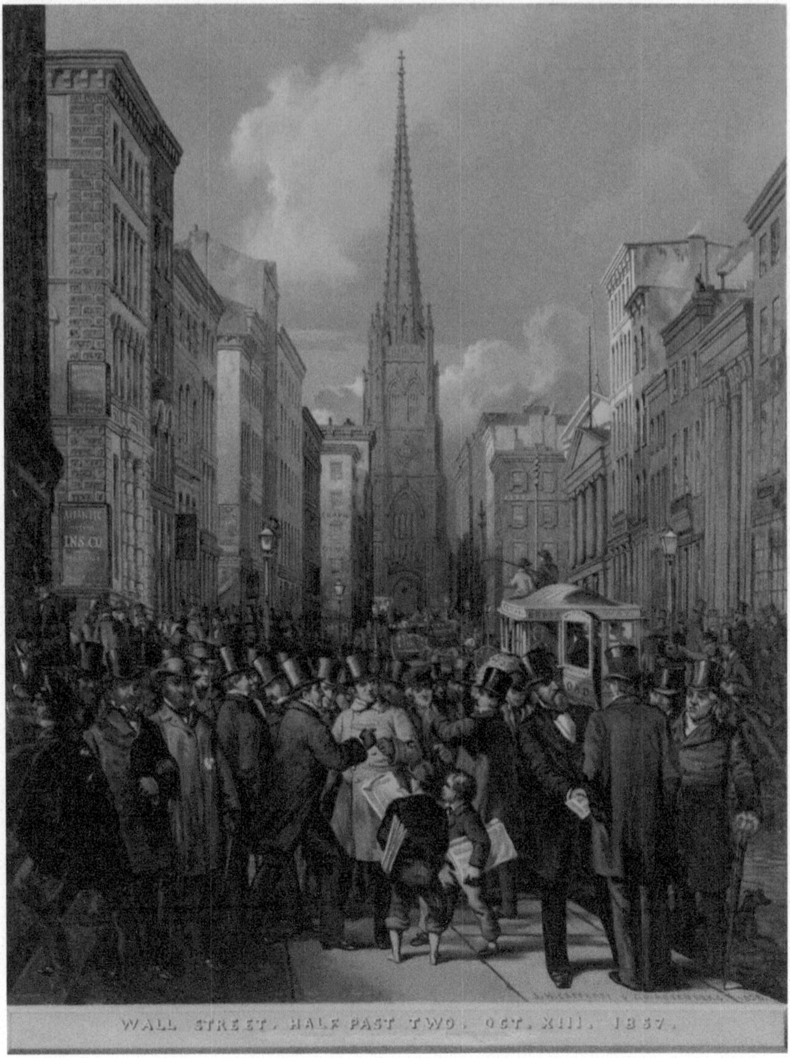

Fig. 6.9 *Wall Street, half past two, Oct. X111, 1857* (Courtesy of LOC)

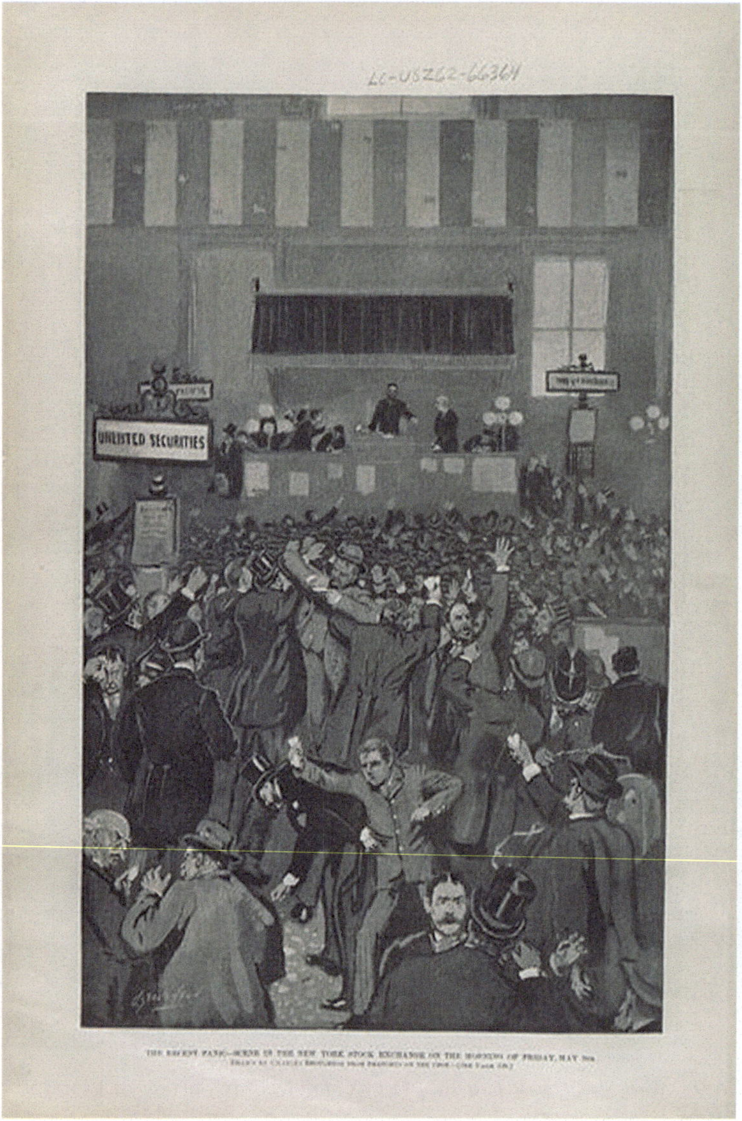

Fig. 6.10 *The recent panic*, *Frank Leslie*, 5 May 1893 (Courtesy of LOC)

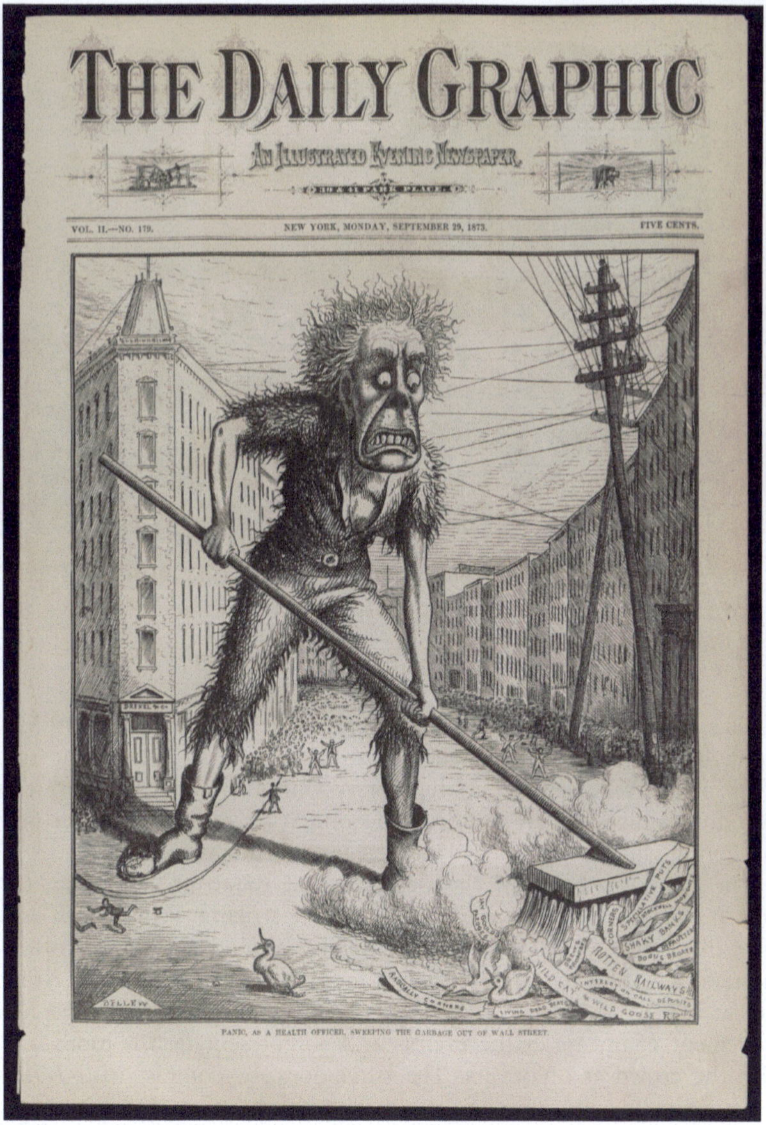

Fig. 6.11 *Daily Graphic, Panic, as a health officer, sweeping the garbage out of Wall Street*, 29 September 1873 (Courtesy of LOC)

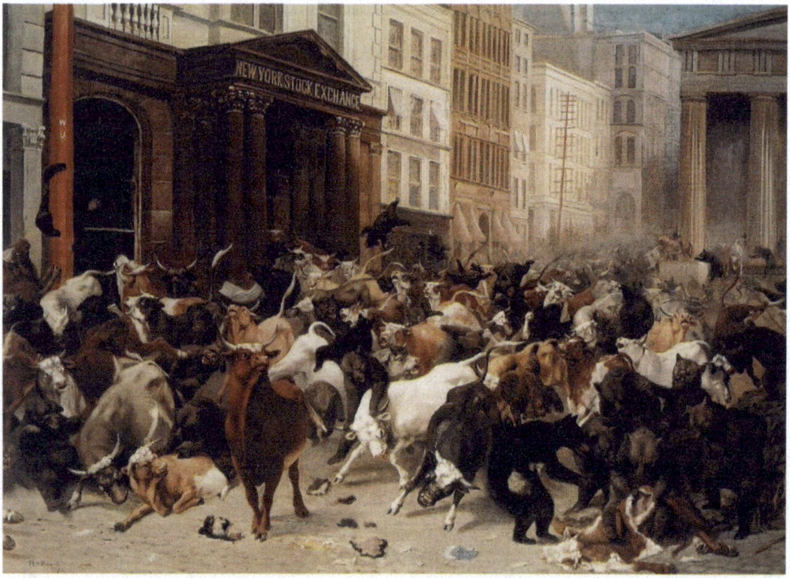

Fig. 6.12 *Bulls and Bears in the Market*, c. 1879 (Courtesy of New York Historical Society)

This image appeared on the front page of the *ILN* edition of 19 May, highlighting the importance that *ILN* placed on the event. The tone of the image reflected the contemporary emotional panic. Sombre top-hatted male investors are frantically peering at the latest newspaper news wondering what had happened to their investments.

The contrasts between the depictions of the bank failure in *ILN* (Fig. 6.13) and *L'Illustration* (Fig. 6.14) are striking. Whilst both associate the bank failure with crowds milling around the bank's offices, the representation in *L'Illustration* is more dynamic. Theatrical gestures indicate the emotional impact of the event, creating the impression of movement of unease at the events. *ILN*'s representation is more static with the crowd as onlookers. The latter does, by contrast with *L'Illustration*, provide more scene setting with the location, O&G's offices, dominating the print.

Figure 6.15, showing investors conducting business on a train that is off the tracks and going off into the clouds, is reminiscent of a similar

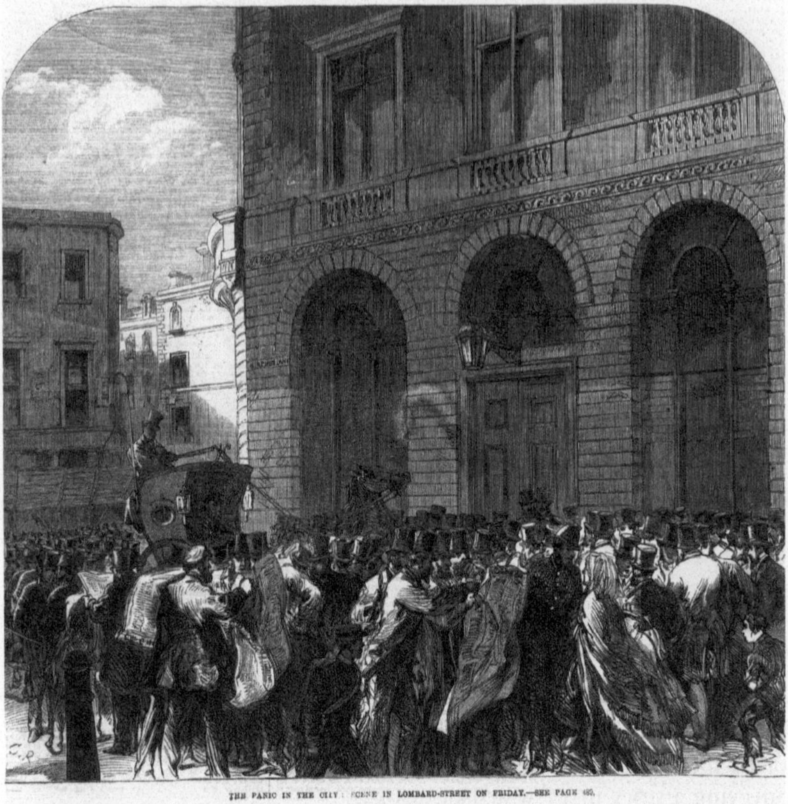

Fig. 6.13 *ILN, The Panic in the City*, 19 May 1866 (© Illustrated London News/Mary Evans)

concept used in the RM itself (see Fig. 6.8). Investors are depicted riding on clouds on a train marked 'speculation'. They clamour to be involved in the latest stock offerings, however preposterous some of their names.

Figure 6.16 is published alongside a long textual commentary warning of the dangers of speculation. A greedy investor wearing a fool's cap (cf. Figure 6.2) has fallen off the crumbling precipice of 'limited liability' in a vain attempt to capture a basket of gold and jewels (the potential rewards from speculation) which has fallen into the abyss below. The

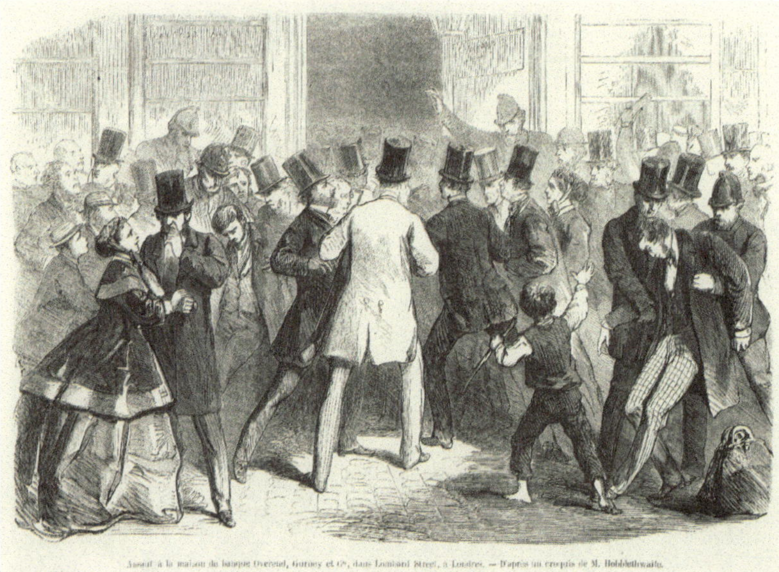

Fig. 6.14 *L'Illustration, Journal Universel, Assaut a la maison de Overend & Gurney,* 19 May 1866 (Courtesy of Hathitrust[10])

resulting outcry after the failure of O&G is depicted here using shock-horror tactics. The feeling of terror illustrates the power of the image, conveying a story in a few artistic strokes.

Krach 1873

This vignette (Fig. 6.17) depicts a crowd of affluent men hurtling to their deaths in pits marked 'Hibernia' and 'Laura' (Laurahutte)—large mining companies in western Germany and Silesia funded by publicly traded shares.[11] A translation reads: 'Recent financial scandal has disproved the adage that "whoever digs a grave for someone else, falls in himself". The Founders (Die Grunder—the founders of the new joint-stock companies) however 'dig all kinds of possible and impossible graves, but only the others- Die Aktionare (the shareholders) - fall in'. This image is reminiscent of the RM image of the railway engine careening over the abyss twenty-eight years earlier (Fig. 6.8).

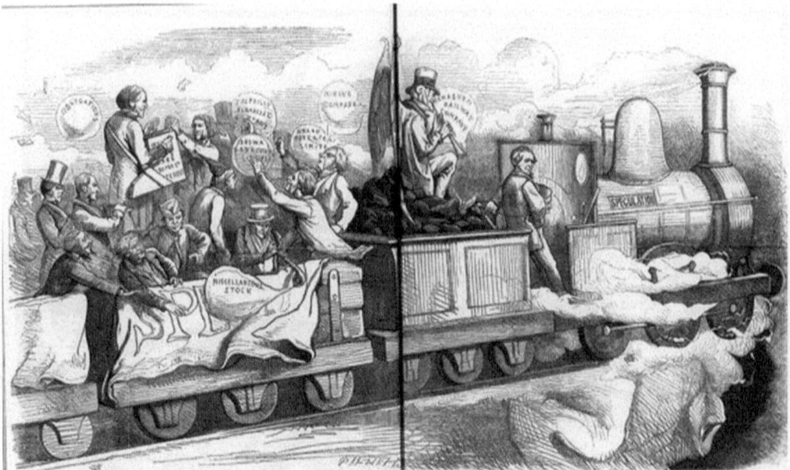

Fig. 6.15 *Fun*, *The Road to Ruin*, 6 July 1867 (Courtesy of UoF)

Ariel uses the image of the railway engine in the 1890s to depict the market/Capitalism driverless, out of control, crushing the poor cow (Labour) whilst throwing the ordinary man (John Bull) out of the carriage because of the speed and instability of the journey (Fig. 6.18).

6.2.3 Financial Institutions

The depiction of financial institutions' buildings in the images under review is always as the setting for describing the impact of financial events, never as stand-alone architectural constructions. There were of course many realistic portrayals and photographs of financial institution buildings. The purpose of my review was to highlight the emotional impact of financial events on investors and depositors, so such pure realistic portrayals have been excluded from the review.

What follows is a summary of the types of images and the events they are depicting:

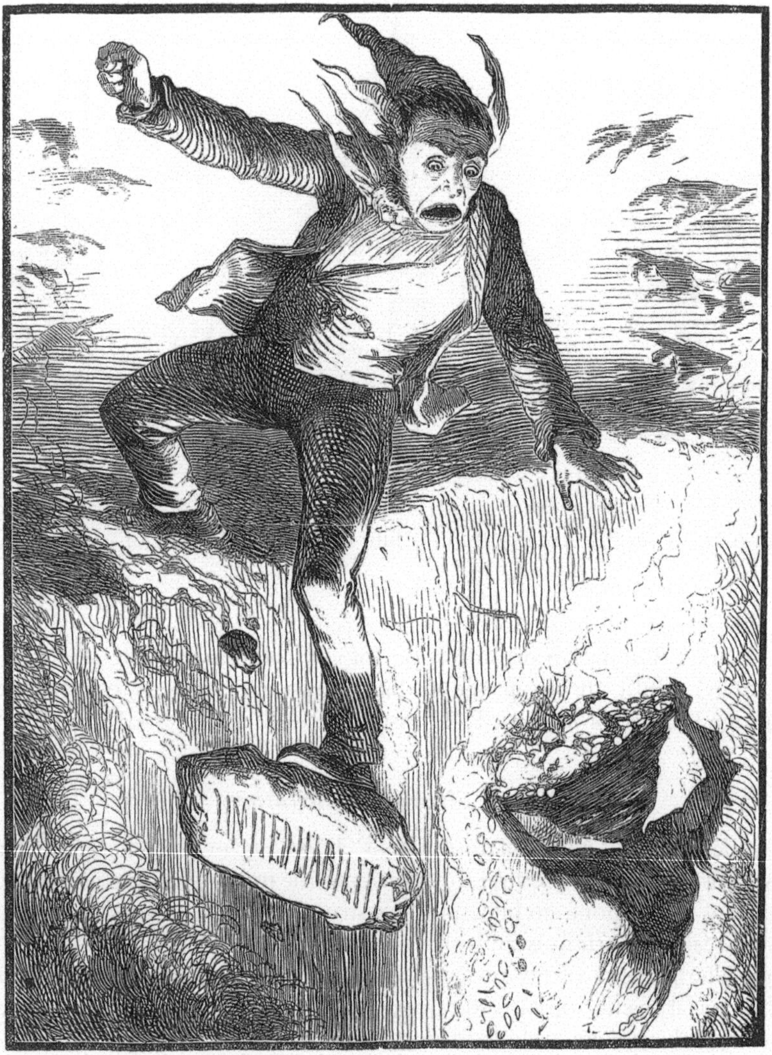

A SERMON FOR THE CITY!

(AFTER CRUIKSHANK.)

[See "The Road to Wealth."]

Fig. 6.16 *Tomahawk*, *The road to wealth*, 31 August 1867 (@ BL Shelf mark, I [31 August 1867], 181)

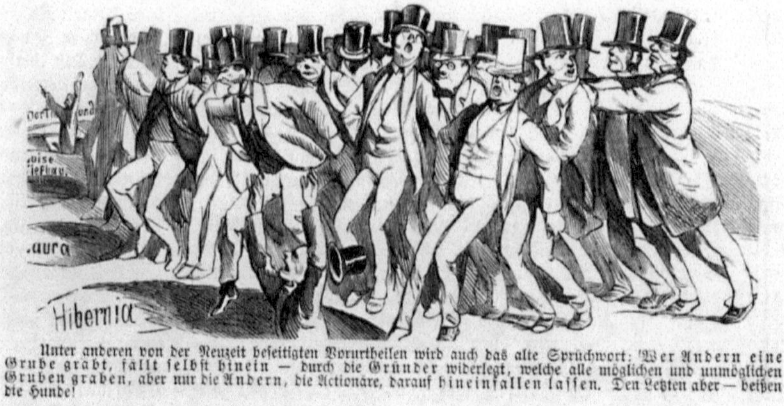

Fig. 6.17 *Kladderadatsch*, vignette, 30 March 1873 (Courtesy of UoH)

1. The interior of a bank vault at the time of the 1825 crisis (*Stout as Ever!!* Fig. 4.8)
2. The exteriors of English banks crashing down at the time of the 1825 crisis (*State of the Money Market* Fig. 6.5)

   This is one of two examples of a collapsing bank edifice (see also vignette in *Overstone's trade cycle*, Fig. 6.1).
3. The interior of a Scottish bank at the time of the 1825 crisis (*State of the Money Market* Fig. 6.5)

   There are reminders here of the Golden Age, for the depiction of bankers behind a counter is reminiscent of Pitt as a bank clerk standing behind a bank counter refusing to accept John Bull's paper money.[12]
4. The interior of the Royal British Bank at the time of the Royal British Bank failure in 1856 (*The British Brigands Bank*, Fig. 6.32)
5. The exterior of Overend & Gurney's headquarters at the time of its failure in 1866 (*The Panic in the City*, Fig. 6.13)
6. The exterior of CGB's headquarters at the time of its failure in 1878 (*The Stoppage of the City of Glasgow Bank*, Fig. 6.34)
7. The empty 'Managers Room' inside CGB headquarters (*The Stoppage of the City of Glasgow Bank*, Fig. 6.34)
8. The Managers Room inside the CGB headquarters: (*The Bank of Virtue: Its Rise and Fall*, Fig. 6.24)

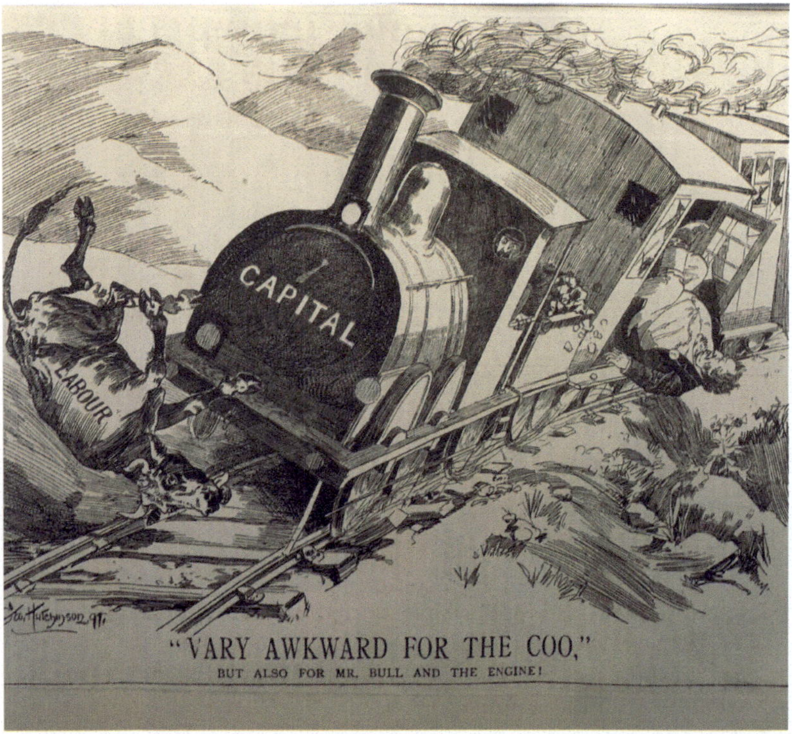

Fig. 6.18 *Ariel, Vary awkward for the Coo', but also for Mr. Bull and the engine!*, Hutchison (own photo) (@ BL Shelf mark, LOU.LON 129 [1892])

9. The bank desk at the Bank of England at the time of the Barings rescue (*Same Old Game*, Fig. 7.11)

In summary, banks are depicted in the main as solid stable institutions. This is reflected in the solid nature of external b,ank edifices (the only example of a bank exterior crashing down is example 2, though for the sake of completeness there is a further example from 1811, BM 11716). The theme of solid edifices representing the exterior of financial institutions is echoed in paintings and cartoons from the US (see, for example, images of the NYSE in Figs. 6.12, 6.25, and 6.27). Bank interiors are depicted as equally stable and unstable. Examples 1, 3, and 9 of stability can be contrasted with the instability depicted in examples 4, 7, and 8 (where bank managers have either fled the premises or are counting their ill-gotten gains).

6.2.4 *Stock Exchange Terminology*

Gambling in the stocks (see Fig. 5.1).

A pun on shares (stocks) also representing the punishment meted out (a spell in the pillory or stocks). The icon of dice symbolises gambling—the use of dice was considered illegal as compared with the legal (or just tolerated) activity of gambling in shares.

In *A king bestowing favours* (Fig. 8.1) Rothschild's ride may end up being rather rocky, and his future uncertain. The febrile atmosphere is evoked by the juxtaposition of the symbols of the pigeon (or dove) and the rook above the bear and the bull, respectively. Just as in his previous print *A New Court Fire Screen* (Fig. 8.2), honest practices are not associated with the bull market, which instead is symbolised by the rapacious representation of the rook.

The Bull, representing the favourable movement of prices, is in the ascendancy, whilst the Bear feels the cold as his time has gone, and his fat has been used up. The sophistication of the imagery is enhanced by the depiction of a pigeon facing a rook, the pigeon saying, 'They have not left me a single feather to fly with', to which the rook replies, 'Where I am there is prey'. The pigeon could symbolise the dove, the virgin part of the Great Goddess, innocence, whilst the rook, the destructive part of the Great Goddess, is ready to pounce on the sacrificial pigeon. It could also signify a play on the good and bad parts of Stock Exchange business practices (echoing Williams again in *New Court*, where the plaques above the porters 'door' represent opposite views of the men standing in front of the doors themselves). Here the pigeon, the good side, is depicted above the bear (the bad times), whilst the rook, the bad side, is depicted above the bull (the good times).

The metaphor of the successful financier casting his web (spinning a web) is evoked in Fig. 6.19 with Rothschild visualised as a spinning top. The figures at the centre of the top depict Rothschild disbursing monies to ladies representing foreign royalty. The bellows on the ground could potentially depict the vision of hot air (speculation) being blown to make the spinning top go round. Rothschild's top half is not depicted satirically, so the overall impact is amusing rather than vicious.

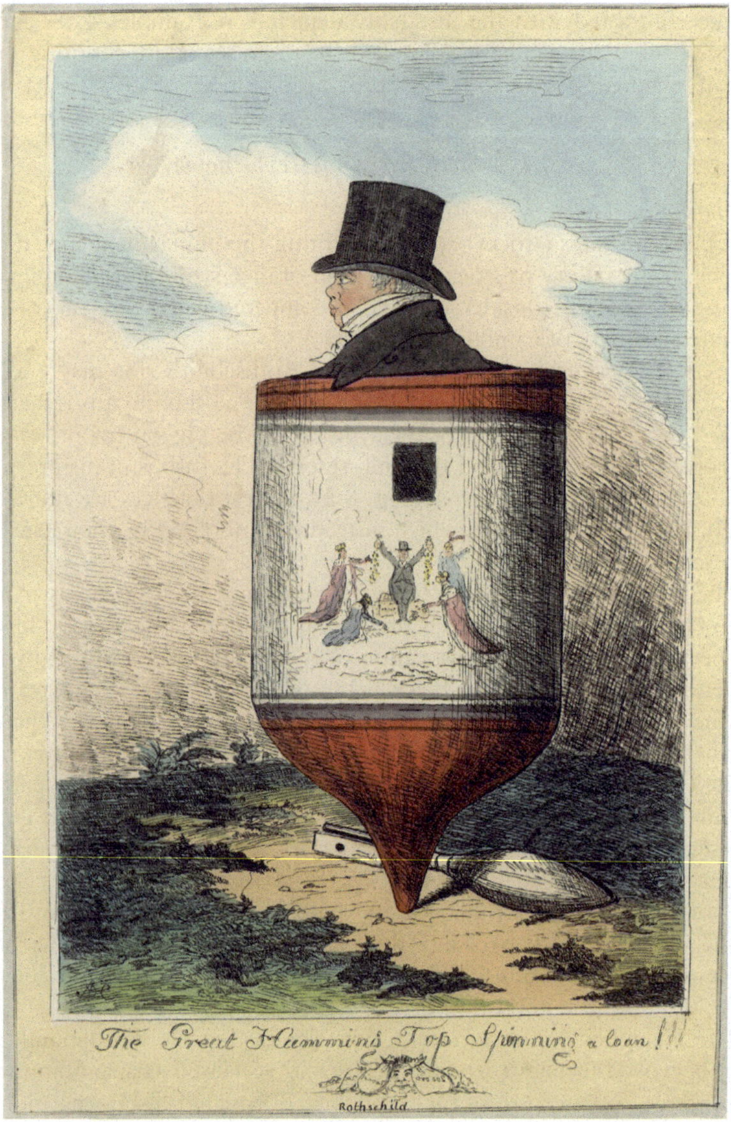

Fig. 6.19 BM 15920, *The great humming top spinning a loan!!!*, 1829 (Courtesy of BM)

What about the actual operations of the Stock Exchange? In the case of the Railway Mania there are several images imaginatively using the term 'stagging'. Officially indicating a large-lot trader, someone engaged in transactions involving large number of shares, it was synonymous with a speculator in shares, someone who drove the prices high by consistently buying when prices were cheap. The link with sport was driven by a recent exhibition the previous year, in 1844, of a painting by Landseer, *The Challenge*. The painting showed two stags locking horns, reflecting the Victorians' love of hunting, and depicting animals (Fig. 6.20).

Several images depict brokers wearing stags' antlers (thus satirising Capel Court the home of the Stock Exchange)—see '*Stag stalking in Capel Court*' (Fig. 6.20), and '*A modern Diogenes looking for an honest man in Capel Court*' and '*the Railway Parliament*'.[13]

The main method which permitted people from all walks of life to take part in these Stock Exchange activities was the ability to buy 'scrips' (see Fig. 6.21). These represented 'margin calls' on shares, the ability to buy into a company for a fraction of the true price of the shares, with the liability to be 'called upon' to meet the full price of the shares later. Several images depict hordes of investors rushing to get hold of these scrips which were depicted as pieces of paper (which they were), with the word 'scrips' written on them. Inevitably investors used the low cost of scrips to increase their exposure to the market for a fraction of their true liability with devastating consequences when the market in railway shares crashed. The image of investors careering lemming-like to their doom over the cliffs above is repeated in *Kladderadatsch*'s image of the 1873 Krach (Fig. 6.17).

The market in railway shares was consistently expressed in terms of a railway engine, invariably out of control representing the periodical's view that the market was out of control. Often the engine was depicted careening into the clouds (itself an image of bubbles associated with speculation), or over a cliff taking investors with it. The engine did not usually have a driver in charge, signifying the lack of control. One of the images (*The Railway Lunatic Asylum*) depicts trains travelling on train lines which all lead to a terminus, marked Lunatic Asylum.[14]

In Fig. 6.22 *Punch* literally pours cold water (retribution) on the bears who it believes precipitated the Overend & Gurney failure and who have failed to profit from it. Other members of the Stock Exchange, the Bulls, are looking on smugly. One of them is literally depicted as a Bull, having bet successfully on the market recovering.

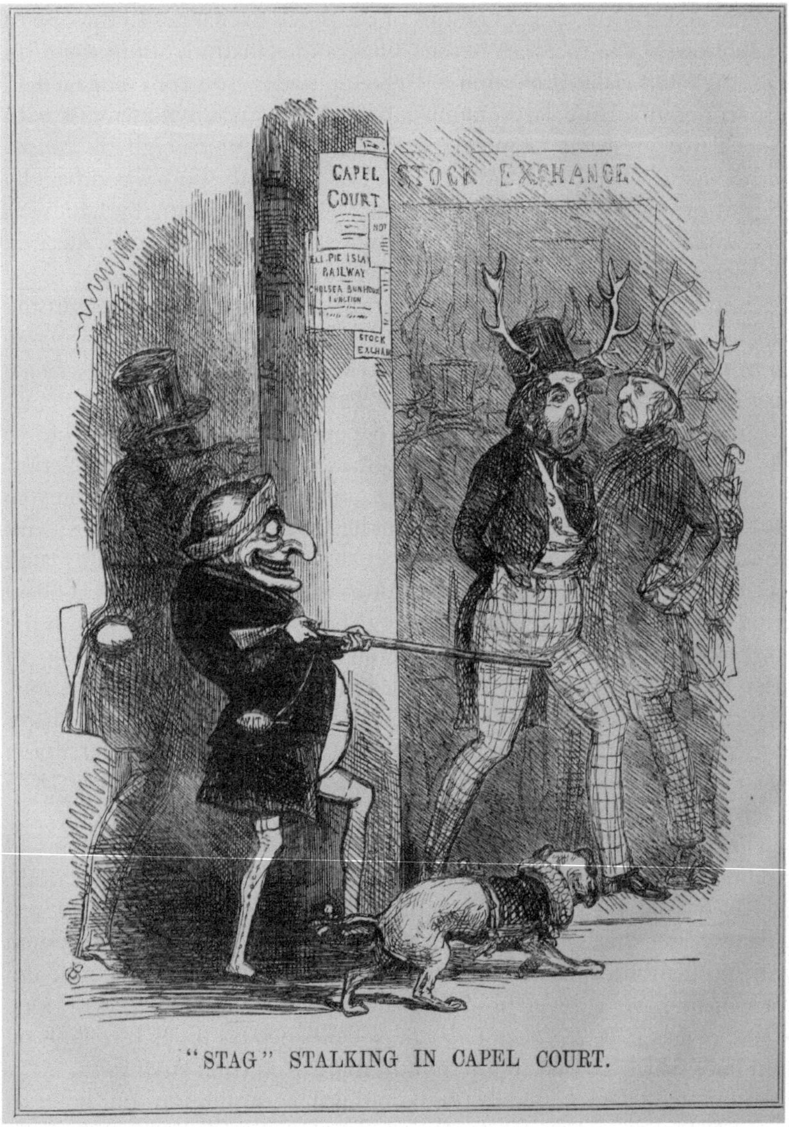

Fig. 6.20 *Punch*, *Stag stalking in Capel Court*, 25 October 1845 (Courtesy of UoH)

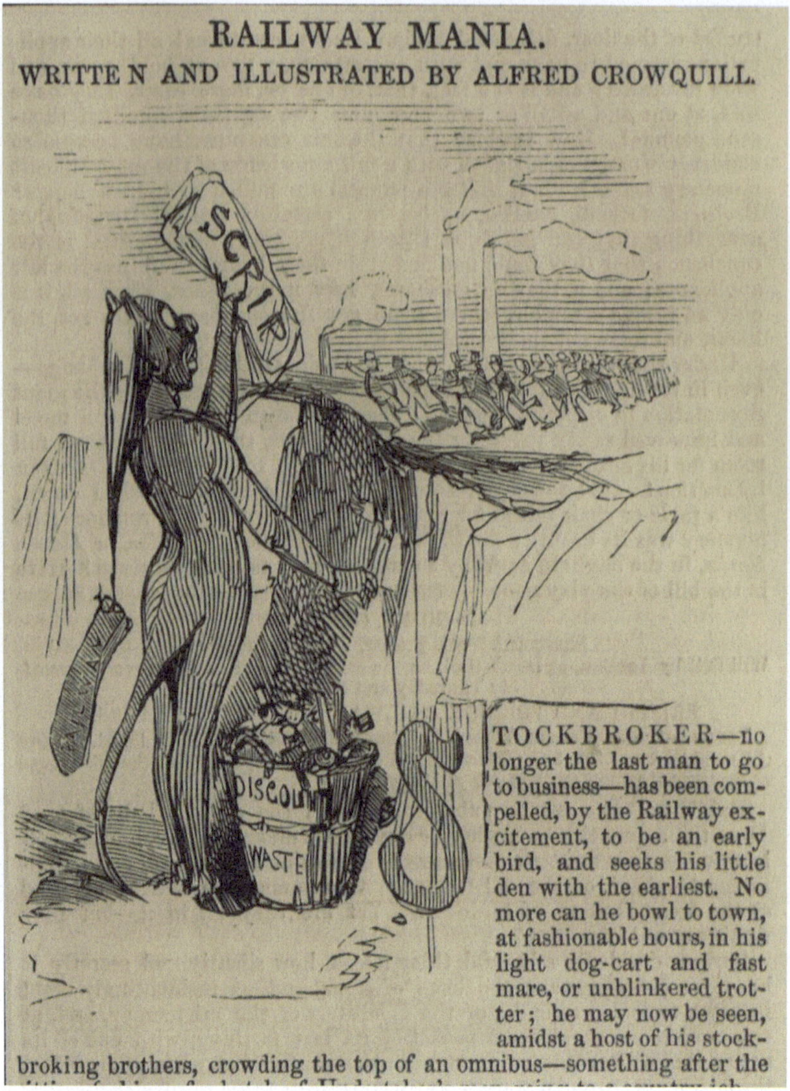
RAILWAY MANIA.
WRITTE N AND ILLUSTRATED BY ALFRED CROWQUILL.

STOCKBROKER—no longer the last man to go to business—has been compelled, by the Railway excitement, to be an early bird, and seeks his little den with the earliest. No more can he bowl to town, at fashionable hours, in his light dog-cart and fast mare, or unblinkered trotter; he may now be seen, amidst a host of his stockbroking brothers, crowding the top of an omnibus—something after the

Fig. 6.21 *ILN*, *Railway Mania*, 8 November 1845 (© Illustrated London News/Mary Evans)

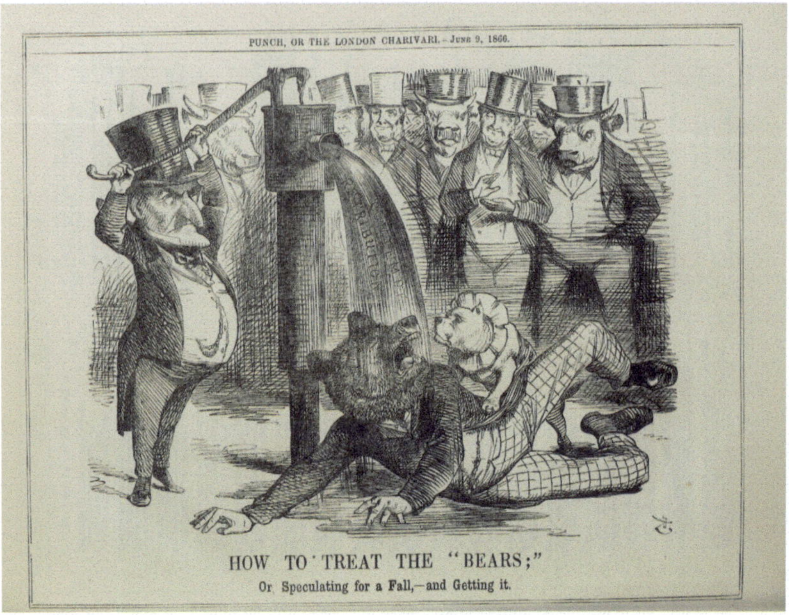

Fig. 6.22 *Punch, How to treat the 'Bears'*, 9 Jun 1866 (Courtesy of UoH)

In *Kladderadatsch* shareholders were often depicted in animal terms. In Fig. 6.23 a shepherd is depicted leading his flock (shareholders depicted as lambs) to the slaughter. The image of shareholders as lambs is repeated in image of Jay Gould *Cut-throat business* (see Fig. 6.25).

By the time of the CGB failure in 1878, financial jargon is evoked both metaphorically (e.g., the use of symbols for speculation, or visualisations of words (cooking the books represented by a cookery book) or else symbols with text bubbles indicating the type of financial misfeasance).

In *Fun* two depictions of the Goddess of Justice (see Figs. 9.4 and 9.5) the pun of cooking the books, or falsifying accounts is represented by a cookery book, with the symbol of the broom sweeping out the muck (cf. clearing out the Augean stables) is used to show puffs of dust being swept away—the puffs with text within their bubbles marked 'credit'.

Even the Banker's attire is depicted as religious (see *Judy* '*By Order*').[15] The images in the storyboard in Fig. 6.24 sequentially describe the hypocrisy (echoes of Regency cant) of Bankers going to Church, and

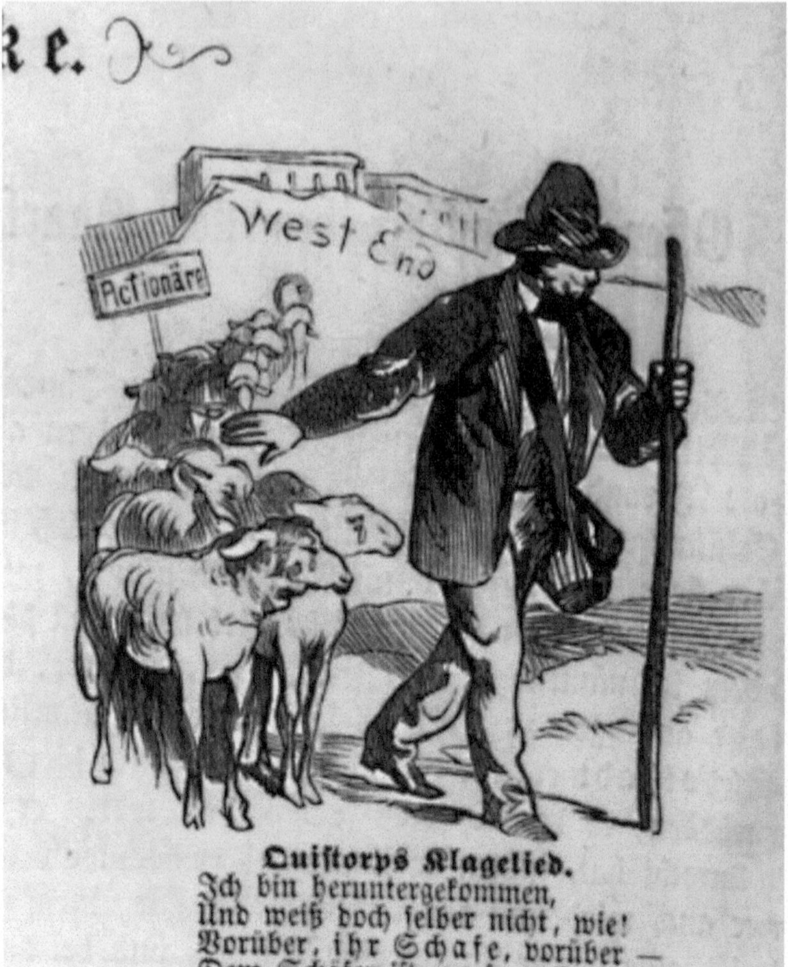

Fig. 6.23 *Kladderadatsch*, *Quistorps Klagelied*, 1873 (Courtesy of UoH)

teaching Old Testament principles to Sunday School children (including Thou shall not Steal, etc.), to the Trust placed in them by investors (echoes of debate over the period over whether investors were in receipt of appropriate information to make informed investment decisions or

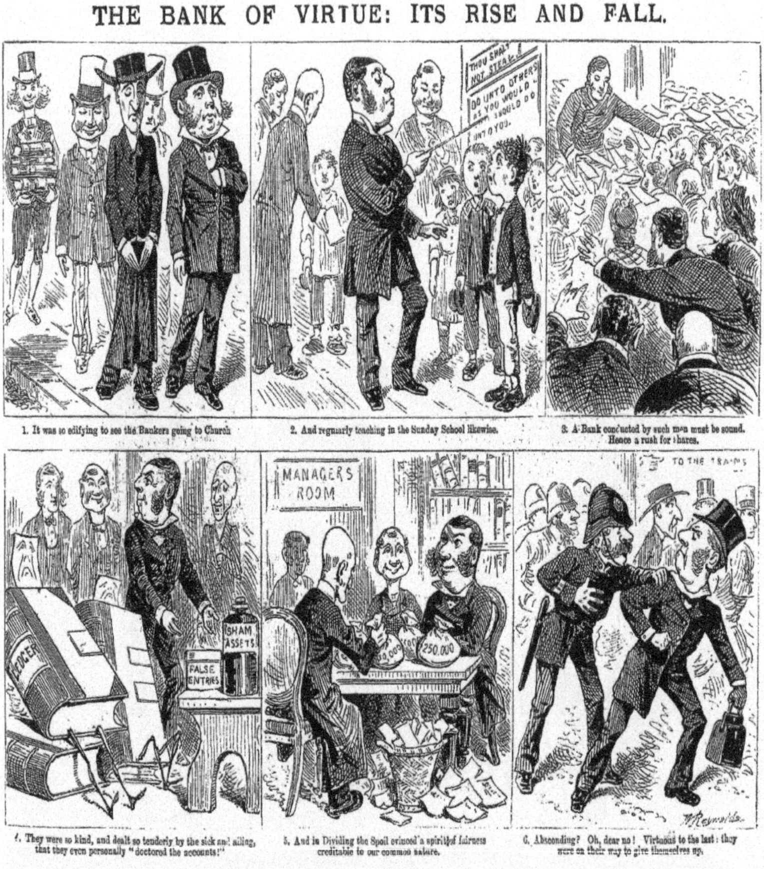

Fig. 6.24 *Funny Folks*, *The Bank of Virtue: Its Rise and Fall*, 9 November 1878 (@ BL Shelf mark, Vol. 4, Issue 206, p. 357)

whether they were swayed by the supposed respectable backgrounds of the bank directors (akin to a herd-like mentality described by Charles Mackay) into following the crowd and investing in the Bank.[16]

The images on the bottom depict visually the solemn undertaking (hypocrisy again) of cooking the books, doctoring the accounts (puns abound here) even to the extent of squashing innocent investors. The final indignity is in the last image where a director fleeing from investors is shown being apprehended by Police, with the Director protesting that he was only fleeing to give himself up to the Police anyway.

This is the only image where there is an overt criticism of the bank directors not in terms of the damage they have caused 'innocent' investors but specifically commenting adversely on their individual morals. The religious hypocrisy referred to above does not feature in any other image. So, in the absence of any similar images, it can perhaps merely be viewed as an indication of the type of reaction that some periodicals had to the events, but it is not possible to attribute any more significance to the views expressed.

In the US contemporary cartoons underscored a dimension of Gould's audacity that has often eluded historians and that was the extent to which Gould's financial wizardry imperilled the commercial world.[17] For the readers of *Puck* and *Judge*, Gould was an agent of destruction—a 'wrecker' as he was often called in the press.

In Fig. 6.25 stock trading on Wall Street is viewed as a '*Cut-Throat Business*' in which Gould and Vanderbilt had the power, by virtue of their inside access to information on market trends, to slit the throats

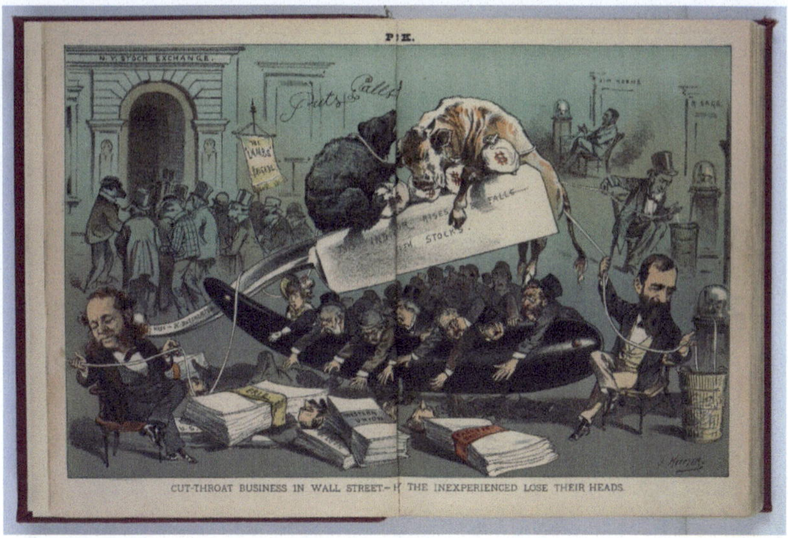

Fig. 6.25 *Puck, Cut-throat business in Wall Street—the inexperienced lose their heads*, 7 September 1881 (Courtesy of LOC)

of the many investors foolish enough to speculate in the shares of highly leveraged corporations like Western Union.

The image further illustrates examples of icons associated with Stock Exchange frenzy (ticker tape, bear and bull, lambs) together with a unique use of razor. Jay Gould (on right) and others are depicted checking ticker tape connected to a large straight-edge razor labelled 'Wade in & Butcher'em' and 'This Indicator Rises & Falls with Stocks' with a bear and a bull and several money bags labelled '$' balanced on the back of the blade; below, draped over the handle are many investors reaching for bundles of 'Pacific Mail, Western Union, [and] Erie' stocks, the blade is poised to drop. In the background another group of investors labelled 'The Lambs Brigade' are headed into the 'N.Y. Stock Exchange'.

In Fig. 6.26 a larger-than-life man labelled 'Promoter' is sitting astride a ticker-tape machine, holding a large butterfly net into which a throng of investors (brokers, merchant, bankers) are tossing money in exchange for balloons labelled 'Sash and Door Combine Stock, American Beet Sugar Co., Distillery and Warehouse Co. Stock, American Caramel Co., Auto-Truck Co. Stock, Print Cloth pool Stock, Chicago Milk Co., Knit Goods Co. Stock, [and] International Silver Co.'

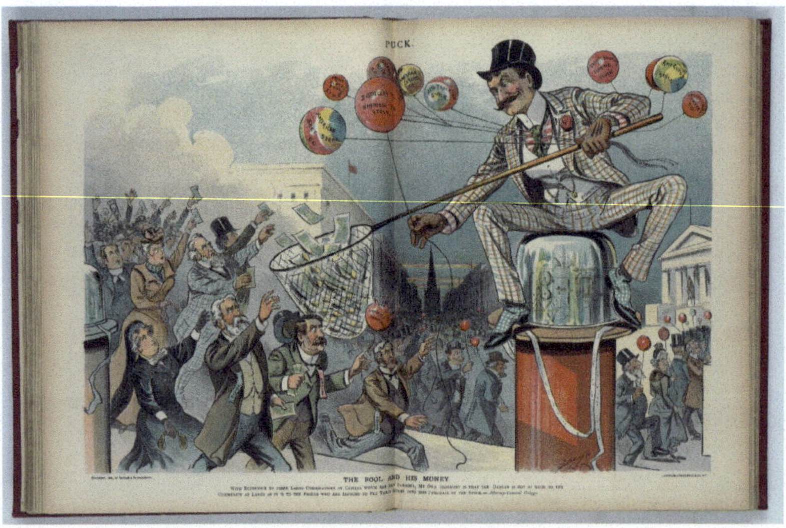

Fig. 6.26 *Puck, The fool and his money*, 26 April 1899 (Courtesy of LOC)

The caption reads: With reference to these large combinations of capital which are now forming, my own judgement is that the danger is not so much to the community at large as it is to the people who are induced to put their money into the purchase of the stock. Attorney-General Griggs.

The malevolence of the ticker tape in this US image is contrasted with the more ironic use in *Vanity Fair*. In the latter image (see discussion on Harry Marks, Fig. 5.14) the ticker tape is seen more as a benign use of increased information. For a similar use of ticker tape as a metaphor for speculation, in this case an ironic view of Jay Gould's own machinations in the stock market—see *Judge*, *I never speculate*, (1886).

The image (Fig. 6.27) depicts a feminine figure, a symbol of probity (cf. *Fun* Goddesses of Justice) cracking her whip to cleanse Wall Street (stock jobbers and stock gamblers) using a large brush.

In Fig. 6.28 a capitalist is depicted playing cards with the Grim Reaper, with disasters all around him. The capitalist, an insurer, is surrounded by vignettes depicting natural disasters. There is a notice marked 'heavily insured' around each of the disasters.

In Fig. 6.29 the cartoonist, Cynicus, is criticising the hypocrisy of peers whose status is being bought by being offered bribes by unscrupulous promoters (who are literally reeling them in using a fishing rod). They are described as 'gulls', easily tricked (this term is used extensively in the Golden Age…).

Figure 6.30 is a typical example of visual representation of common Stock Exchange terminology (e.g., terms such as 'cornering the market', 'a fall in the market', 'turnover', 'discounted'). Like *Punch* earlier, these storyboards appeared in 1880s onwards indicating the depth of financial knowledge of readers of these periodicals (see images of the Old Lady where financial visualisations of 'tightening' and 'loosening' credit can be found—e.g., Fig. 7.6).

Figure 6.31 depicts a dapperly dressed stock trader with the head of a bull eyeing purchases in a china shop. It illustrates a visual pun on 'a bull in a china shop', a term first used in the nineteenth century, and symbolising the clumsiness of the character being depicted. Here it satirises the headlong stubborn antics of stockbrokers.

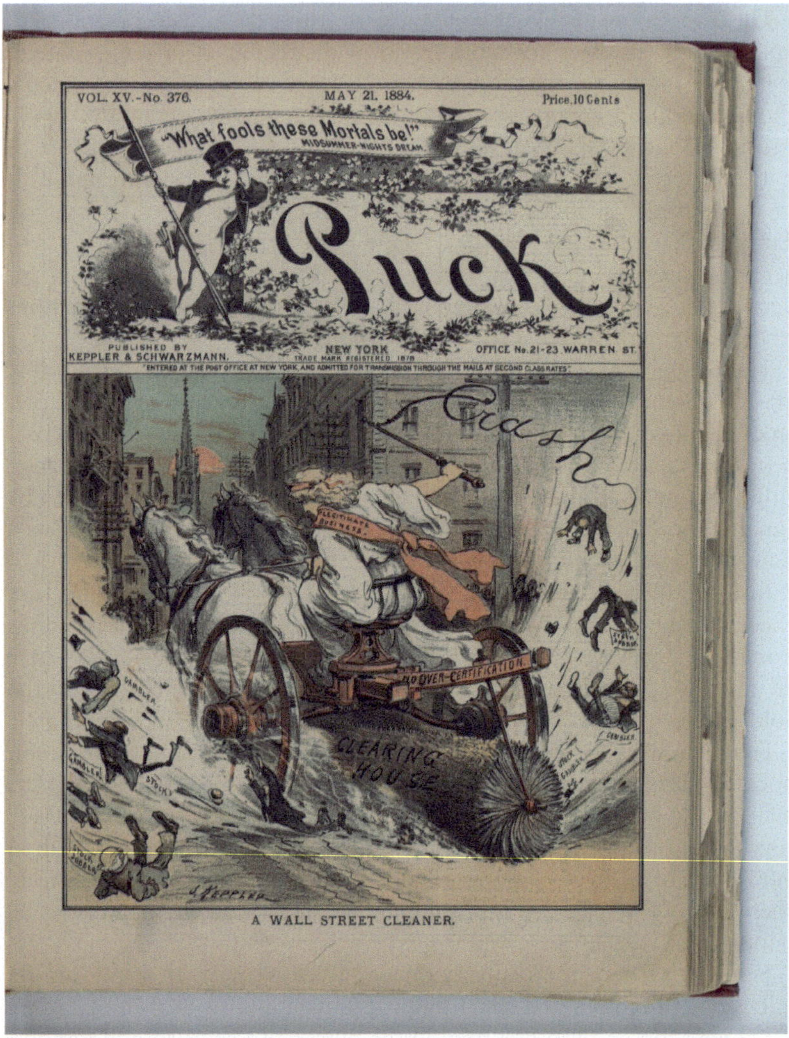

Fig. 6.27 *Puck. A Wall St cleaner*, 21 May 1884, Keppler (Courtesy of LOC)

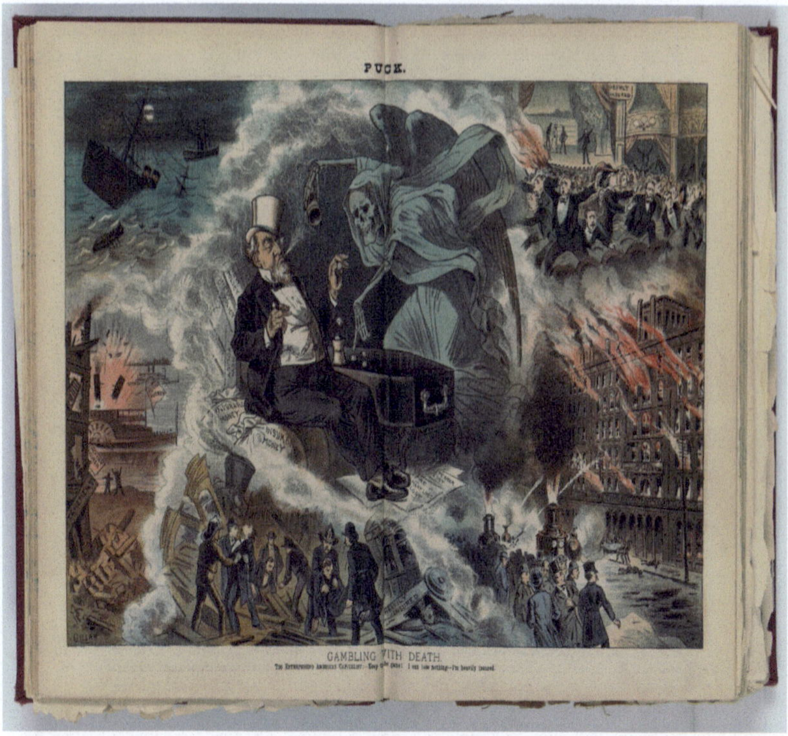

Fig. 6.28 *Puck*, *Gambling with death*, 24 January 1883 (Courtesy of LOC)

6.2.5 *Victims/villains*

Whereas the other themes of speculation concentrated mainly on the victims, there were occasional images where both victims and villains are depicted together. Villains anonymously depicted here also feature in Chapter 9.

The examples illustrate the use of split screens (*A King bestowing favours* Fig. 8.1, as well as *The Brigands' Bank* Fig. 6.32), as well as the emerging use of storyboards (*The stoppage*—Fig. 6.34).

Finally, the depiction of villains gave rise to some colourful icons, that of 'The Spider', 'Napoleon of Finance', and 'Devil-fish'. They conjure up visual puns associated with the web of the spider, the ironic anti-hero of

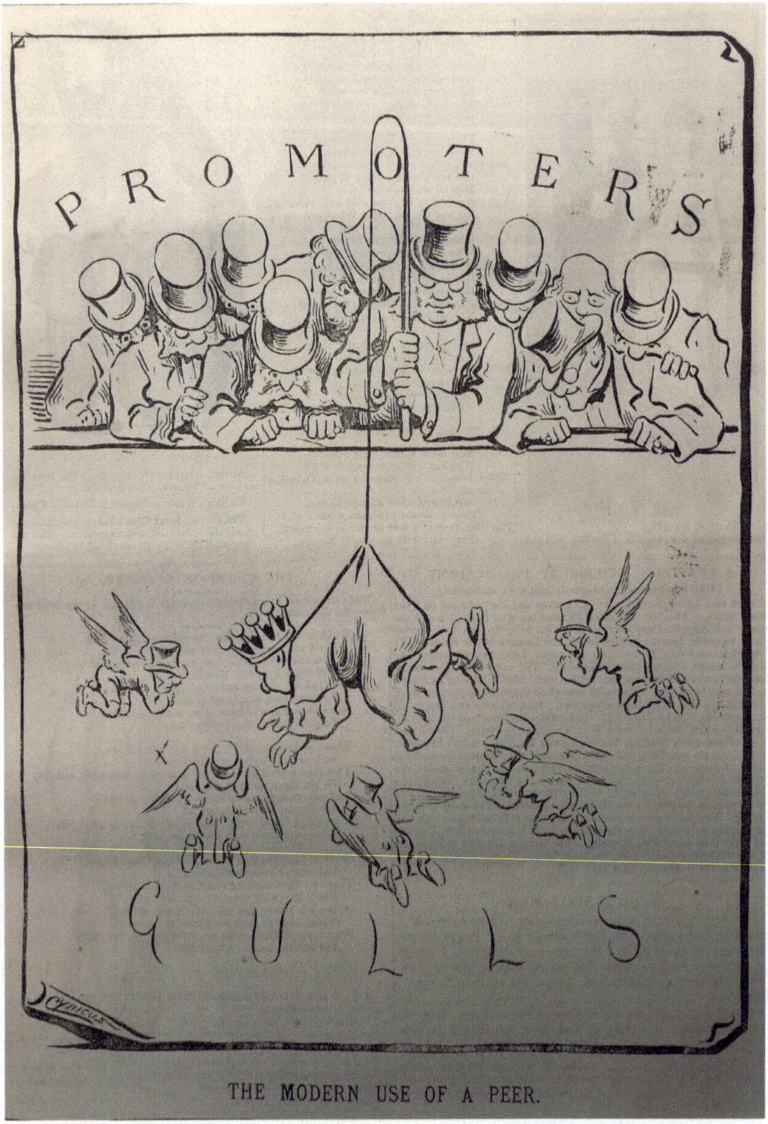

Fig. 6.29 *Ariel*, *Promoters The modern use of a Peer*, 6 June 1891 (own photo) (@ BL Shelf mark, LOU.LON 236 [1891])

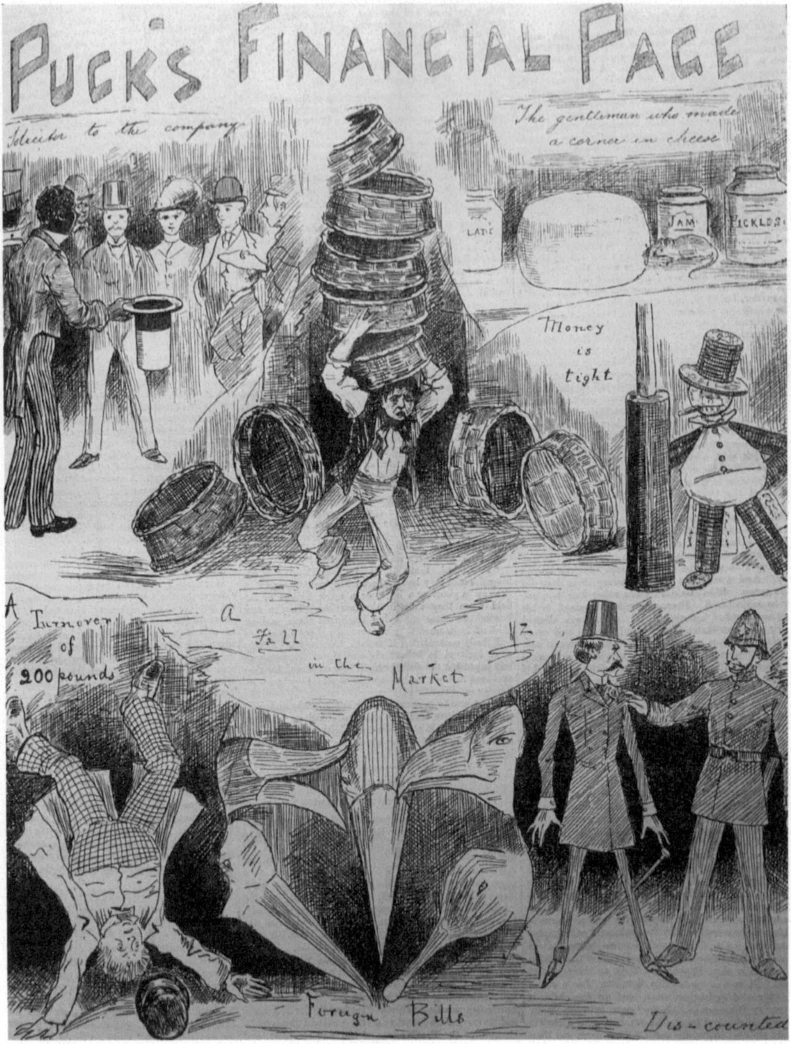

Fig. 6.30 *Ariel*, *Puck's Financial Page*, Cynicus, 12 April 1890 (own photo) (@ BL Shelf mark, LOU.LON 275 [1890])

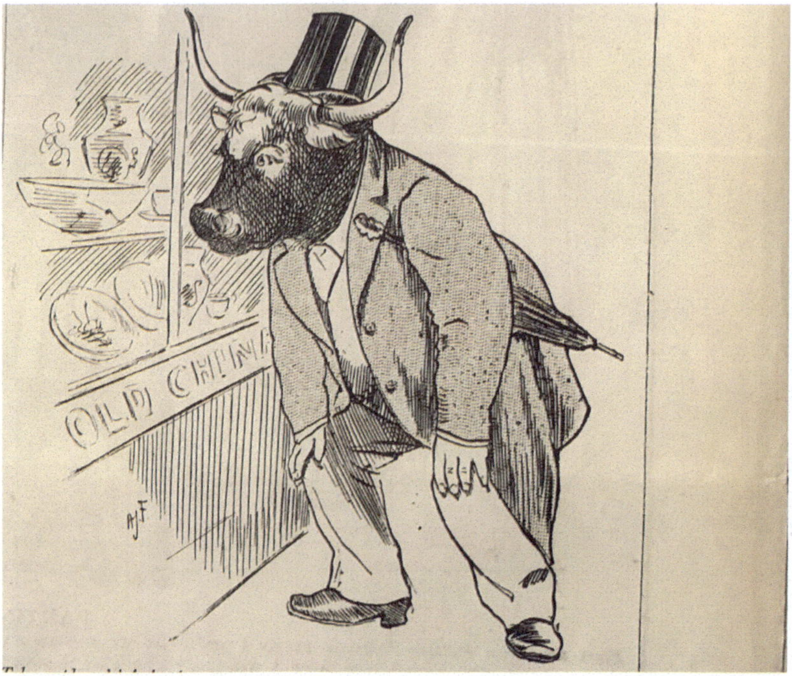

Fig. 6.31 *Ariel*, The Bull (extract) (own photo) (@ BL Shelf mark, LOU.LON 236 [1891])

Napoleon (both despised and secretly admired), and the tentacles of the octopus (the devil-fish).

The victims are depicted as stoically bearing their misfortune, whilst the managers are depicted as sly (school)boys having played a trick on the depositors. Crucially, victims and villains are shown in the same scene. In Fig. 6.32 managers and directors (identified by the bags, full of money, that they are holding) are hiding beneath the clerks' desk, gleefully counting their luck in having swindled the poor investors of their monies. In the subsequent CGB failure, the managers' desk is shown without any managers present.[18] *Punch* is on the side of the depositors, a position not reflected in its initial response to the CGB failure twenty or so years later.

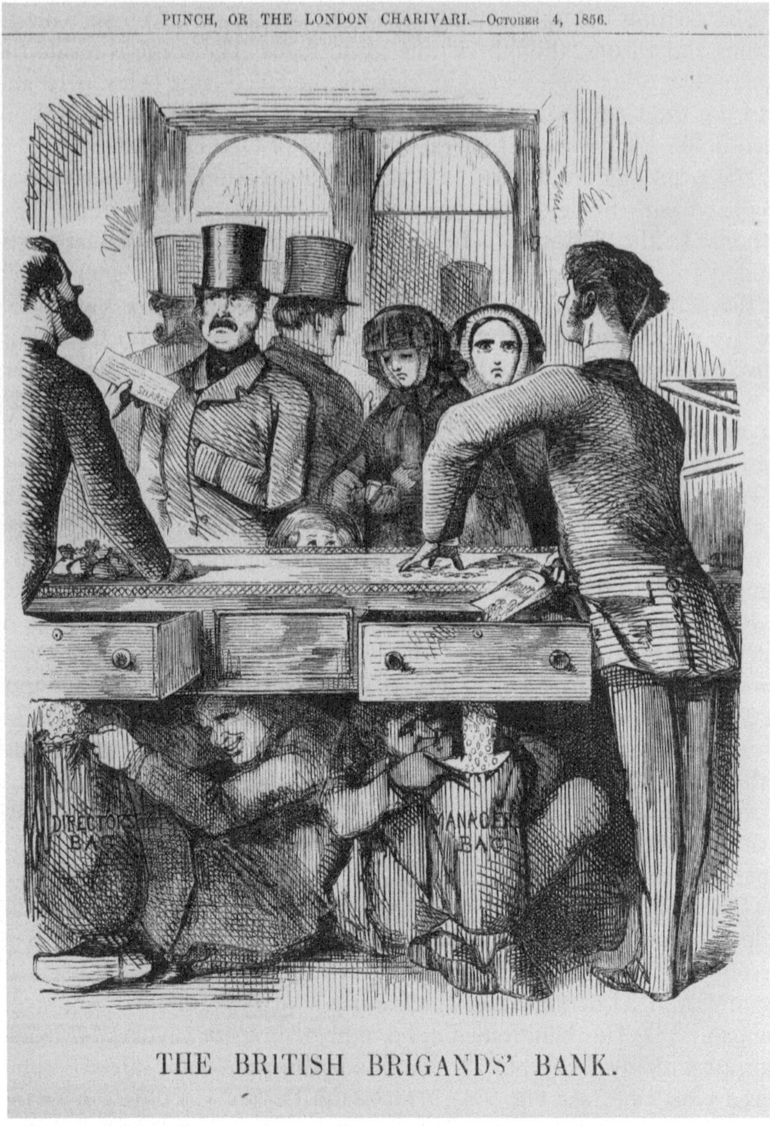

Fig. 6.32 *Punch*, *The British Brigands Bank*, 4 October 1856 (Courtesy of UoH)

The cartoon is a split image—equal prominence is given spatially to victims and villains, though victims are in focus. The scene is inside the bank unlike other representations outside the failed bank (Figs. 6.13 and 6.14 are O&G or Fig. 6.34 in relation to CGB). Their expressions are stern unlike the scenes of hysteria in the case of O&G and CGB.

The main aggrieved party is a gentleman, presumably a war veteran (depicted with his left jacket arm attached to his jacket) waiting for a response to the clerk who is holding a share certificate (presumably just handed to him for repayment). The pull on the emotions is enhanced by the depiction of a child who with pleading eyes, peers up at one of the two clerks who affect haughty, snooty almost supercilious expressions. One of the clerks, unmoved, continues to shovel coins into the drawers of their desks which disappear through a hole in the bags being held by the managers and directors. The failure of RBB was followed within ten years by the spectacular collapse of O&G in May 1866.

When the initial shock of the events had died down, there was a period of almost one year before the periodical press took up popular indignation at what had happened. This reflected in part the emergence of detailed commentary on the failure.

Fun, by contrast, has one generic image commenting on the evils of speculation, *The Road to Ruin* (see Fig. 6.15), and another, *The Ducks (and Drakes) of Directors* (see Fig. 6.33), which rails against contemporary disastrous investments in railway stocks and the rapacious attitudes of railway directors. Both cartoons evoke a period of immense distrust with company promoters, and unscrupulous railway directors. The failure of so many railway companies was linked by the association of railways with the demise of O&G (which owned railway companies in addition to other finance activities).

'*Ducks and Drakes*' (Fig. 6.33) depicts the figure of John Bull as an ordinary shareholder, blindfolded, and being sold worthless shares. The cartoon 'indicates that the image of a beleaguered John Bull could still be employed to demonstrate Englishmen's victimisation by joint-stock companies'.[19] The blindfolded John Bull or investor invokes an ironic contrast with the image of the blindfolded myopic bank director some eleven years later (see Fig. 9.4). 'Ducks and Drakes' is a phrase referring to reckless behaviour, squandering of monies.[20] The words of the chorus come from the popular song 'Pop goes the weasel' which contains the words cited above in line 3; the first registered use of the song dates to 1853.[21]

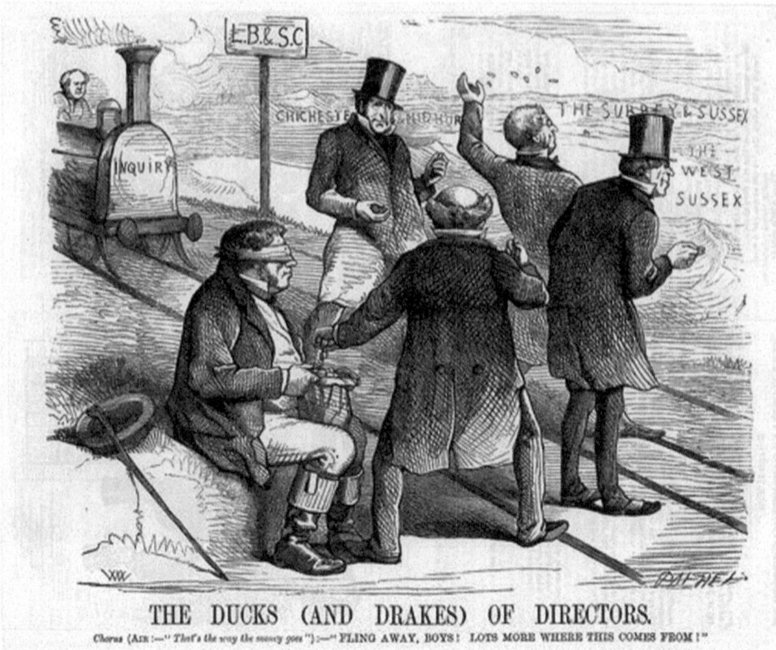

Fig. 6.33 *Fun, The Ducks (and Drakes) of Directors*, 29 June 1867 (Courtesy of UoF)

The *Graphic*'s *The Stoppage at the City of Glasgow Bank* (see Fig. 6.34) is symbolic in its interpretation of the bank failure. The image appears relatively soon after the events have unfolded, providing immediacy and, unusually, is in the form of a storyboard. This format, generally favoured in the more comic periodicals allowed for a dynamic representation of the events, and distanced the *Graphic* from the traditional, static representations prevalent in *ILN* and in photographs of the period (see discussion on Wallace above in Chapter 5). The 'story' is depicted in five parts, another feature of the period, which apes the dramatic impact of five acts in traditional drama.[22]

Movement, essential to depicting the drama and emotions of the events, is illustrated here by the device of showing people pressing against the Royal Exchange Reading Rooms (located in Glasgow) desperate for information, as well as the crowds of despairing shareholders outside

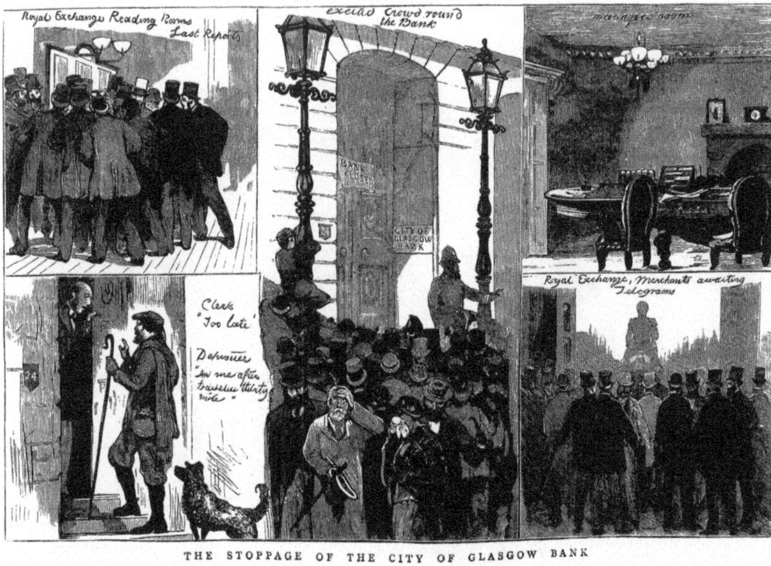

Fig. 6.34 *The Graphic*, *The Stoppage of the City of Glasgow Bank*, 12 October 1878 (Courtesy of © Illustrated London News/Mary Evans Picture Library)

(described in text as 'round', indicating all around) the doors of the bank, which is closed. Some shareholders are trying to clamber up nearby lamp-posts for a view inside the bank, others face the reader despairingly, which adds to the piquancy of the situation.

Similarly, the absence of movement, as in the depiction of an empty Manager's Room, reveals more of the panic (the directors and managers having fled from the public eye, after closing the Bank) and distress. The static nature of the scene where an anxious depositor—a farmer, judging by his clothes and accompanied by his faithful sheepdog—is engaged in conversation with one of the clerks to the Bank (no. 24 was the address of the Glasgow address of CGB), is thrown into question when the words to the scene indicate that the depositor has travelled thirty miles in vain to withdraw his monies. 'Too late' the clerk solemnly, almost sheepishly, tells the depositor. The focus here is on the depositors (who ultimately would all be repaid in full, save any accrued interest), and the farming community, whereas the middle scene is concerned with the impact on the real ultimate losers, the shareholders.

The Spider

In 1880 Frith used the model of Grant in his moralistic series, *Race for Wealth.* Frith was one of the foremost examples of the art of narrative painting that dominated much of the Victorian era. Whilst the cornerstone of narrative painting was an attention to realistic detailed representation, artists were able to express their subjective opinions and moral messages.

In Fig. 6.35 the central figure of the Spider (the villain) is seen talking to interested investors. The satirical metaphorical use of the Spider and the Fly parable was first seen in the nineteenth century with Rowlandson's 1808 *The Corsican Spider in his web.* The words 'Will you walk into my parlour'—the central words from Mary Howitt's 1829 poem—are conjured up here.

It provoked an almost instantaneous riposte from the comic periodical *Fun.* Its chief artist John Sullivan parodied Frith's work in his cartoon *Odds on the Spider* (see Fig. 6.36). As Frith expressed it in his autobiography: 'In the comic paper called *Fun*, the admirable artist of that journal, Mr. Sullivan, laid hold of my puppets, and made them play a different game'.[23]

As Meisel points out, Sullivan's parody showed 'the swindler rolls along in his carriage unpunished and without the least display of sympathy for the poor parson, who is reduced to sweeping a crossing over which the carriage has just passed. But he identifies with the criminal, whom he treats as the tragic representative figure'.[24]

The instantaneous reply in *Fun* illustrates the cross-over between low and high art as well as illustrating the common interests of the two formats.

Sullivan clearly feels the moralist Frith failed to identify the real 'winner', the Spider himself. This he expresses ironically but he pulls the emotional heartstrings of the reader just as effectively as Frith's use of realistic dramatism. Sullivan makes liberal use of puns—'an easy canter' transposes a horse rider to a prison yard with the inversion of the rider (the Spider) indicating that the ride has not gone well—the rider has fallen

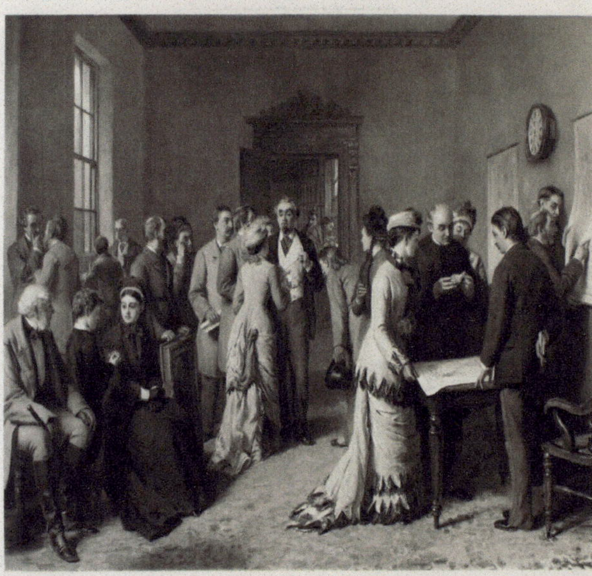

Fig. 6.35 *Spider and the flies*, part of Frith's *Race for wealth* series, 1879/1880 (© Museum of London)

off his horse (i.e., lost the race). The real power of Sullivan's storyboard is the juxtaposition of the Spider's callousness and insouciance in taking monies off unfortunate victims, with his ultimate 'victory' carriage drive in front of his victims. Discussion of Fig. 6.37 is repeated in Chapter 9, The Law, to convey the attitude towards the legal process.

A US treatment of the spiders depicts Gould and William Vanderbilt, and their financial activities centring around the American Union Telegraph Company and the Western Union Telegraph Company. The flies

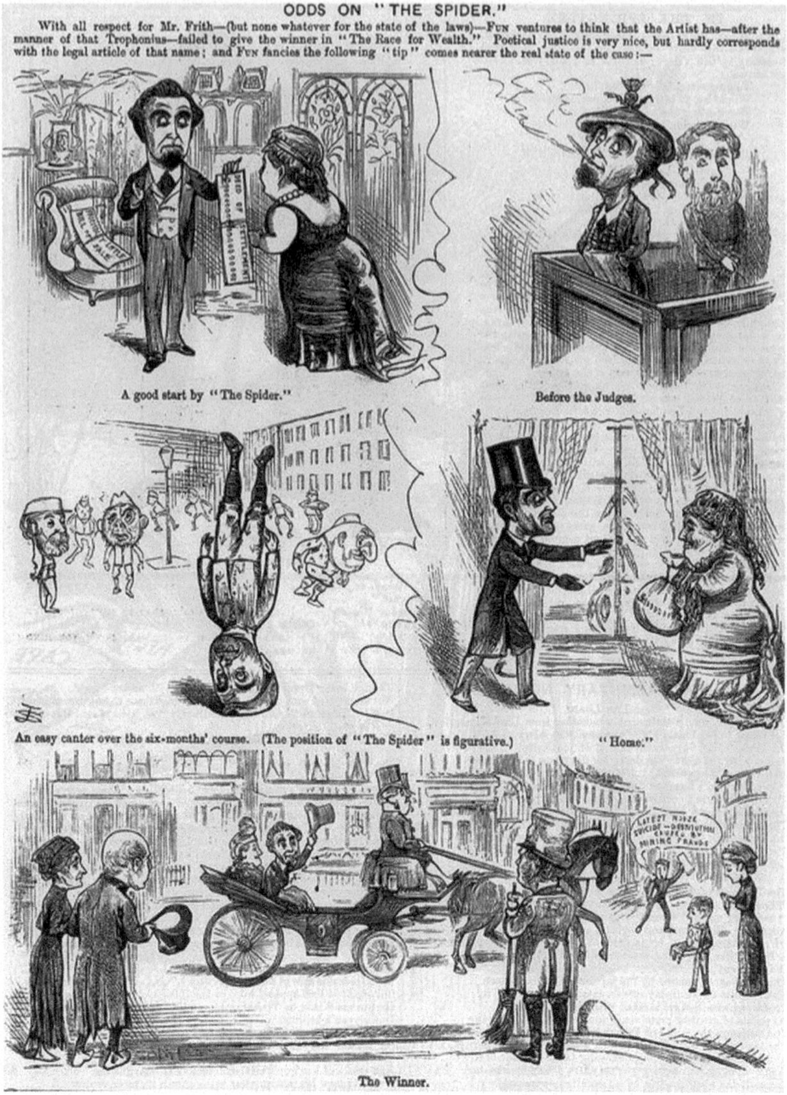

Fig. 6.36 *Fun Odds on the Spider*, 23 June 1880 (Courtesy of UoF)

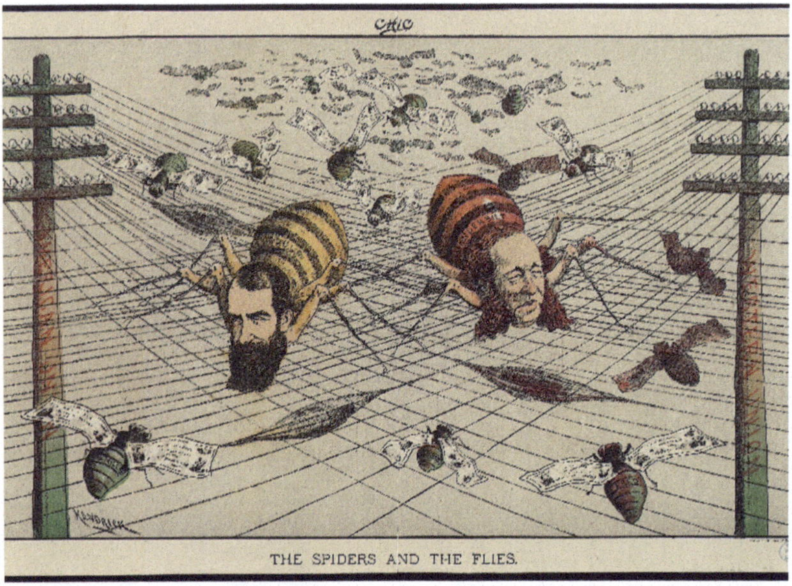

Fig. 6.37 *The Spiders and the Flies* [c. 1880–1889] (Courtesy of Boston Public Library[25])

are symbolised by the dollar bills attaching to them (ready to be sucked into Gould's web).

Napoleons of Finance

As Fraser expressed it in relation to the US robber barons of popular culture: 'Napoleon gripped the romantic imagination of the nineteenth century'.[26] Fraser continued:

> It [the popular view of Napoleon] transformed a hunger for money into a visionary quest by beings blessed with prescience and imagination – nerves of steel, gambler's instinct – the noble upstart, the obscurely risen, the desire for fame with no law, human or divine, could tamper with.[27]

As the *Economist* put it in relation to the UK:

> On the strength of the Dunlop "deal" Mr. Hooley came to be regarded as the Napoleon of Finance, at whose word capital could be created by the million and fortunes could be made as if by a magician's wand.[28]

Yet Hooley was not the only financier to depicted as the Napoleon of Finance. What follows is a comparison of various depictions of financiers as Napoleons of Finance, both from England and the US.

It can be contrasted with his forlorn figure reflecting his fall from grace (see Fig. 9.1).

In Fig. 6.38 Hooley is depicted at the height of his fame, standing surrounded by his fawning acolytes. It is reminiscent of *Punch*'s image of *King Hudson's Levee* over fifty years earlier (see Fig. 5.5).

Whilst both Balfour and Hooley were compared with Napoleon, Balfour's caricature resembled Napoleon in terms of size and bulk, whereas that depicting Hooley reflects his haughty status and the reverence of his investors.[29]

Cecil Rhodes

Figure 6.39 depicts the controversial financier: his figure is squeezed into the diminutive figure of Napoleon; his imperial aspirations can be seen against the backdrop of dead Africans. By contrast the society periodical, *Vanity Fair*, conveys in Fig. 6.40 the prestige and stature afforded to Rhodes in his time by contemporary society.

Figure 6.41 refers to Ferdinand Ward who had established the banking business of Grant & Ward in 1880. He ran an investment fraud which collapsed in 1884, bankrupting the US President Ulysses Grant and other investors.[30]

Devil-Fish

Another image which recurs during the 1880s onwards is that of the devil-fish (a name by which the octopus was also known). A less flattering portrayal of Balfour (reminiscent of French satirical portrayals of the Rothschilds, see Fig. 8.13) appears in W. T. Stead's *Review of Reviews*, November 1893. He was described as the devil-fish who preyed on the savings of innocent investors.[31] The image itself was also used in a *Punch* image of 1881.[32] McKie quotes Spender whose review of Balfour's financial activities appeared in the *Westminster Gazette* in 1893. Spender drew

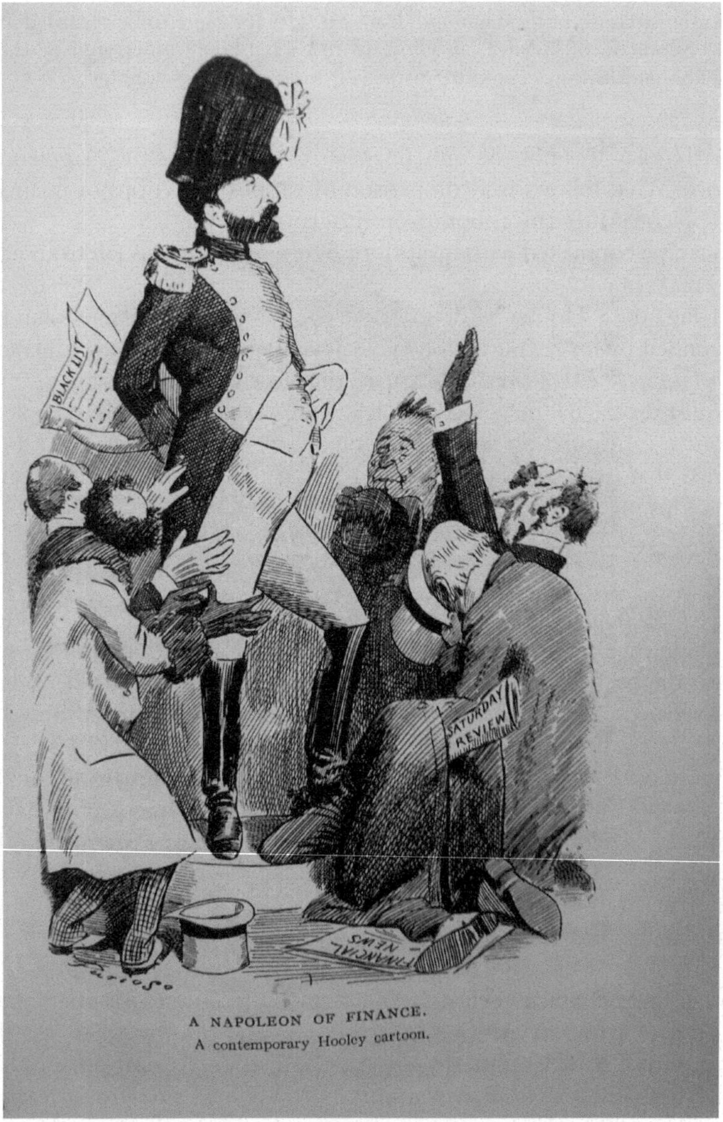

Fig. 6.38 *Hooley as Napoleon of Finance*, from *The Hooley Book*, 1898 (own photo) (@ BL, GRC 10827.bb.36)

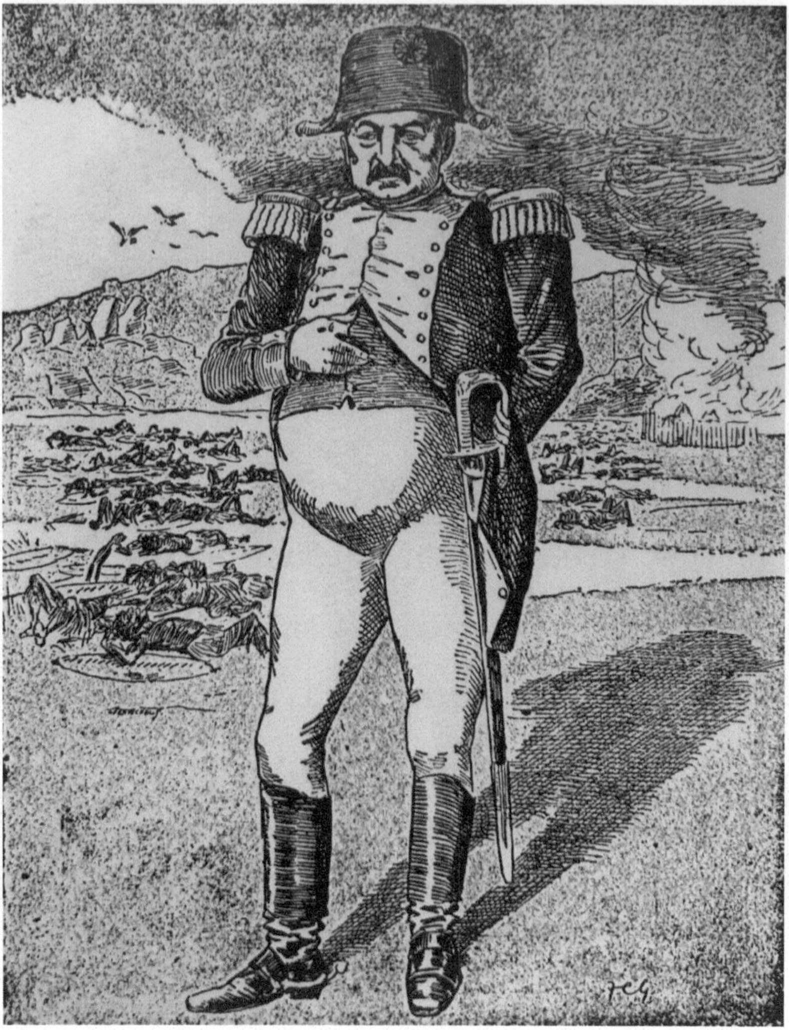

Fig. 6.39 *The Westminster 'Budget', Mr. Rhodes—The Napoleon of South Africa*, from Maurice and Cooper, 1904 (own photo)

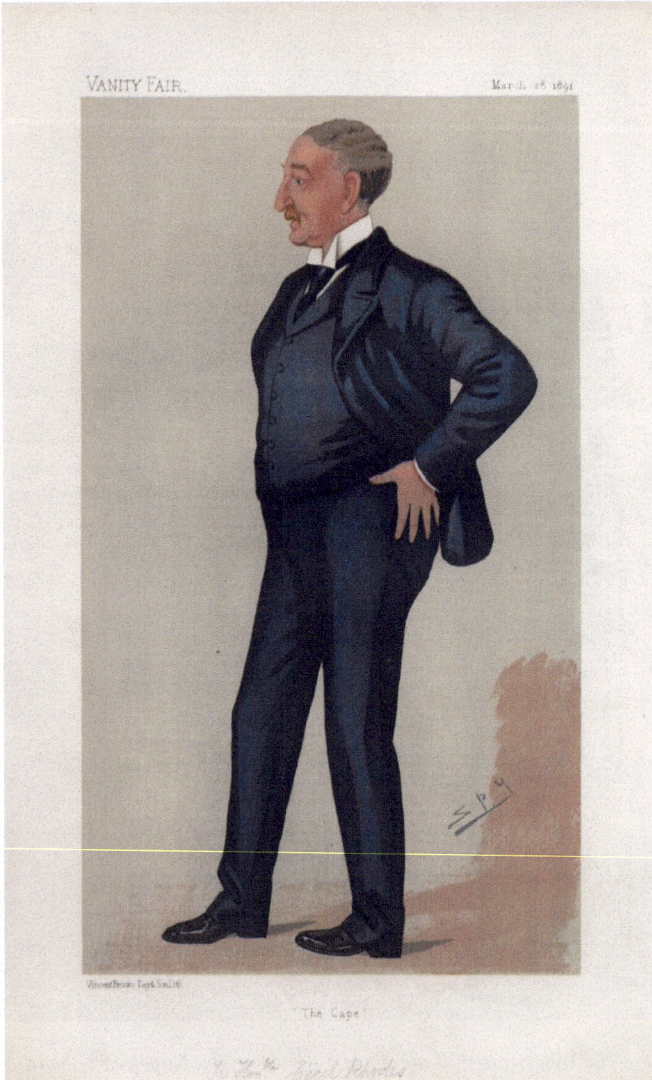

Fig. 6.40 *Vanity Fair*, *The Cape* (Cecil Rhodes), 28 March 1891 (Courtesy of NPG)

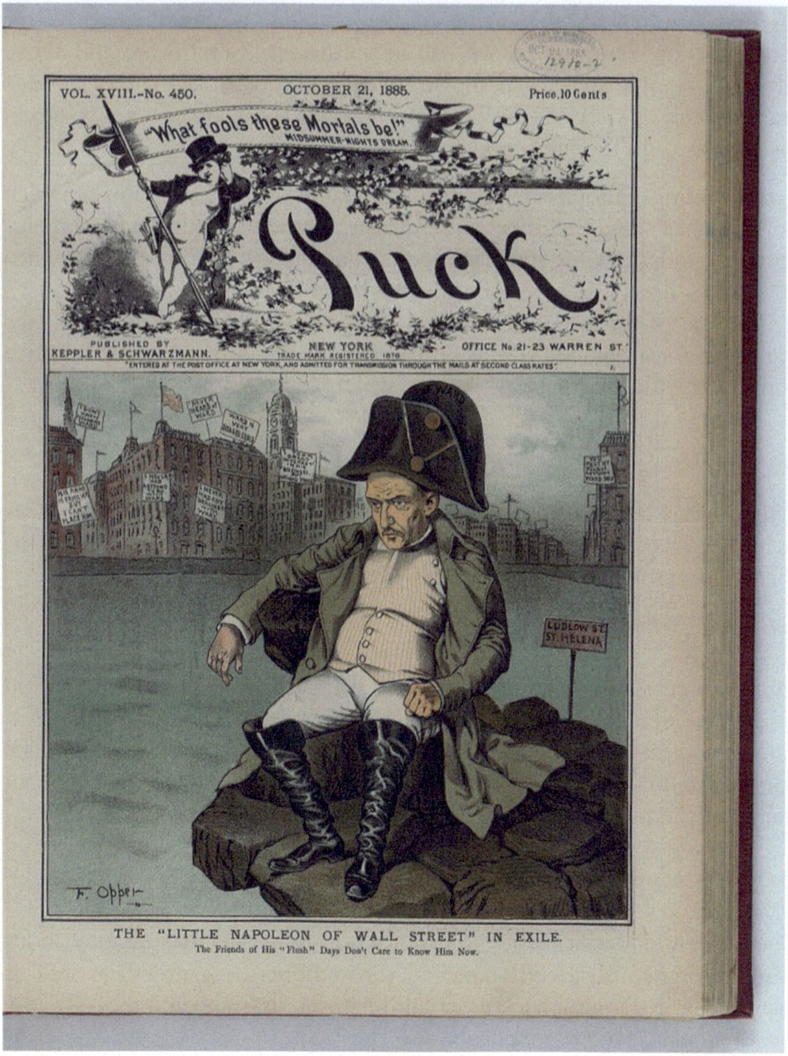

Fig. 6.41 *Puck, The little Napoleon of Wall Street in exile*, 21 October 1885 (Courtesy of LOC)

his inspiration from the image of the octopus as described in Victor Hugo's 1866 *Toilers of the sea*. 'In its softness and craftiness, and above all, in its terrible suckers, is the strength of the octopus. The octopus is crafty- when its victim is unsuspicious it opens suddenly and holds him in his its grasp, till the life-blood is sucked up'.

A grinning Balfour (identified by the name of the institution of which he was chairman, the Liberator Building Society) is depicted with his tentacles (all carrying the names of other failed institutions) about to envelope a desperate investor and drag him down (Fig. 6.42).

The use of the devil-fish imagery in *Musee des Horreurs* in 1899 (see Fig. 8.13 for a detailed review) is more dramatic and extremely negative compared with the image of Balfour which appeared in 1893.

6.3 Conclusion

This chapter has explored the various techniques that editors and artists used to convey the emotional consequences of financial crises, the events themselves as well as the impact on victims and villains.

Editorial Techniques

Editors used a variety of techniques to bring the events to the attention of their readers. The main novelty was using the front page of the realistic periodicals to highlight the events. The comic-serious periodicals, by contrast, emphasised the importance of the events by devoting the main image of the periodical's issue, normally the centre page.

Artistic Techniques

The review identifies the recurrence of financial iconography both contemporaneously (icons repeated throughout the century) as well as historically (harkening back to earlier financial disasters) and globally (the use of similar imagery in Europe and the US).

Moralistic comments are expressed mainly in relation to the portrayals in the comic periodicals (Frith's series of paintings, *Race for Wealth*, being the exception). In the case of the realistic periodicals the commentary is implicit rather than explicit—the setting of the image and the expressions on the faces of the individuals indicate the disapproval of the periodical.

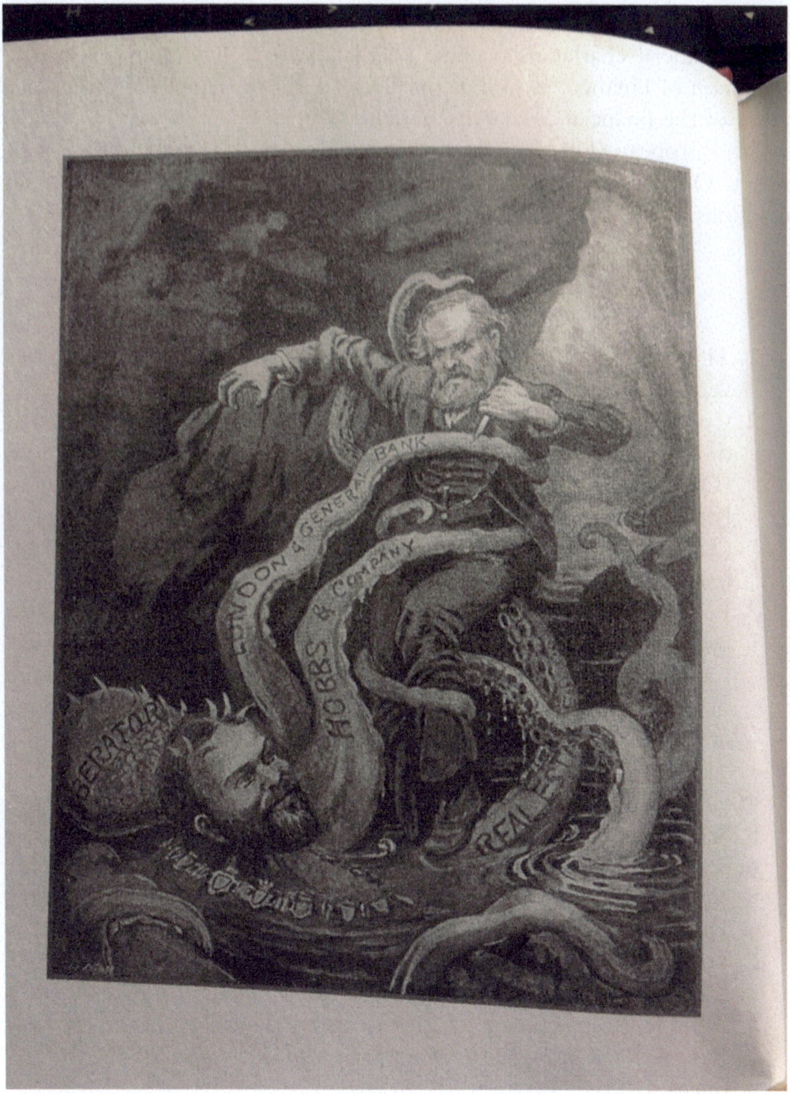

Fig. 6.42 *Review of reviews, The Devil-Fish of Today*, November 1893 (@ BL, GRC PP. 5939. c. 1892–1894)

As new journalism flourishes in the late 1870s more overt criticism of the financial charlatans occurs. This leads to recurrent tropes of the 'Napoleon of Finance' as well as the 'Devil-Fish' to depict the unsavoury nature of the financial charlatans' activities.

The European/US depictions are more satirical and starker in their impact. Only in the 1840s at the time of the railway mania do British depictions reach the visceral emotions of the later international cartoons.

Notes

1. This print is attributed by Besomi to 1858, though an earlier version is dated to 1837.
2. Currency School and Banking School debates of 1830s onwards discussed ways to try and prevent financial crises. Currency school (Overstone, McCulloch, Longfield, and Torrens) favoured note issuance (currency) limited by total gold reserves. Banking school (Tooke, Fullarton, and John Stuart Mill) argued that strict note-issuing restrictions were unnecessary.
3. Besomi argues that modern-day commentators used to 'business cycles' (Burns and Mitchell 1946) have misinterpreted Overstone's trade cycle as support for cycles of trade following one after the other. He argues that contemporary diagrams (Overstone, Longfield, Harvey) referred to the order in which events occurred, to a 'singular' notion of events which is not necessarily recurring.
4. Schama, *Embarrassment of Riches*, p. 150.
5. See De Goede for a detailed explanation of this phenomenon.
6. See *Punch, March of speculation*, 25 October 1845, *A doe in the city*, 1 November 1845, and *The momentous question*, 25 October 1845.
7. Turner, p. 107.
8. Ibid., p. 108. See also Larry Neal, 'The Financial Crisis of 1825 and the Restructuring of the British Financial System', *Federal Reserve Bank of St Louis*, May/June 1998, pp. 53–76.
9. Burns, p. 2.
10. https://babel.hathitrust.org/cgi/pt?id=mdp.39015069785262;view=1up;seq=313.
11. See Morton, p. 200.

12. BMSat.8990, *Gillray's Bank-Notes, –Paper-Money–French-Alarmists –o, the Devil, the Devil! –ah! poor John-Bull!!!*, 1797, at the time of suspension of cash payments of Bank of England paper at the height of war with the French.
13. *Punch*, *A modern Diagones looking for an honest man in Capel Court*, 8 November 1845, *A Railway Parliament*, 8 November 1845.
14. *Punch*, *The Post Office panic* 11 October 1845, *The railway committee man* 27 September, *The railway lunatic asylum*, 25 October 1845.
15. *Judy*, 'By order', 20 November 1878, which otherwise refrains from commenting on the CGB failure here provides a satire on the latest bank attire.
16. Charles Mackay, *Extraordinary Popular Delusions and the Madness of Crowds* (London, 1995)—original published 1852. See also Paul Crosthwaite, Peter Knight and Nicky Marsh (eds.), *Show Me the Money: The Image of Finance 1700 to the Present*, pp. 83/84.
17. Richard R. John, 'Robbers Baron Redux: Antimonolopy Reconsidered', *Enterprise & Society*, 13:1, 2012, pp. 1–38. https://muse.jhu.edu/article/467915.
18. See commentary on *Funny Folks*, *The Bank of Virtue and Vice* (Fig. 6.24) and the *Graphic*'s *Stoppage* (Fig. 6.34) later in this chapter.
19. Ibid., p.136. James Taylor commenting on Miles Taylor's article.
20. "Duck and drake, n". OED Online, March 2019. Oxford University Press. https://www.oed.com/view/Entry/58183?rskey=LhgATJ&result=1 (accessed May 10, 2019).
21. https://www.oed.com/view/Entry/147792?redirectedFrom=pop+goes+the+weasel#eid29227321.
22. Julian Treuherz, *Victorian Painting* (London, Thames & Hudson, 1993), p. 112. The author commented that many artists began to extend their narratives beyond 'the confines of a single time and place' using a serial format derived from Hogarth. Flint quotes Tom Taylor who wrote extensively on Frith and who commented on Frith's *Race for Wealth* as follows: just as Hogarth wrote 'I have endeavoured to treat my subjects as a dramatic writer; my picture is my stage', so 'These five pictures are to be looked at as the five acts of a domestic drama dealing with real life of the day'. See p. 233, FN 78–80.

23. William Frith, *My Autobiography and Reminiscences*, vol. 1 (1887/1888; repr., 2012), p. 144.
24. Martin Meisel, *Realizations Narrative, Pictorial, and Theatrical Arts in Nineteenth-Century England* (Princeton, NJ, Princeton University Press, 1983), p. 392.
25. https://ark.digitalcommonwealth.org/ark:/50959/9880w8480.
26. Fraser, p. 98.
27. Ibid., p. 268.
28. Stratmann, p. 132 quoting the *Economist*, 'The Hooley Failure', 30 July 1898, p. 1113.
29. The Balfour caricature appears in McKie, between pp. 162 and 163. I have been unable to obtain copyright permission to include the image in my book.
30. Fraser, p. 143.
31. Taylor, *Boardroom Scandal*, p. 225.
32. *Punch*, *The Irish devil-fish*, 23 May 1881.

CHAPTER 7

Women

7.1 Introduction

This book reflects a multi-layered view of depiction of female financial figures in the nineteenth century. It ranges from Harriot Coutts, the female head of the respected private bank, Coutts, which withstood the bank crisis of 1825, to depictions of female Goddesses of Justice in the 1870s and images of the Old Lady, representing the stability of the Bank of England. The consistent presence of female investors in financial cartoons of the Victorian age is testimony to the growing importance of women as a shareholding class.[1] *Punch* concentrates on the role of women in the household, subservient to the husband and ignorant of the cost of household expenditure.

7.1.1 The Role of Women

In the late eighteenth century women tended to be depicted in terms of their sexuality[2] and were considered fit only to occupy the private sphere because of it. In the nineteenth century, in the world of money and finance, women do play an important role, even as role models. Mrs Coutts, for all her finery and buxom figure, is extremely rich and there is no suggestion that there is anything wrong with that money. Angela Burdett-Coutts's philanthropic activities in the middle of the century

H. Sless, *Merchant Princes and Charlatans or Makers of Money?*,
https://doi.org/10.1007/978-3-030-86604-4_7

onwards were much admired, and her role in 'advancing' the bank was applauded.

The pictorial depiction of women in finance during the nineteenth century fall into the following categories:

Bankers, Philanthropists

The staggering wealth of Harriot Coutts and the success of her bank in withstanding the 1825 crisis is depicted in the early part of the century. This is followed by the depiction of Angela Burdett-Coutts, and her important role in Victorian philanthropy funded by her inherited banking wealth.

Goddesses of Justice

During the CGB failure and subsequent trial of its directors, images appear of female Goddesses of Justice representing paragons of virtue to which men should be aspiring.

This also includes, on one occasion during the Railway Mania, a cartoon featuring a worldly Queen Victoria admonishing her Consort Prince Albert on succumbing to the temptations of investing in shares.

The Old Lady of Threadneedle Street

The staid respectability of the Bank of England and its importance as an emerging lender of last resort in resolving financial crises. The use of an old woman, a wise crone, to represent the Bank dates to the Golden Age.

Investors

These are often depicted anonymously representing part of the overall investing class.

It also includes numerous images featuring female investors, sometimes quite prominently, adversely affected by the financial crises of the period.

Marriage

The role of married women in society at home, unworldly, features occasionally.

7.2 Bankers, Philanthropists

7.2.1 *Harriot Coutts*

Harriot Coutts (née Mellon) was the scion of the famous Coutts banking family. An actress, she first married the much older Thomas Coutts, the family member instrumental in creating the banking firm. Images commenting on her financial acumen are contrasted with other images making snide remarks about her appearance and greed in seeking to acquire status in society (on the death of Thomas, she married an aristocrat much younger than herself).

The analysis of a series of prints by Cruikshank describing the amorous affair of Harriot Coutts with the future Duke of St Albans reveals a complex picture of contemporary attitudes towards social advancement. Whilst George has analysed this series of prints individually, no one has analysed them as a series. The prints show the rising power of women in business, a facet of life that has not previously been identified.

Indeed, in one print Mrs Coutts is shown with Sir William Curtis in her bank vault surrounded by money bags (Fig. 4.8)—there is no suggestion of envy. In several satires on Mrs Coutts, though, her full figure is complemented by a moustached face.[3] Whilst this could imply ridicule (i.e., not taking care of her toilet), more probably it was to indicate her manliness—her stature as someone in charge of her business affairs. This is further accentuated by *A Visit to Court—or—*, in which Mrs Coutts is being introduced to Court, but instead of being introduced by her then lover the Earl of Burford, the latter acts as a fawning pageboy holding up the train of her dress. Mrs Fry, a member of the Quaker company, is satirised more because of her association with a failed pawn broking company than because of her sex.[4] However, the satire is not addressed at her charitable intentions generally, but more specifically in that she stands accused of pocketing the premium received on the initial subscription for the shares in the abortive company, rather than directing her efforts towards ensuring that the company did commence operations.

Harriot's marriage to Thomas Coutts was one of genuine affection despite their age difference (she was 38 when they married, and he was 82).[5] Perkin comments that Harriot was ridiculed/caricatured for having married someone older for money, for her extravagant lifestyle and her generous giving to the poor. Sir Walter Scott, however, regarded her with 'amused affection'.[6]

During the early 1820s she embarked on an amorous affair with the Earl of Burford, William Aubrey de Vere Beauclerk (1801–1849), later to become Duke of St Albans. She married him in 1827 when she was 50 and he was 26.

Figure 7.1 is a typical complex satire of the period replete with puns. The description of the love affair between Harriot and the future Duke of St Albans is couched in terms of money meeting aristocracy. Money trumps—the scale on the left weighs heavier than the one on the right. The choice of the melon reflected the satirist's depiction of Harriot as a woman of an ample figure, and also provided the opportunity for a number of puns: on her maiden name (Mellon), and on the importance of the dowry (a million) that she brought with her to the marriage. These 'assets' outweighed those of the young Duke who brought with him, by contrast, his aristocratic title and position in society.

Whilst high-profile amorous affairs invited comic satire, this did not mean that the messages conveyed were trivial or unimportant. The staggering wealth of Mrs Coutts made her one of the richest bankers in England, Rothschild being the only one of her contemporaries significantly wealthier. The monied classes had really 'arrived' in society: only a small number of wealthy landowners had more money, and that was based on income from landed estates rather than commercial interests.

7.2.2 *Angela Burdett-Coutts*

In the words of Edward VII, 'after my mother [she was] the most remarkable woman in the country'.[7]

In many ways Angela Burdett-Coutts's life was to imitate that of her step grandmother. She remembered her aunt's happiness in her life with Thomas. The happiness was echoed in her own deep friendship with the Duke of Wellington (it is said that she proposed to him but that he declined politely). In 1844 he was 76, and she was 30.

In an ironic twist, in 1881 she married William Lehmann Ashmead Bartlett, when she was 66 and he was 29. As a result of a stipulation in her step grandmother's will that she should not marry a foreign national, she forfeited three-fifths of her inheritance to her sister.

Healey comments that in her early years she took advice from the Duke of Wellington on how to understand and take care of money, and from Charles Dickens on how to spend it.[8] The Duke advised her to learn the banking business by 'go[ing] through the stationary accounts'. Dickens

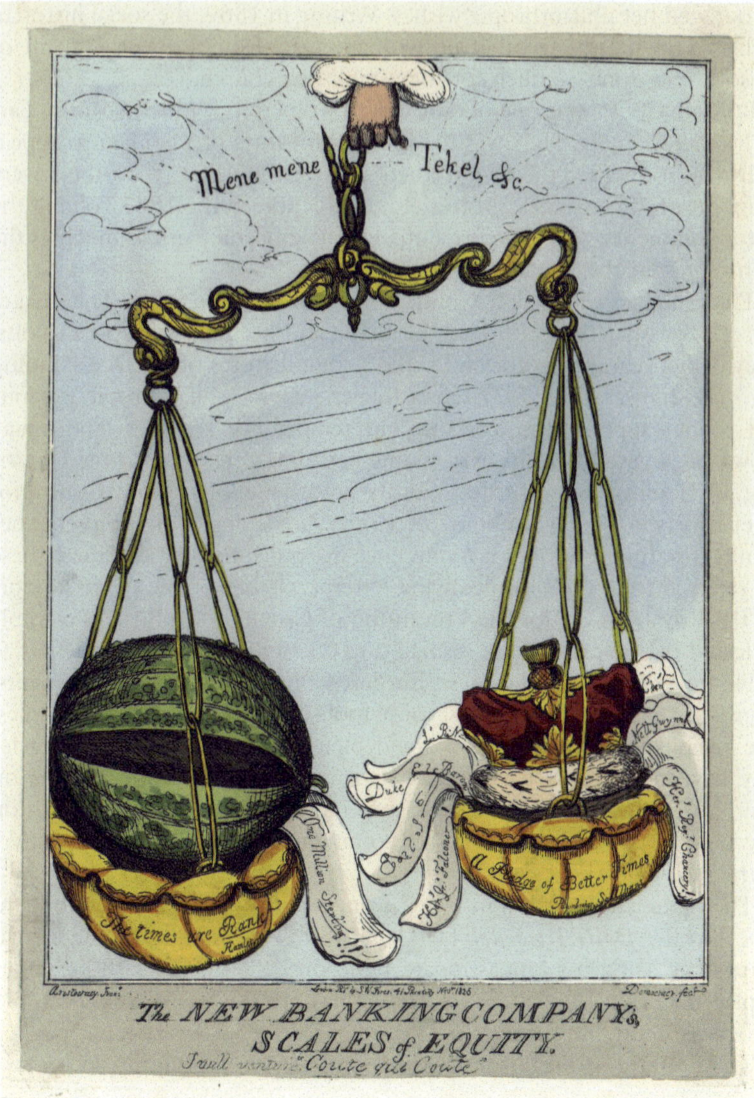

Fig. 7.1 BM14876, *The New Banking Company's Scales of Equity*, Coute qui Coute (Courtesy of BM)

encouraged her philanthropic wishes. Writing in 1869, the social historian William Howitt asserted that no woman, apart from a queen regnant or consort, had done as much for the established church.[9]

Burdett-Coutts was one of only eleven women to feature in *Vanity Fair* in the Victorian era. Hers was the fourth caricature of a woman to appear in 1883—soon after the first women appeared in 1882 (the others were members of the aristocracy). In the introduction to the 1883 volume the editor comments: 'Ladies represent[ing] the graceful truth as much as the Men represent the Brutal truth'.

Three images of Burdett Coutts appear over eleven years. The images reflect her association with both her bank and her philanthropic exploits. They depict her ageing gracefully, the strong features of her face standing out. *The Hornet* (Fig. 7.2) refers to her general philanthropic pursuits and to her support for working and temperance societies (the image shows beggars and drunkards taking her alms). The *Monetary Gazette* (Fig. 7.3) shows how Burdett-Coutts used her money from Coutts for relief efforts in Turkey. In Fig. 7.4, *Vanity Fair*'s depiction represents her dignified stature, but does not reference her philanthropic activities (these are referred to in the accompanying letterpress—see below). Her support for the Royal Society for the Prevention of Cruelty to Animals is possibly indicated by the presence of a small dog on a plush chair to her left.

Figure 7.2 depicts Baroness Burdett-Coutts' philanthropic pursuits. There is some irony in the use of a fool's cap to disburse the monies. The recipients of this largesse are depicted using whatever receptacles they have to hand (a hat, the folds of a skirt) to take the monies on offer. Yet iconographically a fool's cap indicates the folly of speculation (see Fig. 6.2)—perhaps the artist is commenting cynically on the motives of the recipients.

The dignified depiction in Fig. 7.3 appeared shortly after her eloquent appeal in the *Daily Telegraph* (13 August 1877) which led to the formation of the Turkish Compassionate Fund on behalf of Turkish peasantry displaced during the Russo-Turkish War (note the use of the icon of a lifebelt to signify financial help).

The Letterpress on Burdett-Coutts indicated her stature in society:

> heir to a 'stupendous income, 'she occupied herself with the affairs of the bank, and therein displayed a shrewdness and a judgment rare in woman.' Philanthropist….'she is altogether a good woman'.[10]

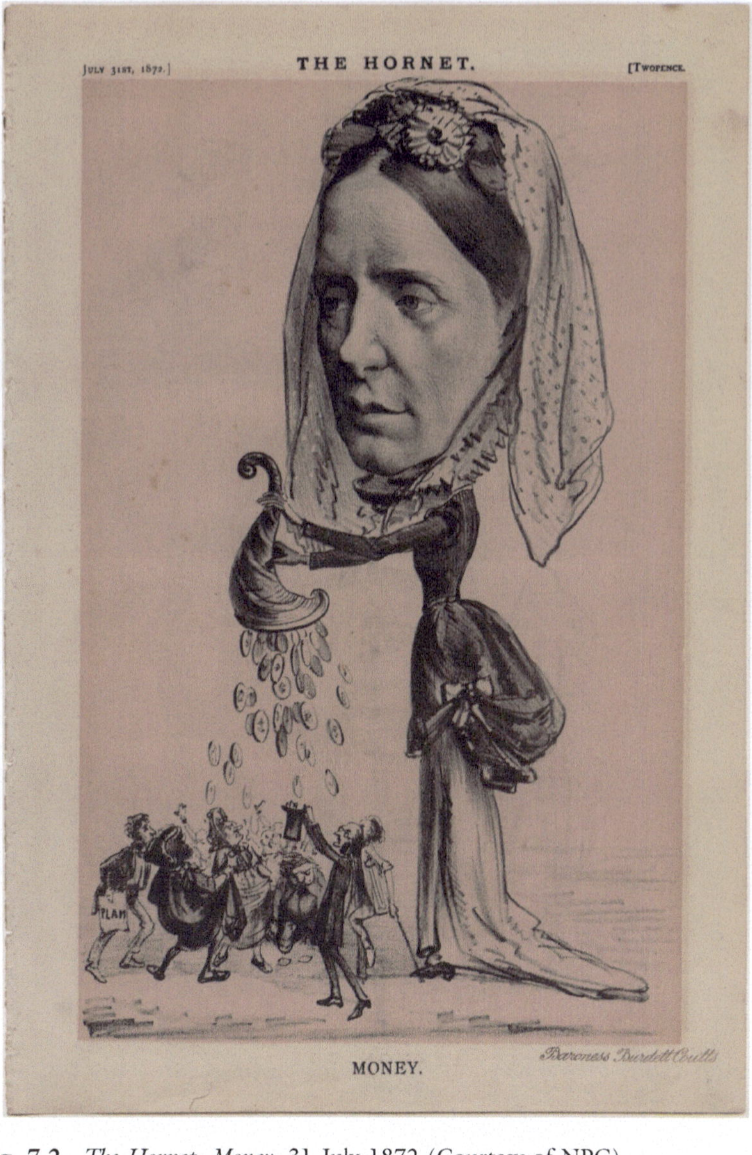

Fig. 7.2 *The Hornet*, *Money*, 31 July 1872 (Courtesy of NPG)

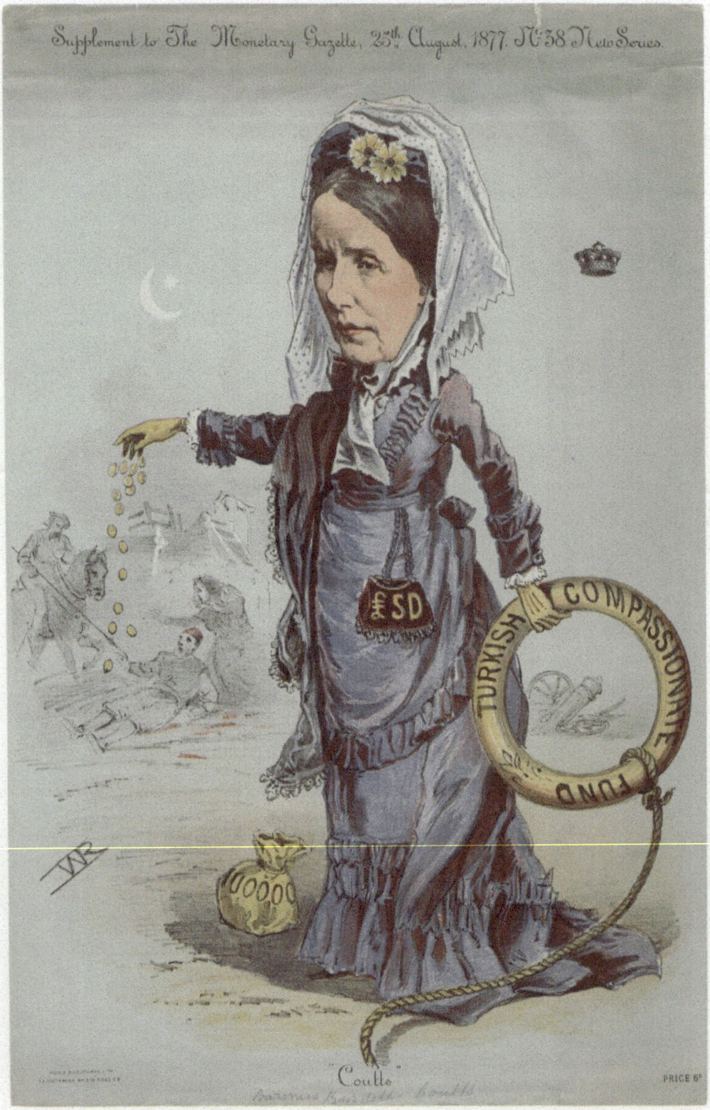

Fig. 7.3 *Monetary Gazette*, *Coutts*, 25 August 1877 (Courtesy of NPG)

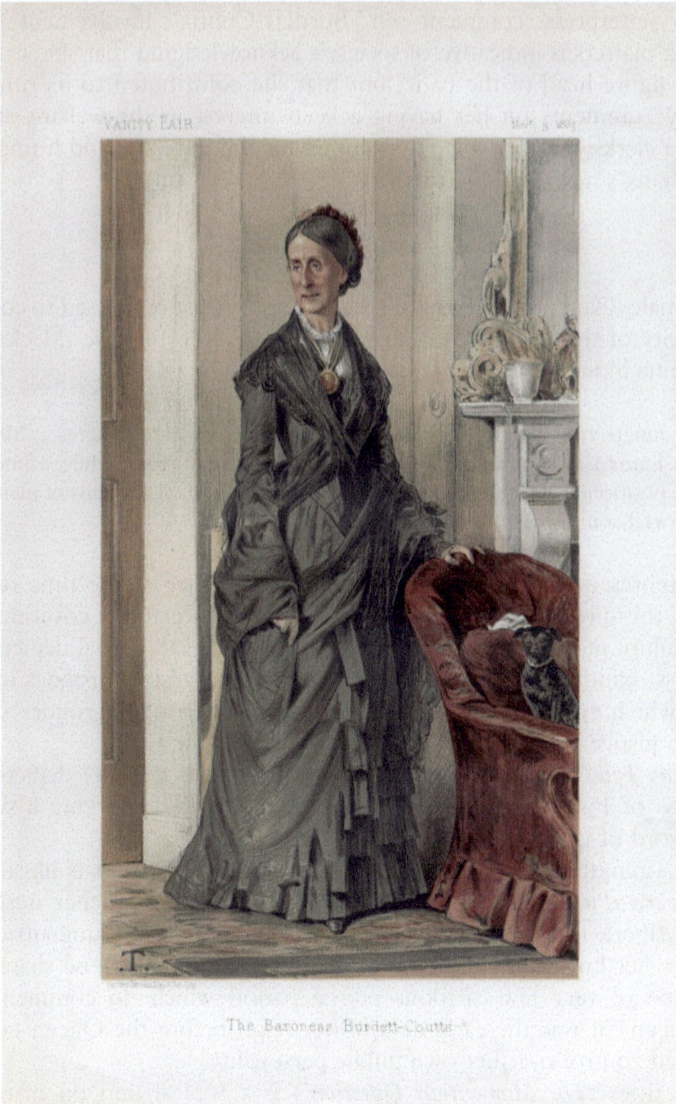

Fig. 7.4 *Vanity Fair*, *The Baroness Burdett-Coutts*, 3 November 1883 (Courtesy of NPG)

The letterpress comment on Burdett-Coutts' involvement with banking matters is indicative of society's acknowledging that she was not a mere figure-head of the bank, but that she contributed to its running (Healey comments on her having a keen interest in the welfare of her banking clerks, and her role in arranging for the purchase and fitting out of the bank's new headquarters).

7.3 Goddesses

The female divine, in the form of the Goddess of Justice, is used to convey the purity of the female as compared with the corrupt male. Mackenzie comments indirectly on the female nature of the divine:

> Mid nineteenth century saw the emergence of separate spheres.....Men were figured as competitors in the amoral, economic realm while women were positioned either as decorative trophies or spiritual guardians of men's immortal souls.[11]

Fun's representation of a female Goddess of Justice at the time of the trial of the directors of O&G is repeated in the cartoons covering the CGB failure nine years later. An image during the O&G trial depicts the Goddess, blindfolded, holding both financial and criminal rogues in her hand, which symbolises her even-handedness in bringing rogues of all sorts to justice.[12]

Funny Folks's '*A Question of Precedence*' (see Fig. 9.14) depicts the Goddess of Justice, strong, feminine, but in this case carrying a sword (the sword of vengeance).

The strength of the female in handling financial matters is illustrated in an early *Punch* cartoon involving Queen Victoria and her husband Prince Albert. In Fig. 7.5, *Punch* depicts Queen Victoria asking anxiously whether her husband, Prince Albert had bought any of 'those shares'.[13] It is one of very few cartoons of the period which do comment on the Queen—it was the early days of her reign before the Queen herself exercised control over her own public personality.

The title ('*The Momentous Question*') is a topical pun on marriage (it was after all Queen Victoria who as sovereign asked Prince Albert to marry her—popping the question). Albert's hunting attire references his stag-hunting exploits, which were reported in the press at the time (see also comments on the use of stags as a financial icon in the next

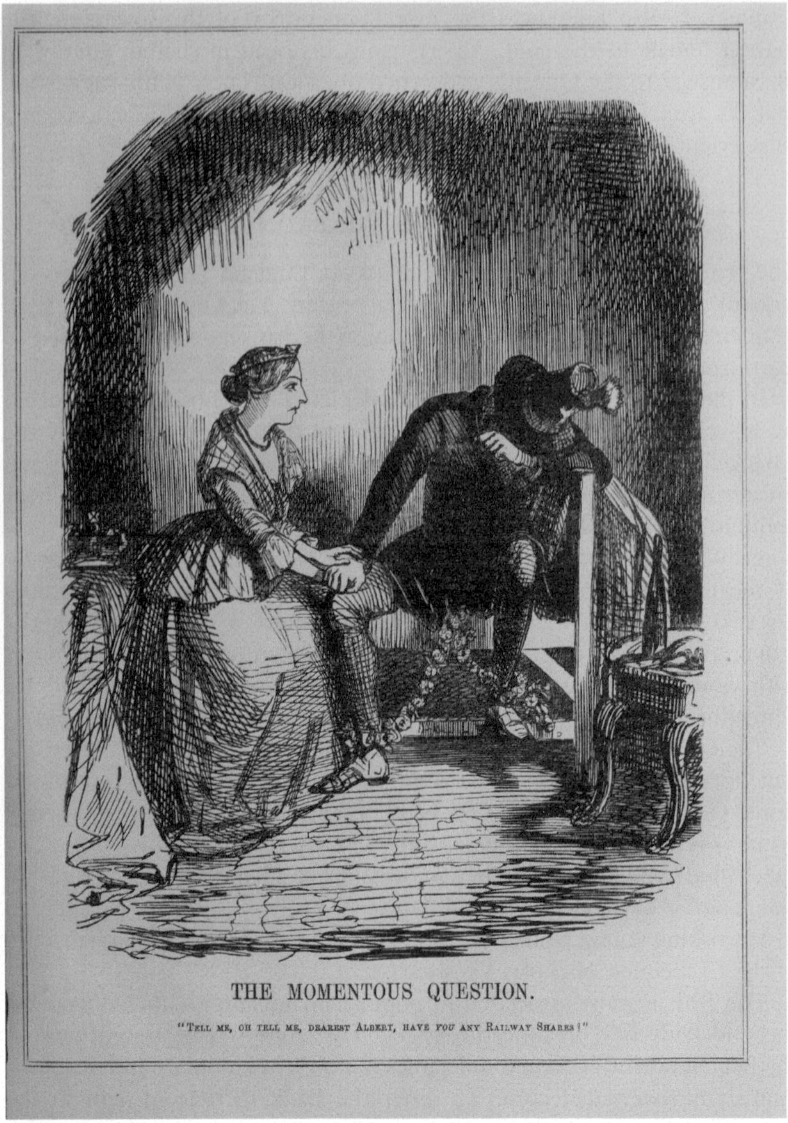

Fig. 7.5 *Punch*, *The Momentous Question*, 25 October 1845 (Courtesy of UoH)

chapter). It also references the moral superiority of the sovereign, the highest female in the land. Albert hangs his head in shame, guiltily, in silent answer to the Queen's concerned question. There is the suggestion that his attire depicts him in chains, held to account for his actions, and subservient to his Queen.

7.4 The Old Lady of Threadneedle Street

The female personification of the Bank of England (BoE)puts the old woman, the crone, on a dais of financial probity. The Old Lady is depicted frequently admonishing her errant pupils (the bankers who have failed to learn from her).

In the case of the BoE, women are depicted both positively and negatively—either the old crone,[14] or a bejewelled lady being wooed by the Chancellor of the Exchequer.[15] In the latter case, the Chancellor has sinister intentions because the print was produced while a parliamentary committee was looking into the conduct of the BoE, and so the lady is really being viewed as not all that pure. Nevertheless, the association of the institution of the BoE with a woman and a crone is revealing for two reasons. First, that the institution itself is associated with the female rather than the male sex, implying that monies are synonymous with women, and second, the character of the crone. The 'Old Lady of Threadneedle Street' which Gillray drew in 1797 in *Political-Ravishment, or The Old Lady of Threadneedle-Street in danger!* is now the old crone. But does the description of a crone carry positive or negative connotations? George refers to 'the Old Lady of Threadneedle Street, an ancient crone' (as in the Gillray 1797 print). 'Crone' connotes miserliness and age,[16] but could it also represent wisdom as in modern-day usage? In *Symptoms of Crim.Con!!!*, a slightly earlier print, the BoE is represented by a ravishing young woman who is being flattered by the then Chancellor of the Exchequer, Nicholas Vansittart.

The BoE is most associated in popular imagination with the trope of the Old Lady of Threadneedle Street. The trope can be traced back to the late eighteenth century and James Gillray's infamous commentary on Peel's controversial decision to order the Bank to redeem debt in the form of paper notes rather than the previous method of paying in gold. Throughout the nineteenth century, the trope is invoked to comment on financial crises, whether generically (without commenting on a specific event) or specifically (commenting on a specific event which, though never named, is implied by the timing of the cartoon).

One important variation is the treatment of the BoE. As Poovey puts it: 'Womening the Bank feminine was conventional in the nineteenth century; ever since James Gillray had used the phrase in an anti-government cartoon as 'the Lady of Threadneedle Street'.[17] Not only was the symbol of financial authority feminine (albeit as an old crone), but the written perception also mirrored this. Poovey quotes McCullough's 147-page encyclopaedia entry on banks in the 1859 edition of his Dictionary: 'Where individuals were weak, powerless they were feminised persons living on fixed income, women, labourers, minors. Where they were strong they were masculinised merchants, bankers, and money-dealers'.[18]

Poovey noted a contradiction: 'Representing the Bank as a woman, of course, did not imply that the institution was weak; instead, like Queen Victoria, the Bank of England could be a martial mother, like Britannia, the female figure, whose image each note bore'.[19] While people generally thought of the Bank as strong, and secure financially, this association contrasted ironically with the physical depiction of the bank—the figure of the old frail crone.

Intriguingly although the BoE became involved belatedly in sorting out the 1825 crisis, there are no images at the time of the Old Lady and the BoE's role. It is the advent of *Punch* in 1841 which sees the trope used firstly to comment on the actions that the Bank undertook to contain the impact of credit squeezes, where suspension of Bank Charter Act of 1844 was required on many occasions to maintain the liquidity of the money market. Secondly, it is used to convey the Bank's disapproval of the activities of bank directors who had caused the BoE to intervene to allay market concerns.

Thus, the apparently cyclical (at least in contemporary eyes) occurrence of BoE interventions, 1846, 1857, 1866, resulted in images appearing mainly in *Punch*, but also in *Fun* in 1866[20] (Table 7.1).

The chart shows that images of the Old Lady appear in response to the financial crises/bank failures of 1846/1847 (the RM collapse), the financial run on the banks post 1856, 1866 (the crisis caused by the O&G failure, and 1890 (when BoE stepped in to organise a rescue fund to be funded by other banks but ultimately guaranteed by BoE on behalf of the government). There is no image for 1878 when the CGB failed because the BoE was not called upon to provide credit facilities; instead, the crisis was resolved by other Scottish banks stepping in to provide extra credit.

Table 7.1 Images of Old Lady by periodical

Publication	*Number of images*	*Year*	*Financial Crisis*
Punch	2	1846/1847	RM
Punch	1	1857	US
Fun	1	1866	O&G
Punch	1	1890	Barings

The characterisation of the Old Lady underwent several iterations during this period. The 25 September 1847 image below (Fig. 7.6) is at the start of the 1847 crisis. Peel is shown desperately trying to maintain the Bank's reserves at £8,915,072.[21] To achieve this, he tightens her waist (a pun on the financial expression 'tightening the money supply'). Her skirt is threatening to burst—i.e., the Bank was being pressed to provide credit, but it was restrained because of the Bank Charter Act. The words being spoken by the Old Lady imply that the bank will go under unless the government allows it to 'loosen' its monetary policy (i.e., to provide credit). The visual depiction of 'tightening' (Peel is depicted trying to prevent the Old Lady's skirts bursting by pulling her waist tight) is juxtaposed against the monetary policy of 'loosening' (or easing), which is described merely in words.

Just over a month later, there is another image of the Old Lady (6 November, see Fig. 7.7), a rare one in that she is not depicted wearing glasses. This time her disposition appears more matronly, as she doles out a soothing syrup (lots of it!) to soothe the cries of the Government (Peel and his nanny). The visual pun arises from the financial expression 'doling out'—in the context of providing credit (here £3m).[22]

In Fig. 7.8, St Stephen's is a reference to the Houses of Parliament, newly built on the site of the former hospital, with Lord Palmerston accompanying the Old Lady. The Old Lady wears the familiar wide crinoline skirt, and her pinafore has banknotes printed on its front referring to the need to provide cash to ease the credit crisis. The cartoon is dated 5 December, i.e., after the crisis had abated. The word 'doctor' is used metaphorically to indicate the Old Lady's needing medical (here financial) help provided by parliament. As befitted the technical requirement for BoE intervention, the text refers to the Old Lady being grateful to the government (in the form of Lord Palmerston) for help in the crisis. Technically the issue of notes by the Bank in the previous weeks had been

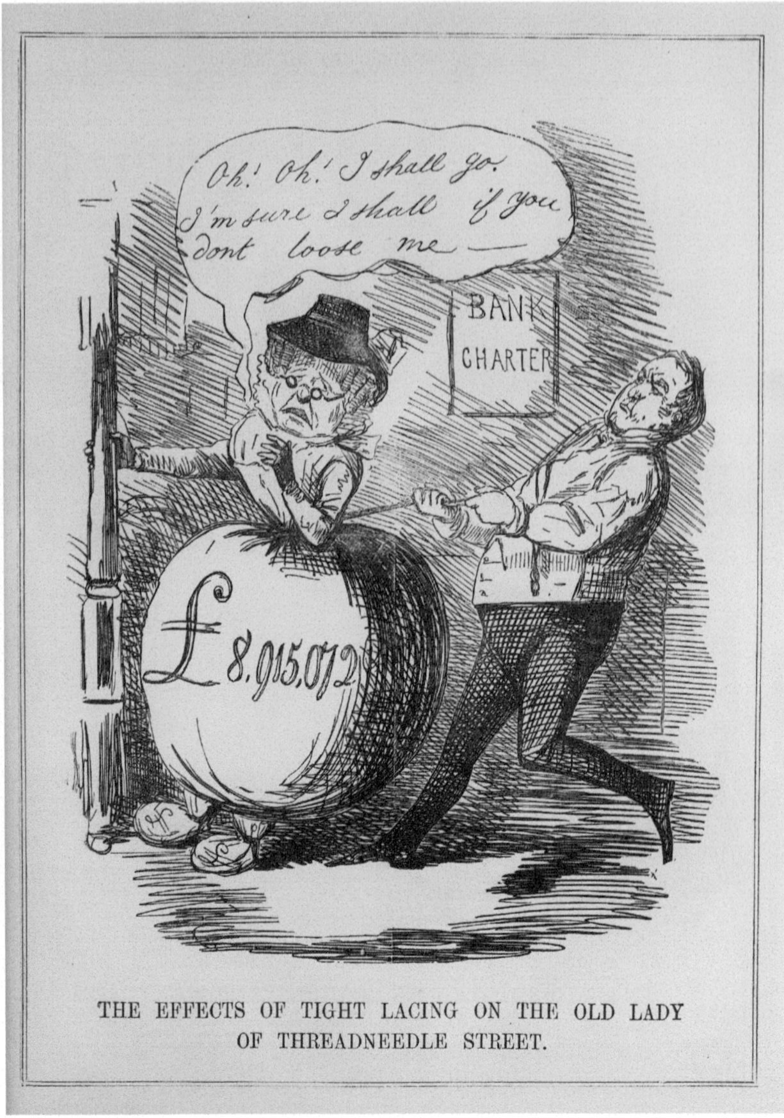

THE EFFECTS OF TIGHT LACING ON THE OLD LADY
OF THREADNEEDLE STREET.

Fig. 7.6 *Punch, The Effects of Tight Lacing on the Old Lady of Threadneedle Street*, 25 September 1847 (Courtesy of UoH)

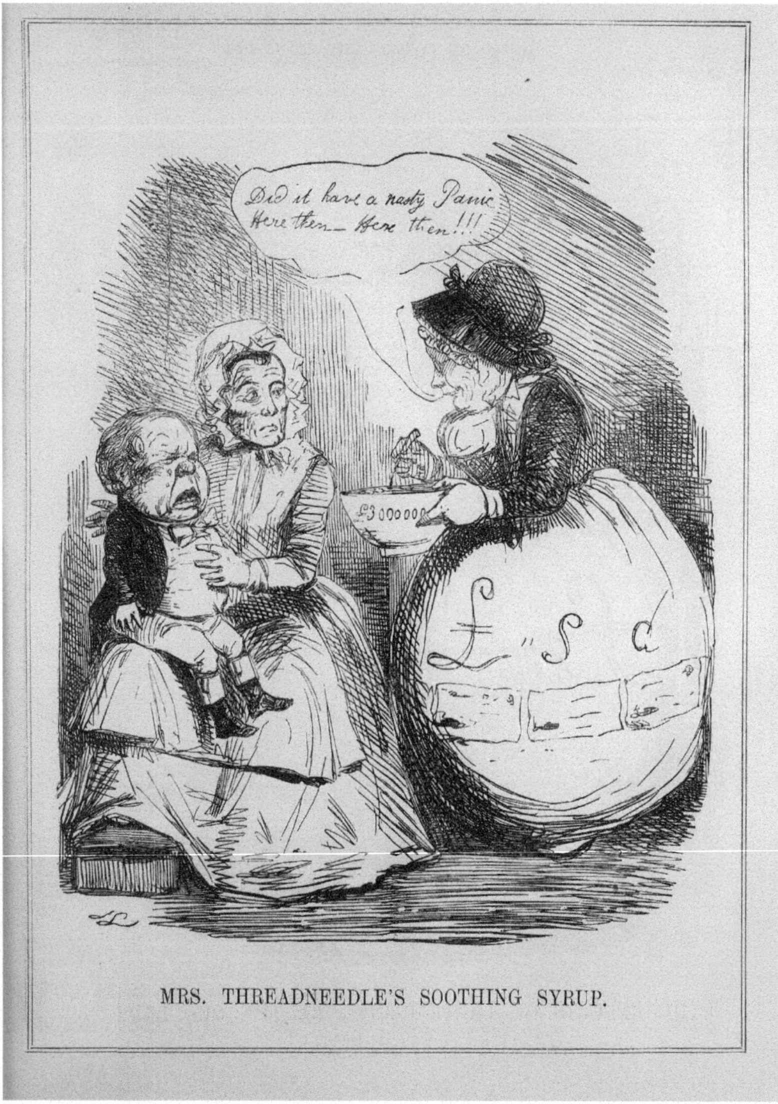

Fig. 7.7 *Punch*, *Mrs Threadneedle's Soothing Syrup*, 6 November 1847 (Courtesy of UoH)

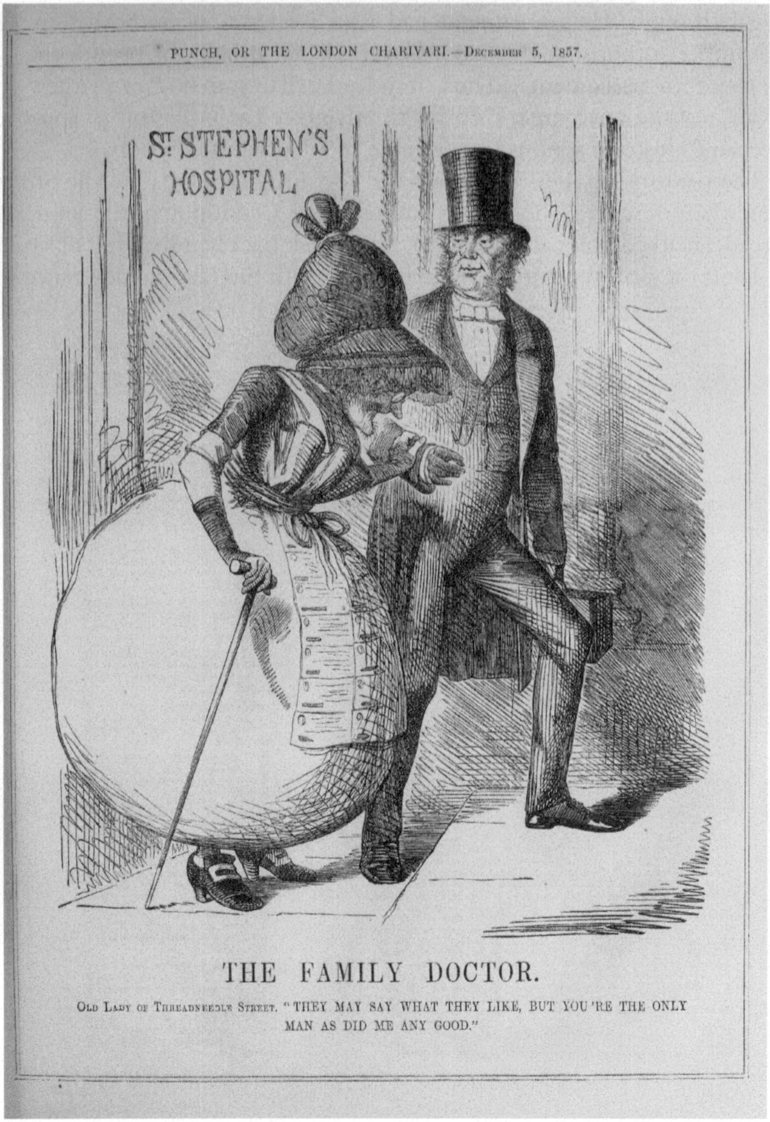

Fig. 7.8 *Punch, The Family Doctor*, 5 December 1857 (Courtesy of UoH)

illegal (though the government had issued a letter of authority on 12 November authorising the actions of the bank, it had not been formally approved in parliament). Thus, it is more likely that *Punch* knew in advance of the government's plans to introduce the provision to approve the bank's historic actions (an example of a journalistic 'scoop').[23]

The next image, Fig. 7.9 shows the Old Lady of Threadneedle Street somewhat obscured, holding a knitted sock (continuing the pun on thread), marked gold, and about to exchange it for a handbag full of silver. In 1860 the BoE was forced to do business with the Banque de France to

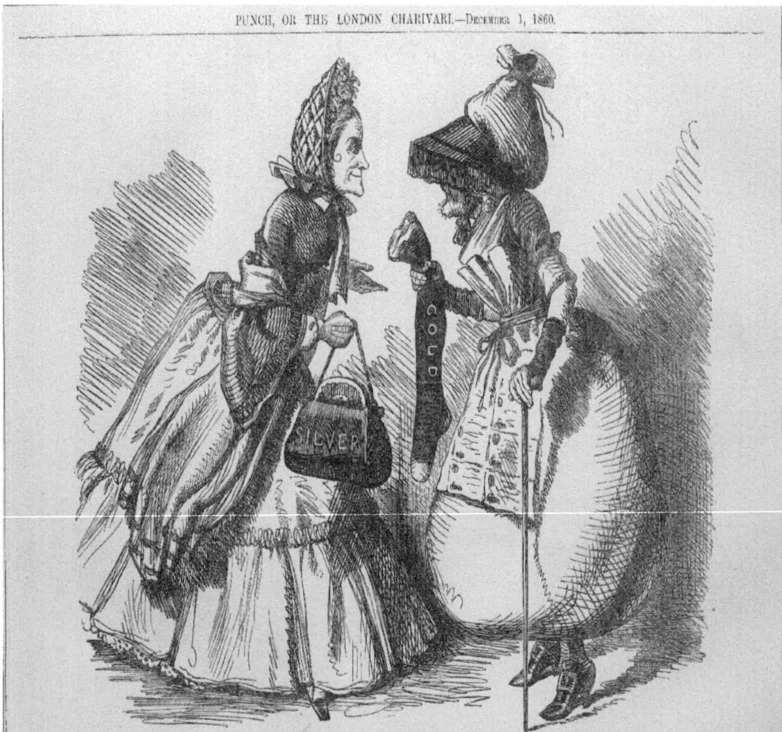

Fig. 7.9 *Punch, Mutual Accommodation*, 1 December 1860 (Courtesy of UoH)

avoid a liquidity crisis which was emerging from the late 1850s. The title '*Mutual Accommodation*' also alludes to a financial pun (accommodation being the need to find financial solutions to a credit crisis).

The Old Lady is depicted in an unflattering pose (with a veil obscuring her face which has traces of stubble on her chin) whereas the Old Lady of France is smartly dressed (both women, however, in large billowy dresses—referencing the crinoline mania pioneered by *Punch* a few years earlier).[24] Madame La Banque is shown carrying a handbag, somewhat smarter and almost certainly a contemporary fashion symbol, as compared with the clichéd knitted sock of the Old Lady of Threadneedle Street.

In Fig. 7.10, it is *Fun* which provides the image of the Old Lady at the time of the O&G failure with a pun on the word 'stock(ing)'. The Old Lady of Threadneedle Street is depicted darning a sock with the word 'Reserve' on it, representing Bank reserves. It is like the *Punch* image at time of the Barings rescue almost twenty-five years later (see Fig. 7.11) The pun plays on the domesticity of the Old Lady's activities (darning a stocking) and the reference to 'stock', i.e., shares, refers to investors' savings in bank stocks being safe—unlike the monies invested in O&G. Here the glasses are back in fashion together with the sock representing the reserves of the Bank of England. In keeping with more domestic imagery, the picture is reminiscent of a school mistress or nanny admonishing her young charges (her naughty boys, the bankers).

The rescue of Barings bank was completely different. Here the Governor of the Bank of England, William Lidderdale, played a pivotal role in keeping the markets calm. The only image depicting the events is a direct copy of the *Fun* cartoon some twenty-four years earlier (as well as a photograph of Lidderdale in *ILN*—see Chapter 4).

As a general point, the speed of the actual collapse of the bank, and the secretive successful attempt to retain public confidence in the financial system, militated against sustained press commentary. The commentary centred around the 'noble' actions of the Barings family in accepting total financial responsibility for the imprudent actions of their bank.

The only visual evidence in relation to the collapse of Barings is a *Punch* cartoon of 1890 which, in keeping with the tradition of attacking the financial community anonymously, merely shows the Old Lady of Threadneedle Street once more admonishing her pupils (the banking community) for engaging in speculation (Fig. 7.11). Yet again, the Victorian view of banking is shown to be ambivalent—praise when the financial system works (legitimate investment), but opprobrium where it fails

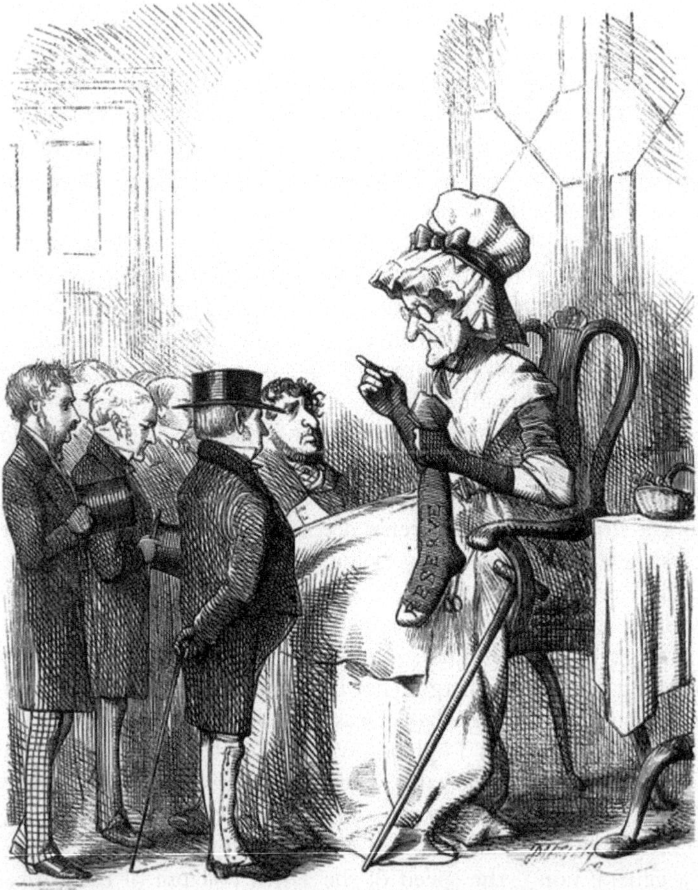

A BANK STOCK(ING).

The Old Lady of Threadneedle Street:—"NOW, MY YOUNG FRIENDS, LET THIS BE A WARNING TO YOU AGAINST RASH SPECULATION. WHAT WOULD YOU HAVE DONE BUT FOR MY LITTLE SAVINGS?"

Fig. 7.10 *Fun, A Bank Stock(ing)*, 26 May 1866 (Courtesy of UoF)

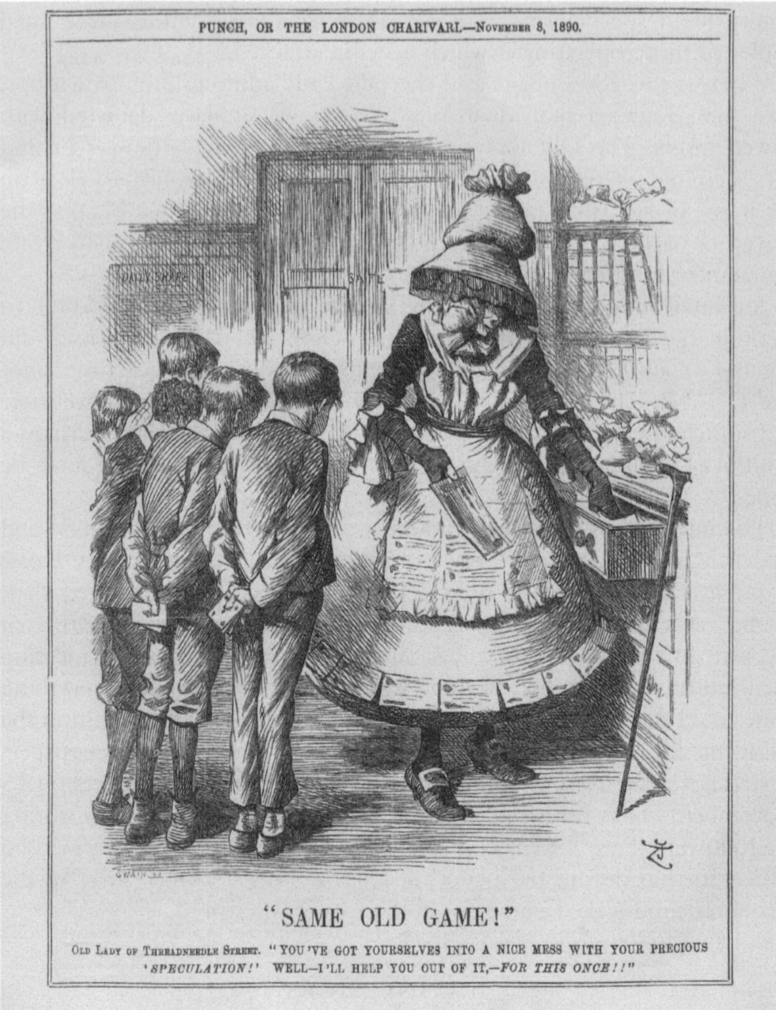

Fig. 7.11 *Punch, Same Old Game!*, 8 November 1890 (Courtesy of UoH)

(improvident speculation). It is not so much the system as the human foibles of those operating it which is being attacked.

Whereas the 1866 image had the Old Lady admonishing grown-ups, here the disgraced individuals are schoolboys, similarly depicted with bowed heads. The Old Lady is taking a cheque from a drawer behind her. Seemingly it represents help to the financial community to clear up the mess. In fact, the cheque was no more than a guarantee because the Governor of the BoE persuaded the financial community at large to create a guarantee fund of its own.

An interesting question is why *Punch* was the only periodical to mention the crisis. How did it get the scoop when the crisis itself did not unfold until the following weekend? Rumours had been rife since mid-October. The probability is that, by the end of October, Revelstoke had sufficiently swallowed his pride to take into his confidence perhaps a handful of leading figures who, in turn, realised that something must be done.[25]

The inference is that the rumours circulating from mid-October, and especially knowledge of a critical meeting on 2 November, led *Punch* to publish its cartoon the following Saturday because it believed that, as the crisis was over, it was appropriate merely to show the role of the BoE in sorting out the mess. Although another important meeting occurred on 8 November, nothing was resolved at that time. Everything came to a head on the weekend of 15/16 November with resolution the following Monday. Banerjee demonstrates that US regional newspapers started coverage from the time of the meeting of London Bankers on 15 November, whilst British newspapers provided commentary only during the following days.[26] Kynaston concluded that the British press practised self-censorship during the period 8–15 November.[27] Once news of the guarantee fund leaked out, calm in the City was restored.

7.5 Investors

> *Widows confided their all to them*, as men of high Christian repute. Guardians gave into their charge the funds of orphan children. *Lonely women, who knew nothing of business, taking them for good men and true, cast their money into their treasury.* [*my italics*]
>
> —From *The Scotsman*, in relation to the CGB failure[28]

Women are depicted during all the financial crises (other than the failure of Barings in 1890).

At the time of the Railway Mania, *The Railway Juggernaut of 1845* (Fig. 6.6) depicts the prominent figure of a female investor carrying bags of gold coin, dressed in black (in mourning)—a symbol of the increasing importance of widow investors or the typical use of women to provoke emotional distress at the outcome of events?

In the *British Brigand's Bank* (Fig. 6.32), at the time of the Royal British Bank failure in 1856, the presence in the picture of two women, one with a veil, one without, indicates again in stylistic terms the prominence of women investors in the bank.

ILN's front page image of the O&G failure in 1866 (Fig. 6.13), depicts a strategically placed solitary female investor in the foreground on the right.

Punch's '*Committed for Trial*' (Fig. 7.12) portrays the impact of the failure on poor shareholders (especially the daughter of the eponymous father). By this time, early 1869, the O&G directors were being committed for trial.

7.6 Marriage

The role of women in the financial discussion around marriage began with the image of Queen Victoria and her scolding of her husband on his foolish speculation at the time of the Railway Mania in 1845.

Punch's *A Doe in the City* (see Fig. 7.13) depicts a young doe-eyed woman's wealth/dowry, represented by the newly increased (potential) value of her railway shares. The uncertain nature of her money is ignored by the young beau who is writing to 'Mr Punch', and who is seduced by the prospect of her paper wealth.

Fun uses the circumstances of the CGB failure specifically to place women in domestic settings where they are perceived as unaware of the financial constraints they are imposing on the household. In *The Effects of the Commercial Crisis* (Fig. 7.14) women (and children) are also seen as naïve—e.g., there is a pun,'going to the dogs', in which a child overhears her father telling her mother that they 'are going to the dogs' (i.e. losing their monies) as a result of the commercial crisis; she interprets this in terms of her parents planning to watch the dog racing, so she asks to come too.[29]

In *Re The Glasgow Bank* (Fig. 7.15), wives are seen to incur 'unlim-

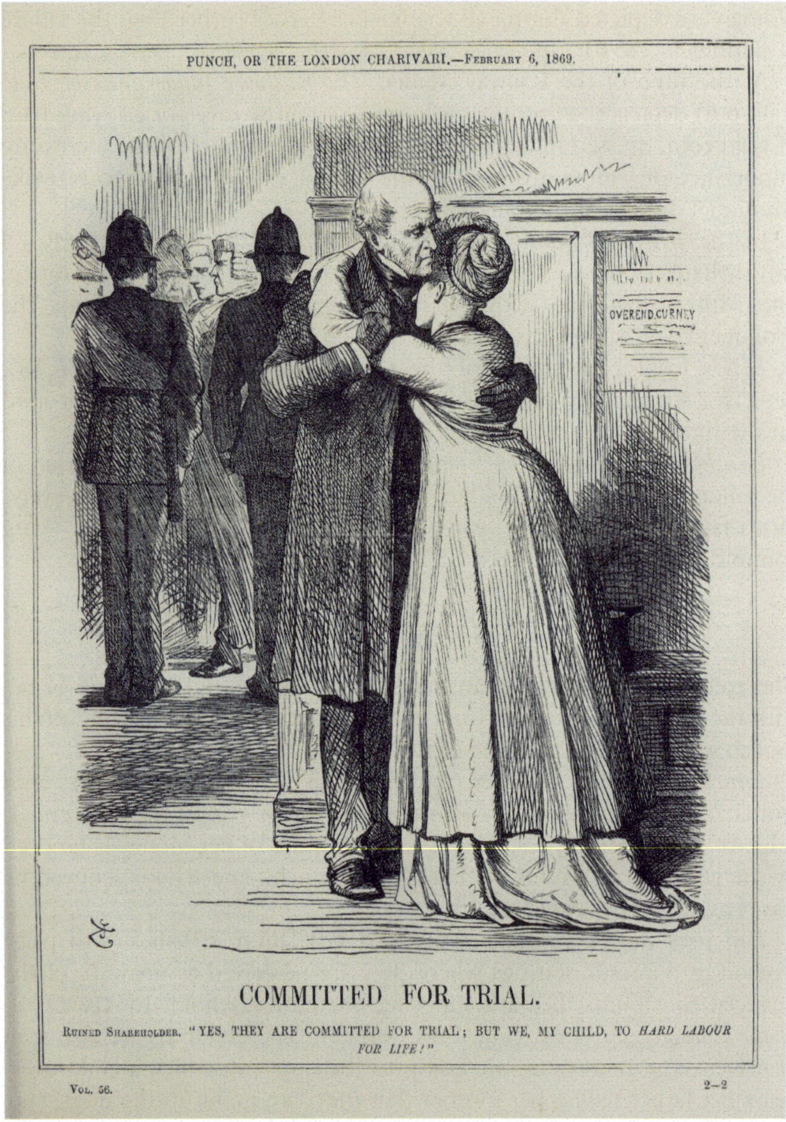

Fig. 7.12 *Punch*, *Committed for Trial*, 6 February 1869 (Courtesy of UoH)

A DOE IN THE CITY.

"Dear Mr. Punch,— "*Holborn Hill, Settling-day, Oct.* 30, 1845.

"As I was going down Stagg Alley yesterday, to sign the Great Didland deed, I saw the prettiest little Brougham in the world pull up at Horn Street—and the sweetest little love of a figure you ever saw, step out of the vehicle. Her appearance created quite a sensation among the stagging gents, and caused even *me* to pause and look round.

"Greatly to my surprise, this lovely young lady tripped by me, walked into the Didland Office, where up comes all the clerks crowding and grinning about her, and signed the deed with the greatest coolness in the world; I peeped over her shoulder, and saw her write—

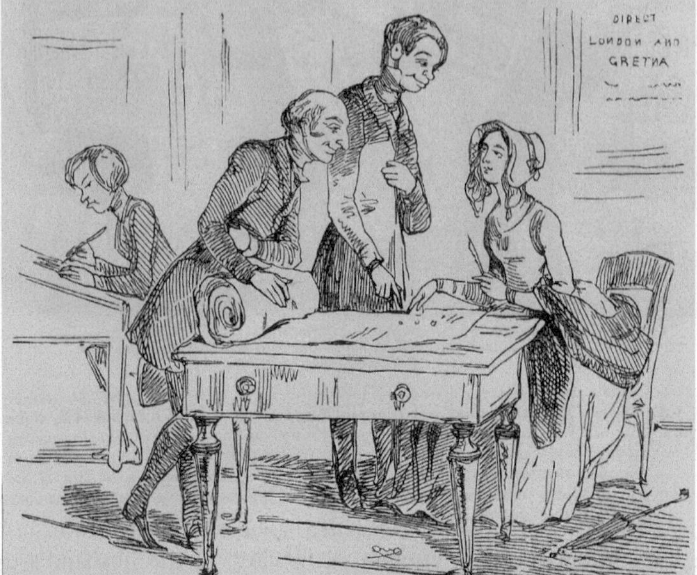

Name in Full.	Place of Residence.	Profession.	Place of Business, if any.	No. of Shares.	Sum.
Katherine Lorimer.	Curzon St., Mayfair.	Spinster.	—	100	£2000

"O, Sir, how my heart beat as she put her sweet little finger on the wafer, and said, in thrilling accents, '*I deliver this as my act and deed!*'

"I have not given her real name here, but if she took notice of a gent. in a green coat and little blue satin stock, light auburn hair and whiskers, diamond pin and brown silk umbrella, and is going to drive in the Park on Sunday next, she will see one at the Achilles statue whose intentions are strictly honourable.

"If you would put this in your widely-extended journal (which I regularly subscribe to) I should be

"Your most grateful Servant,

"Frederick Haltamont de Montmorency.

Fig. 7.13 *Punch*, *A Doe in the City*, 30 October 1845 (Courtesy of UoH)

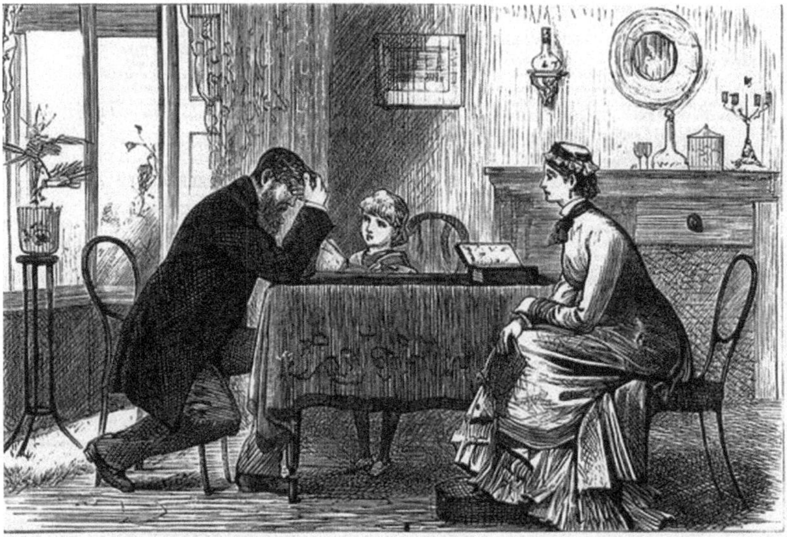

Fig. 7.14 *Fun*, *The Effects of the Commercial Crisis*, 30 October 1878 (Courtesy of UoF)

ited' liability on their husbands' behalf through expenditure on fashion purchases equivalent to the 'unlimited liability' of the husband's exposure to bank shares. Their frivolous behaviour in availing themselves of the latest fashion is contrasted with the serious financial effects of the crisis being faced by the husband.

Women are present in images of the CGB failures—despite recent research that indicates, at least in relation to the CGB failure, that female investors had shunned the risky nature of the investment. Acheson & Turner comment that 'In contrast to the substantial number of female shareholders in many joint stock constituencies by the 1870s (females constituted 31.6 per cent of the average shareholder constituency), only 15.7 per cent of the City of Glasgow Bank's shareholders were women, and they only owned 8.9 per cent of the bank's capital'.[30]

CGB was viewed by its peers as a risky institution so 'it may not be surprising that females invested less in the shares of this bank than they did in the stock of other banks'.[31]

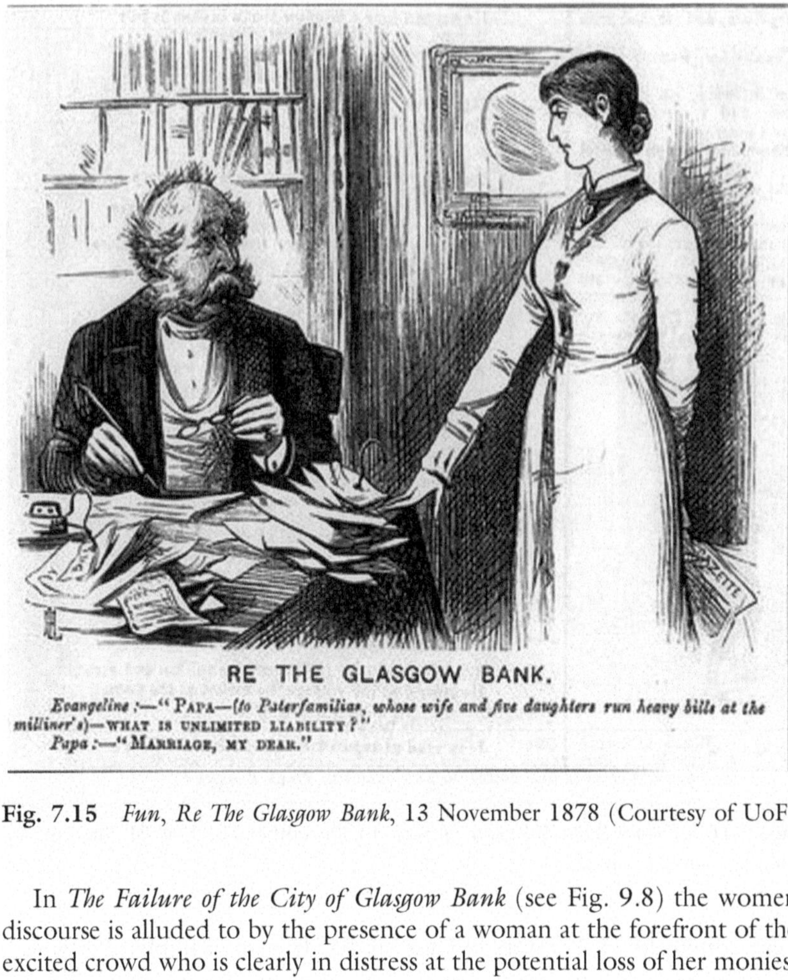

Fig. 7.15 *Fun*, *Re The Glasgow Bank*, 13 November 1878 (Courtesy of UoF)

In *The Failure of the City of Glasgow Bank* (see Fig. 9.8) the women discourse is alluded to by the presence of a woman at the forefront of the excited crowd who is clearly in distress at the potential loss of her monies.

In the *Bank of Virtue: its Rise and Fall* (see Fig. 6.24) there are three female investors in the central part of the image, one visible in black to the right of the image, and two towards the centre of the throng in increasingly dark shades of grey, one seemingly alone, the other with her elderly husband. They are part of the third phase in the storyboard showing the eager investors throwing piles of bank notes towards the smirking bank clerk.

In Fig. 7.16 the image makes fun of female investors even though they

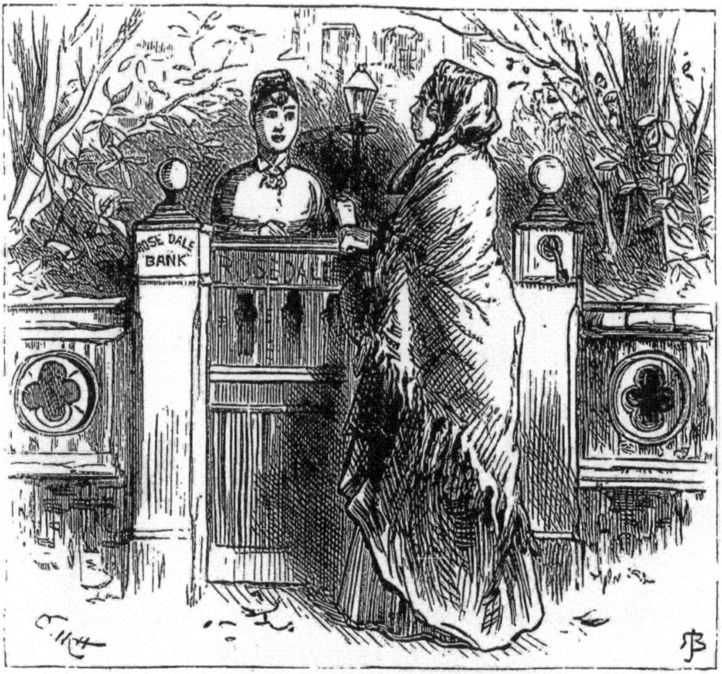

WHO IS TO BLAME?

WHAT IS THIS? ONLY A GOOD OLD COUNTRY STUPID, WHO HAS RUNG OLD JONES'S BELL, AND WANTS TO OPEN A DEPOSIT ACCOUNT WITH HIS HOUSEMAID. BUT THEN WHY DOES OLD JONES GO AND CALL HIS VILLA A *BANK*?

Fig. 7.16 *Funny Folks*, *Who is to blame?*, 14 December 1878 (@ BL Shelf mark, Vol. 4, Issue 211, p. 393)

were a minority of investors in bank stocks. It is an example of a typical linguistic pun on the word 'bank': conjuring up in residential address terms a place of seclusion in the suburbs, as well as the naïve female from the country who thinks it is an address where she can make investments (a joint-stock bank?).

7.7 Conclusion

Editorial Techniques

In the case of the use of the images of the Goddess of Justice or the Old Lady of Threadneedle Street, editors positioned these images of paragons of justice or financial solidity as the main image(s) of the issue.

Equally though there were occasions when women were disparaged as being unworldly and spendthrift, selfish to the serious financial concerns of their husbands. These images appeared in the comic-serious periodicals. On these occasions editors did not position these images as the main image of the issue- instead, they formed part of the smaller set of images which provided light relief throughout the issue.

Artistic Techniques

The depictions reveal the prominent role that cartoonists ascribed to the female during this period. There is an essential dichotomy in the discussions around the role of women in the financial world. On the one hand, she could represent the sound banker at the time of the 1825/1826 crisis, the bastion of financial solidity, or the epitome of justice, the Goddess of Justice during the 1860s and 1870s. The female thus represented the purity of men's souls and thus could be invoked to remind the corrupt male of the lofty virtues to which he should be aspiring. This can be mirrored in the view of Queen Victoria herself; as a woman, she was viewed more as a Goddess, an inspiration for Victorian people.[32]

The key recurring icon of the period, the Old Lady of Threadneedle Street was seized on by artists at *Punch* to convey a message of financial solidity. This consistent positive image of the actions of the BoE throughout this period belies the criticism that was expressed towards the Bank on occasions. Equally the use of imagery associated with school (the Old Lady admonishing her errant pupils) to depict the villains of the crises, the corrupt financiers, understated the growing disquiet at their unscrupulous tactics.

Notes

1. See historiography of the subject in Introduction, p. 27, FN. 90. D. R. Green, A. Owens, J. Maltby, and J. Rutterford (eds.), *Men, Women and Money: Perspectives on Women, Wealth and Investment, 1850–1930* (Oxford, Oxford University Press, 2011), and Acheson and Turner, 'Shareholder liability, risk aversion, and investment returns in nineteenth-century British Banking' in same book, p. 217. See also Robin Pearson, 'Between Madam Bubble and Kitty Lorimer: Women Investors in British and Irish Stock Companies', (Book chapter), in Anne Laurence, James Taylor, and Mark Freeman (eds.), *Women and Their Money: Essays on Women and Finance* (London, Taylor & Francis, 2009).
2. Porter, p. 205.
3. See, especially, BM 14874, *A Beau-Clerk for a Banking-Concern*, and BM 14875, *A Visit to Court—or—*.
4. BM 14653, *The New Combination Pawn Broking Company*, and BM 14654, *Charity begins at home.*
5. Healey, p. 248, 'You are a most extraordinarily good intelligent person: intuitive knowledge from Heaven and a perfect goodness graces every action of your life…. Actions can never repay all your noble & unceasing & most affectionate consideration and love to your own Dearest Coutts.'
6. Ibid., p. 270.
7. ODNB: https://doi.org/10.1093/ref:odnb/32175.
8. Healey, p. 305.
9. ODNB, Ibid.
10. *Vanity Fair*, Letterpress, 3 November 1883.
11. John M. Mackenzie (ed.), *The Victorian Vision: Inventing New Britain* (London, V & A Publications), p. 100.
12. See Fig. 9.2, *Fun, Even-Handed Justice.*
13. *Punch*, *March of speculation*, 25 October 1845, *A Doe in the City*, 1 November 1845, and *The Momentous Question*, 25 October 1845.
14. BM 15119, *The National Pop-Shop in Threadneedle Street*, 1826.
15. BM 13203, *Symptoms of Crim.con!!! Or, a Political Visit to the Heiress in Threadneedle St.*, 1819.

16. The OED online definition is “A withered old woman”. http://www.oed.com.chain.kent.ac.uk/view/Entry/44723?rskey=SY5fAS&result=1#eid (accessed 24 June 2013).
17. Poovey, *Genres of the Credit Economy: Mediating value in Eighteenth Century and Nineteenth Century Britain* (London, University of Chicago Press, 2008), p. 232. The reference is to Gillray’s cartoon, entitled *Political-Ravishment; or, The Old Lady of Threadneedle Street in Danger*, 22 May 1797.
18. Ibid., p. 229.
19. Ibid., p. 229.
20. Mention has already been made of Lord Overstone’s explanation of crises being part of what he called ‘trade cycles’.
21. J. H. Clapham, *The Bank of England: A History, Vol. 11, 1797–1914* (Cambridge, Cambridge University Press, 1944), p. 203 refers to reserves being £8,190,000 as of 25 September.
22. Clapham, Vol. 11, p. 206 refers to £2,255,000 having been advanced in the period 15 September to 23 October.
23. Clapham, Vol. 11, p. 229.
24. See Shu-Chu Yan, ‘Addressing Women: Fashion and Body Image in *Punch*, 1850s–1860s’, *Women’s Studies*, 43:6, 2014, pp. 750–773.
25. Kynaston, Vol. 1, p. 432.
26. Asha Banerjee, ‘The First Modern Bailout: The Barings Crisis of 1890 and the Bank of England’, Undergraduate Thesis, Columbia University, 2017.
27. Ibid., p. 432.
28. *The Scotsman*, 7 October 1878, p. 5. Accessed digitally from www.archive.scotsman.com on 10 October 2015.
29. See *Fun*, *The Effects of the Commercial Crisis*, 30 October 1878, and *Re the Glasgow Bank*, 13 November 1878.
30. Acheson and Turner, p. 217.
31. Wilson, p. 52.
32. Susie L. Steinbach, *Understanding the Victorians: Politics, Culture and Society in Nineteenth-Century Britain* (London, Routledge, 2012), p. 153. She quotes Bagehot who commented that the Queen was wife to Parliament’s Husband. “Victoria, as mother, wife and widow, and spectacle, was the ideal sovereign to lead her country into an age of stable parliamentary democracy while maintaining the strength of her throne.”

CHAPTER 8

The Other

> We resented the introduction of Jews into the social set of the Prince of Wales, wrote Lady Brooke, not because we disliked them... but because they had brains and understood finance. As a class we did not like brains. As for money, our only understanding of it lay in the spending, not the making of it.[1]

8.1 Introduction

This chapter reviews the depiction of financial figures of the Other in British periodicals. The definition of the Other encompasses any race or group viewed as outsiders by the dominant culture. For the purposes of my review of financial figures of the nineteenth century, it initially covers the treatment of the Jews. By way of contrast, and reflecting the rise of anti-Semitism in other parts of the world, it also covers the treatment of Jews in financial images in France, Germany, and the US. It also analyses the treatment of the Irish and the Scots. Depiction of the Irish and the Scots in financial images during the period is limited: the Irish appear only at the time of the CGB failure in 1878, whilst the Scots appear at the beginning of the nineteenth century in connection with the Bank crisis of 1825 as well as the CGB failure.

In Britain it covers the depiction of Disraeli and the Rothschild family, as well as important Jewish financiers. The depiction of Disraeli in his

H. Sless, *Merchant Princes and Charlatans or Makers of Money?*,
https://doi.org/10.1007/978-3-030-86604-4_8

foreign policy, as an alien, a supporter of Asiatic (Turkish) interests, overlaps in this depiction as a financial figure whilst acting as Chancellor of the Exchequer. In Britain, the treatment of the Rothschilds moves from anti-Jewish caricatures in the early 1820s to their depiction as established men of finance in *Vanity Fair* from the 1870s. In comic periodicals, the Rothschilds were generally favourably depicted in the Victorian era. A stereotypical depiction of Rothschild as the Jewish outsider at the time of the parliamentary debates about admitting Jews to parliament in the 1850s gives way to favourable depictions of the role of the Rothschilds in providing finance to the British government during the 1870s and 1880s.

In the case of *Vanity Fair*, numerous caricatures of Jewish financiers are reviewed. These caricatures reflected the gradual acceptance of Jewish financiers into society. The attitude in private was grudging acceptance rather than outright admiration. Queen Victoria's distaste for the financial activities of Rothschild (as compared with the honest industry of manufacturers) is mirrored in the views expressed in the quote that introduces this chapter by Lady Brooke, a member of the Marlborough Set, of which Rothschild was also a member.

This upper-class snobbishness towards the Jews is to be contrasted with the left-wing bias of intellectuals (in turn to be contrasted with the right-wing attacks in France—see later). Ferguson comments that anti-Semitism was rife on both the left and the right of the political centrum during the latter part of the nineteenth century.[2] The anonymous depiction of Jews associated with the Stock Exchange, the figure of the moneylender, is to be found in the comic periodicals. The depiction, whilst it does play on racial stereotypes, does not reach the crude vicious attacks to be found in continental Europe.

The treatment of Rothschild outside Britain is inextricably linked with attacks on high finance and capitalism. Arendt suggests that adverse French attitudes towards the Jews dated to an Enlightenment view that Jews' financial support for the aristocracy was responsible for the evils of the age. Anti-Jewish meant being anti-clerical and anti-establishment. In Europe distrust/resentment of the financial elite was consistent, and specifically in the depiction of the Rothschilds as international financiers. The tone was crude, continuing the tone in England in the 1820s. Whilst 'anti-Semitism' as a term did not appear until the 1870s, the negative view of Jewish financiers is never far from the surface. Whereas the treatment in Britain changed over the century, it did not in Europe. German caricatures from the 1840s onwards presaged the rise of anti-Semitism in the

1870s. This movement, which spread from Austria to Germany to France, spawned the vitriolic caricatures of the *Musee des Horreurs* in France in the 1890s reflecting the antagonism caused by the Dreyfus affair. It also includes a discussion about the avowed anti-Semite, Edgar Degas. In the US, by contrast, Jews were not typically depicted as evil speculators, and French anti-Semitism was attacked.

Stern, in his biography of the German Jewish financier of the nineteenth century, Gerson Bleichroder, summarised succinctly the stages in the anti-Semitic discourse:

> What the anti-Semites did was to convert the particular (Bleichroder's rise to power) into the *general* (all Jews make vast sums of money), the accidental (Bleichroder's ascent into German society) into the *innate* (all Jews can pervade society in this way), and to leap from fact to *fantasy* (the debilitating effect that such prominence could have on German society): they insisted that individual acts proved the existence of a pre-conceived pattern of conspiracy[3] [my emphasis].

8.2 Pre-Victorian

8.2.1 The Jews

Financial figures are depicted as follows:

- Matchstick figures
- Portraits (see Chapter 4)
- Crude caricature
- Financial visualisation (see Chapter 6)

Matchstick Figures

In Figs. 8.1 and 8.2 Nathan Rothschild is depicted in matchstick format, small vignettes which do not reveal any overt anti-Jewishness. The satire is even-handed in its force—in Fig. 8.1 Nathan is applauded for his financial acumen but accused of parsimony in *A King Bestowing Favors* in relation to his philanthropic efforts (his fellow Jews are complaining they are not receiving enough financial support).

In Fig. 8.2 the attire of the three Jewish brokers is more akin to religious garb, which suggests that they symbolise priests gathering in front of their Holy of Holies, the Temple of Solomon, i.e., the temple of Mammon. The document at their feet which refers to their Holy

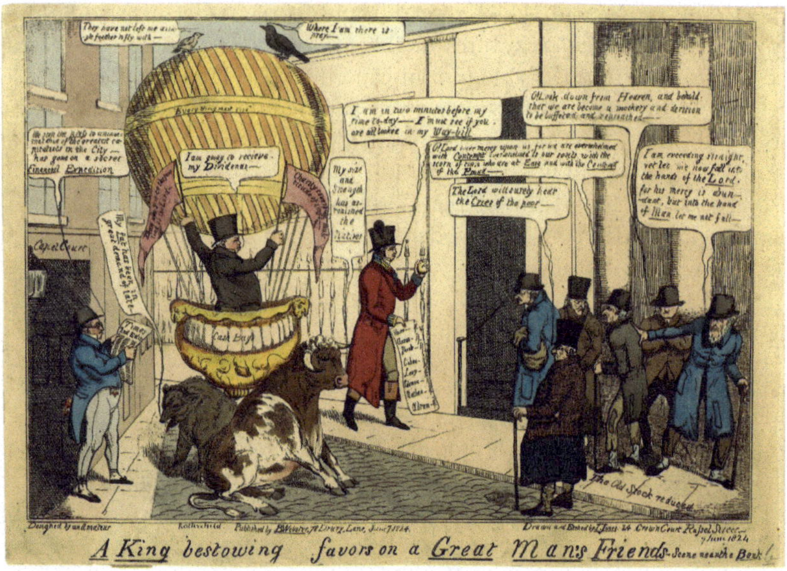

Fig. 8.1 BM 14667, *A King Bestowing Favors on a Great Man's Friends*, 1824 (Courtesy of BM)

Brokers (referencing Rothschild and Montefiore) would then indicate their reverence for the exploits of their kinsmen, but without any negativity or caricature being associated with such references. The depiction is far removed from the portrayal of Jewish stockbrokers in *A Scene on 'Change, London* (Fig. 8.3) two years later.

Crude Caricature

Figure 8.3 depicts two Jewish stockbrokers sitting side by side, their legs confined in penal stocks which are inscribed 4% (the standard government bond issue of the time). Whilst the features are crudely anti-Jewish (the long noses), the tone is playful (the visual pun of 'pulling noses' to settle arguments is reminiscent of children playing games rather than anything vicious). This interpretation is nuanced by the depiction of a whip which is about to be used to punish the other person. The figures in the background represent the alternative way of settling disputes, using pistols by

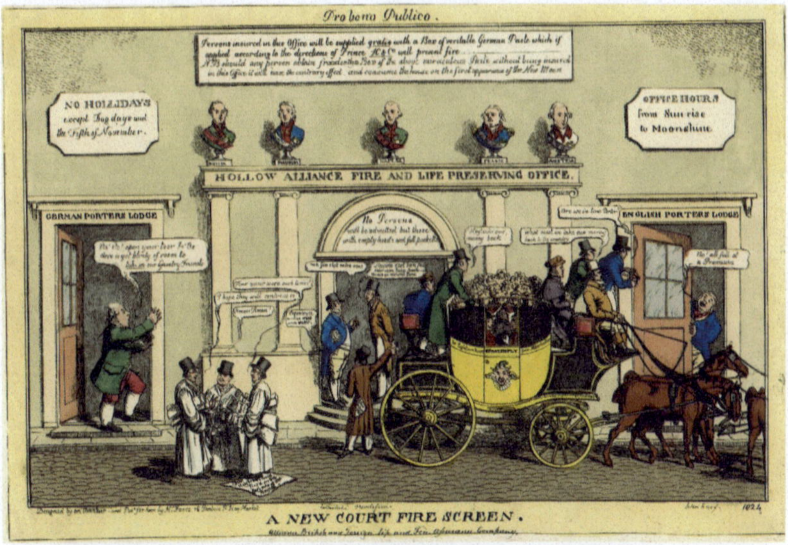

Fig. 8.2 BM 14666, *A New Court Fire Screen*, 1824 (Courtesy of BM)

way of a duel. The device of the stocks is a pun on the word itself—here it relates to stocks on the Stock Exchange (the reference to 4% on the stocks itself)—rather than to any penal inference (see discussion in Chapter 9, 'The Law', for further explanation).

In Fig. 8.4 we see a more stereotypical representation of the Other, i.e., the beard, the use of pidgin English (guttural German transliteration), and the reference to 'Old Rags', signifying a rag-and-bone man, dealing in money.[4] The title is taken from a farce, *The Jew and the Doctor*, by Thomas Dibdin, first produced in 1798. The caricature also refers to a loan of £50,000 which Wellington, through Herries, authorised Nathan Rothschild to make to Dom Miguel, who proclaimed himself King of Portugal in 1828. The caricature refers to a speech made by Mr. Duncombe in the House of Commons, in the course of which he said that in addition to the secret influence behind the Crown (Sir William Knighton, physician and Keeper of the Privy Purse to George IV) 'he trusted that the Duke of Wellington and the Secretary for the Home Dept. would not allow the finances of this great country to be controlled

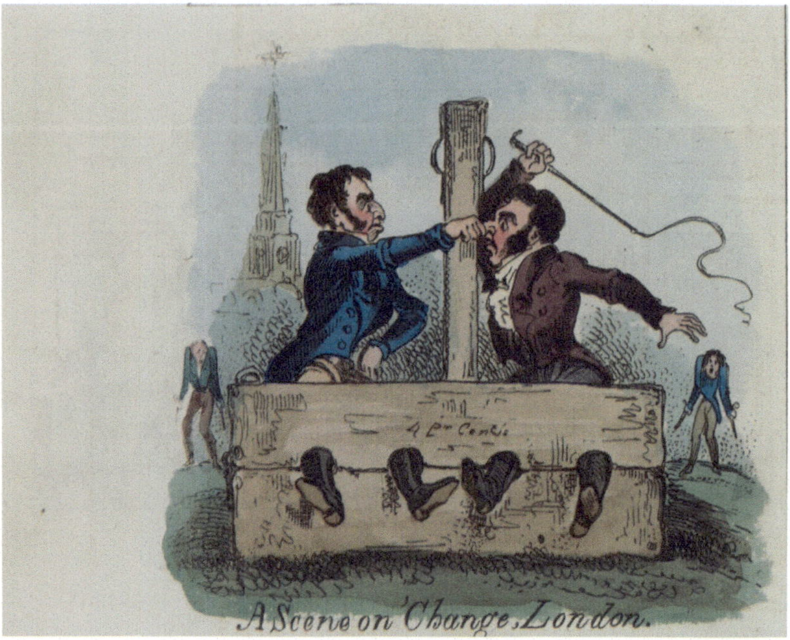

Fig. 8.3 *Northern Looking Glass, A Scene on 'Change, London*, William Heath, Vol. 1, No. XV, January 1826 (Courtesy of UoG)

any longer by a Jew, or the distribution of the patronage of the Crown operated upon by the prescriptions of a physician'.[5]

In *Stout as Ever!!!* (Fig. 4.8), Jews are presented as the evil agents of financial ruin for the rest of the population. They are characterised as avaricious, seeking to deprive Mrs Coutts of the monies proffered as help in the crisis by her fellow banker Sir William Curtis. The text attributed to Sir William refers to those 'd-d Jews'—those 'damned Jews'—who are causing the crisis. Mrs Coutts assures Sir William that her monies are safe from their hands.

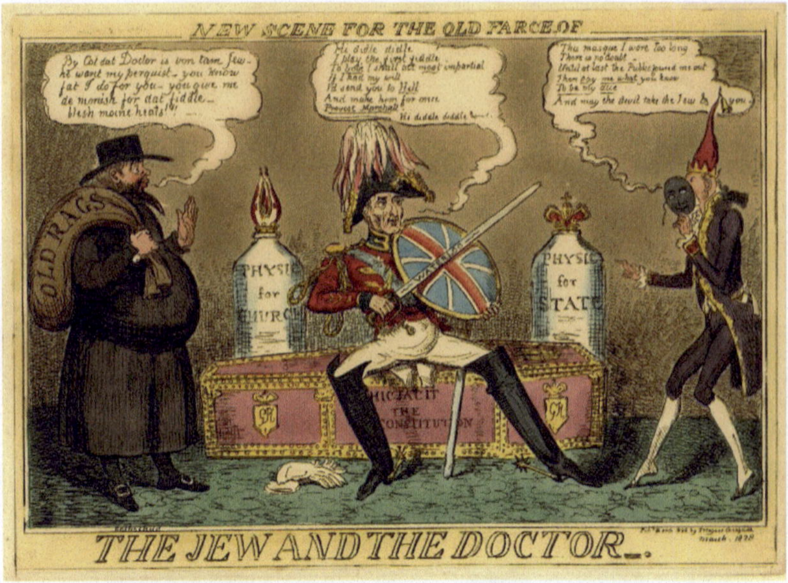

Fig. 8.4 BM 15522, *The Jew and the Doctor*, 1828 (Courtesy of BM)

8.3 Victorian

Compared to the way the Irish were routinely savaged in Victorian cartoons, the portrayals of Disraeli (and indeed of Jews generally) might be seen as relatively mild.

As Wohl expressed it: 'But if Disraeli, and by extension Anglo-Jewry, are not cast in the role of a lower species, missing links, or the sad products of arrested development or degeneration, they are represented in a manner that was potentially equally dangerous, both politically and socially—that of anti-Christians'.[6]

8.3.1 The Rothschilds

Figure 8.5 shows a non-stereotypical depiction of Lionel Nathan Rothschild, wearing a top hat and carrying a gentleman's stick, in contrast to the earlier depiction of Nathan Rothschild as a moneylender with a long coat. However, the depiction of Rothschild with an unkempt beard and

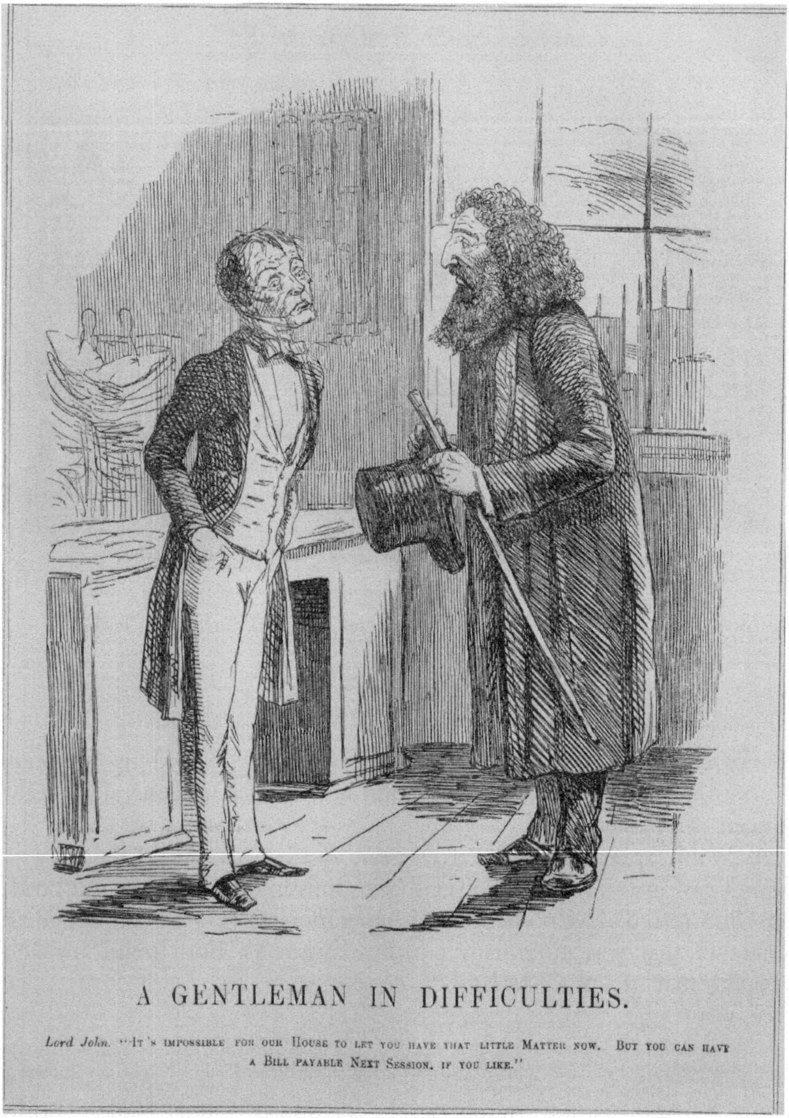

Fig. 8.5 *Punch*, *A Gentleman in Difficulties*, 17 August 1850 (Courtesy of UoH)

straggling hair implies he was not quite yet viewed as a real gentleman. The Lords had scuppered the attempt in the previous year to pass the Jewish Emancipation Bill. *Punch*, despite its avowed liberalism was not immune against the popular prejudices of the day, in this case anti-Jewish feelings….

In Fig. 8.6 Linley Sambourne's cartoon depicts the role of the Rothschilds in arranging four million sterling at short notice to buy shares in the Suez Canal. Rothschild is depicted rather oddly, in colonial clothing, his financial acumen symbolised by the sign on the stake marked 'Bonds'. There is more than a slight implication that Rothschild was reluctant to part with the four million without some form of security (it was reported

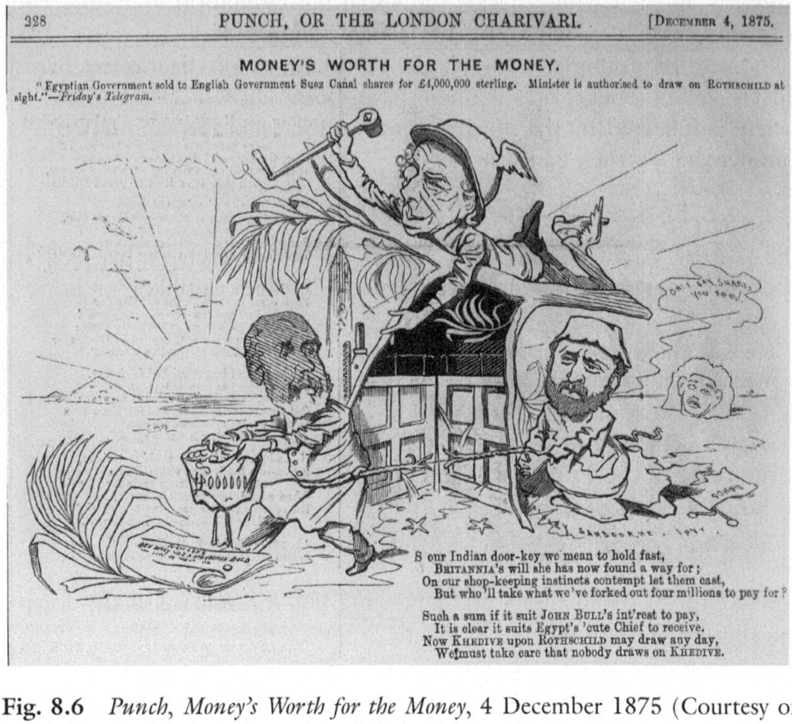
228 PUNCH, OR THE LONDON CHARIVARI. [DECEMBER 4, 1875.

MONEY'S WORTH FOR THE MONEY.

"Egyptian Government sold to English Government Suez Canal shares for £4,000,000 sterling. Minister is authorised to draw on ROTHSCHILD at sight."—*Friday's Telegram.*

S our Indian door-key we mean to hold fast,
BRITANNIA'S will she has now found a way for;
On our shop-keeping instincts contempt let them cast,
But who'll take what we've forked out four millions to pay for?

Such a sum if it suit JOHN BULL'S int'rest to pay,
It is clear it suits Egypt's 'cute Chief to receive.
Now KHEDIVE upon ROTHSCHILD may draw any day,
We must take care that nobody draws on KHEDIVE.

Fig. 8.6 *Punch, Money's Worth for the Money*, 4 December 1875 (Courtesy of UoH)

in the press that Rothschild wanted, and did obtain, a written guarantee from Disraeli and the British government that the monies would be repaid).

8.3.2 Other Jewish Financiers

Even where contemporary anguish over the role of Jewish financiers in overseas activities boiled over into savage caricature in overseas cartoons, visual representations of Jewish financiers based in Britain escaped such criticism. The role of Jewish financiers in South African finance and the ensuing Second Boer War has been covered extensively by Arendt and Hobson (see also comments by Ferguson, N2, above).[7] Despite social snobbery and left-wing attacks, the visual representation in *Vanity Fair* of financiers such as Beit and Barnato was positive.

By way of example, two images of other Jewish financiers, Baron Hirsch and Lionel Louis Cohen have been chosen. Their place in society is reflected by the positive tones of the accompanying letterpress commentary on their caricatures.

Baron Hirsch

The *Vanity Fair* letterpress of Baron Hirsch references his skill in stockbroking which, thus far, has exceeded his skill in gambling on horses.

> He is learning to speculate in blood stock; but he has not as yet made so much thereby as he has made by speculation in other things.

Cynicus's depiction in *Ariel* (Fig. 8.7) references Hirsch's wealth as well as the reliance the Prince of Wales (the figure on Hirsch's right) placed on his financial generosity.

Lionel Louis Cohen

The letterpress commentary accompanying Fig. 8.8 references the acceptance into society of this stockjobber.

> A Jew, a Stockjobber, rich, and a Tory, Mr Lionel Cohen is one of the most reputable of the new members added to the Carlton Club by the last General Election. He... has done a large business on the Stock Exchange, of which he was for many years a member of the Committee, and is even now one of the managers......He is a very respectable person, and very popular in the House.[8]

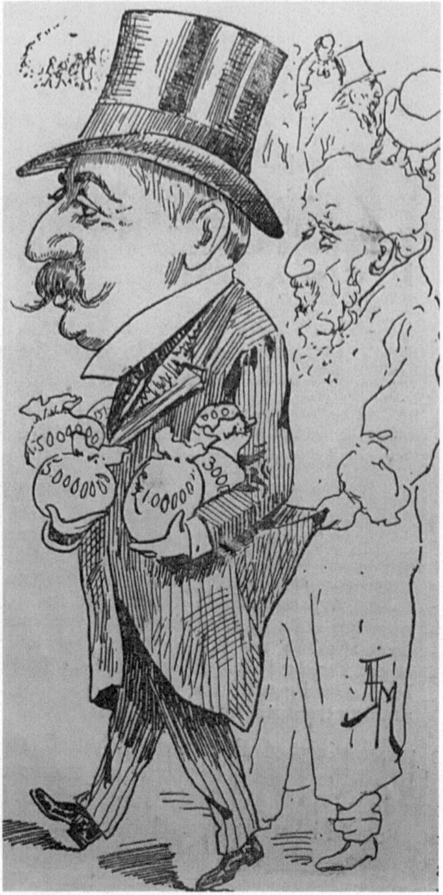

Fig. 8.7 *Ariel, Baron de Hirsch*, Cynicus, 23 May 1891 (own photo from BL) (@ BL Shelf mark, LOU.LON 236 [1891])

Disraeli

Disraeli was Jewish by birth, though he converted to Anglicanism aged thirteen. His Jewish features were often used by cartoonists to express distaste at his upstart ascent into society, and his unpopular (to certain sections of the press) foreign policy views. From its very beginnings, *Punch* used anti-Semitic discourse to attack Disraeli.

Fun provided the most virulent depictions, frequently portraying him with small beady eyes, a bulbous jutting nose, and a weak chin, as a Jewish pawnbroker holding Suez shares as collateral from his Turkish clients, a

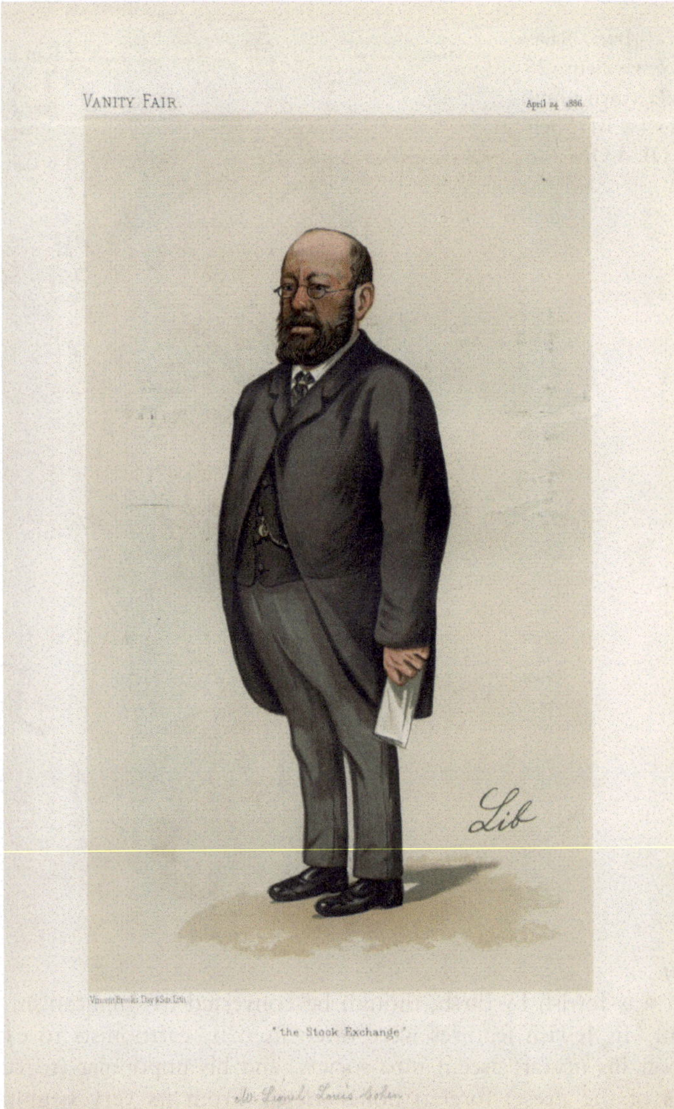

Fig. 8.8 *Vanity Fair, The Stock Exchange* (Lionel Cohen), 24 April 1886 (Courtesy of NPG)

moneylender with a forked tail, or 'Ben Juju', a flunkey servicing the needs of the Ottoman state whilst ignoring the massacres of Christians outside.[9] *Fun* chose to angle in on Disraeli's nose from every perspective in order to distort it and to make Disraeli appear as grotesque as possible. The caricatures of Disraeli really confirm Kris's general theory of caricatures—by destroying any natural harmony in the features, they tend to degrade the subject. In effect they de-humanise the individual.[10]

In Fig. 8.9 Disraeli's Semitic features are exaggerated, and the whole attitude of his body is one of volatile menace. Wohl comments further 'The drawn knife ready to take its pound of flesh, the murderous intent, the lust for some warped version of Old Testament revenge—all speak to Disraeli's allegedly real nature'.[11]

Retrospective evaluations 'took on the shape of reclaiming the eternal Jewish "Other" as a true-born English patriot who had loyally served his country and nourished its dreams of imperial greatness'.[12]

8.4 European

8.4.1 Anti-Semitism

On the continent, by contrast, caricatures of the Jews and the Rothschilds were consistently virulent throughout the nineteenth century, especially from the 1870s. Indeed, anti-Semitism as a term dated from 1879 in Germany (the formation of the anti-Semitic league in Berlin and Dresden), but has its origins in the Vienna Krach (crash) of 1873. This stock market crash pitted clericalism and agrarianism against liberalism, which was supported by Jewish businessmen.

As Ferguson expresses it: popular attacks on the Jews '...were accompanied by numerous hateful caricatures'.[13] Satire is prompted in those European countries (especially Austria and France) where the Rothschilds were viewed as synonymous with international finance (at the expense of domestic financial institutions). When cracks in the international capital markets system occurred in the late 1870s (see comments on Austria and France below), the Jews (often in the form of the Rothschilds) began to be blamed for domestic financial crises.

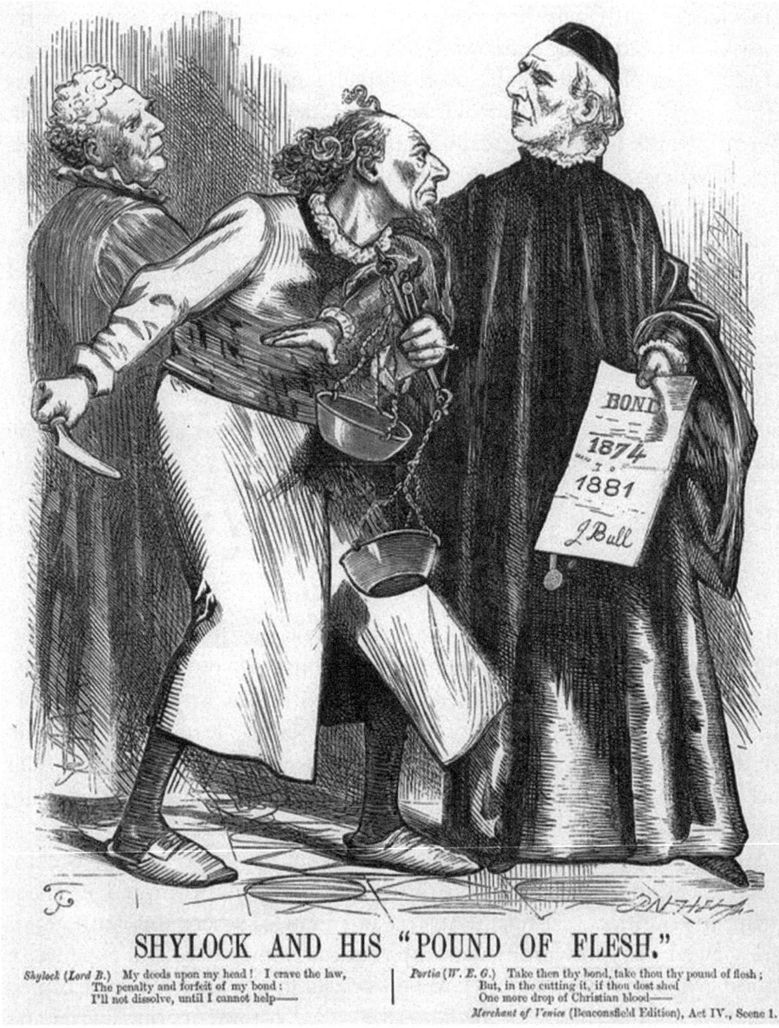

Fig. 8.9 *Fun. Shylock and his Pound of Flesh*, 18 February 1880 (Courtesy of UoF)

8.4.2 Germany

The anti-Semitic movement started in Austria and Germany, in which were the greatest concentrations of Jews in the 1870s (over 6% in Vienna; over 4% in Berlin). In Austria in 1873 Edward Lasker, himself a Jew and a prominent member of the National Liberal Party, drew attention to the imminent dangers of excessive speculation fuelled by the reunification of Germany in 1870, and the rapid payment of the Franco-Prussian War indemnity payment. In response to the crash of 1873 'Jews were held responsible not only for the crisis but for capitalism itself.... No less than 90% of all "capitalist promoters" in Germany were said to be Jews'.[14]

At the beginning of the period a German cartoon from 1845 (Fig. 8.10) depicts a grotesque Rothschild literally acting as a puppet master, *Die Generalpumpe*, a malign force manipulating world events by pumping gold into the grasping hands of statesmen and bankers, whilst foot-soldiers and innocent citizens suffer below. The pun on the word 'pumpen', meaning both to borrow and to lend, is reminiscent of

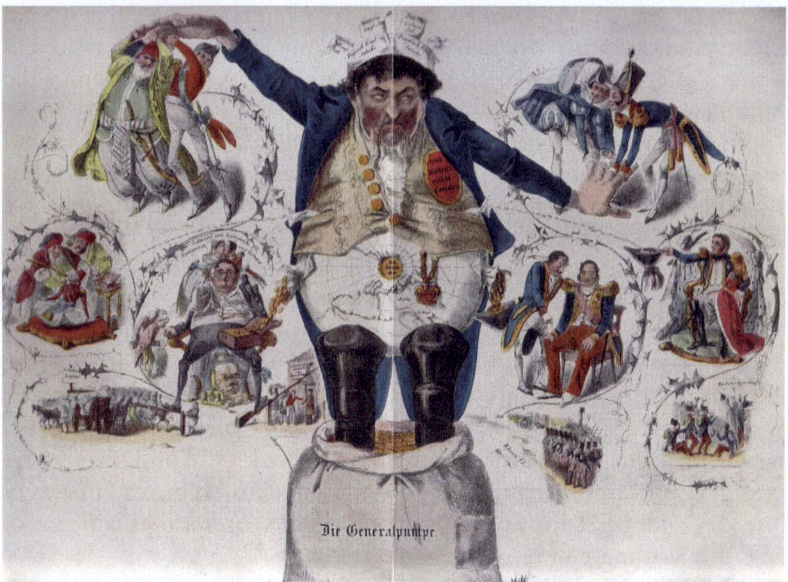

Fig. 8.10 *Die Generalpumpe*, 1845 Christos Varsos (Accessed from the web[15])

Gillray cartoons of the Golden Age. In fact, *Midas Transmuting all into Paper* (which attacked Pitt and his monetary policies) shows similarities. Pumping gold was a frequent trope in the Golden Age to demonstrate how tax was being pumped from poor John Bull.[16]

Whether Fig. 8.10 was published in the 1840s or 1860s, it is probably the earliest pictorial propaganda in support of the myth of Jewish world power. Ferguson attributes this virulent image to c. 1840 because the events depicted occurred at that time.[17]

The Jew was never simply portrayed in *Simplicissimus*, the satirical German weekly, as an ambitious bourgeois, but always as a crude and recognisable racial stereotype, reflecting the innate prejudice of some of its Gentile staff. This demonstrates the ambivalence of attitudes towards Jews even amongst the liberal intelligentsia.

The *Simplicissimus* Jew was almost always rich, successful, and ambitious (ignoring the reality of many poor and lower-middle-class Jews), reinforcing fears of Jewish economic dominance. Perennially insecure, whatever the position of Jews in society they were depicted as 'short, fat, kinky-haired, hook-nosed, thick-lipped'.[18] Stern comments that Gerson Bleichroder was a possible role model.[19] As Allen points out, this type of stereotypical caricature would have, in contemporary eyes, been viewed as no more offensive than caricatures of the overweight businessman or the dumb Prussian noble.

Jewish humour of *Simplicissimus* was popular amongst Gentiles and Jews alike, symptomatic of the psychological and cultural tensions brought about by assimilation. In response to the values of the oppressor, some Jews may have felt that the best defence is laughing at yourself. Similarly, many assimilated Jews might have looked askance at the behaviour of their less sophisticated co-religionists from the East.[20]

The caricature of Jewish financiers in Germany had to take account of the important role of Gerson Bleichroder, a German Jewish financier, who helped Bismarck finance his Prussian military expansion. Bleichroder became hoffahig (a ducal personage allowed to be presented at court)—Stern called him 'the arriviste who never arrived'.[21] Whilst there were occasional caricatures highlighting his closeness to Bismarck, that very closeness, and the success of his financial exploits, meant that criticism of the Other was muted.[22]

Anti-Semitism was deepened by the emergence of a popular and xenophobic myth in the 1870s—the respectability of scientism—notably the notion that the Jew (or the non-white) came to be biologically, and hence irredeemably, inferior (ironically, Bleichroder had none of the typical racial stereotypical characteristics of the Semites, yet people talked about his Jewish physiognomy).

In Fig. 8.11 the use of Gustav Heil's 'The old organ grinder: The song of the sly Jew' evokes the dark humour of the period. The phrase 'Die alte leier', also has an idiomatic meaning (first used around that time, so Heil's audience would have been familiar with it) to signify 'same old shit'—in other words 'same result/here we go again' [i.e., if you grind the organ, you will always get the same tune coming out of it]—in other words, the Jews are always doing the same old thing. The use of the word 'schlimm' embodies the anti-Semitic attack on Jews as sly, dishonest (in other words the typical stereotype of the Jew). The scenes attack Jewish influences allegedly behind the recent stock market crash. In the middle scene, Kaiser Bleichroder 'Rex', is depicted knighting Bismarck and his advisers, the President of the Chancellor's Office, von Delbruck, and the finance minister von Camphausen. The scene is reminiscent of the *Punch* cartoon *King Hudson's Levee* thirty years earlier (see Chapter 5 on Charlatans) as well as the depiction of Cassel at the court of Edward VII (see Cassel image Chapter 6 on Merchant Princes). In the last scene, Jewish stockbrokers are depicted massacring Christians.

8.4.3 France

In France, the failure of the Union Générale, itself established in 1882 as an aristocratic Roman Catholic force to combat the perceived power of the French Jewish and Protestant financiers, resulted in a wave of anti-Semitism. Then followed the Panama scandal of 1892 which involved a rich Jew of German origin, Baron de Rheinbach. He was accused of defrauding the French government, thus reinforcing the concept of wealthy Jews manipulating the government[23] (see Fig. 8.12, *Le Veau d'Or* [The Golden Calf]). The French diatribes came from a clerical conservative anti-progressive bias which associated the Germans and the Jews as agents of foreign finance.

Jones comments on the use of filth, bestial animals, and creatures from other worlds as signs of *fin de siècle* decadence attacking intellectuals and Jews. These included images of the serpent and the octopus, as well as myths like worshipping the Golden Calf (attacking Jews and capitalism).

Nevertheless, there were occasions when the government stepped in to ban publications, such as the virulent attack on Jews, specifically the

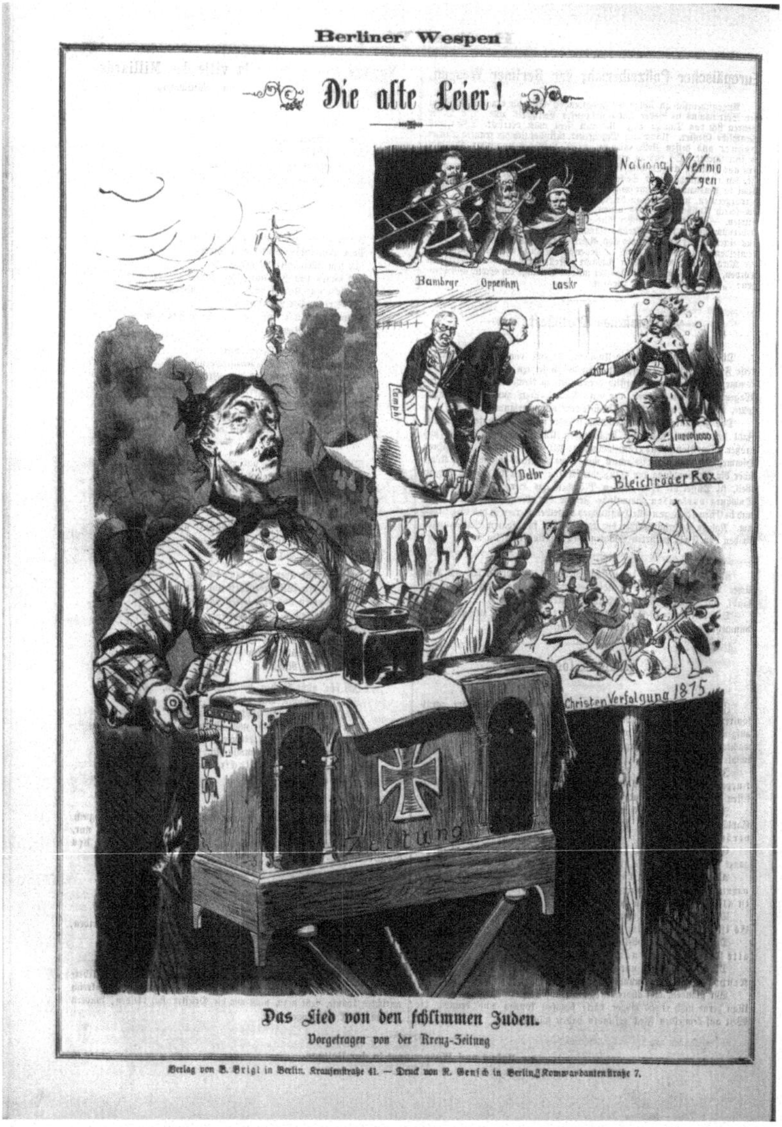

Fig. 8.11 *Berliner Wespen, Die alte Leier, Das Lied von den schlimmen Juden*, Vol. 29, 16 July 1875 (Courtesy of UoH)

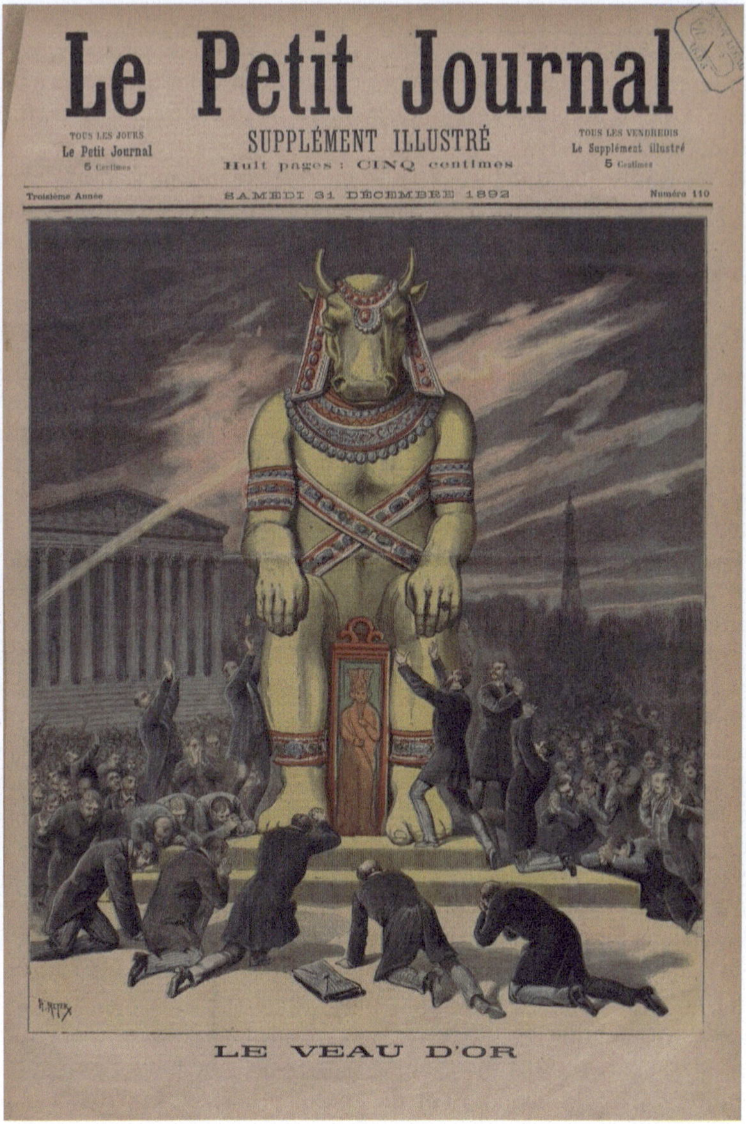

Fig. 8.12 *Le Petit Journal*, *Le veau d'or*, 31 December 1892 (Courtesy of LOC)

Rothschilds, at the time of the Dreyfus affair which began in 1894.[24] One of the periodicals involved was the infamous *Musee des Horreurs.*

Figure 8.13 depicts the same Alphonse de Rothschild who is portrayed in Fig. 4.13 in an amiable light, a member of the elite at ease with his surroundings.

Here, Rothschild is depicted with only one eye, a banker-dealer (literally, a banker dealing in second-hand goods), an octopus with tentacles. He is crudely described as the 'King of Pork', a very unsubtle dig since Jews are forbidden to eat pork. He is also described as a 'trou de balle', a 'bullet hole', or '[arse] hole'. The image of the devil-fish metaphorically evokes the devil in the form of Rothschild incarnate.

Portraits at the Bourse (the Bourse is the Paris Stock Exchange) (Fig. 8.14), is one of the most controversial Impressionist portraits by the French painter Edgar Degas. However, it is widely acknowledged to contain anti-Semitic elements—notably the facial features of the banker Ernest May—based on right-wing anti-Semitic cartoons which were in circulation at the time.[26]

The painting depicts a discreet huddle of businessmen on the trading floor of the Bourse. May is shown in the centre of the composition, wearing pince-nez and a top hat. He is listening to a Monsieur Bolatre, his colleague, who leans over his shoulder. They appear to be discussing the contents of a document being displayed by a third party on the right.

In Degas's hands a portrait of public stock trading has become a representation of shady, back-room dealing.[27] Marnin argues that the setting of the painting is, in fact, the interior trading hall of the Bourse, more precisely a corner of the trading hall, reflecting May's status as a banker not a trader.

Sales of shares in the Union Générale bank and the brand-new Panama Canal company were just opening a decade of frenzied speculation followed by spectacular bankruptcies that came to symbolise the *fin de siècle* French economy. May was certainly at the forefront of the collapse of the two financial worlds, inside and outside the exchange. It gave a sense of how unknowable, secretive, and chaotic finance was coming to be seen. Marnin argues that the painting reflects the emerging, fleeting, fast, and future-oriented economy of the speculative market of the corridor outside the Bourse.

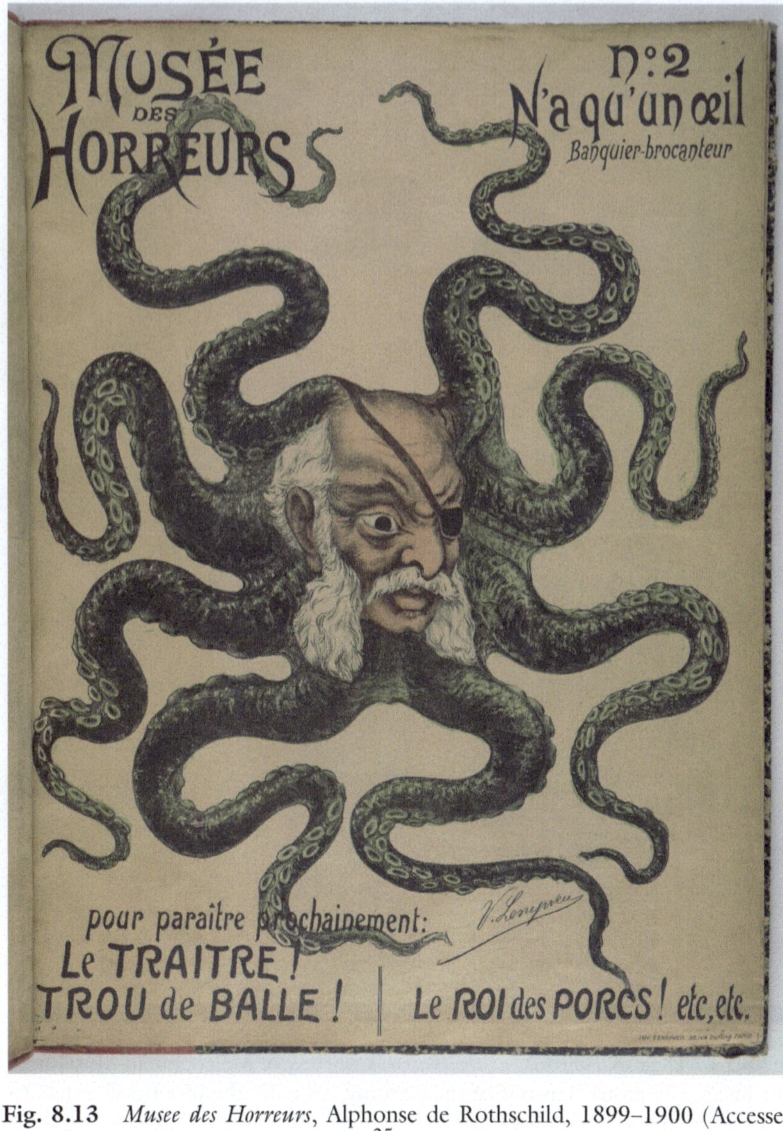

Fig. 8.13 *Musee des Horreurs*, Alphonse de Rothschild, 1899–1900 (Accessed from Duke University Digital Library[25])

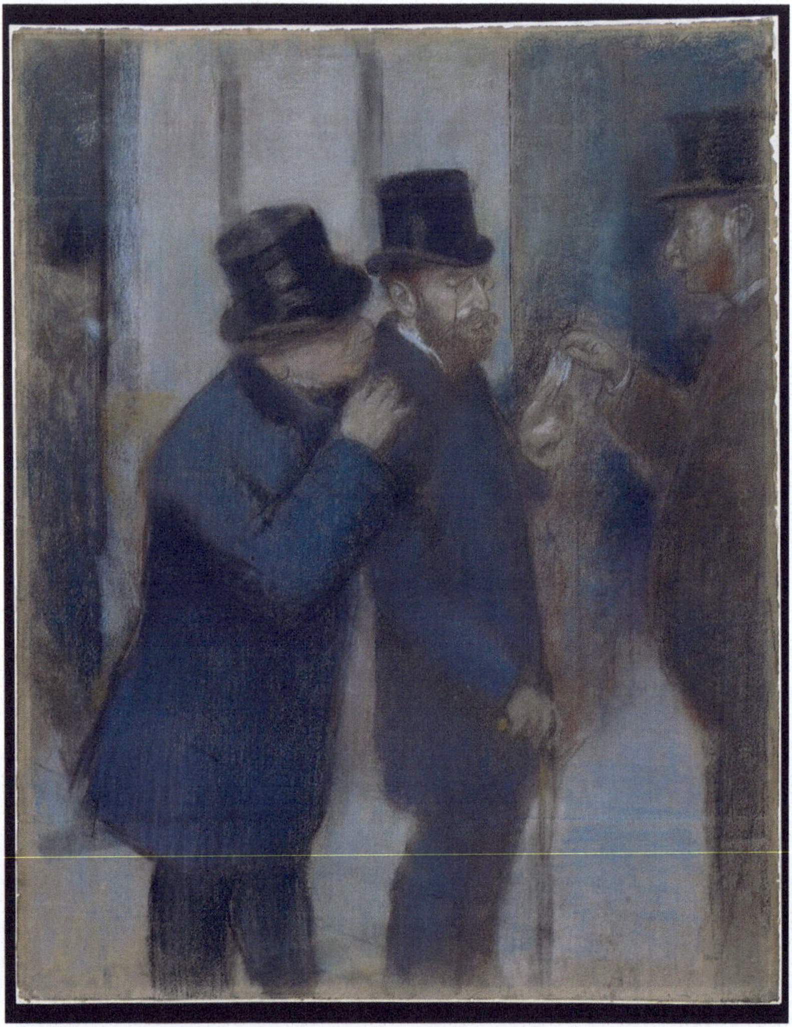

Fig. 8.14 Degas's *Portraits at the Bourse*. Courtesy of Metropolitan Museum[28] (this image is a pastel drawing of the painting, whereas the text below refers to the painting at the Musee d'Orsay)

8.4.4 USA

Banta comments that one of the reasons US periodicals did not caricature Jews specifically in relation to Wall Street was that there were many other Gentile speculators and financiers to attack.[29] Instead, the Jews were attacked as pilfering American history (assigning to themselves the lure of the promised land and corrupting US manners by introducing them to the 'alien vileness' of theatres).[30]

Two examples are shown here, both from *Puck*, one associating Jay Gould, an infamous speculator, with rapacious anti-Semitic traits, and another depicting *Puck*'s negative view of French anti-Semitism of the period.[31]

The caption in Fig. 8.15 is from Shakespeare's *Merchant of Venice*, Act III, Scene I. Jay Gould, as Shakespeare's Shylock, is racing past the Doges' Palace in the Piazzetta di San Marco in Venice, his arms raised overhead, a cane in one hand and in the other a paper that states 'Bond for one pound of Uncle Sam's Flesh'.

Figure 8.16 shows a large frog labelled 'La Ligue Patriotique' and 'Paul Déroulède' sitting on a lily pad called 'Anti-Semitism'; standing on the shore is a man, wearing a Phrygian cap, and holding a paper that states 'Vive La Republique', watching the frog explode.[32]

8.5 Jews and Money

The conflation of the Jew with money lending is an age-old trope. As we have seen in the chapter on Merchant Princes, images of the avaricious Jew (whether anonymous or represented by Nathan Rothschild) were present in the early part of the period. Links to Shakespeare (e.g., Shylock in *Merchant of Venice*) reflect a predilection for classical references. The association continues throughout the century. I have included two examples, one from *Punch* in 1851, and one from *Ariel* forty years later. In the *Punch* cartoon (Fig. 8.17), an evil-looking Jew (shades of Fagin) is depicted handing over a coin for a pawnshop ticket.[33] In the *Ariel* cartoon (Fig. 8.18), the irony is that the image appeared in a periodical which was edited by a renowned man of letters, Israel Zangwill, himself a Jew.

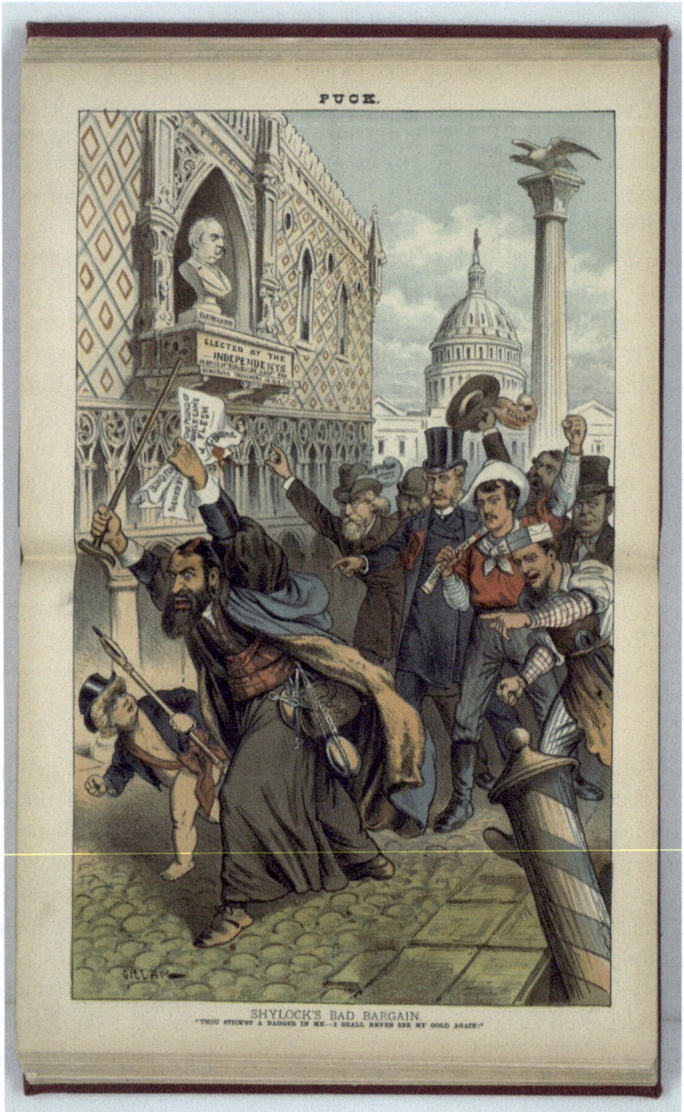

Fig. 8.15 *Puck*, *Shylock's Bad Bargain*, 12 November 1884 (Courtesy of LOC)

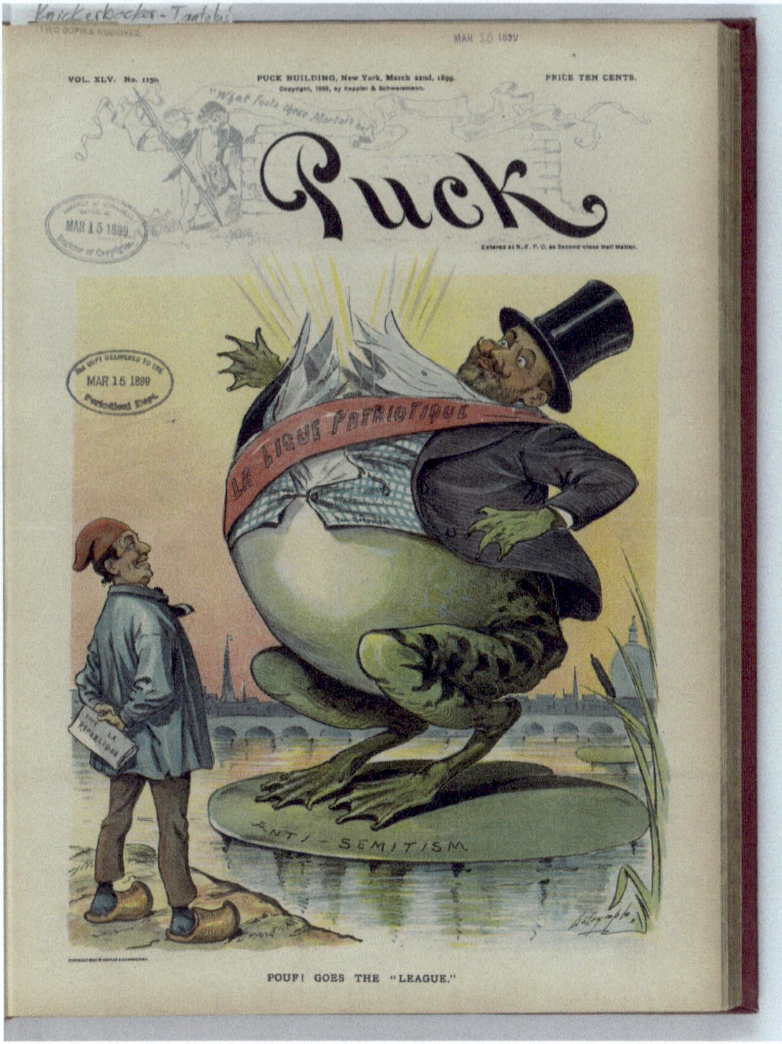

Fig. 8.16 *Puck*, *Pouf! Goes the 'League'*, v. 45, no. 1150, 22 March 1899 (Courtesy of LOC)

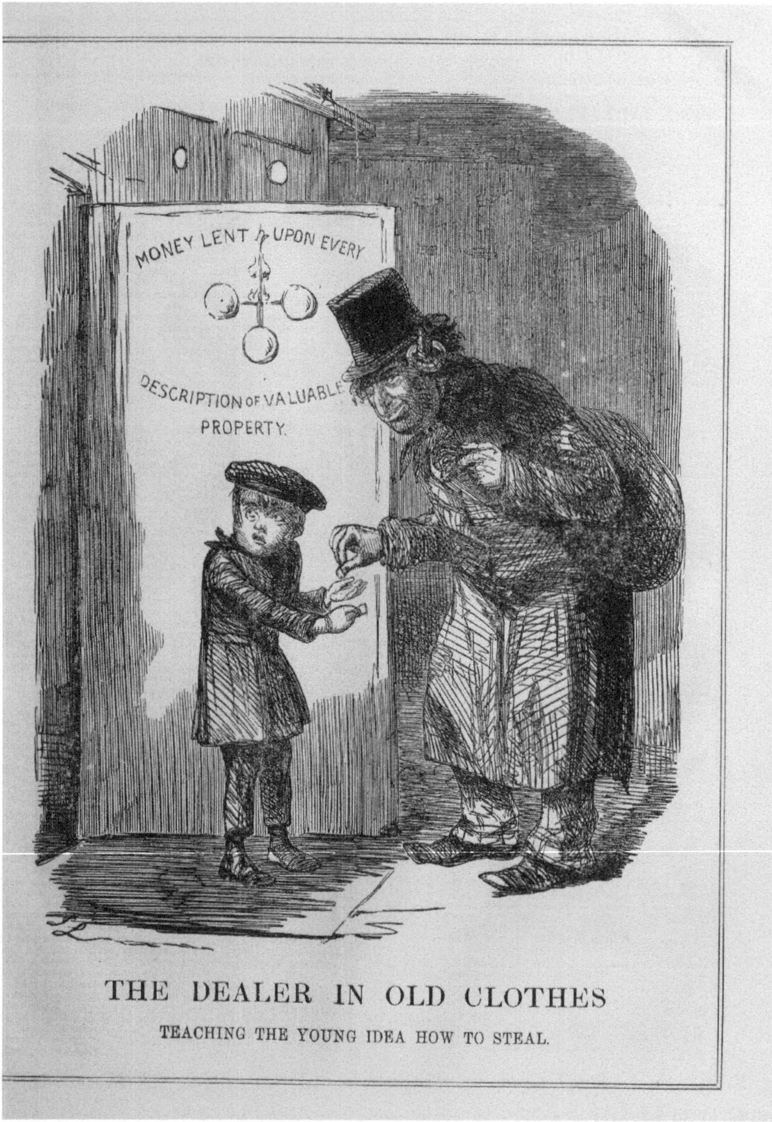

Fig. 8.17 *Punch*, *The Dealer in Old Clothes*, 18 January 1851 (Courtesy of UoH)

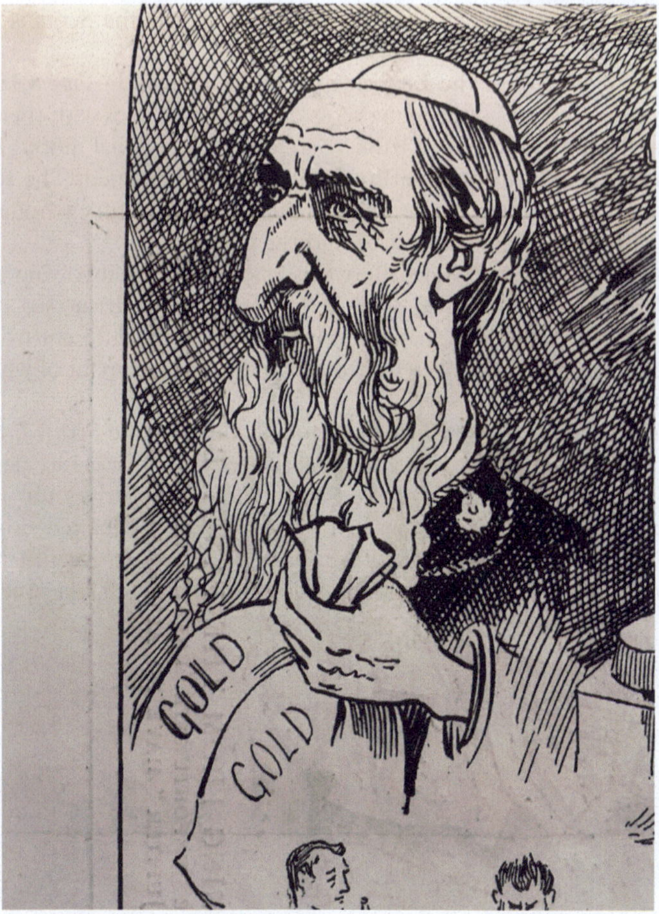

Fig. 8.18 *Ariel or the London Puck, Janus*, George Hutchison, extract from full-page cartoon, 3 January 1891, outlining the hopes and fear for the New Year[34] (own photo from BL) (@ BL Shelf mark, LOU.LON 236 [1891])

8.6 The Scots

Whilst other 'races', e.g., the Jews and the Irish, receive negative depictions during the century, the picture that emerges of the Scots in relation to financial matters is uniformly positive.

The first occasion when the pictorial press depicts the Scots is at the height of the 1825 banking crisis.

The parlous state of the English banks is contrasted in Fig. 8.19 with the jaunty expressions of prudent Scots depositing monies with their local bankers. Both depositors and bankers are depicted in jovial mood. It is as though the crisis south of the Border had never happened. The solidity of the banking counter is a recurring theme in the century (though not always with respectable bankers behind the counter).

As we have seen, the CGB failure was a Scottish crisis involving a large Scottish bank, in 1878. The Scots by contrast to the Irish (see below) are depicted in a dignified manner being viewed as no different from the average investor who has been duped by corrupt management of whatever nationality, sex, or class.

Figure 6.37 uses a storyboard cartoon to illustrate the Scottish nature of the crisis and the impact on the ordinary person. The Scots are depicted in kilts—the personification of the Scots. The farmer arrives too late to withdraw his monies, whilst the Scottish investors are depicted alongside their English brethren. The Scottish element is further accentuated by the two scenes describing events outside the Royal Exchange, the main

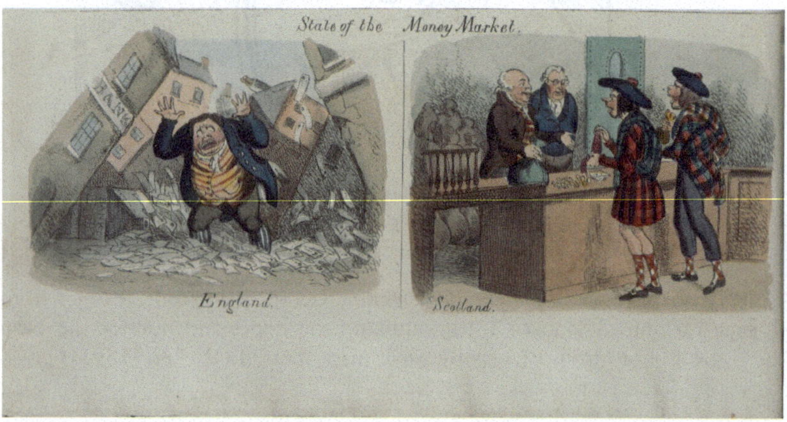

Fig. 8.19 *Northern Looking Glass*, *State of the Money Market*, William Heath, Vol. 1, No. XIII, showing two prints side by side, one captioned *England*, the other *Scotland*. Dated 12 December 1825 (Courtesy of UoG)

Exchange of Glasgow. The Scots are not depicted in satirical tones as representative of an 'Other' discourse, but merely as victims.

The knock-on impact of the failure on related businesses is depicted in the final scene in which Glasgow merchants in front of an equestrian statue of the Duke of Wellington (erected at the front of the Exchange in 1844) anxiously await telegrams indicating what is happening commercially across the country. The statue looms ghost-like in front of the merchants.

In *Fun*'s *The Dream of the Bank Director* (Fig. 9.4), the Goddess is using a broom as a threat to the somnolent corpulent bank director. The shareholders are a mixture of Scots (women and men), their anger at the turn of events evidenced by their clenched fists ready to bang on the door of the closed bank.

In a follow-up, *Fun's The Great Bank Smash* (see Fig. 9.5), the use of Scotia or Scotland for the naming of the Goddess indicates that this is a Scottish matter, to be dealt with by Scotland—reflecting possibly the Scottish solution, as the directors were tried under Scottish law, and it was other Scottish banks that averted any further credit crisis by honouring existing bank notes issued by CGB.

In Fig. 8.20 *Punch* depicts John Bull carrying the burden, literally, beset by the troubles of the time, concentrating on foreign issues, including a dour looking Scot with a note marked 'Glasgow' to symbolise the CGB failure. John Bull here represents the burden of all shareholders in CGB who would have been subject to unlimited liability on the shares they held.

Finally, at the time of the announcement of the verdict in January 1879, in *Funny Folks*'s *The Question of Precedence* (see Fig. 9.20), the female goddess Justice is about to cut off the head of the victim dressed in Scottish kilt but is being remonstrated by the Scottish Chief Justice, Lord Moncrieff, that Justice 'must be in harmony with the law'.

8.7 The Irish

Punch's almost crusading zeal against the Other—those minorities whose characteristics, whether racial, physical, or speech set them apart—has been well documented.[35] Curtis analysed late Victorian political cartoons using physiognomy—he commented that representations of the Irish became increasingly distorted and grotesque as tensions between Great

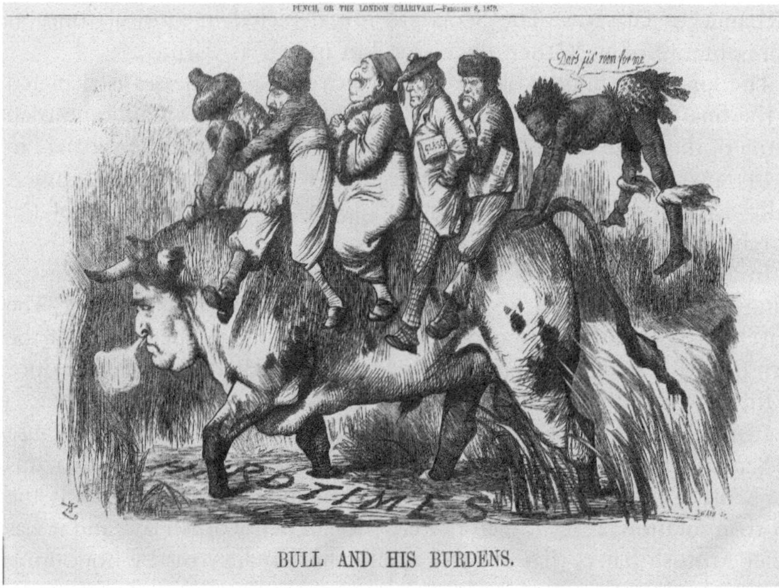

Fig. 8.20 *Punch*, *Bull and his Burdens*, 8 February 1879 (Courtesy of UoH)

Britain and Ireland increased. He concluded that Victorian attitudes towards class mattered more than race or ethnicity.[36]

As Banta expresses it:

> The Irish had suffered the arrogance of British occupiers from before the reign of the first Elizabeth, while the intransigence of the wild men across the Irish Sea – aborted rebellions, economic dependency, agitation for Home Rule, and general blindness to Arnoldian values – was a continuing irritant to Queen Victoria's ministers. *Punch* did likenesses of apelike Calibans into its cartoons as easily interpretable markers for cultural anarchy.[37]

In a financial context, images of the Irish appear only at the time of the CGB failure and are depicted as ignorant of financial matters. Their racial characteristics are not commented upon, save their manner of speaking—the tone is humorous rather than satirical.

In the US, the cartoonists of *Harper's* and of *Puck* used grotesquely simianized types to portray typical Irishmen: peasants sitting before their cottages in Ireland, immigrants, St. Patrick's Day celebrants, and menial labourers. Tenniel borrowed the well-known characteristics of a racial stereotype for his political symbol, and the racial slur was still implicit. *Punch*'s defence of Tenniel's grotesque depiction of the Irish as 'The spirit of lawlessness, Fenianism [radical Irish nationalism], and agrarian outrage' was that they did not imply that Ireland as a whole (Hibernia) was not a beautiful and lovable girl.[38] Hibernia as a national icon was portrayed positively; it was just the individual Irish who were demonised (though not in financial images—see below).

Punch's amusing (for Victorians) link between Ireland and the CGB failure, '*The Last Grievance*' (see Fig. 8.21), puts in sharp focus on both the impoverished nature of Irish investors and their innate stupidity (why is it a bad thing that so few shareholders in the failed bank were Irish?).[39] The image was prompted by a review of the list of shareholders, published in the newspapers a month earlier, who were required to make good the financial deficiencies in the bank.

The Victorians' view of the perceived financial ignorance of Irishmen is satirised in Fig. 8.22 in the form of a complex satire—a dialogue between a bank clerk and a member of the aristocracy. The aristocrat cannot believe his account is overdrawn; the bank clerk refers to his incorrect arithmetic where he has reduced his expenses by casting the thousand column into the pound column. The clerk comments that we would all be rolling in money if we could discount our expenses instead of adding them (addition being shortened to AD with the use of Latin referencing Irish Catholics).

8.8 Conclusion

Artistic Techniques

The treatment of the Other in financial imagery in the nineteenth century in the UK follows a different path from that observed in non-financial imagery. In the case of the Jews, the images are associated primarily with representations of the dominant financial family of the period, the Rothschilds. They show a gradual toning down of the racial stereotypical representations to be found in the 1820s, reflecting the acceptance of the Rothschilds in the 1850s onwards into respectable society, as exemplified by the dominance of the family's presence in the caricatures of *Vanity*

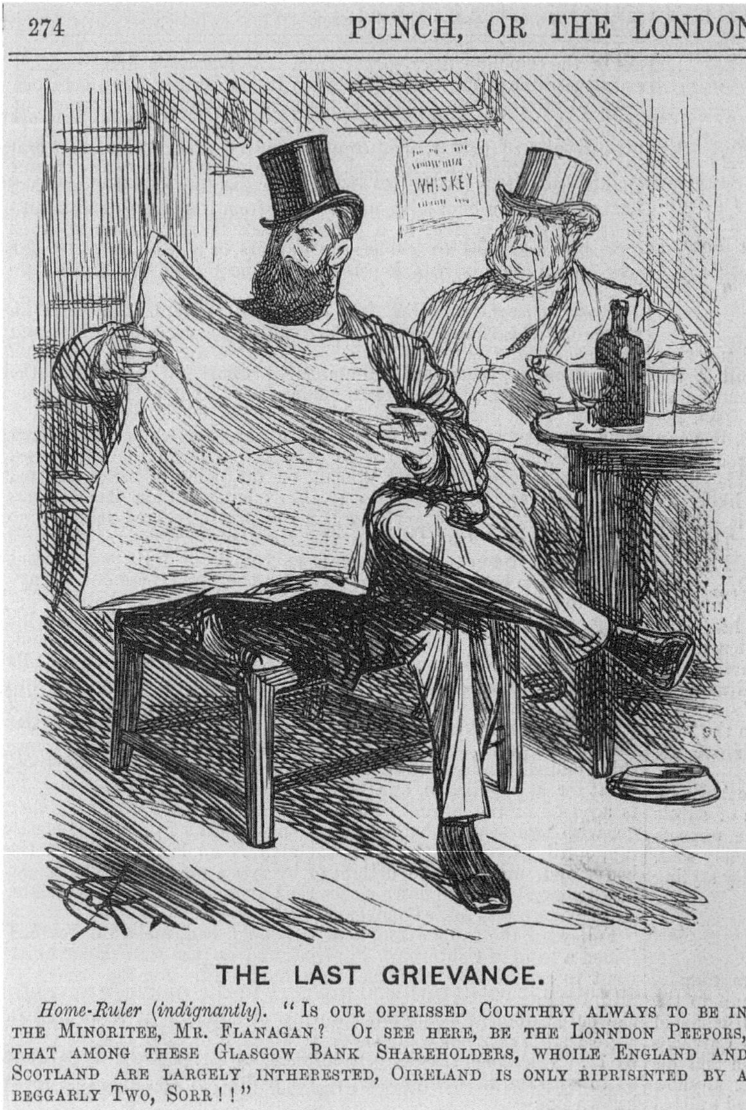

274 PUNCH, OR THE LONDON

THE LAST GRIEVANCE.

Home-Ruler (*indignantly*). "Is our opprissed Counthry always to be in the Minoritee, Mr. Flanagan? Oi see here, be the Lonndon Peepors, that among these Glasgow Bank Shareholders, whoile England and Scotland are largely intherested, Oireland is only riprisinted by a beggarly Two, Sorr!!"

Fig. 8.21 *Punch*, *The Last Grievance*, 14 December 1878 (Courtesy of UoH)

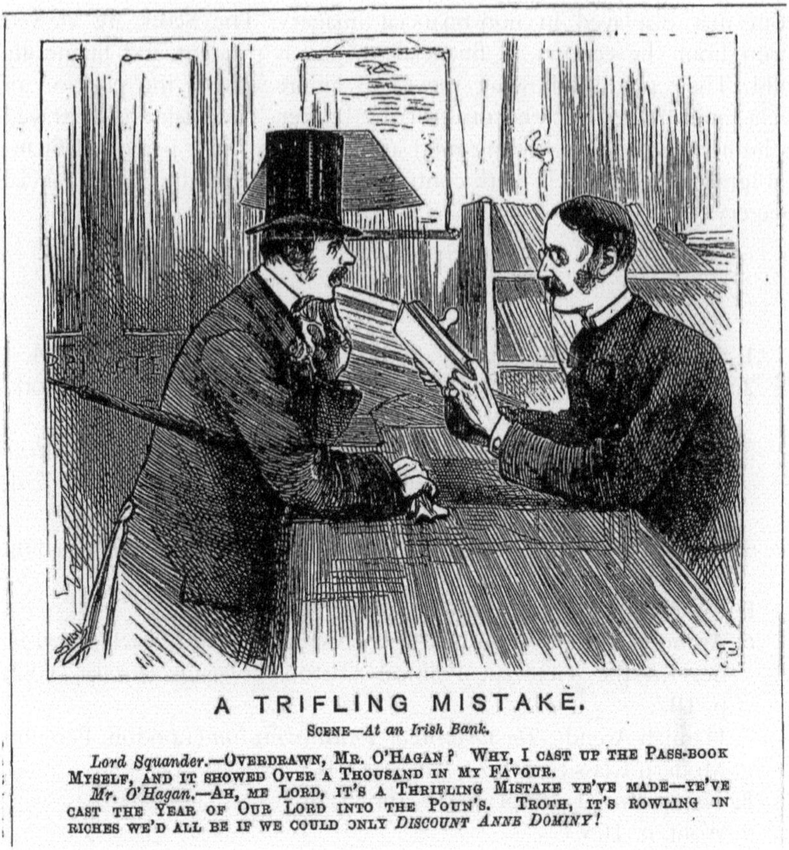

Fig. 8.22 *Funny Folks, A Trifling Mistake*, 19 January 1878 (@ BL Shelf mark, Vol. 4, Issue 164, p. 21)

Fair from 1869 to the end of the nineteenth century. Lingering association of the Jews as a race associated with financial activities continues but the representations are rare and anonymous.

By contrast, the situation in Europe was quite different, reflecting the rise of anti-Semitism. Vitriolic financial images increase towards the end of the century.

The portrayal of other elements of the Other classification—the treatment of other races such as the Scots and the Irish—is markedly different from that displayed in non-financial imagery. The Scots are viewed throughout the century in financial images as prudent and financially solid. Their plight following the CGB failure echoes the position of their English counterparts south of the border. The Irish are portrayed in humorous tones, reflecting mild amusement at their perceived financial ignorance. This is in stark contrast to their portrayal in non-financial imagery.

Notes

1. Quoted in ODNB: https://doi.org/10.1093/ref:odnb/53154.
2. Niall Ferguson, *Vol. 2: The World's Banker 1849–1999* (New York, Viking Penguin, 1999). p. 268.
3. Fritz Stern, *Gold and Iron Bismarck, Bleichroder and the Building of the German Empire* (London, George Allen & Unwin Ltd, 1977), p. 497.
4. Synonymous with Jewish moneylender; also, a colloquial meaning for money.
5. Rubens, p. 12.
6. Anthony S. Wohl, 'Ben JuJu—Representations of Disraeli's Jewishness in the Victorian Political Cartoon', *Jewish History*, 10:2, p. 107.
7. Hannah Arendt, *The Origins of Totalitarianism* (London, Penguin Modern Classics, 2017), Chapter VII.
8. *Vanity Fair*, Letterpress, 24 April 1886.
9. Wohl, p. 105.
10. Ibid., p. 79.
11. Ibid., p. 102.
12. Sandra Mayer, 'Portraits of the Artist as Politician, the Politician as Artist: Commemorating the Disraeli Phenomenon', *Journal of Victorian Culture*, 21:3, 2016, p. 293. https://doi.org/10.1080/13555502.2016.1199323.
13. Ferguson, *House of Rothschilds, Vol. 11*, p. 265.
14. Amos Elon, *The Pity of It All: A Portrait of Jews in Germany, 1743–1933* (London, Penguin, 2014), p. 213.
15. https://upload.wikimedia.org/wikipedia/commons/b/b0/.
16. See, e.g., *Cleaves Penny Gazette*, Applying the Screw. 1842, *Punch, Pencillings XLIX*, *A Political Parallel*, 12 August 1842, *Punch*,

Whig Economy or Screwing at the Tap, Letting out of the Bung, 3 August 1850, and BM 8995, *Midas Transmuting all into Paper*, Gillray, 1797.

17. Rubens, pp. 258–260.
18. Ann Taylor Allen, *Satire & Society in Wilhelmine Germany, Kladderadatsch and Simplicissimus 1890–1914* (Lexington, University Press of Kentucky, 1984), p. 193.
19. Stern, pp. 461–493.
20. Allen, p. 194.
21. Stern, p. 476.
22. Allen, p. 189.
23. Finel-Honigman, p. 54.
24. Ibid., p. 250.
25. https://repository.duke.edu/dc/museedeshorreurs/mdhps0100 1006.
26. Encyclopedia of Art Education © visual-arts-cork.com.
27. Marnin Young, *Capital in the Nineteenth Century: Edgar Degas's Portraits at the Stock Exchange in 1879*, nonsite.org—Issue #14, pp. 1–27.
28. Accessed from Metonline, https://www.metmuseum.org/art/col lection/search/436154.
29. Banta, p. 146.
30. Ibid., p. 151.
31. See also *Shylock's Year 1840*, and *Grand Union* 1877 (LOC).
32. The Ligue des Patriotes was a tightly organised, disciplined, conspiratorial, lower-middle-class organisation led by Paul Deroulede. Its appeal was negative, defensive, fearful, nationalist, in its most exclusive sense, antiparliamentarian, and ultimately anti-Semitic. Peter M. Rutkoff, 'The Ligue des Patriotes: The Nature of the Radical Right and the Dreyfus Affair', *French Historical Studies*, 8:4, Autumn 1974, pp. 585–603, Published by: Duke University Press Stable URL: https://www.jstor.org/stable/ 285854.
33. Altick, p. 269.
34. Meri-Jane Rochelson, *A Jew in the Public Arena* (Detroit, MI, Wayne State University Press, 2008), p. 44. Rochelson comments that the editor, Zangwill, may have felt nervous in the public eye, so went along with anti-Semitic tropes to make his readers feel comfortable.

35. See L. Perry Curtis Jr., *Apes and Angels The Irishman in Victorian Caricature* (Washington, Smithsonian Institution Press, 1997), Marion R. Casey, 'Ireland, New York and the Irish Image in American Popular Culture, 1890–1960', Dissertation, New York University, Graduate School of Arts and Science, 1998. Banta, *Barbaric Intercourse.* Kathleen Diane McGuire, 'The Transatlantic Paddy: The Making of a Transnational Irish Identity in Nineteenth-Century America', Dissertation, UC Riverside, 2009.
36. McGuire, p. 6.
37. Martha Banta, *Barbaric Intercourse: Caricature and the Culture of Conduct 1841–1936* (Chicago and London), p. 141 (see also Roy Douglas, Liam Harte, and Jim O'Hara, *Drawing Conclusions: A Cartoon History of Anglo-Irish Relations 1798–1998* [Belfast, 1998]).
38. Banta, pp. 171/172.
39. Of the 1519 shareholders identified in the report, only 2 were Irish. The accompanying text makes much play on a pun on the word 'Minority', referring both to the minority of Irish investors, but also to the minority in the parliamentary debate over Majority Home Rule for Ireland, which was raging at the time.

CHAPTER 9

The Law

9.1 Introduction

There are two key elements to understanding how visual images were used to depict the legal process. First, there was the portrayal of the emotional reaction to the events giving rise to an actual or potential legal process, and second, the representation of the legal process itself.

Trials of white-collar criminals were rare in the Victorian era until the 1870s (the exception is the trial of Lord Cochrane in 1814). In terms of pictorial depictions, the period before then is characterised by images of the villains in the mid-century and, increasingly, by images of the victims as the century wore on.

9.2 Depiction of the Emotional Response

The judicial process portrayed in financial images differed in high art as compared with low art. In high art, for example Frith's paintings, as part of the *The Race for Wealth* series, convey sentencing and prison in moralistic tones. This depiction, whilst realistic, is deliberately staged for dramatic emotional effect.

In the realistic periodicals (*ILN*, *Graphic*) individual court scenes are either rendered realistically, or presented by way of storyboards to convey selective scenes of the court process. The tone of the latter treatment reflects a more subtle form of morality, the juxtaposition of scenes

H. Sless, *Merchant Princes and Charlatans or Makers of Money?*,
https://doi.org/10.1007/978-3-030-86604-4_9

conveying the periodicals' view of the protagonists (both villains and victims). The comedic effect of similar moralistic comments in comic periodicals mutes the overt emotional effect of the images in realistic periodicals.

9.2.1 *The Image of the Stocks*

The earliest image chronologically in the book is an 1814 image of Lord Cochrane in the stocks (see Fig. 5.1). This image is a visual pun on the word 'stocks' conveying both the cause of his punishment (dabbling in shares or stocks) as well as the result of his punishment (being placed in the stocks though this part of his sentence was not actually carried out). The century ends with an image of Ernest Hooley as a Napoleon of Finance, also in the stocks (see Fig. 9.1). In the latter case, the word 'stocks' is used merely to convey his punishment, caused by bankruptcy. The link to 'stocks' is I would suggest a deliberate device to recall the exploits of Lord Cochrane who was allegedly involved in manipulating the stock market by spreading false rumours about the defeat of the French and the death of Napoleon.

Hooley's glum demeanour can be contrasted with a later image in the chapter *Under Examination* (Fig. 9.23) depicting him at his trial. The image is full of visual puns of financial terms (e.g., whitewash, the birds representing the corrupt aristocracy taking bribes from company promoters like Hooley).

9.2.2 *The Image of the Goddess of Justice*

By the time of the Overend & Gurney failure in May 1866, public interest in the legal process had increased. More and more people were concerned that the process did not punish the real transgressors. The inadequacies of legal remedies were being left bare.

The treatment of bank directors is tied with company directors more generally (notably those involved in railways) as both are viewed as guilty of corrupt practices. The slow process of legal arraignment reached its head in early 1869. *Fun,* in '*Even-handed Justice*' (Fig. 9.2), uses the image of a blindfolded Goddess of Justice grabbing a handful of directors in one hand whilst holding more common rogues in another, ready to put them all in the dock. One of the directors has a roll marked 'prospectus', whilst another roll, which has dropped to the ground, is marked 'private

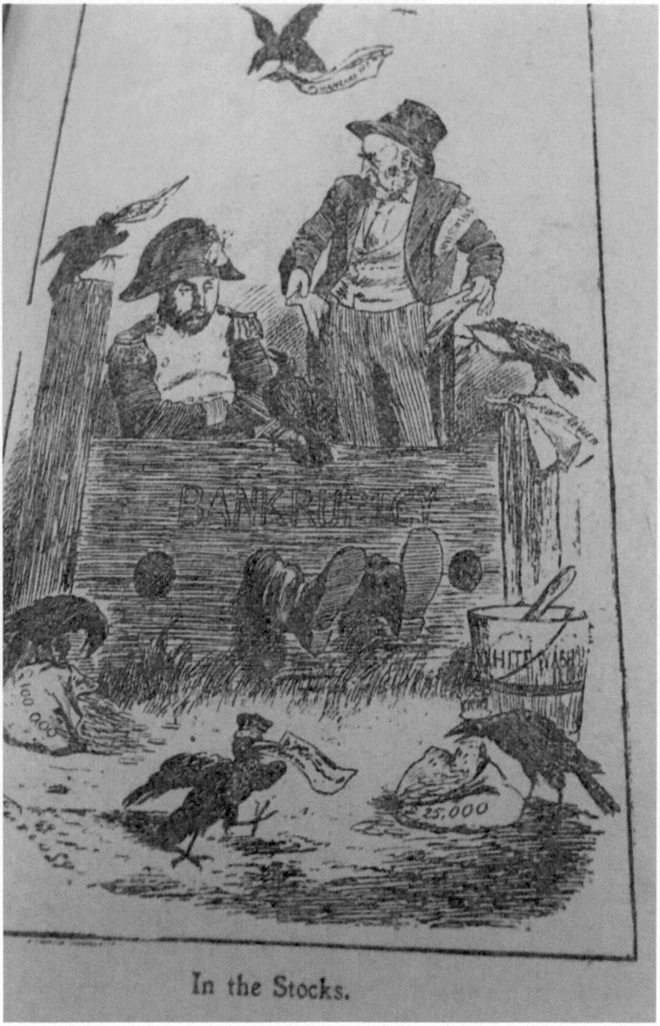

Fig. 9.1 *In the Stocks*, from *The Hooley Book* 1898 (own photo) (@ BL, GRC 10827.bb.36)

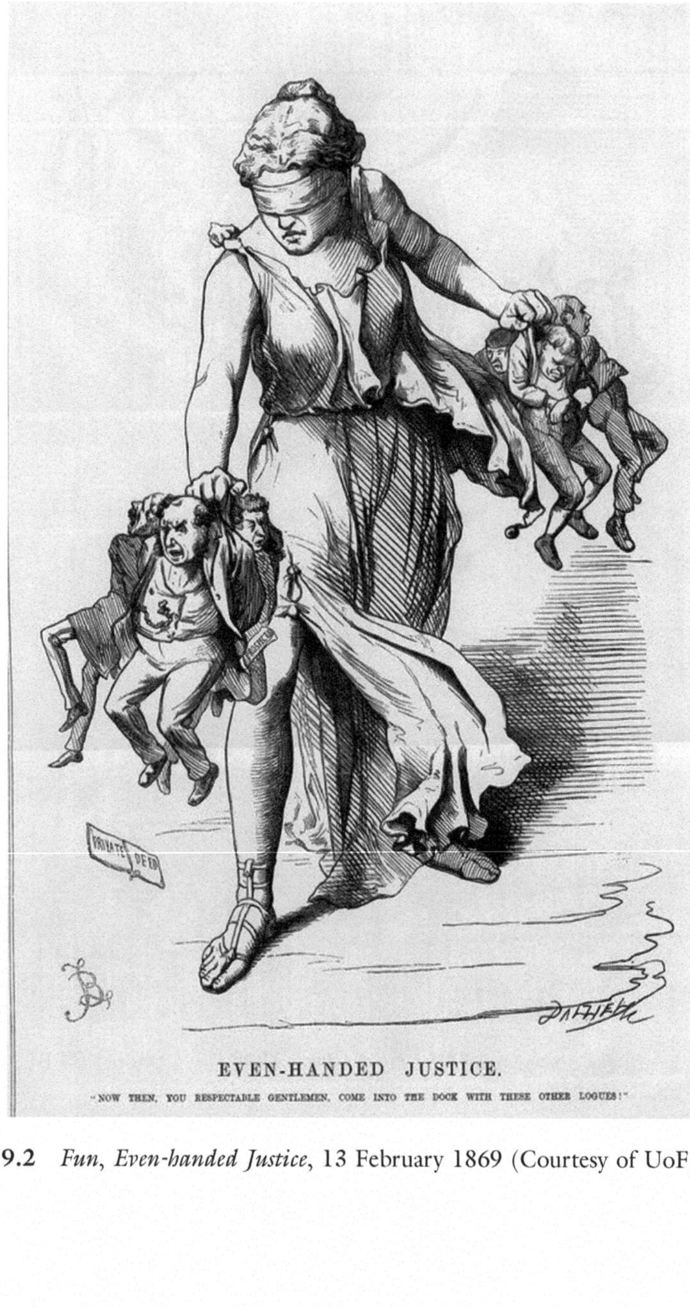

Fig. 9.2 *Fun*, *Even-handed Justice*, 13 February 1869 (Courtesy of UoF)

deed'. For Taylor, this depiction in a Liberal satirical periodical was a 'reassertion of the class blindness of British justice'.[1] However, given the paucity of cases of corporate criminal cases brought against white-collar criminals, the depiction is perhaps slightly ironic and wishful. The title is itself a pun, a nod to an earlier 1872 *Punch* image *Odd-handed Justice* (see Fig. 9.13).

In Fig. 9.3, the text accompanying Fig. 7.12 (the image *Committed for Trial*), *Punch* weighs in with a lament that whilst the directors have been committed (with the sense that they might be ultimately acquitted), a father commiserates with his daughter that as a 'ruined shareholder', they are resigned to a 'sentence' of hard labour for the rest of their lives—trying to make ends meet. *Punch* signals the injustice of the treatment of investors. *Punch* is not concentrating on the villains (the directors), as in *Fun*, but this time on the shareholders. The image is of the poor shareholders, but it is the text which is telling: it indicates *Punch*'s disapproval with the potentially relatively short prison sentence that might be handed down to the directors, whilst the shareholders, having lost all their monies, are affected by this criminality for the rest of their lives. In

COMMITTED FOR TRIAL.

"THE LORD MAYOR said that, after much anxious consideration, he and his colleague had determined to commit the defendants for trial. A cheer rang through the Court at this announcement, which was taken up in Cheapside."—*Report of the proceedings on the charge of conspiracy to defraud, of the Directors of* OVEREND, GURNEY, & CO. *Limited.*

"COMMITTED for trial!" A cheer, long and loud,
From Guildhall and its court, to Cheapside and its crowd!
Pour, virtuous JOHN BULL, pour wrath's bitterest vial;
But let's be quite sure *who's* committed for trial!

On the bench, a Lord Mayor: in the dock, six Directors,
Looking pale in the light of a host of reflectors—
A crowd their committal to Newgate who'd hail,
But for smug *millionnaires*' and M.P.'s eager bail.

Let us own we've sat through an instructive dissection;
Had a "Great House" laid out, by the knife, for inspection:
Neither lens has been stinted, nor scalpel been spared;
All its depths we've had probed, all its nakedness bared,

Watched each gangrene bisected, and handled each sore,
Until the poor "subject" could teach us no more.
Enough! Cover up the dishonoured remains:
Bear a hand with a bucket to wash down the stains.

For if 'twas instructive, 'twas sickening too,
When one thinks that the subject might be *I* or *you*,
The shout of the crowd seems to jar on my ear·
And, do what I will, I can't echo the cheer.

Are they cheering that pride should have come to a fall?
Or that "great" men are made to rub shoulders with small?
Or rejoicing that Justice has one set of weights
For penniless pickers and squires with estates?

Then better were silence of sorrow and shame,
At the thought Justice *could* have had weights not the same:
That 'twas cause for exulting to have it made sure
That the law for the rich was the law for the poor.

Rose the cheer from the victims, their ruin that owe
To blind faith in these names, once so high, now so low?
Then silence were better, and veiling the face:
Theirs the loss, but all England's, methinks, the disgrace.

If they're guilty, no cheer: why insult the bowed head?
Why pour bitter scorn where foul ashes are spread?
If they're guiltless, no cheer: they but went with the throng,
Blind, blundering o'er landmarks between right and wrong.

In no issue a cheer, but a groan and a cry
For the soil'd name of England, that once stood so high—
Stood so high, has so fallen, through gold's abject lust,
That they who would seek it must look in the dust.

A Handsome Commission Expected.

A HINT for an enterprising Art Publisher. Bring out views of a well-known watering-place on the Norfolk Coast in *Cromer*-lithography.

Fig. 9.3 *Punch*, *Committed for Trial* (text), 6 February 1869 (Courtesy of UoH)

fact, although the trial ultimately resulted in the acquittal of two directors concerned, John Henry and Edmund Gurney, *Punch*'s popular view is counterbalanced by the comments appearing in the *Saturday Review* below.

'If investors were naïve enough to be unable/unwilling to properly educate themselves about the dangers of such investments, then why should the law provide more redress for them?'[2] Events over the coming years would swing the sympathy firmly towards shareholders.

The cartoons from *Fun* appear soon after the crisis broke out, with the main theme being the dishonourable conduct of bank directors. Whilst *Punch* used Oliver Twist as the image of thievery (see Fig. 9.12)—with more than a hint of grudging admiration for the criminal exploits of the bank director—*Fun* adopts a classical vein and invokes the spirit and wrath, quite literally, of the Goddess of Justice (see Fig. 9.4). The Goddess becomes the Goddess of Scotland, Scotia, in another image (see Fig. 9.5).

Classically the Goddess of Justice would be blindfolded, holding a set of scales in her left hand and a two-edged sword in her right. These additional icons are what Knox has called 'metonymic tokens'—the absence or existence of which carries resonance with the reader beyond the intrinsic nature of the central figure.[3]

At the same level, the absence of such icons invites the reader to consider the implications of their absence and indeed what replaces them. For example, with no blindfold present, the image can convey the raw emotion, the despair at what has happened, i.e., the total absence of objectivity, and the implication that the Goddess wants vengeance. Instead of empiricism and enlightenment, the Goddess points to the despair of the victims—what has reason come to? It has failed.... Finally, the replacement of the two-pronged sword by a broom is representative of the use of puns and metonymy (sweeping away with a broom) to convey the force and raw emotion of contemporary feelings.

In Fig. 9.4 the Goddess uses a broom as a threat to the somnolent corpulent bank director. The scene evokes the image of a dream the bank director is experiencing, none too concerned about the events being described. The broom is marked 'Enquiry' representing the investigation into the collapse of the bank which had just begun. The puff of dirt marked 'credit' beneath the broom clearly indicates what the collapse has caused (the disappearance or puff indicating in iconographical terms the impacts of speculation). This consequence is further reinforced by

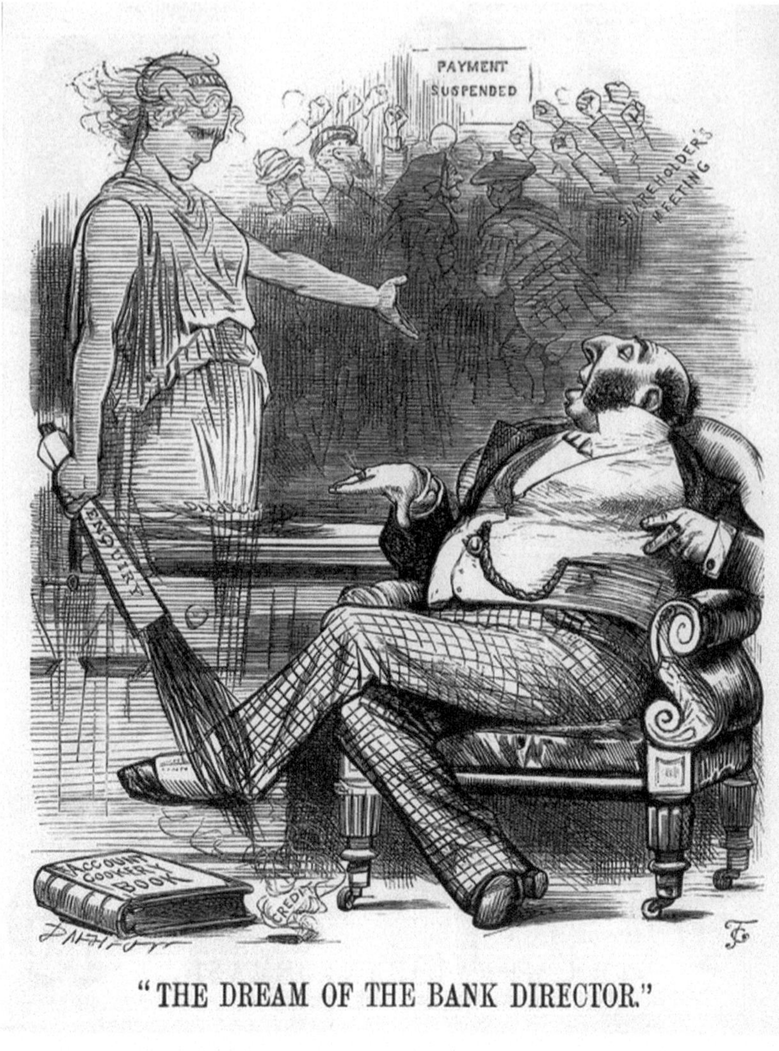

Fig. 9.4 *Fun*, *The Dream of the Bank Director*, 16 October 1878 (Courtesy of UoF)

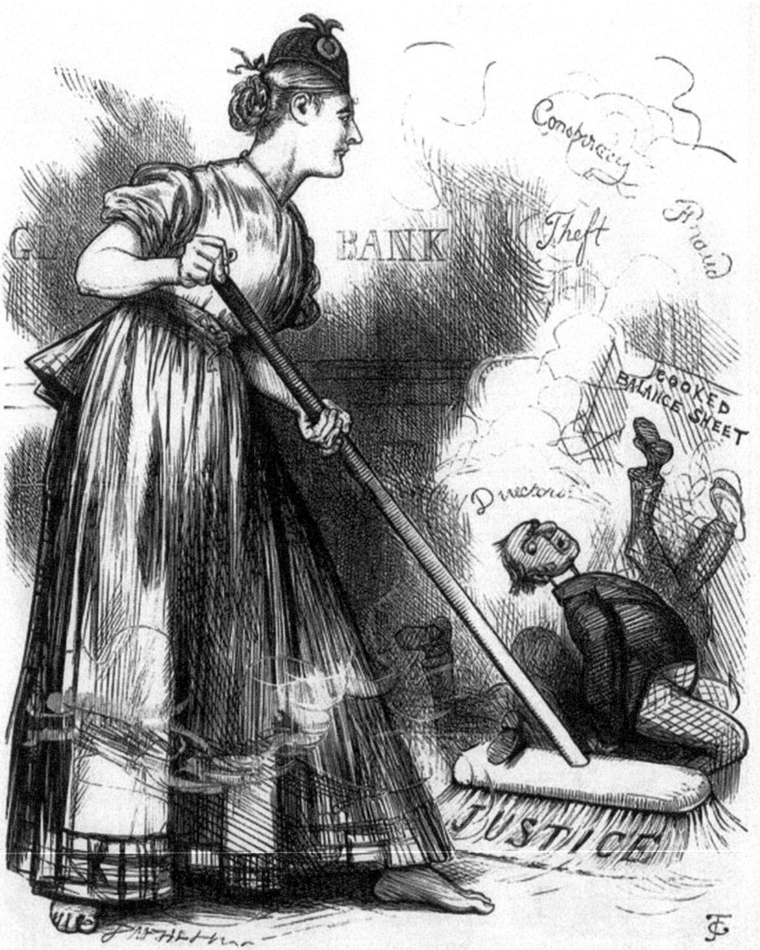

THE GREAT BANK SMASH.

SWEEPING UP THE RUBBISH.

Scotia:—"WELL, IT'S A NASTY JOB, BUT IT'S A GOOD THING THERE ARE NO MORE LIKE IT."

Fig. 9.5 *Fun*, *The Great Bank Smash*, 30 October 1878 (Courtesy of UoF) the Goddess's pointing with her left hand towards the meeting of irate shareholders discussing the fate of their company beneath a sign marked 'payment suspended' (i.e., no cash payments out of the bank). The shareholders are a mixture of Scots, women, and men; their clenched fists, ready to bang on the door of the closed bank, serving as evidence of their anger. Overall, there is a sense of nonchalance, of the director being totally unaware and unconcerned about the impact his actions have had on his victims.

Figure 9.5 appeared two weeks later and shows the Goddess this time as the Goddess of Scotia or Scotland. The Goddess is using her large broom to clear up the mess (by this time the investigation report into the causes and impact of the bank's collapse had been completed and the results published). The size and shape of the broom contrasts with the classical depiction of the broom in the previous image.

The broom (marked 'Justice') is shown sweeping away the bank director (whose eyes are open now, a literal representation of the realisation of his criminal activities), as well as raising the dust (e.g., speculation) thrown up by various consequences of the collapse (conspiracy, fraud, theft, cooked balance sheet). The director is panicking now, having realised that the events were not a dream, as portrayed in the previous image, but real and visceral in their impact. The use of the broom is possibly influenced by a similar image in the *Daily Graphic*, titled *Panic* (see Fig. 6.11), the themes of the broom and dust are both examples of financial iconography and are discussed in greater detail in Chapter 6, Financial Iconography).

Invoking 'Justice' clearly sums up the periodical's point of view, which was to expect the indulgent, insensitive bank directors to pay the price of their cupidity. The puns are kept alive by images of 'cooking the books', here in the form of a cookery book.

The broom serves as a symbol of clearing out the mess caused by the bank directors, with the dust being swept away comprising particles of dirt, theft, conspiracy, and the directors themselves.

9.3 Depiction of the Legal Process

9.3.1 Leopold Redpath

The first depiction of the legal process in relation to white-collar crime is a scene in *Lives of Robson and Redpath*.

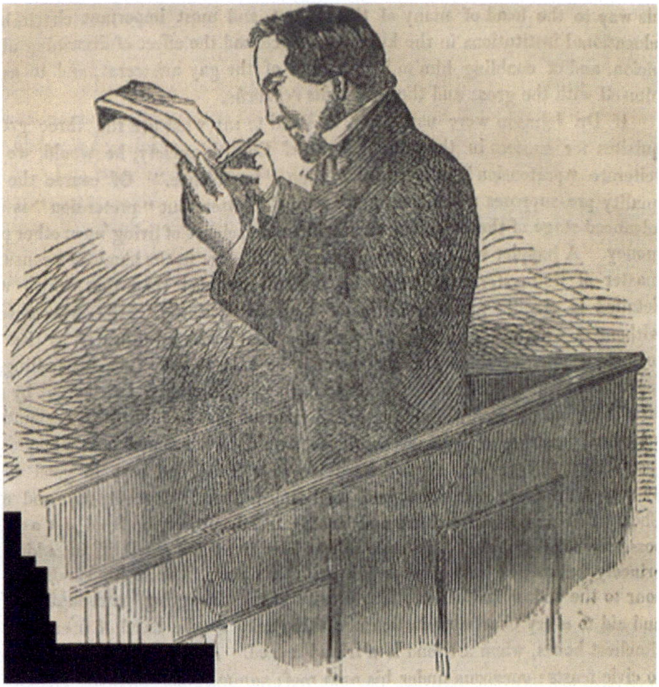

Fig. 9.6 Redpath at the time of his trial (extract from book)—Project Gutenberg

Figure 9.6 shows the only image of Redpath himself in the book. There are no images of his trial (or that of the other villain of the period, Robson). Redpath is depicted, smartly dressed, taking notes of the trial's proceedings. He looks unconcerned about the nature of the crimes of which he is being accused, merely an interested observer. No remorse or emotion is conveyed (unlike the other images in the book described in Chapter 5, The Charlatans).

9.3.2 The Trial of the Scotland Yard Detectives (the Harry Benson Case)

The view from the side in Fig. 9.7 imagines the scene that members of the viewing public would see. The general composition of the depiction of

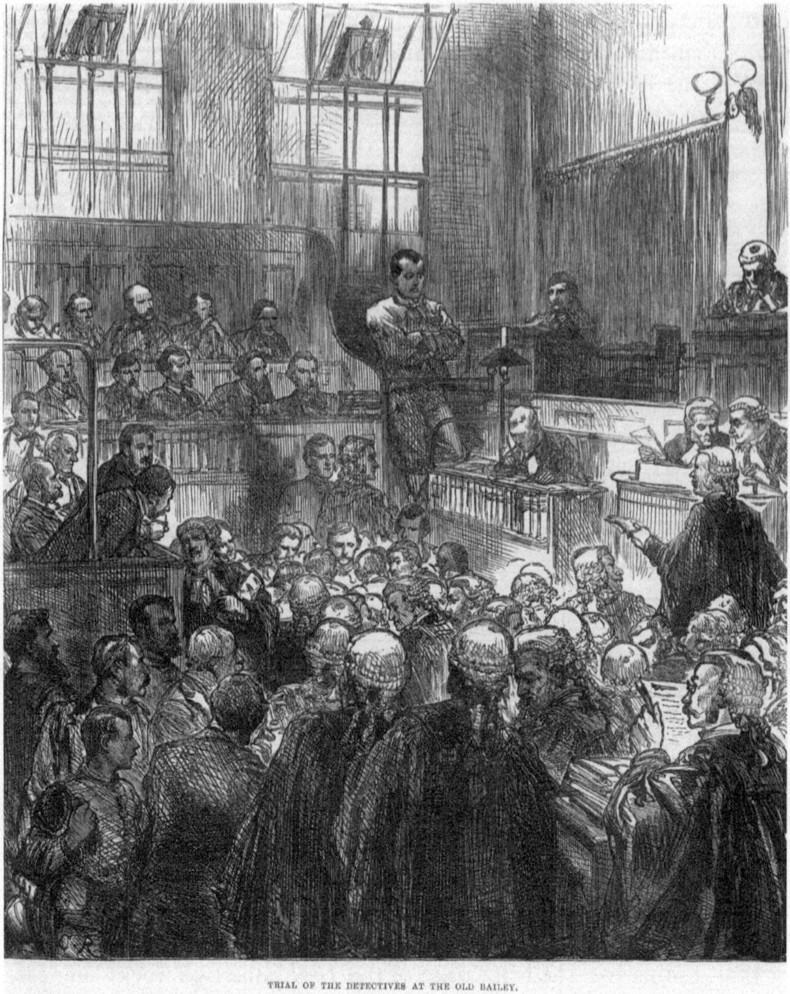

Fig. 9.7 *ILN*, *The Trial of the Scotland Yard Detectives*, 3 November 1877 (© Illustrated London News/Mary Evans)

court proceedings followed a common format reflecting the actual setting in Victorian times.[4] The view accentuates the hubbub of bewigged legal teams at the front, with the jury centre stage at the back. By narrowing the view of the court participants, the effect is claustrophobic, accentuated by the larger-than-life image of one of the accused in the witness dock.

9.3.3 The CGB Failure

The realistic periodicals really began to focus on trials of white-collar criminals at the time of the CGB failure in 1878. They covered the various stage of the trial process, from early November when the examination of the accused began, through to the trial and judgement in early 1879. As has been mentioned previously, the sheer number of images relating to the CGB failure is testimony to the interest that readers—from both realistic and comic-serious periodicals—took in the trial. This was even more noteworthy given that the editorial space for images had to be split between the domestic sensation of the CGB failure and the exotic foreign images of the first Afghan War, which began in November 1878 (see Fig. 5.13 for an illustration of this 'competition' for editorial space).[5] Almost half the images of the CGB failure came from the realistic periodicals indicating that the new journalism, with its predilection for sensationalism and images, had truly arrived.[6]

This chapter deals with fourteen images of the CGB failure, covering the emotional responses to the initial failure (see Figs. 9.4 and 9.5) as well as the depictions of various elements of the trial process. It includes a detailed analysis of one *Punch* image, *At the Head of the Profession* (Fig. 9.12), which conveys a sense of the in-depth review possible in interpreting such images and which is illustrated in Appendix 1.

Figure 9.8 displays the front page of the *Graphic,* which depicts the directors being brought to the Central Police Court to be committed for trial. Rather like the front page of the *IPN* issue two weeks later (see Fig. 5.13), the novelty of a white-collar criminal case led the editors of the two periodicals to position the events on their front pages. The *IPN* issue headlines the sensational nature of the events, whilst the *Graphic* issue merely emphasises that the editor felt its readers should realise the importance of white-collar criminals being brought to court. The emphasis is on the accused, lined up opposite the reader. Like the *ILN* image in Fig. 9.9 the artist uses the superimposition of larger-than-life depictions of the accused to frame the court scene in the lower image. The artist

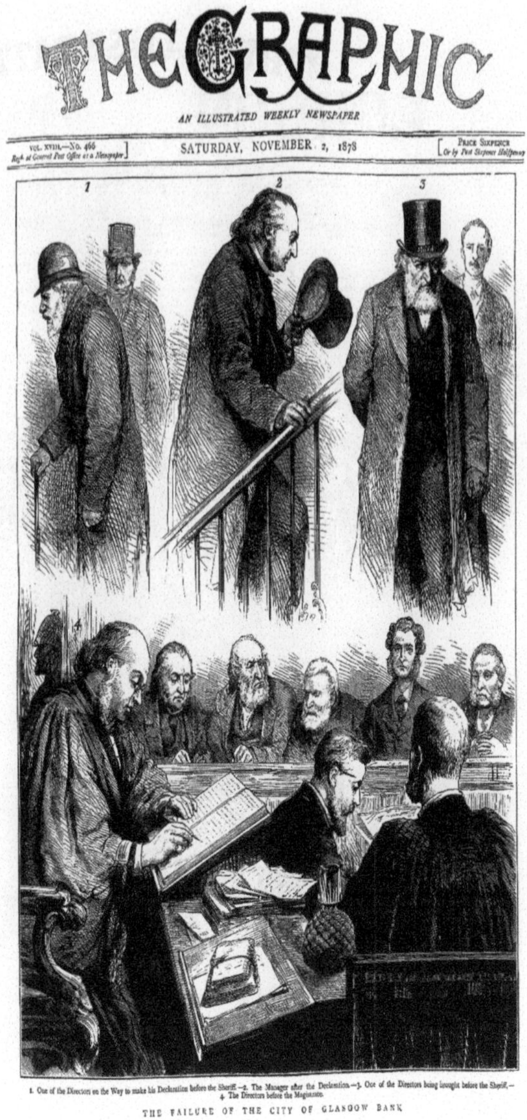
THE GRAPHIC

AN ILLUSTRATED WEEKLY NEWSPAPER

VOL. XVIII.—No. 466 Regd. at General Post Office as a Newspaper

SATURDAY, NOVEMBER 2, 1878

PRICE SIXPENCE Or by Post Sixpence Halfpenny

1. One of the Directors on the Way to make his Declaration before the Sheriff.—2. The Manager after the Declaration.—3. One of the Directors being brought before the Sheriff.—4. The Directors before the Magistrate.

THE FAILURE OF THE CITY OF GLASGOW BANK

Fig. 9.8 *The Graphic, The Failure of the City of Glasgow Bank*, 2 November 1878 (© Illustrated London News/Mary Evans)

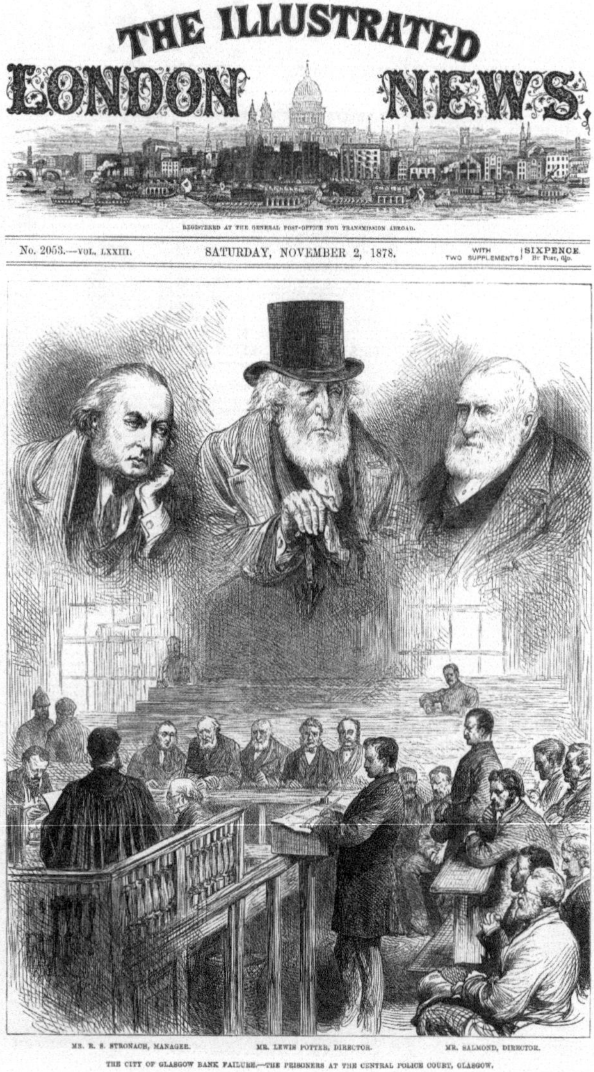

Fig. 9.9 *ILN, The City of Glasgow Bank—The Prisoners at the Central Police Court Glasgow*, 2 November 1878 (© Illustrated London News/Mary Evans)

is seeking to stress the age and sombre expression of the accused. In the *Graphic* the directors are depicted arriving at the court, and the emphasis of the court scene is on the Sheriff examining the accused.

In Fig. 9.9, the images of the directors are less distinct at the Sheriff's Court; the artist is placing more emphasis on the superimposed images above. The accused is depicted in sombre, serious mood, not shocked by the unfolding events. In the *ILN* image the larger size of the superimposed accused figures compared with the similar depiction in the *Graphic* accentuates the emotional impact.

It is instructive to compare the images of the accused in the realistic periodicals with photographs at the trial in late January 1879 contained in Wallace's book.[7] The trial evidence is interspersed with photographs not just of the accused and the judges as in *ILN*, the *Graphic*, and *Funny Folks*, but also of the Defence Counsel and the Crown Prosecuting Counsel. All the Wallace photographs show the protagonists in static portrait mode, with no props or setting as in the images in the periodicals.

Figure 9.10 conveys the age of the accused, most of them in their sixties, like Salmond, who was 74, and Potter, who was 72. Whether intended or not, the portrayal of such figures would have evoked some sympathy in the minds of readers. This was a point not lost on counsel for the defence; on more than one occasion mention is made of the advancing years of some of the defendants and the impact that has had on their ability to understand the complex financial affairs of CGB. See Fig. 9.11 for an example of a Defence Counsel representation.

In *Punch*'s *At the Head of the Profession*, Fig. 9.12, a bank director is depicted in a waiting room outside the Criminal Court waiting to be examined. The use of sensationalist criminal headlines on the notice board as well as the presence of fictional 'criminal' low-life characters from Dickens's *Oliver Twist* alongside the fictional accused bank director provides a stark juxtaposition of white-collar crime alongside low-level crime.

The caption in Fig. 9.12 is ambiguous as 'profession' could refer as much to the profession of criminals as to that of bankers (as may at first sight be indicated). The title also places the Director at the head or pinnacle of his profession, banking at one level, so *Punch* appears to be attacking banking, and bank directors especially—a possible indication of the attitude of *Punch* towards the events unfolding. The Institute of Bankers in England and Wales had only just been established (in 1878)—the first time that bankers had a professional organisation to represent

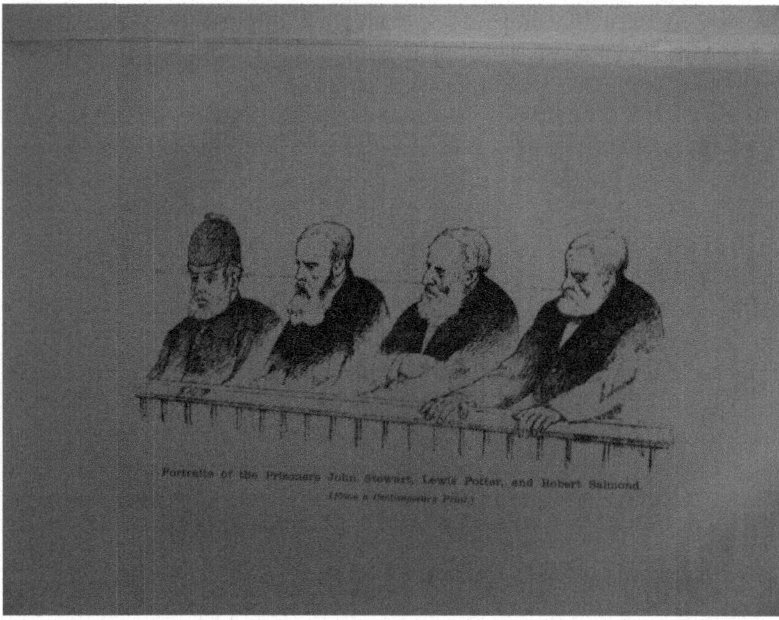

Fig. 9.10 *Wallace, Portraits of the Prisoners John Stewart, Lewis Potter, and Robert Salmond* (own photo)

them and to run examinations and establish codes of conduct.[8] Accordingly, there is a sense of irony implicit in the notion of unscrupulous directors just as a professional organisation is trying to impose ethical standards of behaviour upon them (it should be borne in mind that the Scottish equivalent was formed three years earlier making the irony arguably even more poignant).

The scene is the waiting room adjoining the Police Court (Glasgow). *Punch*'s composition of the scene is altogether more melancholic and fearful than similar images in *ILN* and the *Graphic,* which show the accused appearing before the magistrate. In the latter images, the accused are depicted as elderly bewildered gentlemen, confused at the proceedings. Who is the 'eminently respectable Director' depicted in the scene? Comparing him to portraits of the actual accused in Chapter 5, the director in Fig. 9.12 appears to be a generic (London centric), rather than

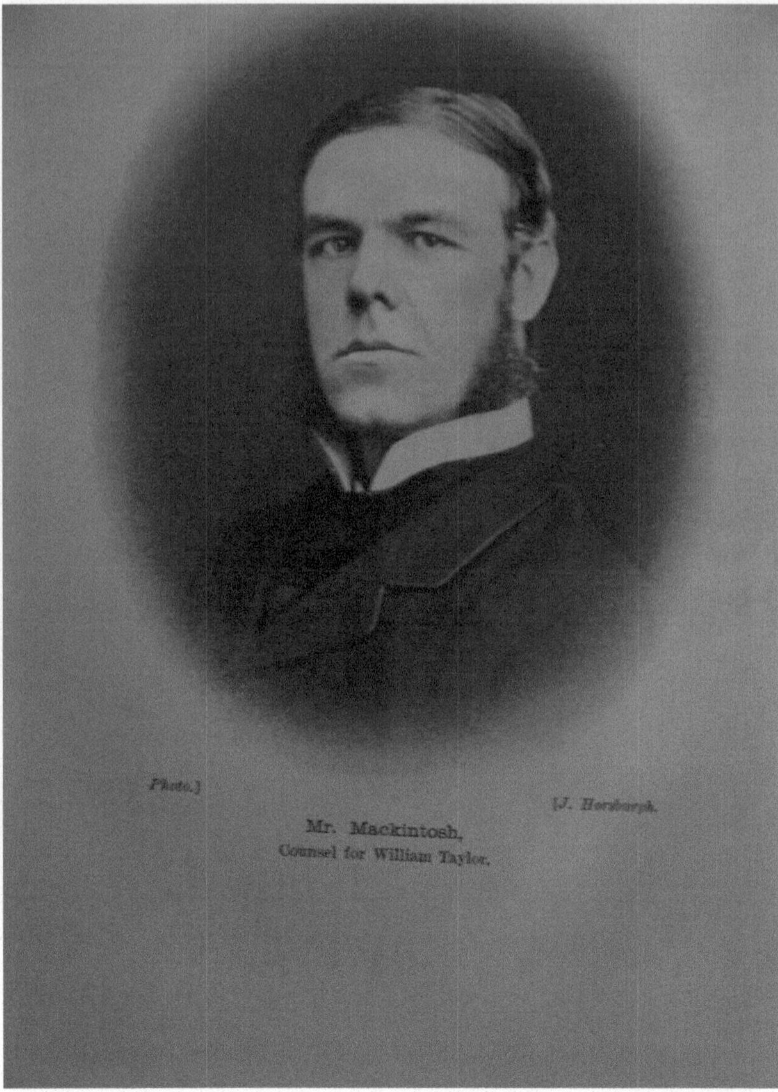

Fig. 9.11 *Wallace, Mr Mackintosh, Counsel for William Taylor* (own photo)

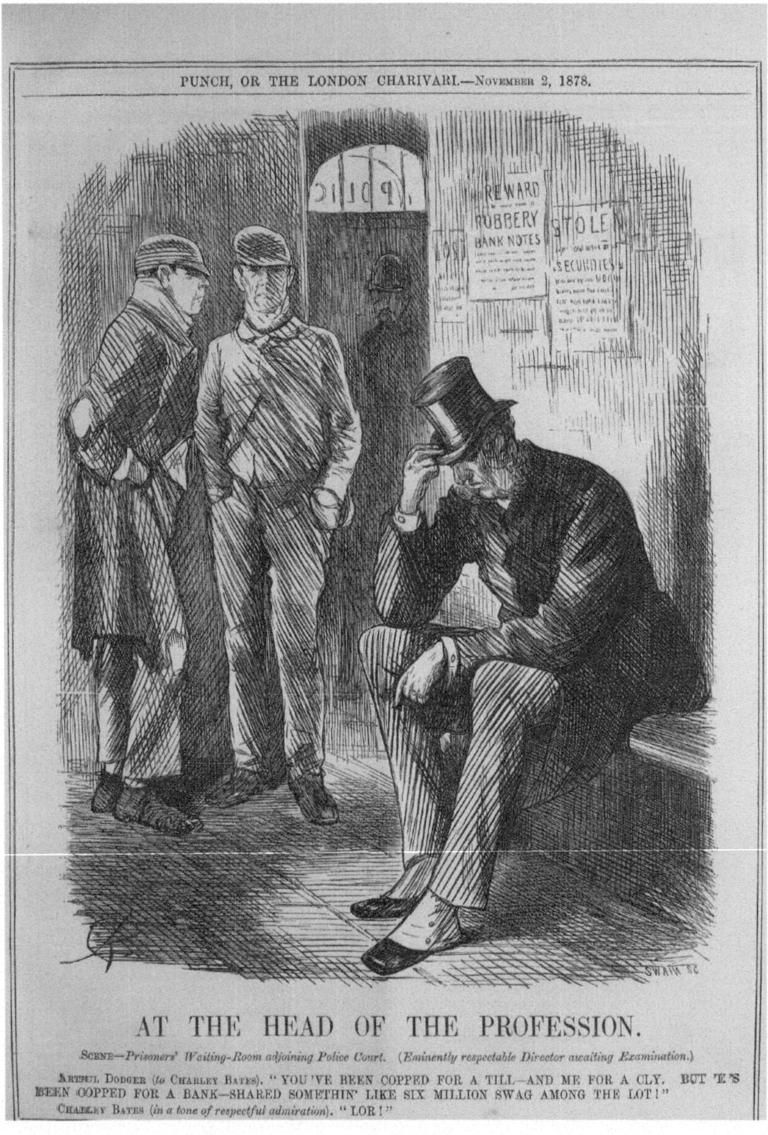

Fig. 9.12 *Punch, At the Head of the Profession*, 2 November 1878 (Courtesy of UoH)

a specific, representation. The depiction in *Punch* is of a smart distinguished businessman (indicated by his frock coat, lighter trousers, and galoshes) whereas the CGB directors (see Chapter 5) are dressed in a long coat. He is disconsolate, almost trying to hide his face from any onlookers. Behind him is a wall with notices about rewards for bank-note robbery and theft of securities. There is no doubt where the publication's sympathies lay, but it is interesting that the notices are for crimes in respect of which no CGB director was ever actually accused. It is probably more a case of what the artist thought would be most redolent for a reader: something sensationalist (e.g., a bank-notes robbery) and reminiscent of bank crimes of a few years earlier (theft of securities)—allusions to CGB losses.

The two individuals conversing behind the director are key protagonists from Dickens's *Oliver Twist*, the cunning leader of Fagin's gang of pickpockets, the Artful Dodger, and one of his young gang members, Charley Bates.

Punch evokes the spirit of Dickens and anti-speculation type activities by using the *Oliver Twist* analogy.[9] Though serialised forty years earlier the story would have been powerful enough to have prompted memories of Dickens's distaste of money, and its impact on the poor, and in so doing cause readers to have far less sympathy for the bank director than the poor urchins. It chimes with the Victorians' sense of morality—an adherence to a code of conduct both personally and professionally. As Searle remarks, this sense of morality was at the heart of the Victorians' dilemma. Morally, bankers were viewed less favourably than manufacturers. From a business perspective, by contrast, bankers enjoyed greater social prestige.[10]

Readers would have had to understand the use of slang (*till, cly, swag, copped*) to indicate the working-class nature of the onlookers. (*Till* signifies taking monies from a till, *cly* is slang for pick pocketing,[11] *swag* means monies or goods taken by a burglar,[12] *copped* means having been nabbed, or arrested).

Charley Bates, on learning from the Artful Dodger that the gentleman is being examined in connection with the stealing of six million pounds expresses deep professional respect, one criminal to another; it also signifies a class distinction, given the paltry amounts both Charley and the Artful Dodger had stolen in their fictional representations. After all, six million would have been worth £500m in today's terms.[13]

And it is this almost 'hero worship' by the two petty criminals which makes *Punch*'s view of the bank director somewhat ambivalent. There is a sense of solidarity with the criminal class which elevates the bank director beyond opprobrium towards a grudging admiration for his exploits. The main thrust of *Punch*'s image is the disgust felt towards the dishonourable conduct of the bank director, and not the impact of this fraud on investors.

If readers of Fig. 9.12 were aware of the setting of the earlier Fig. 9.13, then the irony would be significant. Figure 9.13 dealt with the iniquity of justice handed out to crimes of violence and robbery as compared with crimes of wife-beating.

The inference from reading both the 1872 and the 1878 images together is a criticism that white-collar crime is equated with low-level prison sentences—there should be higher sentences. But the irony is perhaps too subtle for some of *Punch*'s readers?

Did *Punch* regret this sympathetic portrayal of a bank director? By the following week (9 November), see Fig. 9.14 the tune had changed. Relegated to a small image, with accompanying text predominating, the

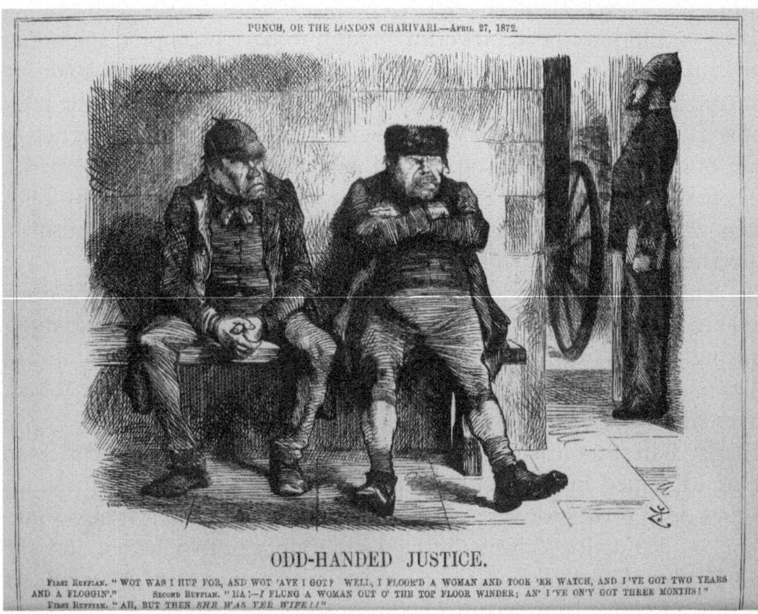

Fig. 9.13 *Punch, Odd-Handed Justice*, 27 April 1872 (Courtesy of UoH)

AMAZING!

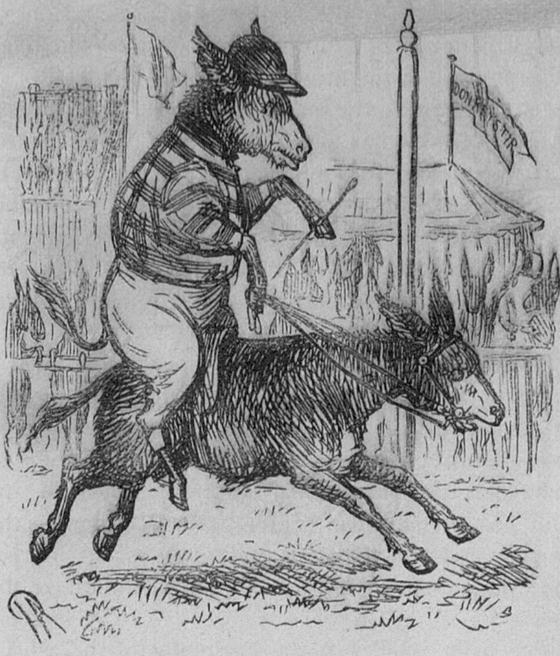

"AGAINST folly," SCHILLER says, "the gods themselves fight in vain!" Why, then, should *Punch* hope to contend successfully with this irresistible adversary? At what desperate odds he dares the contest will be apparent, he hopes, to some, at least, of his readers, when he tells them that his last week's Cartoon, branding the villany of the Directors of the City of Glasgow Bank, has been construed by an indignant correspondent—a Scotchman, he is sorry to say—into an outrageous and unfeeling attack on the unhappy sufferers by that gigantic swindle—the very objects, *Punch* need scarcely point out, of his deepest sympathy as helpless and innocent victims of these thieves on a colossal scale, whom his Cartoon presents in their true character as heads of the plundering profession.

Fig. 9.14 *Punch*, *Amazing!*, 9 November 1878 (Courtesy of UoH[14])

article *Amazing!* is now more concerned with the impact of the scandal on duped investors than it is with expressing disgust at the bank director. The main image is that of a donkey (a poor investor) being ridden flat out by an overweight jockey (representing the bank director, whose full figure this time alludes to the depiction in *Fun* a few weeks earlier) disguised as a horse.

In Fig. 9.14 reference is made in the text accompanying the image to an apparently fictional letter from a Scot berating *Punch* for its treatment of bank directors. As indicated above in the context of other depictions of bank directors, *Punch*'s depiction in its 2 November image is too dignified and does not reflect clearly enough the moral indignation that it displays a week later in the text accompanying the image of 9 November. The text expands on *Punch*'s view of banking as 'heads of the plundering profession'. It almost feels like an apology for any misrepresentation implied in Fig. 9.12. But the contrast in depiction and style is striking—the possible ambiguity in the tragic-comic depiction in Fig. 9.14 is replaced with outright condemnation of the behaviour of the directors whose characterisation as a horse, whipping a poor donkey, is clearly ironic. Whilst the 'horse' has won the race, the image implies that there has been an unacceptable cost, the cost to the poor victim, the 'donkey'.

A metonymic pun 'being taken for a ride' is also reflected in the image, with the 'race' being held at one of the most prestigious racecourses in the country (Doncaster—Donkeystir—Donkey). Doncaster was home to one of the major classic events on the annual horseracing calendar, the St Leger.[15] It had only just been run (in September) so combining the image of a donkey (a poor investor) with this prestigious race is another example of the complex puns used by *Punch* and other periodicals of the time.

The use of the quote from Schiller at the beginning of the article, commenting that even the Gods cannot prevent humans falling prey to folly, is indicative of the view *Punch* took of the actions of the bank directors. However, such comments are in the text, not reflected in the image, which is more comical than biting in its satire. Having shot its bolt, so to speak, with its initial potentially mistimed response to the failure, *Punch* falls back on gentle humour going forward in dealing with the rest of the events.

The importance of the CGB failure can be gauged by the positioning of the images in the periodicals (invariably at the beginning of an issue), the size of the images (invariably taking over the whole front page), or in some cases, merely the existence of images of the CGB failure in the periodical itself. In *IPN* for example the only images of the failure appear in the 16 November 1878 issue where four of the directors are shown framed in a sensationalist fashion in keeping with the style of the periodical (see Fig. 5.13).

Superimposing individual vignettes of some of the accused at the top of the image stirs the readers' emotions. The age, eminence, and contrition of the accused is made clear, and whilst the crimes may be serious, there is more than slight degree of empathy for the accused.

In Fig. 9.15 a two-page spread in *ILN* (a typical device used by periodicals for important events) provides a dynamic representation of the various elements present at the trial. The different 'episodes' are shown framing the main figure of the Prosecuting Counsel arguing his case in front of the Judiciary.

The representation of the same trial in the *Graphic* (Fig. 9.16) offers a different view.

In Fig. 9.16 the *Graphic*'s use of 'realistic' storyboards provides an almost epic quality to the unfolding events and differentiates itself from its staider rivals (such as *ILN*). Nevertheless, both *ILN* and the *Graphic*

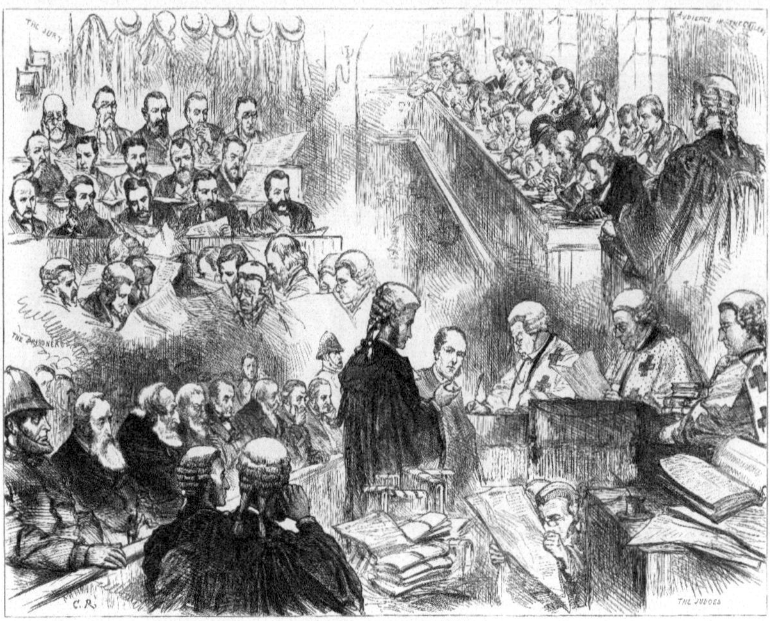

Fig. 9.15 *ILN*, *Trial of the Glasgow Bank Directors*, 1 February 1879 (© Illustrated London News/Mary Evans)

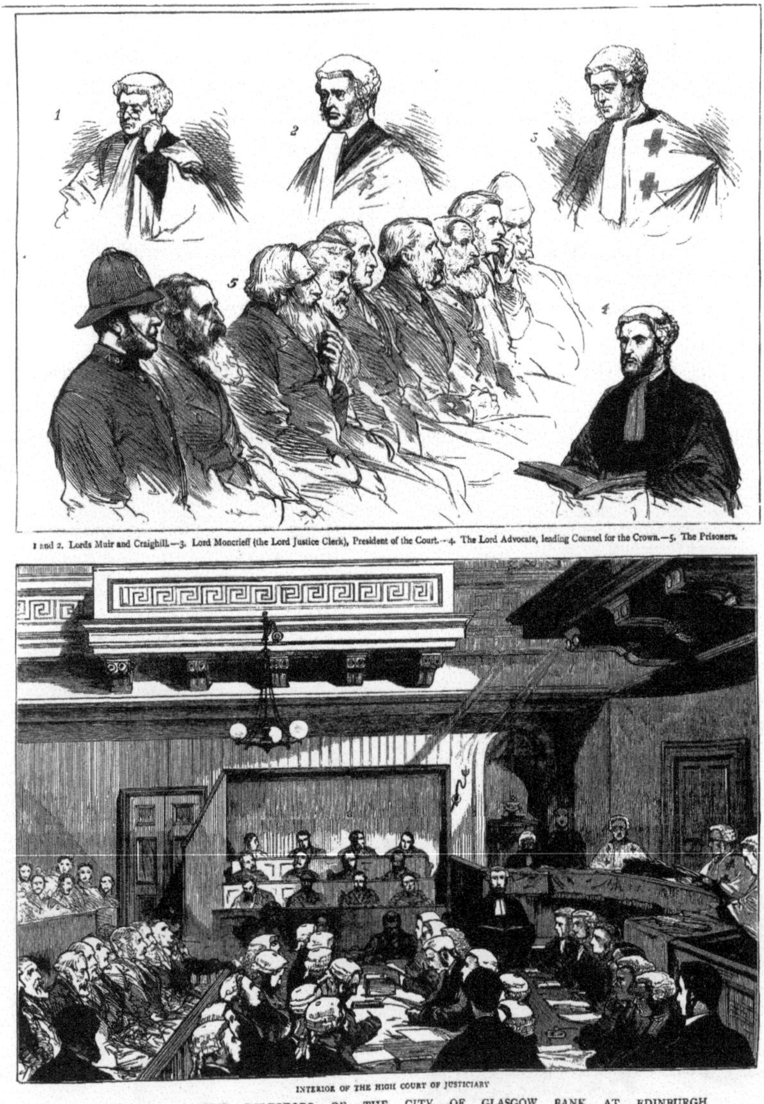

Fig. 9.16 *The Graphic*, *The Trial of the Directors of the City of Glasgow Bank at Edinburgh*, 1 February 1879 (© Illustrated London News/Mary Evans)

also provide a social commentary, lacking from the Wallace account of the CGB trial, which consisted of photographs only.[16] Providing a setting (such as the Police Court or the trial location) for the accused evoked more of the anguish of the events than did the pure 'staged' photographs (without props or setting) as seen in Wallace. Using different angles in the courtroom (drawing the eye of the reader to either the Jury or Prosecuting Counsel) provokes differing emotional responses (the solemnity of the responsibility placed on the jurors on the one hand, and the desire for Justice on the other, reflected in all eyes gazing—almost burning in intensity—at the Prosecuting Counsel delivering his comments).

Both *ILN* and the *Graphic* depict the accused at their pre-trial hearing, and again at their trial. The composition of the figures is again revealing for the readership is drawn to different aspects of the images on the page depending on the angle of sight chosen by the artists. Is it the judges, or the accused, or the setting itself, which is being highlighted?

In Fig. 9.16 the *Graphic* moves into a storyboard mode for the events, allowing a dynamic rather than a static representation of the events. The series of images in the edition of 2 November permit a free-flowing story reflecting the sudden movements of the day with anguished shareholders and despairing depositors depicted in animated form. These staged episodes contrast with the staged portrait depiction of photos of the time.[17] *ILN*, *IPN,* and the *Graphic* can show the anguish and despondency of the accused—emotional elements which are entirely absent from contemporary photos.

In Frith's *The Race for Wealth* (Fig. 9.24) and the *Graphic*'s representation (Fig. 9.16), images of the trial depicting twelve jurors indicate that this was an English trial, whilst *ILN* depicts the trial of the CGB directors correctly as being held in Edinburgh in front of 15 jurors (see Fig. 9.15).[18] The other difference is that the reader is invited, by the positioning of the various protagonists, to imagine it is the jury who is key to the events unfolding. The use of different angles of viewing the trial proceedings, whilst on the one hand an artistic device to 'lead' the reader, also provokes emotional responses not apparent when viewing photographs of the individual accused. In both the *ILN* and *Graphic* representations, the artist is provoking the reader to examine closely the events unfolding and to agree or disagree with the prominence of either the Prosecuting Counsel (*ILN)* or the jury (*Graphic*). Do these differences in composition elicit either objectivity (imagine you the reader were members of the jury) or the desire for Justice (imagine you the reader were in the role of the Prosecuting Counsel in seeking convictions for the crimes of the accused)? The *ILN* image certainly puts the figure of prosecuting counsel at the centre, whilst the *Graphic* image puts the jury foremost dominating the proceedings in the centre. In both cases the images do not concentrate on the accused, although another image in the *Graphic* does show a detail from the main image which conveys the sober elderly nature of the accused.

Alongside images of other buildings in the main judicial complex, the drawing of the scene of the cell (Fig. 9.17) provides a sense of the ghoulish (and emotional) settings beloved by Victorian readers (see commentary on juxtaposition of CGB directors with exotic animals in *IPN* (Fig. 5.13). The commentary is at pains to stress the lack of privileged status for these upstanding members of the financial community. The description in Fig. 9.18 indicates the lengths to which the periodical went to depict scenes of the trial.

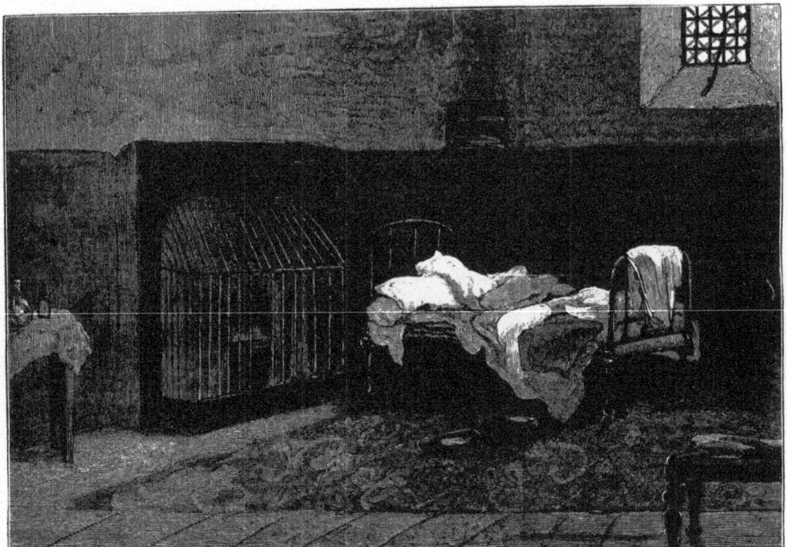

THE TRIAL OF THE CITY OF GLASGOW BANK DIRECTORS—CELL BENEATH THE HIGH COURT OF JUSTICIARY, OCCUPIED BY HENRY INGLIS

Fig. 9.17 *Graphic, The Trial of the City of Glasgow Bank Directors—Cell Beneath the High Court of Judiciary, occupied by Henry Inglis*, 1 February 1879 (© Illustrated London News/Mary Evans)

THE GLASGOW BANK TRIAL

THE trial of the manager and directors of the City of Glasgow Bank was concluded on Friday, when the jury found Lewis Potter and Robert Stronach guilty of fabricating and uttering the false balance-sheets, and the other five prisoners guilty of using and uttering them, knowing them to be false. Judgment was deferred until next day (Saturday), when Potter and Stronach were sentenced to be imprisoned for eighteen months, and Stewart, Salmond, Taylor, Inglis, and Wright for eight months, the judge specially remarking that the imprisonment they had already undergone had been taken into consideration. The sentence was received with great surprise in Court, and with evident satisfaction by the convicts, some of whom seemed much excited. When the news got to be known outside there were loud murmurs of disapproval, and the prisoners were driven off in the police van amidst the howls and execrations of the people. In Glasgow a large crowd assembled at the Royal Exchange, awaiting the arrival of the news, and on the telegram being posted, one man expressed his readiness "tae hang the lot o' them on the gibbet." Many persons in the crowd evidently sympathised with the indignation thus roughly expressed. The general opinion of the Press appears to be that the punishment is far too lenient, and though it may be urged that, as the prisoners are men of culture and social position, the exposure and consequent disgrace makes them feel keenly a sentence which would be thought ridiculously light by persons of less refinement and susceptibility, yet it must be remembered that that very social position placed them to a great extent above temptation.

Our illustration shows the nature of the accommodation afforded to the prisoners while in confinement during the trial. Potter and Stronach are now in Perth Penitentiary, and the five others in Glasgow Prison. The *Scotsman* says that they are kept in ordinary cells, supplied with the usual fare, and subjected to the customary discipline of the prison.

NOTE.——Mr. C. Scott, Clerk of Justiciary, Edinburgh, desires us to contradict the statement we made last week as to the reason of the Lord Justice General having nothing to do with the case. He informs us that Lord Glencorse is in no way related to the prisoner, Henry Inglis, and that the duty of presiding at the trial fell to Lord Moncrieff in the ordinary course of judicial business.

Fig. 9.18 *Graphic*, *Our Illustrations*, 1 February 1879 (© Illustrated London News/Mary Evans)

The only comic depiction of the trial itself is to be found in *Funny Folks*, which offers a humorous take on the trial proceedings based on the transcript of the trial published in the daily newspapers of the time (see Fig. 9.19). The storyboard highlights that all relevant parties—jurors, judges, defence and prosecuting counsel, and spectators—were crammed into a tiny space (notice the repetition of the word 'economy' of space on two occasions). The sheer volume of evidence, as well as the dramatic location of the trapdoor out of which the prisoners emerged from their cells, contribute to the emotional sensational nature of the trial.

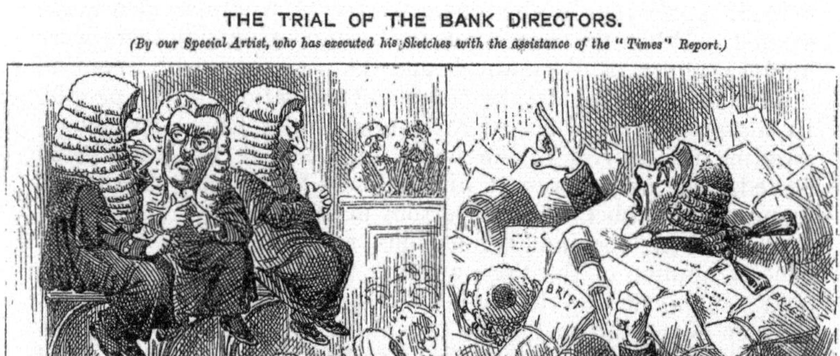

Fig. 9.19 *Funny Folks*, *The Trial of the Bank Directors*, 1 February 1879 (@ BL Shelf Mark, Vol. 5, Issue 218, p. 35)

By the end of the CGB trial *Funny Folks* could invoke the spirit of the Goddess of Justice, this time with her sword of Justice, about to cut off the head of one of the Bank Directors (see Fig. 9.20). But presciently the cartoon shows the Lord Justice-Clerk (Moncrieff) calmly telling the Goddess that the Law must have precedence, and act as a precedent. The accused could not be convicted based on popular distaste but on the state of Company Law at the time. The Goddess is clearly meant to represent here contemporary opinion, moral indignation, and the Christian virtues of divine law rather than man-made law. The type of sword, two-edged, provides another layer of metonymy and pun. As a metaphor of divine justice, it implies both defensive, protecting the innocent, as well as offensive, actions, dealing out justice. But it also conveys popular justice as the head of the Judiciary intervenes before the Goddess can administer popular justice to invoke the sanctity of man-made laws which must be obeyed first. This visceral sense of injustice, of the divine law being unable to override man-made law, reflected public indignation at the light sentences being handed out. White-collar criminals escaped with minor sentences, whilst thieves and other blue-collar criminals were subject to draconian sentences including death or exile to penal colonies (e.g., the example of Leopold Redpath, twenty years discussed in Chapter 5).

As has been discussed above in relation to the women trope, the image displays the conflict between Justice (depicted as a Goddess) and the Law. Whilst Justice must run its course, it must not be seen to be conflicting with the Law. So, the Law must take precedence over Justice—Justice here represents moral as well as legal justice. The Scottish victim looks rather manly, if elderly, and is more a symbol for the accused rather than reflecting any realistic personification.

After the CGB failure in 1878, the next major legal trial of white-collar criminals was that of Jabez Balfour in 1895. The intervening period as indicated in Chapter 2 (Financial Context), had seen the tightening of the role of the BoE and more investor protection in the form of company law reforms. Nevertheless, dubious business practices continued and Jabez Balfour's exploits at the Liberator Building Society provoked another outcry from the press (See discussion in Chapter 5).

9.3.4 *Jabez Balfour*

Figure 9.21 represents a staged drawing of Jabez Balfour's trial. The image concentrates on the face of Balfour as he listens intently to evidence

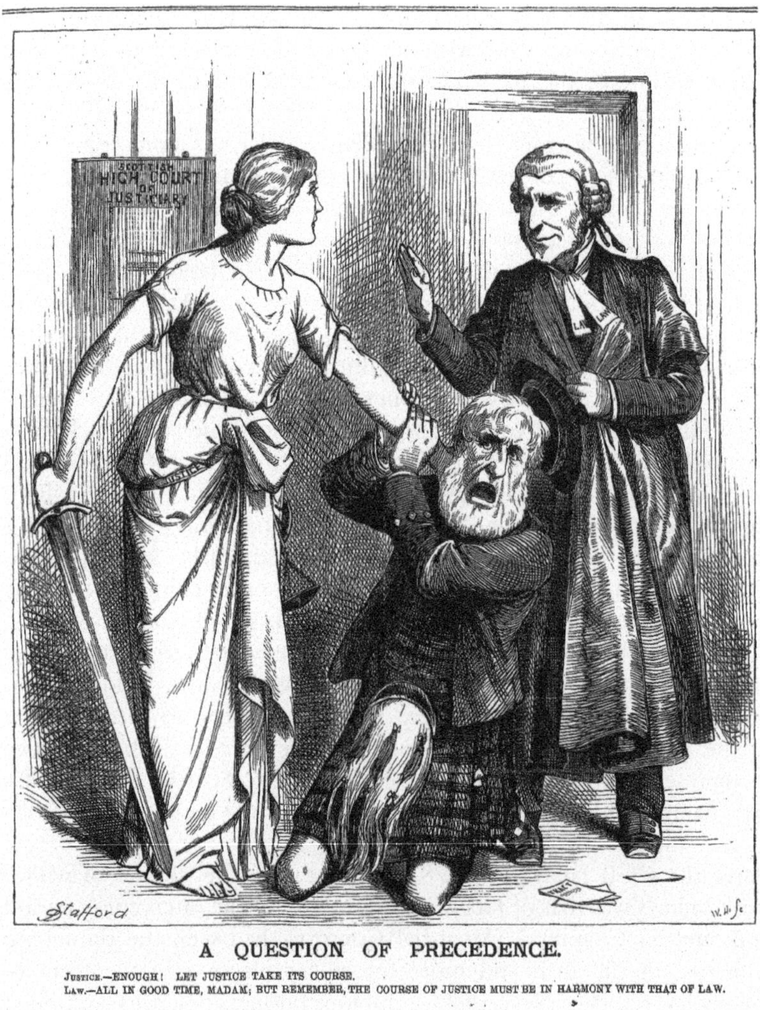

Fig. 9.20 *Funny Folks*, *A Question of Precedence*, 1 February 1879 (@ BL Shelf Mark, Vol. 5, Issue 218, p. 33)

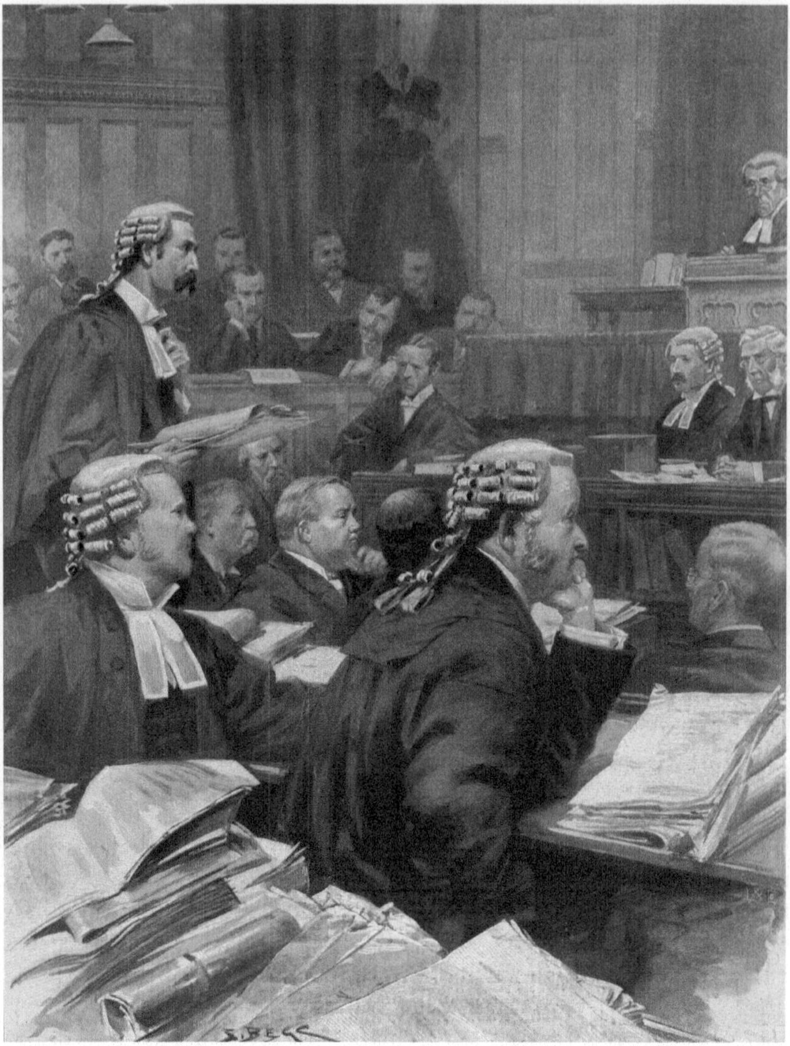

Fig. 9.21 *ILN*, *The Alleged Liberator Companies' Frauds; The trial of Jabez Balfour*. 1895 (© Illustrated London News/Mary Evans)

of an unseen witness. Positioning Balfour sitting with his defence team was unusual for depictions of trials of financial figures at the time. Together with the caption entitled '*The **Alleged** Liberator Company Frauds*' (my emphasis) it indicates that the periodical was unsure at this point in time about Balfour's guilt (though of course it could indicate the periodical's following the maxim of 'innocent until proved guilty').

Three years later the last major white-collar criminal trial of the nineteenth century took place—the trial of Ernest Hooley in 1898 (further detail can be found in Chapter 5).

9.3.5 Ernest Hooley

In Fig. 9.22, the staged depiction of the court scenes features the dominant figure of Hooley arguing his case alone. Hooley 'describes his solicitorless and lonely condition'. The judge and various counsel for the case are all depicted staring at him. He is smartly dressed, arguing his case passionately with demonstrative outstretched arms. There is no contrition, nor remorse. The use of the term 'solicitorless', literally without a solicitor, indicates Hooley's dismissal of the legal process and confidence in his own legal position (i.e., arguing his own defence).

This is another staged trial scene (contrast the *ILN* image of Balfour's trial three years earlier Fig. 9.21), this time with Hooley centre stage dominating the proceedings. The storyboard seems rather stiff, with characters all seeming to play to the courtroom.

As we have seen in the chapter on Charlatans, the figure of Ernest Hooley attracted the attention of the comic-serious periodicals, and the Hooley book contains over thirty cartoons from these periodicals illustrating the text of his life. Figure 9.23 has been chosen to indicate how his character was portrayed at his trial by the comic periodicals. It displays both verisimilitude (the accurate portrayal of the villain in this case being the cornerstone of the artistic method of the realistic periodicals), as well as the satire prevalent in the 1890s.

Figure 9.23 is a satirical representation of Hooley. His stoic disposition, common to several other cartoons of Hooley, is seen here with his head being examined (both literally and figuratively). Phrenology (a popular belief at the time that sought correlation between certain characteristics of the skull and the mental faculties contained within) is alluded to; the judge holds a form of screwdriver in his left hand with which he

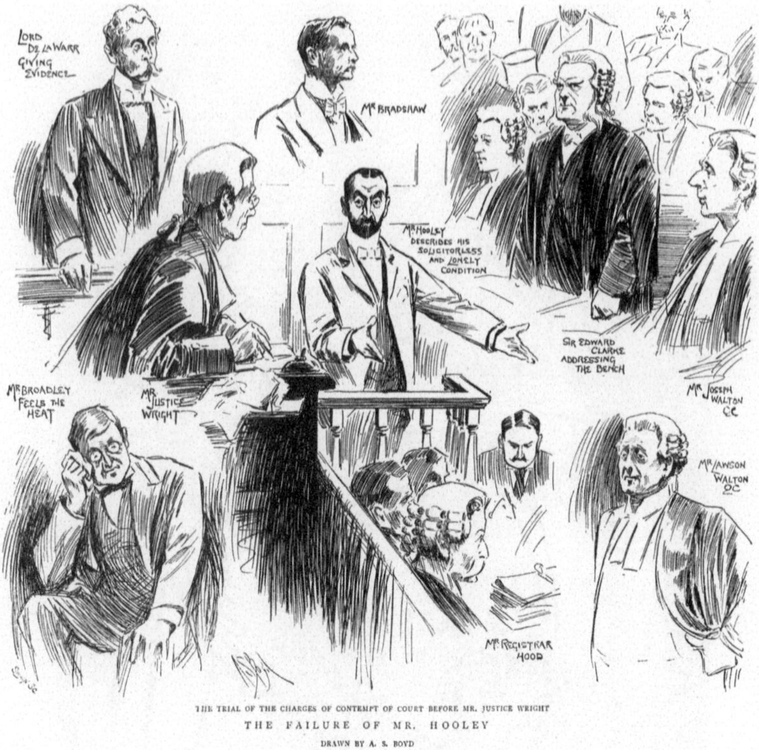

Fig. 9.22 *The Graphic*, *The Failure of Mr Hooley*, 20 August 1898 (© Illustrated London News/Mary Evans)

has created a hole in Hooley's head. In his right hand he holds a magnifying glass through which he peers, to understand what he is seeing inside Hooley's brain [mind].[19]

At the top left of the picture, Hooley's boards of directors, packed with aristocrats, are shown crumbling. At the bottom left, images of cheques are shown drifting in the air. The vignette of a bull under water possibly indicates that investors have lost their monies as the bull market has ended. The whole image is replete with financial iconography ('bulls', 'under water', as well as visual puns ('sinking' of the board directors, 'under examination' i.e., under the knife, which conjures the ghoulish portrayal of a live operation or examination).

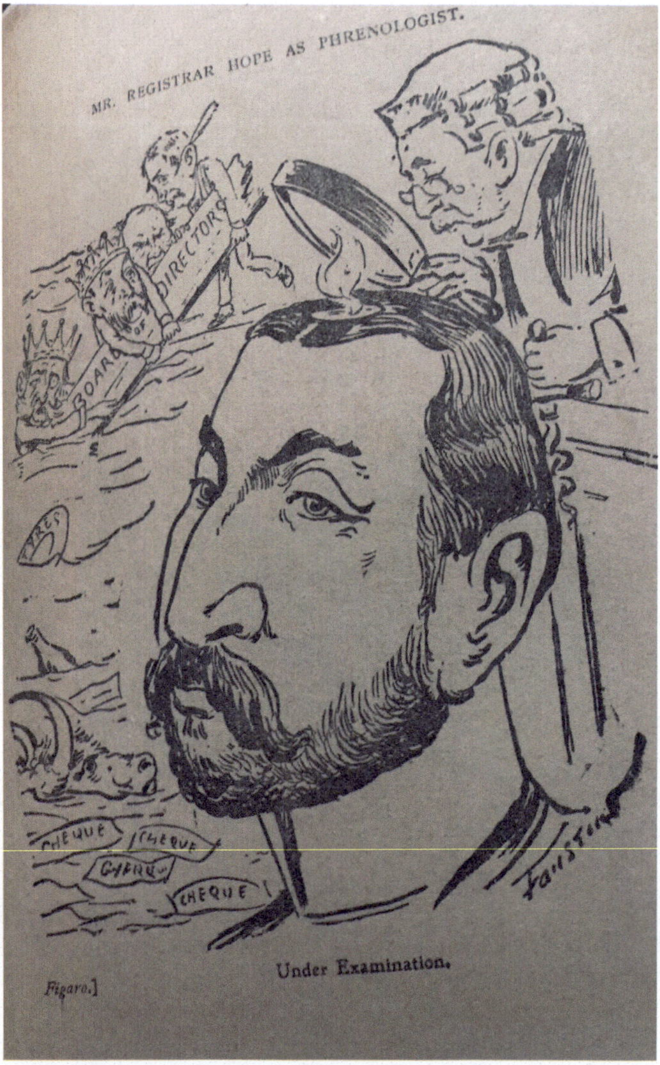

Fig. 9.23 *Under examination*, own photo from *The Hooley book*, 1898 (@ BL Shelf mark, GRC 10827.bb.36)

9.4 Cross-Over Between Realism and Comedy

9.4.1 Frith

Frith's *The Race for Wealth* provides a mixture of realism and moral attitudes representing a cross-over between the message conveyed in the realistic periodicals and those in the comic periodicals. This series contained court scenes as well as a rare scene of a villain, the Spider, dressed in prison clothes.

The last two images of *The Race for Wealth* illustrate the final two phases of the artist's fictional representation of the rise and fall of a typical financier. The first, *Judgement* (see below), depicts in realistic detail the trial of the Spider.

Frith was thwarted in his attempt to use real-life settings for several of his scenes. However, in *Judgement*, he was able to base the court scene and the representation of the judges on real life. In his attempts at verisimilitude, albeit whilst depicting scenes and individuals anonymously, Frith went to great lengths to provide exact likenesses of individuals and places. In *Judgement,* Frith aimed 'to realise the impression that the sight of the judge, with the sword of justice over him, together with a crowded court, would produce on the half-dazed eyes of the poor wretch (the accused)'.[20]

Figure 9.24 conveys the scene at court. Whilst the Spider is in the dock, contrite, his victims wait to tell their stories.

In *Judgement*, the angle of the viewer is steered towards the villain, with the jury members behind him. The emphasis is on the face of the villain, his contriteness, whilst he is being addressed by one of the counsels, with a judge looking on. The viewer is drawn to the distraught victims in the bottom right of the picture. They are witnesses ready to accuse him of crimes.[21]

The second, *Retribution* (Fig. 9.25), depicts the Spider, in convict garb, walking around a prison courtyard. The depiction of the villain in convict garb can be compared with the earlier caricature of Harry Benson in *Vanity Fair* (Fig. 5.11), which depicts the prisoner in sombre, reflective mood, though less penitent than Frith's representation.

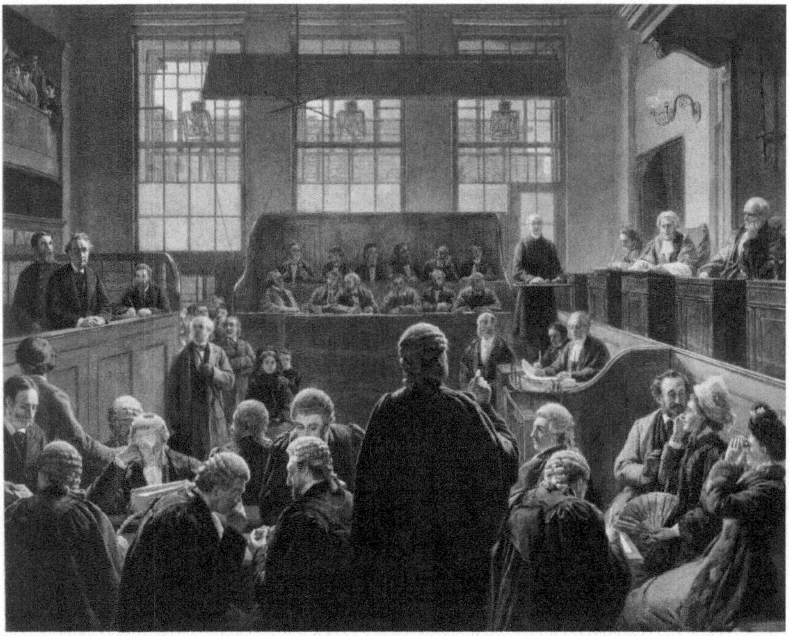

Fig. 9.24 W. P. Frith, *Judgement*, part of *The Race for Wealth*, 1880 (© Museum of London)

9.4.2 Sullivan

The comic periodicals often commented on the latest art exhibitions and in this case Sullivan, the editor of *Fun*, was moved not to just comment on Frith's series but to offer his own comic response.

In Fig. 6.35, *Odds on the* Spider, Sullivan comments that justice was not certain for white-collar criminals. Only sentenced to six months' imprisonment, the Spider (the name of the criminal in Frith's *The Race for Wealth*) is soon back on his feet, both literally and figuratively, firmly in the bosom of his family. The victims, by contrast, are left to clear up after him.

But which version was the truer, if either?

The text accompanying Sullivan's cartoon refers to the artist's (Frith) aping Trophonius. The latter was, in Greek mythology, an oracle to whom people came via a cave of nightmares. He was variously viewed as a God,

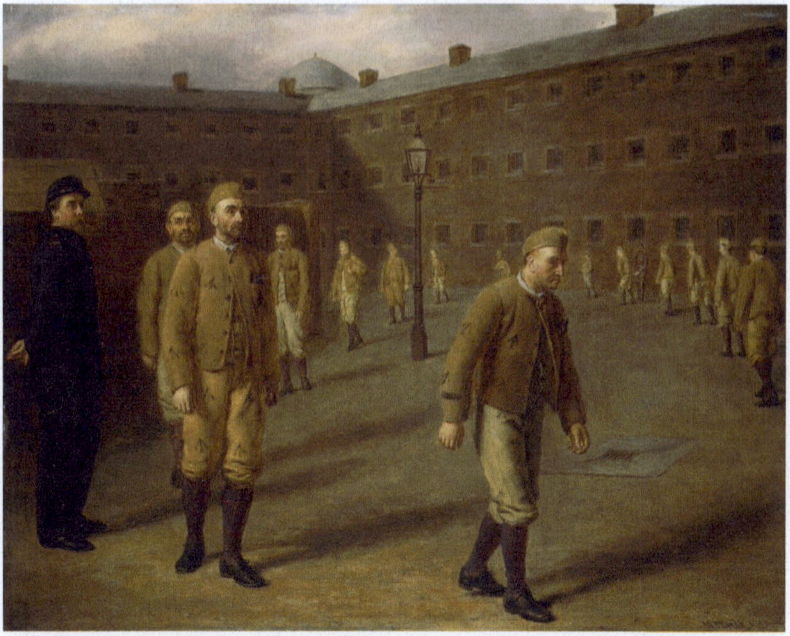

Fig. 9.25 W. P. Frith, *Retribution,* part of *The Race for Wealth*, 1880 (Photo by Birmingham Museums Trust licensed under CC0)

a thief, and a hero. Sullivan was supposing a different ending to that of Frith and appeared to leave it to the viewer as to the morality of their respective representations. Consulting an oracle often meant reflecting on one's own values—as the answers from oracles were often vague.

As mentioned in Chapter 6, Frith makes liberal use of puns. These reflected the nuances of the story as the verdict, six months, could be viewed as a mockery of the knavery of the Spider, a reversal (indicated by the Spider's 'standing on his head') of the real position. Note the comment on the position of the Spider, upside-down, as 'figurative'. Similarly, the words 'an easy canter over the six-month course' are used to dismiss the seriousness of the sentence. Was the Spider the real villain and did the sentence fit the crime?

But how to compare Sullivan's representation with that of Frith? Sullivan, unlike Firth, makes no pretension at artistic verisimilitude, instead he presents a wittier, arguably more realistic moral perspective.

Frith's moralistic stance is unequivocal, the 'bad' should be punished. Sullivan represents an ambivalent situation more attuned to real life. He invites viewers to make their own judgements on the rights and wrongs of the story.

9.5 Conclusion

Victims or villains, the coverage of the legal process underwent a transformation during the nineteenth century.

As public interest in white-collar trials increased mid-century onwards realistic periodicals devoted more and more images to depictions of the proceedings. The ambivalence of the depiction of Leopold Redpath at trial (more as an interested observer, a journalist, rather than the villain) gives way to more social commentary as the cry for prosecution of the white-collar criminals grew.

Editorial Techniques

Though less irreverent than their comic-serious counterparts the realistic periodicals' use of editorial techniques did provide pointed social commentary. Positioning images of events and financial figures on the front pages of issues in the realistic periodicals helped to 'sell' copy as much as it did highlight the sensational consequences of white-collar crime.

Artistic Techniques

The century begins and ends with the icon of the stocks to convey the retribution being meted out to financial villains.

The selective use of 'story boards' to highlight events and emotional responses elevated the realistic periodicals' coverage above the more formal use of photographs at the time.

The cross-over between the high art of Frith's narrative painting, to the realistic depictions of the realistic periodicals, and to the irreverent depictions in the comic-serious periodicals is made clear in this visual image analysis of the legal process. All three media made their points in different but ultimately similar ways. The villains were not to be applauded; sympathies were with the victims.

Notes

1. Taylor, 2013, p. 144.
2. 'The Overend and Gurney Case', *Saturday Review*, 25 December 1869; 28, 739; British Periodicals.
3. Bradly A. Knox, 'The Visual Rhetoric of Lady Justice: Understanding Jurisprudence Through "Metonymic Tokens"', *Student Pulse*, 6:5, 2014. From http://www.studentpulse.com/a?id=896.
4. 'To the left of the dock is the witness-box, and to the left of that the jury-box—an arrangement which enables the jury, as well as the judges on the bench, to see at one glance the faces both of the witnesses and the prisoners.' *The Dictionary of Victorian London.*
5. The number of images which I identified as relating to the CGB failure (34) was eclipsed only by the number of images attributed to the Railway Mania (37) which lasted for two years compared with the four months in the case of the failure of CGB from its suspension to the ultimate sentencing of its directors.
6. 'New Journalism' as a term is usually attributed historically to an article by Matthew Arnold in 1887.
7. William Wallace (ed.), *Trial of the City of Glasgow Bank directors* (Edinburgh, William Hodge, 1905).
8. Edwin Green, *Debtors to their Profession: History of the Institute of Bankers, 1879–1979* (London, Financial World Publishing, 1979).
9. Irene Finel-Honigman, *A Cultural History of Finance* (Abingdon, Routledge, 2010), p. 129.
10. Geoffrey Searle, *Morality and the Market in Victorian Britain*, Chapter 'Criminal Capitalism', p. 16, accessed from Oxford Scholarship Online, 13 April 2015, http://www.oxfordscholarship.com.idproxy.reading.ac.uk/view/10.
11. http://www.oed.com.idpproxy.reading.ac.uk/view/Entry/34907?rskey=ZyXOaA&result=1#eid (accessed 31 August 2015).
12. http://www.oed.com.idpproxy.reading.ac.uk/view/Entry/195335?rskey=nNJnax&result=1#eid (accessed 31 August 2015).
13. See www.moneysorter.co.uk/calculator_inflation2.html#calculator.
14. The reference to Schiller is from the Maid of Orleans. The word 'Dummheit' in the play is normally translated in English to stupidity, whilst 'Torheit' signifies folly. https://www.goodreads.

com/quotes/1358074-gegen-die-dummheit-k-mpfen-selbst-die-g-tter-vergebens-against-stupidity.

15. Judith Flanders, *Consuming Passions Leisure and Pleasure in Victorian Britain* (London, Harper Press, 2006). "In 1888 nearly 100,000 race goers travelled to the St Leger by train," p. 430. All freight trains were stopped by GNR on the day of the race.
16. Ibid.
17. See Figs. 9.8 and 9.9.
18. This is almost certainly due to the differing geographical jurisdictions. Whilst Scotland had a 15-man jury system, England had only 12.
19. See, e.g., the discussion in Jonathan Smith, *Charles Darwin and Victorian Visual Culture* (Cambridge, Cambridge University Press, 2006), pp. 198–204.
20. Frith, 2.143.
21. https://www.victorianlondon.org/legal/oldbailey.htm.

CHAPTER 10

Conclusion

In this conclusion I will summarise the key conclusions and outline areas of future research which may inspire readers to undertake their own research.

10.1 Themes

10.1.1 The Charlatans and Merchant Princes

Charlatans were viewed ambivalently during the century. They were at times viewed positively as 'Napoleons of Finance', the derring-do exploits of the French general personified as positive, if ruthless, characteristics. The use of sinister animal personifications (e.g., the devil-fish) is reflected in British cartoons of charlatans (as in the case of Balfour), as well as in European cartoons of Merchant Princes (e.g., Alphonse de Rothschild).

As crude satire was aimed only at the unliked, typically Merchant Princes in Britain were immune to ridicule in the comic periodicals. When they were caricatured it was part of a rite of acceptance in society—the inclusion of so many financiers in *Vanity Fair* is testimony to that acceptance. Their treatment by caricaturists was mild and amusing—reflecting their personal foibles (rather than depicting any racial or distorted physiognomic characteristics).

H. Sless, *Merchant Princes and Charlatans or Makers of Money?*,
https://doi.org/10.1007/978-3-030-86604-4_10

10.1.2 Iconography

The iconography of financiers reflected a more nuanced commentary than the uniformly negative view in literary works which dominated British, and French works for most of the century. Real-life white-collar criminals who provided the inspiration for Trollope or Frith were depicted favourably in the periodical *Vanity Fair*. Towards the end of the century the comic periodicals in Britain began to satirise charlatans using the age-old tropes of bubbles and balloons to signify the ephemeral and disastrous impact of speculation.

The recurring imagery to depict financial crises (bubbles, balloons, corrupt bank interiors) reflects both the recurrence of the events themselves, as well as the potential impact on readers of artists using images from the past consistently to convey the emotional impact of these crises. As such these images reinforce the contemporary view of writers such as Mackay in stressing the 'herd' instinct now used by behavioural economists to seek to explain why investors react in irrational, deluded fashion to financial crises (both exuberantly at times of financial bubbles, as well as despairingly when the bubbles burst).

10.1.3 International

The constant recurrence of similar imagery to depict financial crises in both British and foreign periodicals indicates the cross-fertilisation of ideas that took place. The satire was more biting internationally than in the UK. This reflected local political and economic contexts (e.g., the rise of anti-Semitism in France and Germany, the abolition of censorship in France, or the dominant role played by the Robber Barons in the US) as well as artistic developments (the rise of artists such as Keppler and Nast in the US, or Wilhelm Scholz in Germany).

10.1.4 Women

The images reveal a detailed interest in women in prominent financial positions both at the beginning and in the latter half of the nineteenth century (Harriot Coutts at the beginning; Angela Burdett-Coutts at mid-century onwards). This is interspersed with 'matchstick' representations of women in crowd scenes at times of financial distress. Whether this overall truly reflected artists' cognisance of the role of women in financial decisions is unclear (other evidence from contemporary works evidencing the existence and importance of women in visual images of finance would be required to comment more effectively on this point).

Punch and *Funny Folks* themselves downplay this possibility by referencing the stereotypical vanity and financial ignorance of women at the time of the CGB failure.

Yet for all this repudiation of the role and importance of women in general financial matters, the depiction of the Old Lady as the personification of the Bank of England, and financial solidity, is present throughout the century. The loftiness of the position of the 'woman' is exemplified in the depiction of unscrupulous 'impure' bank directors being admonished by the 'pure' Goddess of Justice during the CGB financial crisis.

10.1.5 The Other

Jews are depicted as inextricably linked to financial matters. In Britain, the representations undergo a softening of caricature with the cruder named representations of Rothschild in the 1820s giving way to images signifying acceptance into society in the 1870s onwards. Despite this, racial views of the Jews remained, whether in the representations of the facial features of Disraeli, or the association of Jews as moneylenders at times of stock exchange turbulence.

Internationally, where Jews were associated with Stock Exchange transactions, they were blamed as representatives of the capitalist system which spawned the mania for speculation. In Germany and in France, depictions of the Jews as symbols for decadence and immoral behaviour reached their apogee in the financial events that occurred from the 1870s, which corresponded with the growth of anti-Semitic attitudes. The blame for financial crashes such as the Krach of 1873 in Germany/Austria, or the scandals of the failure of Union Generale, and the Panama share scandal in France in the early 1880s were laid at the door of Jews, whose deep involvement in German and French financial transactions engendered resentment and hatred. In the US, by contrast, satirical cartoons of financiers centred on the Robber Barons, who were predominantly not Jewish.

Other representations of the Other, involving the Scots and the Irish reveal contrasting depictions. The Scots are viewed as bastions of financial solidity at the time of the 1825 banking crisis, and as part of the collective investor despair at the time of the CGB failure. The Irish do not show the racial stereotypes prevalent in non-financial depictions. Instead, their financial ignorance (which is echoed in depictions of women at the same time) is displayed (echoing the stereotypical depictions of their ignorance generally which is prevalent in images in the comic periodicals of the period).

10.1.6 *The Law*

The depictions of the legal process involving financiers prosecuted for financial improprieties undergo a transformation in the century. The crudeness of the Golden Age is reflected in the visual pun of 'stocks' at the time of the trial of Lord Cochrane in 1814 and is continued in the 1820s. Succeeding financial scandals did not reference any depictions of legal proceedings until the aftermath of the Overend & Gurney failure in 1866. Thereafter the realistic periodicals reflected public interest in white-collar criminal trials by depicting the legal process in realistic if staged representations. The use of storyboards allowed the juxtaposition of 'scenes' from the legal process to enhance the dramatic impact of the events unfolding.

The comic periodicals are cruder in their representations of the legal process—stressing initially the emotional impact on victims, whilst reserving increasing opprobrium for the villains, the bank directors and unscrupulous company promoters as the century wears on.

10.2 Pearl

10.2.1 *Publishers' Political Bias*

Such a bias is not readily visible in this book as political debates about finance were rare after mid-century. Laissez-faire business policies were accepted by the two political parties; regulatory reform was a necessary evil as the century wore on. By contrast, the comic periodicals delighted in exposing the foreign policy differences of Disraeli and Gladstone (*Punch* being generally pro-Disraeli, and *Fun,* for example, pro-Gladstone), but in finance Gladstone's fiscal rectitude was followed by the Tories as well.

10.2.2 *Editorial Techniques*

The nineteenth century sees the emergence of periodicals and newspapers featuring cartoons. The book illustrates the various techniques used by editors to 'sell' copy ranging from displaying images on the front page, to key cartoons appearing as one- or two-page centre spreads, to juxtaposing financial images alongside other sensational events, or using text (whether in the cartoon itself or accompanying the cartoon) to 'explain' a cartoon. What is intriguing is how financial events were considered important enough to warrant such prominence in the face of other events—overseas (especially wars), and domestically (consider for example, the 'fight' for editorial space for financial cartoons at the time of the CGB failure in late 1878/early 1879 when confronted with competing news stories such as the First Anglo-Afghan War which started at the same time).

10.2.3 *Artistic Techniques*

Cartoonists generally did not depict the techniques of financial transactions in visual terms. Where they did depict financial transactions, they used linguistic puns to convey stock exchange terminology rather than the details of the financial machinations which gave rise to the numerous financial scandals of the century.

Instead, they concentrated on depicting the emotional response to financial events using icons from earlier financial disasters (bubbles, balloons, crowds, bulls, and bears), as well as new icons such as the railway engine and bank interiors and exteriors.

10.2.4 *Readers' Response*

As I have mentioned earlier only *Punch* obliquely refers to the influence of readers in providing cartoon commentary. Contemporary biographies and autobiographies do provide tantalising glimpses into this world, but there is a need for a detailed forensic review of comments about cartoons, and specifically about images of finance, which may be apparent from researching contemporary literary sources (in novels, or autobiographies for example) using datamining referred to later.

10.2.5 Legal

Britain was able to escape the legal rigours of censorship which affected the dissemination of images on the Continent. For the most part, British publishers exercised self-censorship when permitting caricatures of famous personalities. With the advent of *Vanity Fair*, caricatures came into vogue, but their style was more humorous than satirical so legal interventions were not required.

10.3 Future Areas of Research

Using almost exclusively digital resources enabled a comprehensive homogeneous review to be undertaken. Limiting the images to be researched to cartoons in the main enabled a broad comprehensive selection of images to be identified. But for instance, a detailed review of paintings and photographs could be undertaken to supplement the cartoon coverage.

The choice of cartoon images was both selective and subjective. It was based almost exclusively on digital rather than hard copy images, and inevitably the choice of which images to use in this book was subjective. A study of hard copy sources could also help address the London-centric nature of coverage.

Other areas of visual culture, such as architecture or posters, have been ignored on the grounds of space. Yet the study of what is called the Spatial turn, as well as the Geographic turn could yield interesting results in exploring further aspects of the lives of financiers.[1] For example, the type of buildings used to attract customers and demonstrate the confidence that customers should place in the banks with which they were doing business. Or the geographical significance of the areas of London and the surrounding areas (from the changing nature of the City of London to the West End bank premises of the private banks, to the type of country residences that the 'aristocratic' banking families used to promote their social connections); understanding where financiers lived and worked, from the lowly clerks and accountants to the retail and merchant bankers, is surely a fruitful area for future research.[2]

In the digital area the whole field of datamining has not been covered. This is particularly relevant when considering the potential impact of memory which has been discussed briefly in the book. For example, readers' responses to the appearance of cartoons could be assessed by reviewing the quantity and quality of references in nineteenth-century British works held at the British Library. Whilst the repetition of icons of finance over the nineteenth century did occur (within the UK and abroad), the understanding of why artists chose these icons, and the degree of resonance in the minds of their readers remains elusive. This would also tie in with the current debate amongst cultural historians about the impact of the collective unconscious.

The book provides a complementary approach to traditional academic works on nineteenth-century financial history. It establishes that visual sources can be used effectively to interpret historical financial events, especially when analysing long periods of time. I echo Burke's comment on the importance of 'images serielles', the cumulative impact of reviewing numerous images over a period. He ends his book *Eyewitnessing* with Panovsky's words (quoting Flaubert and Warburg) 'Le bon Dieu est dans le detail'. In-depth study of visual images can be extremely rewarding and stimulating in historical research.[3]

Notes

1. See, for example, Iain Black, 'Spaces of Capital: Bank Office Building in the City of London, 1830–1870', *Journal of Historical Geography*, 26:3, 2000, and Charles W. J. Withers, 'Place and the "Spatial Turn" in Geography and in History', *Journal of the History of Ideas*, 70:4, 2009.
2. Garrett Ziegler, 'The City of London, Real and Unreal', *Victorian Studies*, 49:3, Spring 2007.
3. Burke, *Eyewitnessing*, p. 189.

Appendix 1: Analysis of Moon-Rise and Sun-Set

Appendix 1 outlines the research methodology used in my critical evaluation of the images in this book. It involves a forensic analysis of the various elements of the print, using historical background to contextualise what contemporary readers could have 'read' into the image.

As a representative example, I have chosen the 1825 print, *Moon-Rise and Sun-Set with John Bull, A Picture for the Times* by the artist Charles Williams.

Whereas in the post Golden Age I refer to the PEARL acronym (publisher, editor, artist, reader, and legal restrictions if any) to describe the interconnecting dynamics of the artistic relationship, in the Golden Age itself there are no editors, so the dynamics reflect only the PARL acronym.

Stages in Review

Description of Print

A detailed exposition of the print revealing key areas for underlying research.

Significance of title(s)

The first area for research is to understand the significance of the title, and in this case the sub-title.

Publisher

H. Sless, *Merchant Princes and Charlatans or Makers of Money?*,
https://doi.org/10.1007/978-3-030-86604-4

The role of the publisher in commissioning or agreeing to publishing a specific print needs to be understood. This would include a discussion about the location of the publisher, and any information about their commercial dealings.

Artist

In this case the name of the artist has been attributed. It might be necessary to understand the political leanings of the artist, their typical themes, etc.

Date

The date could be significant as it may provide a historical context to understand the nature of the event(s) being depicted.

Size

The size of the print can provide context as to the ease of viewing of the print.

Reader

Historical context can be provided by analysing what types of reader viewed such prints—whether passers-by gazing through print-sellers' windows, or the educated upper middle classes reviewing prints in salons, either singly or as part of bound volumes.

Legal

Censorship was an important consideration during the Golden Age. In respect of financial images, it does not play a part, as the images were of events rather than satirising individual financiers. (For consideration of the impact of censorship on images of the Rothschilds see Chapters 4 and 8 for any relevant commentary).

Major themes in the print

Finally, the major themes in the print can be analysed.

Description of Print

Figure A.1 reveals that there are two titles to the print: at the top, the words "*Paper versus Gold*", and the main title underneath "*Moon-Rise and Sun-Set with John Bull. A Picture for the Times.*" In the print, the larger-than-life figure of John Bull is shown dressed in a plain country smock, kneeling with his hands outstretched imploringly, his hair standing on end in fright, addressing someone to his right with the words "O Lord preserve us!" Though dressed in a smock, he is well heeled with smart dark-coloured boots, and a coloured kerchief around his neck. Despite his distress he appears well fed, with a rotund figure; his knees are pressed

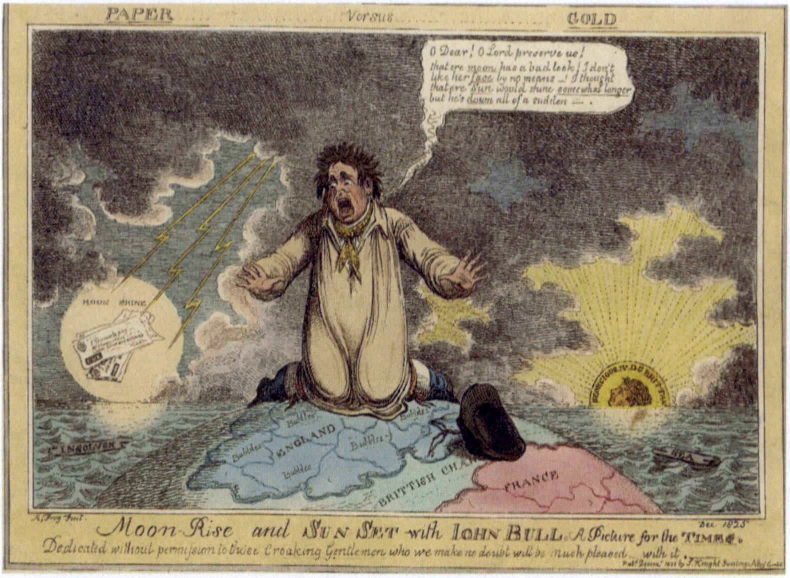

Fig. A.1 *Moon-Rise and Sun-Set with John Bull. A Picture for the Times*, artist Charles Williams, publisher John Knight, Sweetings Alley, Cornhill, December 1825. Dimensions 245 mm × 341 mm, hand-coloured etching

together making his smock taut and accentuating his plump belly. The words "I thought that 'ere Sun would shine somewhat longer but he is down all of a sudden," suggest John Bull's surprise that it has suddenly set. He is concerned, too, about the moon: "that 'ere moon has a bad look! I don't like her face by no means!" On either side of John Bull are representations of the moon and the sun. The moon on his right, which is larger than the sun on his left, is shaped like a sun, and is seen as rising. It is of an insipid, whitish-yellow colour with a picture of £1 Bank of England bank notes and the words "Moon Shine" above the notes. Three yellow forks of lightning are striking the moon, emanating from huge menacing black clouds which dominate the skyline of the print, and extend behind the figure of John Bull, encircling the gap in the clouds on his left, which is coloured yellow from the rays of the setting sun. The sun is in the shape of a gold sovereign with the face of George IV depicted on it, gazing at John Bull

John Bull is kneeling on the arc of a globe which shows the southern part of England, depicted in pale blue and showing individual counties—some inscribed with the word "Bubbles", some blank. The arc also contains parts of northern France, coloured in pink. John Bull's hat, topped with a feather, has been flung to the ground in despair but lies positioned between England and France, spanning the Channel. The Channel is depicted in a slightly lighter blue than England. The area beyond the immediate coastline of England is represented by a greyish-black sea. Beyond the globe the sea becomes increasingly choppy. A spar, broken in two pieces, drifts by with the word "Insolven" on the piece underneath the moon, and the word "Sea" on the piece below the sun.

The Title(s)

The two titles of this print reveal the perilous state of the country. The main title, *Moon-Rise and Sun-Set with John Bull,* reflects the uncertainties of the times.

The addition at the end of the main title "*A picture for the Times*" implies that the scene is an allegory, symbolic of the state of the nation at that time.

Publisher

Samuel Knight was a publisher of satirical prints. Little is known about him: for more information about publishers of the period see commentary on Thomas Tegg and Hannah Humphrey in Gatrell.[1]

Artist

Dorothy George who catalogued most of the prints and satires to be found in the BM of this period viewed Williams as a journeyman artist not on a par with Gillray, Rowlandson, and Isaac Cruikshank.[2] He did depict numerous financial prints of the period and they are discussed in the main body of the book.

Date

The date of December 1825 indicates that the print was produced at the height of the 1825 banking crisis. By December country banks had begun to fail, and there was a domino effect with London correspondent banks who arranged credit for the country banks being dragged into financial distress.

Size

Gatrell comments on the myriad of sizes to be found in satirical prints of the time.[3] The actual size of this print is tiny, equivalent to the length of a hard back book. It is hard for a modern reader to comprehend how painstaking the review of such an image would have been for a contemporary reader. Using a magnifying glass or reading glass would have been essential to appreciate fully the intricate iconography employed.

Reader

See Gillray's *Very Slippery Weather* (BMC 11100) for depiction of how the public viewed the expensive prints that only the well-off could buy.

Major Themes

As with any form of visual art, the key to historical analysis is to analyse the elements of the print in the light of historical information. In prints, the obvious starting point is to review written material of the time (e.g., newspapers or autobiographies).

Historical Context

It is possible that the print reflects the arrival in Britain of gold sovereigns from France (reported by the *Morning Chronicle* and other papers on Friday, 21 December).[4] My support for this interpretation is based on reviewing the following elements of the print:

- the positioning of John Bull's hat,
- the depiction of France in the print, and
- the words at the bottom left of the print, attributed to the anonymous artist, "A, Frog Fecit."

The hat has been flung down by John Bull, signifying his cry for help. The positioning of the hat, firstly in its placement in the Channel between

England and France, and secondly in being shown with its open side uppermost—like a beggar asking for alms—symbolises, I would contend, seeking help from France. The *Morning Chronicle* of 21 December reported "one hundred and fifty thousand sovereigns were paid in, in the course of the morning, by a great capitalist, which had been received from the Continent, and further large arrivals are expected,"[5] and Clapham and Pressnell both state that the sovereigns did come from France at that time.[6] Clapham states, "It was not a direct transaction between the Bank of England and the Bank of France but no doubt the Bank was cognisant of it and may have supplied the gold, the English Gold: for when the consignments did come, they mostly came in (gold) sovereigns."[7] If that is so, then the print reflects the hope that aid would be, or had been, forthcoming from France. Mrs Arbuthnot, a close confidante of the Duke of Wellington, reported, "Rothschild has made most gigantic efforts to assist the Bank and he told Mr. Herries that, if he had been applied to sooner, he wd [sic] have prevented all the difficulty. As it is, if they can hold out till Monday or Tuesday, he will have enormous sums over in sovereigns from Paris, & the pressure will be entirely relieved."[8]

Finally, the words attributed to the anonymous artist translate as "A Frog made (it)"—a Frenchman made it—another clue that France might be helping, or had helped, in the crisis. Could this signify that a Frenchman (a frog) made the print, i.e., were the French the ultimate saviours? Williams was known to sign anonymously.

Artistic Devices

Juxtaposition (Paper v Gold/Sun vs Moon)

Instead of the usual astrological movements of the rise of the sun in the morning, its setting in the early evening, followed by the shining of the moon in the late evening, the order here is reversed. Since the moon is placed underneath "Paper" in the title, and the sun underneath "Gold", the inference can be drawn that paper, and not gold, is in the ascendancy. The association of "paper" with "moon" may give rise to another deeper meaning in that paper can be associated with forgery, something that is worthless.[9] The implication is that though the moon, wan in colour as it is, is in the ascendancy, it represents something that is just paper, therefore worthless.

The second title at the top, "*Paper versus Gold*", would have immediately reminded an educated audience of the fierce debates inside and outside Parliament in the aftermath of the Napoleonic War about the nature of Britain's monetary policy, and whether it should return to a gold standard, i.e., paper money backed by convertibility in specie (gold).[10] The title refers to a paper by William Cobbett, the radical, who prophesied catastrophe in the immediate post-war period if Britain were to return to the old standard without repudiating the mountain of National Debt accumulated during the war years.[11] The text accompanying the subtitle almost certainly refers to Cobbett and his supporters—"those croaking gentlemen"—who foresaw financial collapse, and who have been proved right. "Croaking", here, probably means to talk despairingly about, to prophesy trouble or evil, or to grumble.[12]

This is reflected in the debate between the Bullionists, who believed that paper notes should be made convertible to gold on demand, and the Anti-Bullionists, who believed that bank notes would not be issued more than commercial demand.

The text at the top of the print invites discussion as it implies a conflict between paper and gold—there is a choice, one or the other. This is evidenced by the events depicted in the scene. There is no depiction of paper as being backed by gold (the actual state at the time, with Britain being on a gold standard, with gold backing the issue of paper), more that the issue of Bank of England paper appears to be in the ascendancy, and that gold sovereigns have failed to stem the crisis. Consumers would most likely have immediately recognised the double entendres and verbal puns on display. The events in late 1825 caused so severe a crisis of confidence that the Bank of England was forced to issue low denomination (£1) notes to ease the credit contraction that had taken place. The key for investors in Bank of England paper was the convertibility into gold specie, so the depiction of a gold sovereign sinking into the stormy sea would have suggested that the issue of paper was not going to be an effective solution, as there might not be enough gold sovereigns to meet repayment.[13] There were rumours that the Bank of England was on the brink of suspending cash payments on its debt, a situation like that in 1797 when cash payments were first suspended. The rumours began circulating on Monday, 19 December, because of a report in the *Times* of a Cabinet Council meeting the previous Friday evening that had lasted well into Saturday morning that stated: "The determination was adopted of suspending, for a short time, the payments in specie at the Bank."[14]

Moon-Shine

This is a visual pun. The insipid nature of the colour of the moon implies that the paper notes within it are not of good quality—indeed, the presence of forks of lightning attacking the moon reinforce this suggestion. Just as importantly, the pun "moon-shine" suggests both the shining of the moon, and that the issue of paper was illegal, counterfeit, and akin to illicit moonshine liquor.[15]

John Bull

Is this a typical representation of John Bull? Normally depicted as burdened by national debt or taxation, impoverished as a result, here is he is depicted as a rotund farmer in despair.[16] An indication of the ambiguity in the depiction begins with the smock, which would indicate that it is the labourer, the country worker, who is suffering. But the labourer is wearing good boots, and is clearly not suffering from any lack of food.

He carries no tools and speaks in an educated manner, quoting from the Psalms ("O Lord preserve us" is from Psalms 12:7). John Bull may be defenceless in the current crisis, but he is not the ordinary peasant.

The second clue is the map of England beneath John Bull's knees. It represents, in the main, the south and south-west of England—the heart of England's agricultural industry at the time. I would suggest that it is with his fellow agriculturalists in that area of England that John Bull sympathises. A relatively well-off John Bull (see his rotund figure) is depicted as being the victim of the banking crisis, reflecting the economic distress affecting the agricultural towns in the south and west of England. John Bull here suggests more of the gentry farmer, not working the land himself, but living off it and doing well out of it. The label "Bubbles" in many of the counties is also indicative that it was those with surplus cash—the relatively wealthy, rather than the ordinary (poorer) man—who have been severely affected by the crisis, and who are symbolised by the John Bull figure.

Geographical Turn

Why is the globe depicted only in part, concentrating mainly on southern England and to some extent France? With England being at the top of the arc, does it represent in some way an Anglo-centric view of the world, and its importance? With the globe surrounded by stormy seas, it could indicate that England, and in particular the south and south-west, were beset by enormous problems, which threatened to leave John

Bull shipwrecked. The combination of the two words "INSOLVEN" and "SEA" is an obvious pun on "INSOLVENCY", but there is also a further pun on "SEA" as the spar is floating on the sea. What does the broken spar represent? As the two spars span the part of the globe representing England, could the spar represent the state of the nation, broken in two and shipwrecked?

If the print could be interpreted in this way, then it can represent the economic impact of the 1825 crisis on the country banks servicing the areas of England depicted in the print.

In *Moon-Rise* Williams depicts the geographical impact of the crisis. This is achieved by using maps—of England beneath John Bull's outstretched feet—and of Scotland, northern England, and possibly Ireland to the left of John Bull's outstretched left hand. The maps may represent in an allegorical fashion the impact of the crisis during the latter months of 1825, when the credit crisis spread from the country to London and back again.

The agricultural areas tended to be cash rich, especially in the years of economic boom leading up to the bank crisis in 1825, as landlords earned income from rents and crop yields (as contrasted with the industrial north which constantly needed capital to fund investments in heavy machinery, plant, and factories). The country banks acted as intermediaries, sending the surplus cash generated by the agricultural south to London to be redistributed to the cash-hungry northern counties.[17] As Bagehot put it: "Agricultural counties tend not to employ as much money as they save: manufacturing counties, on the other hand, can employ much more than they save; and therefore the money of Norfolk or of Somersetshire is deposited with the London bill brokers, who use it to discount the bills of Lancashire and Yorkshire."[18]

Some of the English counties represented on the map contain within their outlines the word "Bubbles" as text; others do not. The crisis hit some counties more strongly than others, and this map may reflect the actual areas where the effects were greatest. Of interest here is that the artist identified the cause of the crisis as "bubbles", the word having been synonymous with speculation ever since the South Sea Bubble a hundred years earlier.[19] Speculation was indeed one of the causes of the crisis, though various commentators, including modern ones such as Bordo and Neal,[20] attribute the crisis partly to the role of the Bank of England in cutting the supply of credit, and partly to the country banks in issuing an excess of country bank notes. These notes were required to fund the ever-growing demand for increased yield for investors' surplus cash in the boom years following the successful transition from a wartime to a peacetime economy after the Napoleonic War.[21]

So, it is possible that the print depicts the speculation and greed of gentry in the counties shown in the print who invested their surplus cash in speculative investments, either in the counties marked with the word "Bubbles" or in the financial projects promoted in London. Accordingly, the word "Bubbles" could refer either to projects in the counties concerned or to London-originated projects.

Conclusion

This is a brief analysis of one specific financial print by Charles Williams. It illustrates the multi-layered interpretation that can be gleaned from a detailed review of background information, whether from primary (in the case of contemporary newspapers, and autobiographies), or secondary sources (etymologies of words, and academic articles on the 1825 crisis).

The images shown in the rest of the book are not analysed in the same degree of detail, but salient points of interpretation have been identified.

Appendix 2: List of Victorian Periodicals

The range of Victorian periodicals that I consulted was firstly determined by those periodicals carrying financial images digitised in the Gale Vault database of nineteenth century periodicals. This excluded several periodicals which were available only in hard copy.[22] These were then categorised as shown below to provide further insight into the significance of the images by reference to the targeted audience, the style of the periodical, its political leaning, and its circulation (Table A.1).

The political leanings of individual periodicals were obtained from a review of the entries for the various periodicals in the Dictionary of Nineteenth-Century Journalism.

I then subdivided the periodicals in to two categories:

1. Comic serious (*Punch, Fun, Funny Folks, Judy, Western Mail, Picture Politics, Pall Mall Gazette*), and
2. Realistic (*ILN, IPN, The Graphic*)

This distinction reflects what Clement Shorter, a journalist and editor of *ILN* in the 1890s, referred to when commenting on developments in *ILN* and the *Graphic*: 'I am treating here solely of illustrated journalism in its literal sense—as it applies to the actual presentation of current news.'[24]

One implication of Shorter's comment, to be tested by reviewing the images I have selected, is to assess the style of representation of financial

H. Sless, *Merchant Princes and Charlatans or Makers of Money?*,
https://doi.org/10.1007/978-3-030-86604-4

Table A.1 List of periodicals/newspapers consulted

Periodical	*Date*	*Circulation'000s*	*Price*	*Type*	*Readership*
Fun	1861–	20	1d	Comic	Lib/MC
Funny Folks	1874–1894	60	1d	"	MC/WC
The Graphic	1869–	200–250	6d	Realistic	MC
ILN	1842–	300	6d	"	MC
IPN	1864–	300	1d	"	MC/WC
Judy	1867–	40	2d	Comic	Cons/MC
Moonshine	1879–	NK	1d	Comic	Cons/MC/WC
Pall Mall Gazette	1865–	8–12	1d	Comic	Cons/MC
Picture Politics	1894–1894	NK	NK	Comic	Lib/MC
Punch	1841–	50–80	3d	Comic	Apol/MC
Vanity Fair	1869–	2.5	6d	Comic	MC/Cons
Western Mail	1869–	12	1d	Comic	Cons/MC

Key
Lib—Liberal
Cons—Conservative
Apol—apolitical
MC—middle class
WC—working class
NK—not known
Note The circulation figures are approximate for this period[23]

imagery that appears in the 'realistic' press compared with that in the 'comic' periodicals, and the degree of overlap between the two.

As can be seen from Table A.1, *Fun*, *Judy* and *Punch* were relatively long-established periodicals, whereas *Moonshine* and *Picture Politics* were more recent additions. Two newspapers were identified—the *Western Mail*, a Cardiff based daily, and *Pall Mall Gazette*, a London based daily—both of which produced images in respect of the coverage of Harcourt's 1894 budget. Most of the periodicals were published weekly (*Picture Politics*, a monthly periodical, being the exception). They were also mainly Conservative, as distinct from the Liberal-leaning *Fun* and *Picture Politics*. I also used the digital database of the National Portrait Gallery to provide additional information on some of the financial figures in *Vanity Fair*. In addition, I have analysed photographs contained in Wallace (1905)—a detailed account of the CGB directors' trial proceedings.[25]

Appendix 3: Analysis of *Vanity Fair* Caricatures

I have designated all the caricatures in *Vanity Fair* for the period under review under the following headings:

a. MPs
b. Men of Finance
c. HOL (House of Lords, essentially the aristocracy)
d. Military
e. Church
f. Law
g. Literature and the Arts (including actors etc.)
h. Sport (horse breeders, jockeys, rowing, cricket,)
i. Statesmen (here includes all diplomats, whether UK or foreign)

For the purposes of my analysis, I defined Men of Finance as follows:

a. Financial figures who held Government posts (as Chancellor of the Exchequer, Financial Secretary to the Treasury, Financial Secretary of War, Financial Secretary of the Admiralty, Chancellor of the Duchy of Lancaster, Paymaster General). Often people with non-financial expertise (typically lawyers) held several financial posts (especially the Chancellor of the Duchy of Lancaster). I have not included those posts nominally associated with finance, namely the

H. Sless, *Merchant Princes and Charlatans or Makers of Money?*,
https://doi.org/10.1007/978-3-030-86604-4

Junior Lords of the Treasury, who were invariably key Government appointees acting as Government Whips in a non-financial capacity.

b. Financial figures who held Royal appointments which indicated financial responsibilities (Treasurer of the Household, Comptroller of the Household, Keeper of the Privy Purse).
c. Other financial figures were identified as involved in banking, finance, stockbroking, commodity, or merchant trading, or who were members of a banking family.
d. Gamblers. Many individuals were identified in the accompanying letterpress as involved in gambling, predominantly in horse racing, either as owners or as those placing bets. The classification also includes those involved as speculators in shares. I have included these two categories of gambling and speculation under one heading because the distinctions between them (as I have demonstrated) were problematic for Victorians.

The analysis required a review of ODNB entries relating to all the *Vanity Fair* caricatures, a list of bankers and businessmen in *Vanity Fair* identified by NPG, and the list of banking families that Cassis used in his survey of *City Bankers 1890–1914*.[26] The *Vanity Fair* captions accompanying the caricatures often do not identify the profession/Government position of the person (unless they were a Judge, or MP). The initial identification was supported by the text accompanying the individual caricatures (the so-called *letterpress* in *Vanity Fair* itself). Thus, the use of ODNB and other information available from the internet, as well as Cassis's own sample of banking families, was used to identify/corroborate the information in *Vanity Fair*.

Having assembled this information, Chart A.1, portrays visually the results of the quantitative exercise.

Individual classifications result in a degree of double counting because there are numerous figures who appear in more than one category. As the aim of the classification is directional, i.e., it is designed to illustrate in broad terms the size of each category, the double counting has not been considered critical. Although 1763 images are included in the above chart, the number of actual caricatures was 1695—a reduction of 68.

The analysis of financial figures from *Vanity Fair* required me to establish criteria for the inclusion of figures in the dataset. A broad definition

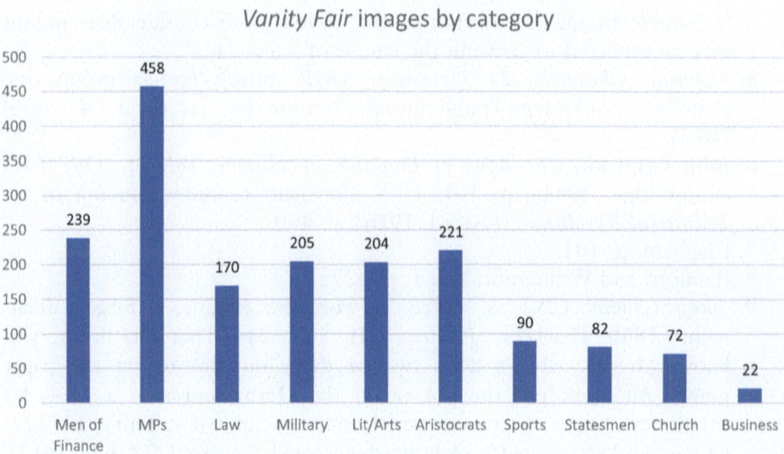

Chart A.1 *Vanity Fair* images by category

of the financial community was constructed and from a total of 1695 caricatures covering the beginning of *Vanity Fair* in 1869 to the end of the Victorian period in January 1901, 239 figures were identified as financial.

The dataset also enabled me to carry out my own original work to subdivide the figures not only to identify specific financial professions (stockbrokers vs. merchant banks vs. private banks, etc.) but also to establish the extent to which the major players in each financial sector were represented in *Vanity Fair*.

Notes

1. Vic Gatrell, *City of Laughter Sex and Satire in Eighteenth Century London* (London, Atlantic Books, 2006). See section Brief Lives, pp. 597–604.
2. M. Dorothy George (ed.), *Catalogue of Personal and Political Satires in the British Museum*, Vol. viii, p. xxxviii.
3. Gatrell, pp. 230–234.
4. There is conflicting debate as to the amount of sovereigns brought over, as there were numerous shipments. The *Times* reported on Saturday, 16 December "A large amount in sovereigns said to be near £300,000 was delivered at the Bank yesterday by an eminent capitalist, who had imported them from Paris, and it is said as the rate of exchange continues

favourable to such an operation, that a still more considerable amount may be expected to arrive in the course of a few days."

5. *Morning Chronicle*, 21 December 1825. http://find.galegroup.com.chain.kent.ac.uk/dvnw/publicationByLocation.do (accessed 4 April 2013).
6. John Clapham, *The Bank of England: A History, Vol. 11, 1797–1914* (Cambridge, 1944), p. 101. L. S. Pressnell, *Country Banking in the Industrial Revolution* (Oxford, 1956), p. 490.
7. Clapham, p. 101.
8. Bamford and Wellington, Vol. 1, p. 427.
9. *Slang* (chiefly *U.S.*). A forged or worthless cheque; a forged document. 1850 Thackeray *Pendennis* II. xxiv. 244 That kite-flying, you know, Mr. M., always takes two or three on 'em to set the paper going. Altamont put the pot on at the Derby and won a good bit of money. http://www.oed.com.chain.kent.ac.uk/view/Entry/137122?rskey=eo4nYs&result=1&isAdvanced=false#eid (accessed 23 July 2013). OR **b**. That exists only in written form; 'on paper', rather than in reality; theoretical, hypothetical, unrealized. 1814 J. Austen *Mansfield Park* III. xii. 227 It is impossible to put an hundredth part of my great mind on paper, so I will abstain altogether.
10. Boyd Hilton, *A Mad, Bad, and Dangerous People? England 1783–1846* (Oxford, 2006), pp. 262/263 summarising the debates within Parliament in 1819 which resulted in the resumption of convertibility within five years. Lord Sheffield's words "notwithstanding that extraordinary unanimity, everybody seems to differ" (p. 262) summed up the divisions at the time and the tensions still apparent years later.
11. "At the same time Cobbett became increasingly obsessed with financial issues, especially the national debt and the government's increasing reliance upon paper money. He opposed these trends for the rest of his days, regularly decrying government debts and paper currencies in his writings, notably in his Paper Against Gold (1815)." Ian Dyck, 'Cobbett, William (1763–1835)', *Oxford Dictionary of National Biography* (Oxford University Press, 2004), http://www.oxforddnb.com/view/article/5734 (accessed 3 April 2013).
12. 1780 F. Burney *Lett.* 24 August, "A Croaking Prophet, Foretells Nothing but Utter Destruction', croaking, adj. OED Online. March 2013. Oxford University Press. http://www.oed.com.chain.kent.ac.uk/view/Entry/44622 (accessed 3 April, 2013).
13. Francis Bamford and The Duke of Wellington (eds.), *The Journal of Mrs. Arbuthnot 1820–1832*, vol. 1 (London, 1950), p. 426. Mrs. Arbuthnot reports on her meeting with Mr. Herries: "Mr. Herries told us that such had been the extraordinary demand for gold to supply the country bankers and to meet the general run on them that the Bank of England

was completely drained of its specie and was reduced to 100,000 sovereigns…".

14. 'The Money-Market', *The Times* [London, England] 19 December 1825: 2. *The Times Digital Archive*. Web. 1 July 2013. http://find.galegroup.com.chain.kent.ac.uk/ttda/infomark.do?&source=gale&prodId=TTDA&userGroupName=uokent&tabID=T003&docPage=article&searchType=BasicSearchForm&docId=CS347549638&type=multipage&contentSet=LTO&version=1.0.
15. See OED online definition. http://www.oed.com. For contemporary comments on danger of illegal notes see Hansard. http://parlipapers.chadwyck.co.uk/hansard/27June1825.
16. Examples are *Leap Year or… 1816*, where John Bull is depicted as a fat "cit", bridled, carrying two panniers representing extravagant Royal expenditure; "*The Blessing of new Taxes*", 1819, where John Bull is in a bare room being deprived of his last comforts, a drink and his last shilling; or *Johnny Mooncalf's Back*, 1820, where John Bull has his legs shackled, his lips are padlocked, and he hobbles on crutches named "Credit" (presumably lack of it) and "Bank Notes" (presumably forgeries). See also Miles Taylor, 'John Bull and the Iconography of Public Opinion in England c. 1712–1929', *Past & Present*, no. 134, February 1992, pp. 93–128.
17. Pressnell, p. 76.
18. Walter Bagehot, *Lombard Street: A Description of the Money Market* (US, 2010—on demand print edition), p. 121.
19. Charles Mackay, *Extraordinary Popular Delusions and the Madness of Crowds* (Ware, 2006), p. 45. Mackay, writing in the 1840s very soon after the 1825 Bank crisis, wrote of previous speculation in the South Sea Company in 1720, "In the meantime, innumerable joint stock companies started up everywhere. They soon received the name of Bubbles, the most appropriate that imagination could devise. The populace are often most happy in the nicknames they employ."
20. Michael Bordo, 'Commentary', *Federal Reserve Bank of St Louis Review*, May/June 1998, Larry Neal, "The Financial Crisis of 1825 and the Restructuring of the British Financial System", *Federal Reserve Bank of St Louis Review*, May/June 1998. See also discussion in chapter Financial Context.
21. Bordo, p. 77.
22. See James Taylor, 'Business in Pictures: Representations of Railway Enterprise in the Satirical Press in Britain 1845–1870', *Past & Present*, no. 189, November 2005, FN 12, pp. 114/115 for an exhaustive list of periodicals consulted by Taylor.
23. Richard D. Altick, *The English Common Reader: A Social History of the Mass Reading Public 1800–1900* (Chicago, Chicago University Press,

1957), pp. 391–396. See also Alvar Ellegård, 'The Readership of the Periodical Press in Mid-Victorian Britain II: Directory', *Victorian Periodicals Newsletter* 3 (September 1971).

24. Clement K. Shorter, 'Illustrated Journalism: Its Past and Its Future', *The Contemporary Review*, January 1, 1879, 75, p. 488.
25. William Wallace, *Trial of the City of Glasgow Bank Directors* (Glasgow, William Hodge and Company, 1905).
26. Youssef Cassis, *City Bankers 1890–1914* (New York, Cambridge University Press, 2009).

The manufacturer's authorised representative in the EU is Springer Nature Customer Service Centre GmbH, Europaplatz 3, 69115 Heidelberg, Germany. If you have any concerns regarding our products, please contact ProductSafety@springernature.com

Printed and bound by CPI Group (UK) Ltd, Croydon, CR0 4YY
30/09/2026
02225492-0008